The United States *and*
the Transatlantic Slave Trade
to the Americas,
1776–1867

The United States *and* *the* Transatlantic Slave Trade *to* *the* Americas, *1776–1867*

LEONARDO MARQUES

Yale UNIVERSITY PRESS/NEW HAVEN & LONDON

Published with assistance from the Annie Burr Lewis Fund and from the foundation established in memory of Calvin Chapin of the Class of 1788, Yale College.

Yale University Press books may be purchased in quantity for educational, business, or promotional use. For information, please e-mail sales.press@yale.edu (US office) or sales@yaleup. co.uk (UK office).

Set in Minion type by Integrated Publishing Solutions.
Printed in the United States of America.

Library of Congress Control Number: 2016942711
ISBN 978-0-300-21241-9 (hardcover)

A catalogue record for this book is available from the British Library.

This paper meets the requirements of ANSI/NISO Z39.48–1992 (Permanence of Paper).

10 9 8 7 6 5 4 3 2 1

To Iraci

Contents

Acknowledgments

This book is a revised version of my PhD dissertation, defended at Emory University in 2013. I therefore start by thanking the many colleagues, friends, and professors I have met and learned from since 2007 at Emory. A very special thanks goes to David Eltis, whom I had the honor of having as an adviser and friend. It is impossible to describe how much I have learned from him over the years. This book would not exist without his mentorship. James Roark and Thomas Rogers read a previous version of this work and provided invaluable comments. I cannot thank them enough for all their help over the years. Susan Socolow is one of the greatest professors I ever had, and I thank her for everything she has done for me. Nafees Khan, Rachel Lambrecht, Brad Lange, Joe Renouard, and Cari Williams have not only helped me with various issues, but have also been fantastic friends. Thanks also to Sarita Alami, Marcy Alexander, Patrick Allitt, Alex Borucki, Barb Brandt, Erica Bruchko, Richard Cook, Joe Crespino, Robert Desrocher, Daniel Domingues, Bob Elder, Melissa Faris Gayan, George Kientzy, Steve Lamb, Jeffrey Lesser, Kristin Mann, Phil Misevich, Francis Musoni, Alex Neundorf, Craig Perry, Fabrício Prado, Bianca Premo, Marina Rustow, Andrea Scionti, Elizabeth Stice, Patricia Stockbridge, Lena Suk, Ariel Svarch, Jorge Troisi-Melean, Juan Viacava, Katie Wilson, and Steve Witte.

Before I attended Emory, I had the honor to study with and learn from a number of people at the Universidade Federal do Paraná and at the University of North Carolina at Charlotte. I must start by thanking my first adviser, Carlos Alberto Medeiros Lima, to whom I owe eternal gratitude. I also wish to thank Rafael Benthien, Luiz Adriano Borges, Mabel Borges, Hilton Costa, Cesar Cundari, Rogério Cunha, Rodrigo Gonçalves, Maria Thereza David João, Athos Maia, Ana Paula Vosne Martins, Allan de Paula Oliveira, Jonas Pegoraro, José Roberto Braga Portella, Claudio Guga Rovel, Helder Cyrelli de Souza, Luiz Geraldo Silva, Rodrigo Turin, and Bruno Zorek. A very special thanks goes to my good old friend Bruno Santos Alexandre, who has actually read parts of this work and with whom I have had regular discussions on a number of issues. At UNC Charlotte I had the honor of studying with Lyman Johnson, Robert Smith, and the same Thomas Rogers. I cannot thank them enough. A special thanks goes to Martha LaFollette Miller.

In recent years I had the opportunity to discuss this work with a number of people at Brown University and at the Universidade de São Paulo. I would like to thank Valerie Andrews, Paula Dias, Natalie Deibel, Alexandre Dubé, Kittya Lee, Derek Miller, Margot Nishimura, Marcy Norton, Kimberly Nusco, Gabriel Paquette, Seth Rockman, Ken Ward, and Ted Widmer. Nancy Kougeas was especially helpful during my research at Bristol. In São Paulo, I thank Rafael Marquese and Tâmis Parron for their friendship and great discussions, which were fundamental for many of the arguments developed in this book. Gabriel Aladrén, Fernanda Bretones, Marcelo Ferraro, Marco Holtz, and Priscila Lima, Waldomiro Jr., and Alain Youssef read parts of this work and helped me improve it. I also thank João Paulo Pimenta and the members of the Lab-Mundi at USP.

André Luiz Bertoli, Ida Camila Dantas Granja, Andrei Dignart, Elisa Freitas, Marcy, Laura and Felipe Marques, and Kenny, Cari, Miles, and Georgia Maes received me in their homes during research trips to Providence, Bristol, Rio de Janeiro, Piracicaba, and Lisbon, and for this I'll be forever thankful.

I thank Marcos Abreu, Lorena Avellar, Edward Baptist, Sarah Batterson, Celso Castilho, Stephen Chambers, Luiz Alberto Couceiro, Aisnara Perera Díaz, Carlos and Bia Dignart, Seymour Drescher, Sharla Fett, João

Escosteguy Filho, Frederico Freitas, Fábio Frizzo, María de los Ánge-
les Meriño Fuentes, Graciela Garcia, Tiago Gil, Dale Graden, Mariana
Guglielmo Martha Hameister, John Harris, Richard Huzzey, Anthony
Kaye, José Knust, Thiago Krause, Marcia Kuniochi, Jane Landers, Thiago
C.P. Lourenço, Beatriz Mamigonian, Katherine Marino, Karl Monsma,
Mariana Muaze, Paulo Henrique Pachá, Walter Luiz Pereira, Ian Read,
Ricardo Salles, Ynaê Lopes dos Santos, Lise Sedrez, Rejane Valvano Silva,
Dale Tomich, Oscar de la Torre, Marial Iglesias Utset, Scott Webster, David
Wheat, Nicholas Wood, Michael Zeuske, the Felix and Peixoto families,
Derry, Marcy, and all the people at the Bristol Historical and Preservation
Society, the John Carter Brown Library, the National Archives at Atlanta,
the National Archives at Boston, the Rhode Island Historical Society, the
Arquivo Nacional do Rio de Janeiro, the Arquivo do Itamaraty, the Brit-
ish National Archives, the Arquivo Histórico-Diplomático at Lisbon, the
Arquivo Nacional da Torre do Tombo, the Emory Laney Graduate School,
and the Santos Futebol Clube.

Since 2015, I have had the chance to meet and work with a number of great colleagues and students at the Universidade Federal Fluminense. I thank them for receiving me so well. A special thanks goes
to Maria Verónica Secreto Ferreras, Norberto Osvaldo Ferreras, Renato
Júnio Franco, Jonis Freire, Carlos Gabriel Guimarães, Alexandre Santos
de Moraes, Silvia Patuzzi, Ronald Raminelli, Alexandre Vieira Ribeiro,
Giselle Martins Venâncio, Carlos Eduardo Valencia Villa, and Marcelo
da Rocha Wanderley.

A very special thanks also goes to Chris Rogers, Erica Hanson,
Kristy Cottrell, Laura Jones Dooley, and everyone at Yale University
Press who made this book possible.

Last, I thank my family, starting with my mother, Iraci Mailde
Ramos, without whom none of this would have been possible, and
Gisele Batista Candido, who was literally by my side during the writing
of this book. Infinite love for these two. I also thank the entire Marques,
Batista, and Candido families, Jalmar, Jalmara, and Pérsio Torres, and all
my friends in Brazil and the United States. Unfortunately, João Ramos
da Silva Filho, Antônio Augusto Marques, Milce Mailde Marques, and
Luíz Candido did not live long enough to see this book in print, but I
wish to acknowledge my gratitude for having had them in my life.

The United States *and*
the Transatlantic Slave Trade
to the Americas,
1776–1867

Introduction

In 1841, an Englishman and his American friend, John Gardiner, decided to unearth the grave of James D'Wolf in Bristol, Rhode Island. Having arrived that year in the country, the Englishman learned about the deceased man after attending a lecture against slavery given by a visiting abolitionist woman. There he learned that D'Wolf had worked at a young age as mate onboard a vessel engaged in the transatlantic slave trade and that, after becoming its captain, he accumulated "property rapidly, until he became very rich and owned . . . large plantations in the Island of Cuba." According to legend, D'Wolf later became associated with Charles Gibbs, a Rhode Island pirate who captured a vessel leaving Spanish America for Europe with seven coffins of silver. James D'Wolf was alleged to have been buried in one of these.

Before breaking into the tomb, the invaders wrote an alternative version of William Cowper's poem "The Negro's Complaint" on the wall (or the coffin, the deponent could not really remember):

> Forced from home and all its pleasures,
> Afric's coast, I left forlorn—
> To increase "old De Wolfe's" treasures,
> O'er the raging billows borne.

But then came the frustration: there was no silver coffin. According to Gardiner, "The sons had cheated the old man out of the coffin and had doubtless melted it up and coined it into hard dollars before that, as there had been much dissension among them about an equal division of the property after his death." James D'Wolf had in fact left a large fortune to his descendants. In 1836, when he prepared his will, he had two cotton manufacturing companies, ships and vessels involved with whaling, capital stock in Rhode Island banks, two textile mills, and lands and real estate in Rhode Island, Massachusetts, New York, Ohio, Kentucky, and Baltimore. Along with other New Englanders, he was also directly implicated in the continuation of slavery overseas with his four Cuban plantations and all their coffee, sugar, and enslaved Africans. A senator for Rhode Island in the 1820s, D'Wolf is usually remembered as the largest slave trader in the history of the United States. And indeed, much of his fortune had come from his activities as a slave trader. Between 1791 and 1808, he financed at least forty-three slave voyages to Africa, captaining several of them.[1]

Perhaps the most famous US slave trader other than James D'Wolf is Nathaniel Gordon. Gordon illegally captained a few slave voyages to Brazil in the early 1850s but was arrested only in 1860, when US authorities found 897 Africans tightly packed below the deck of the *Erie* off the coast of Africa. At the time of Gordon's capture, the Buchanan administration was cracking down on the slave trade in response to mounting British pressure, but there were no indications that punishment according to the law of 1820—which had turned the slave trade into a crime of piracy, therefore making it punishable by death—would be carried out. A number of slave traders had been convicted since 1820; none had been punished with death. A few years earlier, a captain convicted under the law of 1820 had merely been ordered to pay a two-hundred-dollar fine and serve a two-year jail term, and in 1857, President James Buchanan granted him a pardon. When Gordon was judged, however, not only had the Republican Party just been elected under a platform that called for immediate measures to suppress US participation in slave traffic, but a civil war had started around the issue of slavery. Bad timing, perhaps, but President Abraham Lincoln refused to grant Gordon a pardon after his conviction, and on February 21, 1862, Nathaniel Gordon became the only slave trader to be legally punished with death in Western history.[2]

D'Wolf's and Gordon's destinies could not have differed more. One became so rich that people believed he had been buried in a silver coffin. The other died by hanging one day after trying to poison himself in his cell in a New York prison. Their distinct trajectories are indications of the deep transformation in the nature of US involvement in the transatlantic slave trade between the American Revolution and the Civil War. James D'Wolf and other Rhode Islanders were involved in almost every aspect of slave-trading operations, from the production of the rum exchanged for slaves in Africa to the financing and organization of the voyages. Because a number of Rhode Island slave traders used those gains to purchase coffee and sugar plantations in Cuba in the early nineteenth century, many of them also received the African captives when they stepped off the slave vessel. Nathaniel Gordon and other US slave traders of the 1850s, on the other hand, rarely if ever amassed fortunes comparable to those made by Rhode Island slave traders. They engaged in many aspects of the trade, such as providing the US flag and papers or captaining US vessels on voyages to Africa. On the whole, however, these actions were part of their activities as *employees* of the major Portuguese, Brazilian, and Spanish slave traders. A few occasionally had some interest in slave voyages, but this was a tiny fragment of the traffic, which had gone through radical transformations since the early 1800s.

The creation of the US branch of the transatlantic slave trade took place in the context of profound structural transformations initiated by American independence. The political, economic, and sociocultural changes that characterized the last quarter of the eighteenth century culminated, on the one hand, in the events that were pivotal to the crisis of the French and British colonial slave systems, namely the Haitian Revolution and the British abolition of the slave trade. On the other hand, trade liberalization on a global scale and industrial development in parts of the North Atlantic, with the consequent growth of cities and working classes, drove demand for New World exports—and, consequently, slave labor—to new heights. Not only did the consumption of coffee and sugar dramatically increase, but also cotton became an essential part of the ongoing Industrial Revolution. By 1850, slave societies in the United States, Cuba, and Brazil had become, respectively, the main producers of cotton, sugar, and coffee for a world market, in what Dale Tomich has called the "second slavery." The integration of these new zones into the less regulated world economy of the nineteenth century led to the adoption of new technologies, novel forms of labor organization, and their growing specialization in the production of specific crops, as planters strove to remain competitive in this new context. This book is in part an exploration of how US slave traders contributed to (and were affected by) the emergence of this new world, which can be seen as an innovative moment in the history not only of slavery in the Americas but also of historical capitalism as a whole.[3]

In terms of labor supply, Cuba, Brazil, and the United States followed divergent trajectories. All three formally prohibited the transatlantic slave trade. However, whereas the United States effectively closed its doors to the importation of enslaved Africans (leading to the emergence of a massive domestic slave trade), Brazil and Cuba continued to heavily depend on imported slaves. By the mid-nineteenth century this traffic had become so internationalized that the old national divisions of the business that had characterized the eighteenth century had nearly disappeared. The British financial innovations that had been favoring British merchants in the previous century became accessible to any slave trader. United States–built vessels became a mainstay of the traffic, and by the 1850s a number of British steamers also entered the business. A growing share of the slave-trading cargoes was composed of products manufactured in the North Atlantic, from Swedish iron bars to British arms and gunpowder. The captains and crews found aboard slave ships had always been largely multinational, but the passing of anti-slave-trade policies in the new world of sovereign nation-states of the nineteenth century transformed the issue of citizenship into an strategic tool for slave traders. The famous slave captain Théophilus Conneau, for instance, was once described as "an Italian by birth, a Frenchman by descent, a Spaniard by semi-naturalization and trade, an African in habit, and somewhat an American by early association and apprenticeship."[4]

On the key issue of ownership, however, the traffic became highly concentrated in the hands of Portuguese, Spanish, and Brazilian slave traders. This was a direct consequence of the slave trade acts of 1807 in Britain and in the United States. By the 1850s, the traffic to Cuba had US elements all over it: most ships were not only built in the United States but flew the US flag, voyages were frequently outfitted at New York, and American citizens actively participated in them as captains, crews, and agents. In almost every case where it is possible to track the ownership of the voyage, however, a major Portuguese or Spanish slave trader is uncovered as the actual owner. Employing a wide range of strategies to circumvent the authorities, these traders opened opportunities for profits to American citizens and others in a number of ways. But unlike earlier in the century, US participants rarely managed to ascend within the structure of a business increasingly in the hands of fewer and larger owners.

Participation in the transatlantic slave trade could assume a variety of forms, from the direct organization of slave voyages to the consumption of slave-grown produce. The first wave of British abolitionism attacked all these forms, completely blurring their lines. Some depicted the slave trader as the employee of sugar consumers in Britain. Lurid images associating sugar and the blood of slaves abounded, at times resulting in stories of Caribbean planters entombing slaves in sugar casks to give the product a better taste. Though Thomas Clarkson's estimate that three hundred thousand Britons abstained from the consumption of sugar from the West Indies during the 1790s may be an exaggeration, later historians have confirmed the strength of the movement during that decade. The acts of 1807 abolishing the slave trade in Britain and in the United States had an impact only on the most direct forms of participation in the slave trade, mainly the organization of slave voyages to Africa. Boycott movements continued in Britain after 1807, with a revival in the early 1820s and later, but they never reached the point of affecting slavery in the Americas. In the United States such movements were much smaller, despite similar denunciations by such eminent figures as the poet Ralph Waldo Emerson. In a famous address delivered in 1844 to a Massachusetts audience, Emerson sarcastically praised the qualities of products grown by slaves across the Americas: "The sugar they raised was excellent: nobody tasted blood in it. The coffee was fragrant; the tobacco was incense; the brandy made nations happy; the cotton clothed the world. What! All raised by these men, and no wages? Excellent! What a convenience!" Emerson exposed Northern audiences to the direct connection between their consumption at home and slavery overseas precisely when New Englanders were cementing the narrative of a white New England barely marked by slavery. Boycott movements and the establishment of "free produce" shops, however, never really took off in the United States.[5]

The nineteenth century was, therefore, marked by tensions in the English-speaking Atlantic around the boundaries defining what constituted legitimate and illegitimate forms of involvement with the transatlantic slave trade. The laws passed both in Britain and in the United States could certainly be interpreted as instruments to curb the indirect involvement of merchants from both countries in the contraband slave trade. This is precisely what a few opponents of the traffic did. The British foreign affairs secretary Lord Palmerston, for example, followed a number of leads on British indirect involvement in the slave trade, some of them resulting in legal prosecutions. None, however, resulted in convictions. As David Eltis argues, the British could have eliminated the legal loopholes that allowed these merchants to escape or banned trade with certain parts of Africa, but such acts "would have run counter to their beliefs in the moral effects of honest trade and would have caused widespread loss of markets as merchants and manufacturers pulled back from any transactions that might conceivably have resulted in merchandise ending up in the slave trade." One consequence, as Eltis shows, was that British credit continued to be found in the transatlantic slave trade after 1807. Broader attitudes to trade were certainly at work in the United States, too, but the issue was complicated by rising suspicions of British motives. A number of US diplomats in Brazil during the 1840s would denounce British profits from the traffic, and some, in fact, saw their own actions against the slave trade as a struggle against British global domination. A few proposed new measures, such as prohibiting the sale of US vessels in Africa or Brazil, but it was unlikely that the US government could adopt such a policy in a world of expanding markets and competition. Drawing the line on the direct purchase and selling of slaves as a crime effectively took hold in the North Atlantic, but expanding this line to include the indirect participation of merchants in the selling of vessels and goods to slave traders ultimately failed. Just like British credit, US-built ships became a hallmark of the contraband slave trade. Until the complete suppression of the slave trade to the Americas, US, British, and French merchants would profit by aiding Portuguese, Brazilian, and Spanish slave traders.[6]

Many historians in the past several decades have labored to explain the origins and dynamics of abolition. As Thomas Holt and Christopher Brown have noted, this discussion can involve at least three levels of analysis: abolitionist sensibilities, abolitionist movements, and abolitionist state policies. All three levels of analysis appear and inform this book. They are fundamental, for example, to an understanding of how a strong opposition to the transatlantic slave trade finally took hold in the South by 1820. Shifting sensibilities toward violence and cruelty had an impact on slaveholders in the English-speaking Atlantic, who increasingly styled themselves as enlightened masters. Some openly sought to distance themselves from the traffic and employed a humanitarian language in attacks against it. Developments such as the Haitian Revolution in the 1790s, the dramatic growth of a domestic slave trade in the United States over the 1810s, and the US nationalist upsurge in the aftermath of the War of 1812, however, were fundamental elements for the consolidation of anti-slave-trade attitudes in the South. By the 1840s, diplomats from the US South in Brazil were some of the strongest militants against the participation of US citizens in the transatlantic slave trade. Some of the articulations that led to the creation of new governmental policies and the limits to their implementation are also explored here. It is impossible to understand these actions and limits without reference to the increasingly predominant laissez-faire ideals or to the growing competition for markets among North Atlantic powers in the aftermath of the Napoleonic Wars.[7]

The focus of this book, however, is less on the precipitants of abolitionist action or government policies and more on their main targets: the slave traders. The shifts in the organization of the trade and in the forms of US involvement that form the core of this work have been nearly ignored in the historiography of the US slave trade, despite the renewed interest on the subject brought by the two hundredth anniversary of the abolition of the slave trade in Britain and the United States in 2007–8.[8] This is largely a product of the persisting influence of W. E. B. Du Bois's classic study *The Suppression of the African Slave Trade.* This work remains one of the most complete resources on US participation in the transatlantic slave trade. Two fundamental problems, however, come with it. First, Du Bois conflated the numbers of the transatlantic slave trade to Brazil, Cuba, and the United States. Most historians now agree that the number of slaves smuggled into the United States after the passing of abolitionist legislation was radically smaller than the figures presented by Du Bois (the recent work of Ernest Obadele-Starks stands as an exception).[9] This near consensus has led to the conclusion that the slave trade legislation was more effective in stopping the importation of slaves into the country than in curbing the participation of US citizens in the slave trade to Cuba and Brazil, which was indeed the case. However, owing in part to the persisting influence of Du Bois, a possible interpretation connected to this overestimates the size and, more important, misrepresents the role of US participation in the contraband slave trade to other countries.[10]

A more serious problem in the literature is the general characterization of US slave trade laws as dead letters, first established more bluntly also by Du Bois. The half-century between the passing of anti-slave-trade legislation and the condemnation of Nathaniel Gordon in 1862 stimulated the widespread view that US slave trade legislation was largely ineffective. Part of the reason for such a persisting view is that most works on the US slave trade deal either with the few decades after the American Revolution or with the last years before the Civil War. Thus, Jay Coughtry concludes, in his work on the pre-1808 Rhode Island slave trade, that the D'Wolfs' political alliances rendered the slave trade act of 1807 ineffective. Warren Howard, whose book remains an essential resource, also concludes that the slave trade legislation of the early nineteenth century was completely ineffective. Howard describes a very different organization of the traffic in the 1840s and 1850s but does not explore the causes or implications of this change. His emphasis is on the participation of US captains and agents in the traffic as examples of loopholes in the legislation. That such loopholes and problems of enforcement existed is beyond doubt, but this should not lead us to treat the slave trade legislation passed between 1794 and 1820 as having had no historical impact. Not surprisingly, two studies that deal with the US slave trade in the entire period between the American Revolution and the Civil War—Don Fehrenbacher's *Slaveholding Republic* and David Ericson's *Slavery in the America Republic*—offer more balanced views of the impact of slave trade legislation. Yet, too often interpretations of the US slave trade come associated to a "racial consensus," to borrow a term used by James Oakes, a product of the racism that united Northerners and Southerners. Historian Robert Conrad, for example, explains the widespread presence of US vessels and citizens in the traffic to Brazil by referring to the pervasive existence of racism, slavery, and a domestic slave trade in the United States. These elements, Conrad argues, "blunted the nation's sensitivity to the suffering of black people and perhaps intensified widespread disrespect for the laws that prohibited the participation of United States citizens in the international slave trade."[11]

Two main arguments developed in this book are related to the discussion outlined above. First, the slave trade legislation of the early nineteenth century affected the participation of US citizens in the transatlantic slave trade. To track these changes, I explore the history of slave-trading communities with some form of US connection against the changing background of new attitudes to the traffic. Second, some of the enforcement problems were connected to broader issues related to the emergence of a world of nation-states regulated by international laws and the ideals of laissez faire that characterized the post-1815 world. These problems were faced not only by the US government but also by Britain and France, and in order to fully understand them we need to frame them within this broader Atlantic context. On a more general level, I also explore the role that economic and political developments in the United States had over the two other main slave societies of the nineteenth century, Brazil and Cuba, and vice-versa. Leaving aside the direct contribution to the contraband slave trade by US citizens in multiple roles, the economic growth of the United States turned the country into the largest consumer of the slave-grown produce exported from

Brazil and Cuba as well as the main providers of vessels for the traffic to both countries (and indeed in many other branches of maritime
commerce before the steamship revolution). The growth of the United
States as a slaveholding republic in international relations, in turn, was
perceived and explored not only by Brazilian and Cuban planters but
also by slave traders across the Atlantic.

Many works have shaped the ideas developed in this study. Some
have already been cited, but three groups of historians, and a few studies
among them, must be mentioned. First, this book would be inconceiv-
able without the previous research of such historians as Philip Curtin,
Herbert Klein, David Richardson, David Eltis, and Manolo Florentino,
to name only a few, who have explored the volume, routes, and other
aspects of the transatlantic slave trade to the Americas. Much of their
research is stored on *Voyages: The Trans-Atlantic Slave Trade Database*
(www.slavevoyages.org), a database with information on almost thirty-
five thousand slave voyages that took place between 1514 and 1866. My
own research has added both new voyages and substantial new information to at least four hundred previously logged voyages, including places
of vessel construction, itineraries, and ownership.[12]

Also important are the works of historians of slavery and politics in the United States, such as Donald Robinson, Don Fehrenbacher,
Paul Finkelman, and Matthew Mason, among others. Despite their differences, their discussions were fundamental in my understanding of
the status of the transatlantic slave trade in the United States and the
issues at stake in the debates leading to the passing of new regulations.
The Slaveholding Republic, by Don Fehrenbacher, has been particularly
important for a number of other reasons. His two chapters on US involvement in the transatlantic slave trade are certainly some of the finest
interpretations of the topic and influenced many of my own arguments.
Using mainly diplomatic documents, Fehrenbacher makes important
suggestions regarding the broader social history of US involvement in
the traffic that asked for more solid research. Many of these became
starting points for my research, and I was not surprised to see many of
them confirmed by different sets of sources. Moreover, his discussion of
the emergence of the United States as a slaveholding republic in international relations inspired me to explore not only the ways this develop-

ment was received in Brazil and Cuba but also how it was perceived and explored by the slave traders themselves.[13]

From this last point came my interest in the works of a third group of historians, all of them exploring the mutual influences between nineteenth-century United States, Brazil, and Cuba under the concept of "second slavery." Studies by Tâmis Parron and Rafael Marquese were particularly important for my understanding of the political configurations that allowed for the emergence of a massive contraband slave trade to Cuba and Brazil and how these developments had larger ramifications. Their descriptions of how the growing slave power of the US South was received by planters in Brazil and Cuba and, more generally, their efforts to treat nineteenth-century slavery in the Americas as an integrated whole have shaped much of my discussion. The mutual influences among the three slave societies of the nineteenth century also affected the form and direction of the contraband slave trade itself. And perhaps even more important for some of my conclusions were their explorations of the limits to these hemispheric connections.[14]

Approximately five million enslaved Africans were disembarked in the Americas between 1776 and 1867. Of these, more than a hundred thousand went to the United States, almost all before 1808, when the US slave trade was abolished. This separation between US slavery and its African source paved the way for the emergence of the most powerful proslavery ideology in the Americas. The participation of Americans in the slave trade to other countries, however, continued in multiple ways, contributing to the illegal disembarkation of more than a million slaves in Cuba and Brazil during the nineteenth century. Most of the traders and planters responsible for these disembarkations would never be brought to justice for their crimes, yet almost all of their illegally disembarked captives would remain enslaved until death or the abolition of slavery in Cuba and Brazil in the 1880s. And the US participation in the slave trade ultimately contributed to shattering the separation between US slavery and slave trafficking, increasing the tensions that marked the 1850s and led to the Civil War. It is to this history and its broader economic, political, and social implications that we now turn.

North American Slave Traders in the Age of Revolution, 1776–1807

I n a famous passage of his presidential message of 1806, Thomas Jefferson noted that the time was coming for the United States to prohibit the participation of its own citizens in "those violations of human rights which have been so long continued on the un-offending inhabitants of Africa, and which the morality, the reputation, and the best of our country have long been eager to proscribe." A sub-stantial number of US vessels had indeed been carrying captives from Africa to the Americas since independence, including the *Thomas Jefferson,* a slave ship that disembarked 156 enslaved Africans in Havana four years earlier. A newspaper from Pennsylvania—home of one of the most active abolitionist societies in the early Republic—published a short note about the case, saying that the vessel belonged to a Democrat from Rhode Island and concluding that "it is DE 'WOLF in sheep's cloth-ing' that thus traffic in human flesh, contrary to the laws of nature and humanity." The cryptic reference was to Charles D'Wolf, owner of the *Thomas Jefferson* and a few other slave ships. President Jefferson could have replied that he had "De Wolf by the ears," but that was not the case. Charles D'Wolf and his brother, James, had managed to transform their hometown, the small city of Bristol in the state of Rhode Island, into one of the greatest slave-trading ports in US history. The transforma-tion could not have happened without a contribution from Jefferson himself, who attended to the requests of the brothers to appoint their associate, the slave trader Charles Collins, as the collector for Bristol. The gesture showed Jefferson's appreciation for the political loyalty of Charles and James, active Republicans in a New England increasingly dominated by Federalists.[1]

The D'Wolfs became the largest slave traders in US history, following the lead of other Rhode Island merchants who had been engaging in the commerce since the colonial era. When the Revolution began, Rhode Island was the largest slave-trading colony in British America. In the decades following the American Revolution, the scale of ventures (as well as the existing sources documenting them) improved. Between the decades 1766–75 and 1801–10, the number of slaves embarked per vessel increased 20 percent. The number of people involved in the slave-trading business also increased between 1765 and 1807, which is exactly what one would expect of a US slave trade whose mean annual volume was three times larger in 1804 than in the last decade before the Revolution (1766–75). In fact, the years 1804–7 saw the highest annual average number of slaves ever carried off on vessels from Rhode Island. As historian James Rawley notes, "Rhode Islanders, with just over 1,000 square miles of land to live on, naturally took to the sea." And that included slave trading, one of the most profitable maritime activities of the modern era. The business was, of course, highly competitive and marked by many bankruptcies, but the great profits for the successful stimulated US slave traders—most of them from Rhode Island—to enter aggressively into the transatlantic commerce in Africans, hitherto the domain of European colonial empires (of which they had been part until 1776).[2]

Broader transformations ensured that demand for slaves would continue to rise, opening new opportunities for US slave traders in the aftermath of the American Revolution. In his classic work of 1962, historian Eric Hobsbawm argues that at the center of the transformations that reshaped the world between 1789 and 1848 was what he called a "dual revolution": an economic revolution in Britain and its political counterpart in France. From the perspective of the history of slavery in the Americas, many revisions to his model have been made, above all the incorporation of the events in Saint Domingue, which ultimately led to the foundation of Haiti, as a pivotal moment in the history of the French

Revolution. But his emphasis on these processes is indeed central to a comprehension of the reconfiguration of nineteenth-century slavery. On the one hand, the Industrial Revolution boosted the consumption of slave-grown products such as sugar, coffee, and cotton in the largest cities of the North Atlantic. The Haitian Revolution, on the other hand, brought the largest colonial suppliers of those products to an end. The confluence of these forces led to the dramatic growth of slavery in the Americas, transforming what had been societies with slaves—the Vale do Paraíba in Brazil, states in the US South, and Cuba—into full-blown slave societies.[3]

The greatest opportunities for US slave traders were to be found in the Spanish Empire. While slave-trading patterns of other empires such as the British and the Portuguese generally followed the shape of a parabola between the seventeenth and the nineteenth centuries, the Spanish slave trade had a U shape. After a first slave-trading peak in the seventeenth century—largely a product of the Iberian Union (1580–1640)—the traffic to Spanish colonies decreased and came to be carried mainly by non-Spanish slave traders under exclusive contracts called *asientos* before the late eighteenth century. The number of slave disembarkations remained small compared to other European empires, especially because the main export of the Spanish colonies, bullion, was mainly worked by the large Amerindian population that the Spanish first encountered in Mesoamerica and the Andes in the sixteenth century. With the growing interest of the empire in large-scale plantation agriculture by the second half of the eighteenth century, attempts to create a stronger Spanish slave trade—in the sense of having Spanish dealers as the main carriers of captives—were made without success. The Treaty of San Ildefonso between Portugal and Spain in 1777 settled some of the disputes over territories in South America and transferred to Spain the islands of Fernando Po and Annobon, both located off the coast of Africa. The main goal was transforming these islands into outposts of the Spanish slave trade, but Spanish expeditions successively failed to colonize them in the following two years. Cuba continued to depend on foreign slave traders, a demand that US merchants were eager to supply. Broader geopolitical tensions—namely, the successive wars between European powers, especially Britain and France—also favored the activities of US slave traders, who were largely able to operate as neutrals in the first decades after independence.[4]

The widening base of US participation in the slave trade before abolition took place within a changing legal and social environment in the North Atlantic that constrained their activities. In the United States, all states had prohibited the introduction of Africans by 1798, and the volume of smuggling thereafter had not been significant. But the re-opening of the traffic to South Carolina in 1803—largely a consequence of the Haitian Revolution—added to the existing Spanish demand for slaves and stimulated the entrance of other traders into the business. During the four years of unabated traffic to South Carolina, a number of Southern and European merchants joined the Rhode Island dealers and turned the southern port into the capital of slave disembarkations in the Americas. The expansion of these activities met growing anti-slave-trade pressures in other parts of the country, with slave traders developing a large range of strategies to circumvent the law. The great profits accrued from the traffic ensured that they would continue in the business, a few of them, in fact, past its formal abolition in 1808.[5]

Slave Trading in the Early Republic: Size and Direction

The American Revolution dealt one of the first blows to North American involvement in the transatlantic slave trade by immediately inter-rupting the traffic. Although present estimates point to the disembar-kation of 1,739 slaves in the mainland in 1776, in the seven years that followed to 1783, perhaps fewer than 1,000 Africans were disembarked in the country. Another consequence of independence was closing the major outlet for North American slave traders in the colonial period, the British Caribbean. The old imperial connections between the main-land and the British Caribbean encompassed much more than the slave trade; all commerce from the mainland was completely reconfigured after the Revolution as the British now excluded the vessels of the newly independent nation from their ports. British Caribbean planters could not get access to subsistence goods from the mainland, and US slave traders could not sell them the captives they brought from Africa.[6]

Within a decade of independence, however, the end of British colonial restrictions stimulated the growth of long-distance trade in the United States. These slave traders can be seen as "inheritors of the Revolution," to cite Joyce Appleby, entrepreneurs who launched ventures in multiple directions. The successful entrance of US dealers into the slave trade was part of the emergence of a strong maritime trade sector in the early Republic that explored different markets over the world. These traders embarked slaves in ports as distant as Quelimane, in Mozambique, and disembarked them in South Atlantic cities such as Rio de Janeiro and Montevideo. Between 1782 and the abolition of the slave trade in 1808, estimates are that US merchants were responsible for the embarkation of 165,394 enslaved Africans (out of the 2,336,563 African captives embarked by all nations during that period) (table 2.1). Although their participation was small compared to the 794,107 captives embarked by the Portuguese or the 925,198 embarked by the British, it was marked by a more rapid growth than either of these. Estimates are that in 1807, in fact, US vessels embarked more enslaved Africans (36,217) than the British (36,127) and came very close to the Portuguese (40,138). The rapid growth of US slave-trading activities becomes evident when we compare the years 1782–94 to 1795–1807. The participation of vessels flying the US flag rose from 2.9 to 11.6 percent. The successful entrance of the US merchant fleet in the slave trade was also due to its faster, cheaper, and smaller vessels, which carried fewer captives per voyage than other nations. The average number of slaves carried aboard US vessels never passed 150 between 1782 and 1807, whereas all other nations, with the exception of Denmark between 1795 and 1807, had averages higher than 200 slaves per vessel. Portuguese vessels carried almost 400 slaves per voyage between 1795 and 1807.[7]

Before 1808 there is evidence of at least three vessels disembarking slaves in Brazil under the US flag. Writing in 1797 from Rio de Janeiro, a slave captain told William Vernon and his associates—all notorious Rhode Island slave traders—about the prices of slaves and sugar in the city, and of an offer from a Mozambican merchant willing to buy their ship, the *Ascension*. That same year the ship disembarked 208 enslaved Africans from Mozambique in Montevideo. Thus US merchants took advantage of opportunities that ranged from the carrying of slaves to the selling of ships in the southernmost part of the Atlantic, although

Table 2.1. Estimated number of vessels and the slaves they embarked by flag flown at point of departure from the Americas to Africa, 1782–1807

Country	1782–94				1795–1807			
	Voyages	Average number of slaves	Total slaves	Percentage of trade	Voyages	Average number of slaves	Total slaves	Percentage of trade
Spain	17	237	4,013	0.3	33	231	7,545	0.7
Portugal	1,131	311	351,174	29.0	1,150	385	442,933	39.3
Great Britain	1,416	300	424,518	35.1	1,680	298	500,680	44.4
Netherlands	84	258	21,633	1.8	7	269	1,874	0.2
United States	270	128	34,565	2.9	920	142	130,829	11.6
France	1,059	336	356,400	29.5	36	301	10,972	1.0
Denmark	56	312	17,338	1.4	199	161	32,087	2.8

Note: For methodology, see table 2.2.
Source: www.slavevoyages.org

Table 2.2. Estimated number of vessels and the slaves they embarked by country of ship construction, 1795–1807

Ship construction	Voyages	Percentage	Slaves
Europe	2,953	74.6	840,759
North America	563	14.2	160,386
Caribbean	347	8.8	98,764
Portuguese America	6	0.1	1,688
East Indies	89	2.2	25,324
Total	3,958	100	1,126,921

Note: This table is based on a sample of 1,409 voyages for which the place of construction of the vessel is available (1,335 voyages for 1795–1807 and 74 for 1808–20). First, I extracted the total number of embarked slaves from the estimates page on *Voyages* for the two periods (1,126,921 captives for 1795–1807 and 840,754 for 1808–20). Second, I divided this number by the average of embarked slaves per vessel for both periods (284.7 for 1795–1807 and 333.4 for 1808–20) to derive the total number of voyages (3,958 for 1795–1807 and 2,522 for 1808–20). Third, I divided these voyages by the percentage of voyages by each place of construction in the sample of 1,409 voyages, getting the estimates for each place of construction. The fourth and final step was to multiply the number of voyages by the average of slaves carried on board each vessel to reach the number of slaves carried by place of construction. One voyage that had Spanish Central America as the place of construction of the vessel was included in the Caribbean category. Two other voyages that had India as the place of construction of the vessels were included in the East Indies category.
Source: www.slavevoyages.org

slavery in this region was still incipient compared to its size in the mid-nineteenth century. About 14 percent of all slave voyages between 1795 and 1807 were on vessels built in North America, resulting in the embarkation of 160,386 enslaved Africans (table 2.2). There is a small discrepancy between the number of Africans carried by North American vessels and those carried on vessels flying the US flag, which may be due to the large number of vessels built in Canada that were included in the category North America. Estimates for this same period are that vessels flying the US flag embarked 130,829 enslaved Africans (see table 2.1). In general, US-built vessels flew the US flag during this early period, as most countries at that time required ships using their flag to have been built in home ports or captured from another country in war.[8]

The other three documented slave voyages of the *Ascension* disembarked Africans in Havana, Cuba. While the British had closed their Caribbean parts to US merchants, Spanish America, as well as parts of the French, Danish, and Swedish Caribbean, did just the opposite. Cuba became the main destination for slaves carried on vessels flying the US flag before South Carolina officially reopened the traffic to the state between 1803 and 1807. Unlike their sporadic presence in Rio de Janeiro, Rio de la Plata, and other parts of the South Atlantic, US slave traders established strong connections with Cuba that persisted well into the nineteenth century. Up to the last decades of the eighteenth century the Spanish colony had great strategic importance but only marginal productive significance within the Spanish Empire, producing some tobacco with little slave labor. By the 1750s the production of sugar on the island had increased, but it still lagged well behind the levels of the neighboring British and French Caribbean territories.[9]

A confluence of events would completely change the history of Cuba and its place in the world economy. The first transformation was brought by the Seven Years' War and the British occupation of Havana in 1762. Spain's recovery of Cuba under the terms of the Peace of Paris in the aftermath of the war, argues John Elliott, "made Cuba an ideal laboratory for trying out a programme of comprehensive reform." Thus, from the 1760s on, restrictions on slave imports were gradually loosened as part of the Bourbon reforms. As ties with the British Caribbean withered, Cuba emerged as one of the most promising markets for US merchants. The second pivotal event was the slave uprising that led to the end of the French colony of Saint Domingue, the largest sugar and coffee producer in the world, as well as home of a substantial cotton and indigo production by the late eighteenth century. The end of the French colony catapulted Cuba into the world economy as an important coffee and sugar producer. This shift was enhanced by the suppression of the transatlantic slave trade (1807) and ultimately slavery (1833–37) in the British Caribbean, opening the way for the expansion of sugar and coffee production in the Spanish island. The dramatic rise in the demand for labor reflected in the large number of slaves disembarked on the island between 1783 and 1820, a total of 225,594 captives.[10]

These changes also combined with a few others to spawn a radical transformation of the US South. The country had already taken advantage of interimperial rivalries in the Treaty of San Lorenzo with Spain (also known as Pinckney's Treaty, it granted navigation rights on the Mississippi River to the United States). The economic growth of the country received another boost with the purchase of Louisiana from France in 1803, which opened a vast land for the expansion of cotton— on the rise since the development of the cotton gin by Eli Whitney in 1793—and sugar production. The demand for labor in the new republic reached an unprecedented level, with present estimates pointing to the disembarkation of almost 100,000 enslaved Africans between 1783 and 1807. The changes brought by the purchase of Louisiana in 1803 also reflected in South Carolina's decision to reopen the slave trade, with the port of Charleston alone witnessing the disembarkation of approximately 40,000 Africans before 1808.[11]

During the two decades after the Constitutional Convention, Rhode Island slave traders had been the main slave merchants but not the only ones. As historian James McMillin shows, European (especially British) and Southern merchants, some of them already involved in a few slave importations in the early 1780s, took advantage of the opportunities that emerged with the reopening of the traffic to South Carolina in 1803. Estimates are that British vessels carried 20,285 enslaved Africans (31 percent) out of the 65,159 disembarked in Georgia and, especially, South Carolina between 1803 and 1807. Of these, 44,788 captives were brought by Rhode Islanders and Southern merchants. One strategy to estimate the participation of each group is to use the place of registration of slave voyages. The *Voyages* database contains 281 voyages that had South Carolina as their place of slave disembarkation, of which 213 have the place of registration of the vessel. Charleston is the city with the largest number of vessels registered, 81 (38 percent). Very close to it, however, were vessels registered in New England, 78 (36.6 percent). The vast majority of these New England vessels were registered in Rhode Island, more specifically in the cities of Newport (31 vessels) and Bristol (34 vessels). The remaining vessels were registered in Europe (38 vessels) or other US ports (16 vessels, 11 of which have unspecified US ports). Thus, despite the growth and diversification of US participation in the slave trade between 1803 and 1807, Rhode Island slave traders continued to be the main dealers in the early Republic. While a number of Charleston and Savannah companies had withdrawn from the slave trade in 1785, Rhode Island merchants continued to disembark large numbers of enslaved Africans in Cuba through to and beyond the turn of the century. By 1803 they simply expanded the range of their operations to include the growing demand from the Lower South, strategically choosing between Charleston and Havana according to circumstances.[12]

The slave-trading networks of Rhode Island were connected not only to specific ports in the Americas but also to specific parts of Africa. Links between particular regions in Africa and in the Americas actually formed a major feature of the transatlantic slave trade as a whole. Tastes for individual products, along with winds and ocean currents, all helped create such links. For Rhode Island slave traders, the Gold Coast would become their main source of captives. Vessels that had started their voyages in Rhode Island ports embarked 40,221 enslaved Africans on the Gold Coast between 1783 and 1807, the equivalent of more than half of all captives carried by vessels departing Rhode Island (table 2.3). From the perspective of the Gold Coast, that meant 83.7 percent of all captives taken from the region by vessels flying the US flag. The main ports in the region, Anomabu and the Cape Coast Castle, together accounted for over 95 percent of all embarkations by US slavers. By contrast, vessels departing South Carolina (which as we have seen were owned by Southerners, Britons, and a few Rhode Islanders) went mainly to Sierra Leone and West Central Africa, which together supplied 65 percent (41,900) of all captives carried by them. The reopening of the slave trade to South Carolina was therefore marked by the juxtaposition of multiple slave-trading networks.

Despite the centrality of the Gold Coast, Rhode Islanders had important connections with other parts of Africa. The Upper Guinea region formed the second most important source of their slaves. The Gold Coast and Senegambia—and West Africa as a whole—were located in a privileged position to serve North American slave markets, given the clockwise North Atlantic gyre. This widespread US presence was due largely to the success of New England rum as a trading good on the coast of Africa. Products forged transatlantic connections as much as did winds and ocean currents. The historical connection, for instance, be-

Table 2.3. Estimated number of embarked slaves by US region of departure and region of embarkation, 1783–1807

			Region of embarkation			
US region of departure	Sierra Leone	Gold Coast	Other West Africa	West Central Africa	Southeast Africa	Total
Rhode Island	16,708 (37.5%)	40,221 (83.7%)	10,208 (31.4%)	1,486 (7.5%)	9,325 (46.6%)	77,948
South Carolina	23,771 (53.3%)	1,208 (2.5%)	15,333 (47.1%)	18,129 (91.3%)	5,508 (27.5%)	63,949
Other United States	4,123 (9.2%)	6,644 (13.8%)	7,011 (21.5%)	241 (1.2%)	5,160 (25.8%)	23,179
Total	44,602 (100%)	48,073 (100%)	32,553 (100%)	19,855 (100%)	19,993 (100%)	165,077

Note: The category "Other West Africa" includes Senegambia and Offshore Atlantic, Windward Coast, Bight of Benin, and Bight of Biafra. The category "Other United States" includes New Hampshire, Massachusetts, Connecticut, New York, Pennsylvania, Virginia, Georgia, and unidentified North American regions. This table was created based on the estimates for all voyages carried under the US flag from the *estimates* interface in the Voyages database between 1783 and 1807. I cross-tabulated the data from the *search* interface for region of departure and region of embarkation, calculated the percentages, and used them to divide the estimates.

tween Rio de Janeiro and Angola or Bahia and the Bight of Benin, relied heavily on specific products of these regions. Rum was the Rhode Island counterpart to Bahian tobacco or Rio's *geribita*. The "rum-men," as New Englanders came to be known on the African coast, developed important ties based on the heavy exportation of the product starting in the 1730s. The governor-in-chief of the Cape Coast Castle told his London associates that "West India[n] rum never will sell here while there is any Americans here." The outbreak of the American Revolution meant no more Rhode Island rum, which generated anxiety for English slave traders on the coast of Africa. When US merchants eventually reentered the trade, they found a ready market on which to reestablish their own triangular trade and gain access to the forts dominated by Europeans. A few US merchants also became integrated to Euro-African communities, especially on the Upper Guinea coast, and operated as middlemen for many US slave traders. Some of them came from British colonies in North America and, after the American Revolution, became US citizens, owning factories around the Rio Pongo with names such as Charleston, South Carolina, and Boston.[13]

Notwithstanding the role of winds, ocean currents, and the demand for rum that made possible a strong network connecting Rhode Island to the Gold Coast, Rhode Island slave traders did venture into the South Atlantic in both Africa and the Americas. The third most important region of purchase for Rhode Island slave traders in the period was Southeast Africa. From 1782 to 1807 there is evidence of at least nine voyages organized by US slave traders to Mozambique and one to Quelimane, carrying more than 2,000 slaves to the Americas. About 900 of these captives were disembarked in Cuba, 217 in the Dutch Caribbean, and 548 in Montevideo. American slave traders in fact carried about 11 percent of all transatlantic slaves disembarked in Montevideo during those years. This unusual connection, which straddled North and South Atlantic gyres, was another expression of the world of freer trade that US slave traders were helping to create.

Early Attempts at Regulation

A growing number of historians interpret the American Revolution as the source of contradictory forces that eventually clashed over the issue of slavery more often than previously thought. While, on the one hand, revolutionary ideals fueled abolitionist movements in the country, on the other, they became the basis of proslavery discourses based on the right of property, including property in human beings. These tensions marked the history of the US slave trade in complex ways, punctuating it with conflicts and compromises that involved a multiplicity of material and moral interests. Besides the moral condemnation of the slave trade coming mainly, but not only, from Quakers and other religious groups in the North, some opposed the trade for fear of the threat posed by a large African population. Moreover, slaveholders in the Chesapeake welcomed the abolition of the transatlantic slave trade as a strategy to increase the value of their own surplus slave population. "Without the prior anxiety about the impact of slave imports on colonial society, and the lack of necessity for African newcomers in most places," Philip Morgan argues, "the moral case against the Atlantic slave trade would have carried far less weight." This context resembled, in some aspects, the British case. At the turn of the century an increasing number of West Indian planters portrayed themselves as enlightened paternalists and believed that the better treatment of their captives would lead to a natural growth of their enslaved population. Those in older islands also opposed the traffic in order to raise the value of their captives. Some of their interests, therefore, converged with those of abolitionists, although their ultimate goal was the strengthening of slavery, not its destruction.[14]

The tensions brought by these multiple forces permeated political debates in the United States from day one. In a well-known passage of the draft of the Declaration of Independence, Thomas Jefferson indicted the British king for waging a "cruel war against human nature itself" in his support of the slave trade to the colonies, but the Continental Congress ultimately excluded the paragraph from the final version. Jefferson would later observe that the passage was eliminated because of pressures coming from South Carolina and Georgia, which still wanted to import slaves, and from "our Northern brethren," who although having very few slaves themselves, "had been pretty considerable carriers of them to others."[15]

Despite this early indication that the emerging condemnation of the slave trade was not consensual, it was during the debates of the Constitutional Convention that these disagreements—as well as the shared interests of people in New England and in the Lower South—would come to the forefront. When the convention met in 1787, only Georgia had not prohibited the importation of African slaves into its territory yet. Massachusetts and New Hampshire had abolished slavery altogether, while all other ten states had prohibited the traffic or imposed prohibitive duties (Pennsylvania and North Carolina). In South Carolina's case, however, the legislation was considered a temporary measure. That its opposition to the trade was contingent became evident during the debates, when figures such as John Rutledge and Charles Pinckney united with representatives from Georgia in protecting the traffic and turning its acceptance into a nonnegotiable condition for the integration of their states into the Union.

New England states joined their Lower South counterparts on crucial votes prohibiting the taxation of exports and the importation of slaves. The line of reasoning from South Carolinians and Georgians, which proved to be politically effective, was that the people from New England were the main carriers of their slave-grown exports. This alliance led to the rather peculiar event of a New Englander, Oliver Ellsworth of Connecticut, defending the right of South Carolina and Georgia to buy African slaves against the attacks of the Virginian George Mason. The final outcome of these debates was section 9 of the first article of the US Constitution, which limited the power of Congress to regulate the slave trade until the year of 1808 and left to each individual state the decision regarding the introduction of enslaved Africans into their territories. The Constitution did not refer to the involvement of US merchants in the slave trade to foreign territories, dealing exclusively with the importation of slaves to US ports.[16]

Despite the compromise, calls for new regulations of the trade continued. Already in 1789, during the First Congress, Josiah Parker of Virginia called for a ten-dollar tax on every African imported into the country as a necessary measure to discourage the traffic. The bill generated debates and a critique of slavery by James Madison in support of Parker. The reaction from the Georgia and South Carolina congressmen was almost immediate, showing, as historian Donald Robinson argues, "the pain that was felt whenever this sensitive nerve received the slightest touch." In one of the most radical responses of the time, James Jackson of Georgia argued that Africans were better off as slaves in America than as free people in Africa. The bill offered by Parker would be forgotten until the Eighth Congress, when the reopening of the slave trade to South Carolina brought the question back to debate.[17]

Northern abolitionists, nonetheless, continued to pressure for new regulations of the traffic, with the Pennsylvania Abolition Society sending at least ten petitions related to the issue between 1787 and 1820. Already in February 1790, Congress received three petitions related to slavery, two from societies of Quakers and one from the Pennsylvania Abolition Society. The petition sent by the abolition society was one of the most radical documents of its own history, calling for federal action against the slave trade for humanitarian and religious reasons. The petition, signed by Benjamin Franklin, in fact, went a step further and asked for the government to act against slavery altogether, arguing that since the federal government was invested of powers to promote welfare and secure "the blessings of liberty," its actions should be "administered without distinction of colour to all descriptions of people." Seventy years later the Georgian slaveholder Thomas R. R. Cobb would refer to that petition as the first act of a never-ending agitation against slavery in the US government.[18]

The Southern reaction was immediate and furious. Representatives from South Carolina and Georgia stressed that the petition had made an unconstitutional request, since Congress was prohibited from interfering in the slave trade before 1808, and that it ultimately aimed at Southern slavery, which was indeed the case. These congressmen argued that petitions should be returned to abolitionists and the issue of slavery avoided altogether. A committee was formed to investigate the powers of Congress over slavery and the slave trade as well as its limits. Whereas the first three clauses of the report the committee produced pointed to the limits of federal action against slavery (prohibiting the interdiction of traffic before 1808, emancipating slaves, or interfering in the internal policies of slave states), the following three showed that some room for action had nonetheless been made (rights to pass a ten-dollar tax on imported captives, to prevent foreigners from using US ships or ports for the slave trade, and to pass laws to ameliorate the conditions of the Middle Passage). A seventh clause was a nod to the "humane objects" of the petitioners, which should, according to the report, be addressed by Congress in the future.

A long debate ensued, with William L. Smith of South Carolina further developing some of the arguments made by James Jackson the previous year. Slavery suited Africans because they were by nature "averse to labor." Emancipation in turn stimulated their laziness and, perhaps even worse, brought dangerous ideas to the existing slave population. His arguments also touched on the sexual mixing of races that would come with emancipation and, drawing on the ideas of the racial inferiority of blacks espoused by Jefferson in *Notes on Virginia*, stressed

the disaster that this intermingling would be for whites. After the debates the report of the committee was revised and a simpler form passed
with three provisions: the first two showed that Congress could neither
prohibit the slave trade before 1808 nor interfere in domestic slavery;
the third allowed it to prevent the participation of US citizens in the
slave trade to non-US territories and to pass laws demanding better conditions aboard slave ships.[19]

The Pennsylvania Abolition Society changed the tone of its petitions after 1790 and limited itself to emphasizing those aspects of the
slave trade that Congress reportedly had the power to regulate. In 1794,
without much debate, new legislation was passed to attend those requests. The act of 1794 ("An Act to Prohibit the Carrying on the Slave
Trade from the United States to Any Foreign Place or Country") made it
illegal for any US citizen or foreigner residing in the country to "either
as master, factor or owner, build, fit, equip, load or otherwise prepare
any ship or vessel, within any port or place of the said United States," to
the slave traffic to other countries. The act specified a fine of two thousand dollars, forfeiture of the vessel, and a two-hundred-dollar fine for
every slave found aboard. Half of the money from fines would go to the
prosecutors. Further federal legislation was passed in 1800 strengthening the federal restrictions of the 1794 act. The specification to US ports
present in the act of 1794 was gone. It was now unlawful for US citizens
and residents to participate in any slave voyage, even if it did not involve
US ports. Convicted investors would have to pay double the value of their
interests on the vessel and on the slaves found on board. US captains and
sailors found aboard slave ships could receive fines of up to two thousand
dollars and be sentenced to up to two years in prison. The amendment
also permitted the US navy to seize US slavers, with half of the value of
forfeited ships going to the crews of the captors.[20]

The Pennsylvania Abolition Society used these laws to pressure slave
traders and the government. Members of the society tracked more than
fifty cases of slave-trading violations, compiling lists that included the
names of captains, destinations, and numbers of slaves carried. With the
act of 1794, US slave traders, according to federal laws, were allowed to
deliver their captives only in Georgia and after 1798, when that state outlawed the traffic, not even there. Thereafter, the society frequently used

the act to prosecute individuals engaging in the traffic to other countries. In one case one of its members traveled to South Carolina to serve a writ against a captain accused of carrying 300 captives to foreign merchants. The society also became responsible for the 134 captives found by the US Navy on board two US ships, the *Prudent* and the *Phoebe,* off the coast of Cuba in 1800. Both vessels were taken to Philadelphia, where Judge Richard Peters made the Pennsylvania Abolition Society the guardian of the seized captives. The society then indentured them to farmers in Philadelphia and nearby counties. These laws thus provided tools to abolitionists in other parts of the North, who though they could not bring the traffic to an end before 1808, did create new pressures and force US slave traders to adopt novel strategies to circumvent them.[21]

Bristol, a Slave-Trading Enclave

The effects of anti-slave-trade actions on US slave traders are particularly clear in the history of Rhode Island, where dealers became increasingly isolated in specific locales. We can tabulate the number of voyages, slaves disembarked in the Americas, and the main ports of departure of the main slave traders in US history, including the colonial period, from information in the *Voyages* database (table 2.4). The prominent role of the D'Wolf family and, consequently, the small city of Bristol is evident. Besides James D'Wolf, three other D'Wolfs figure among the top slave traders in the country. It is important to note that these voyages were usually joint ventures. For the 517 voyages made under the US flag for which evidence of ownership exists, 299, or 58 percent, were joint adventures. It is reasonable to infer, however, that many others were also jointly owned and that only the name of the principal owner has survived. Given the high risks involved in the slave trade, cost sharing had always been an important strategy in these voyages. As Rachel Chernos Lin has shown, joint ventures also opened the opportunity for many occasional investors who were not necessarily part of local elites. This also explains, to a large extent, the hegemonic role of the family within Bristol.[22]

The history of the D'Wolfs in the slave trade started with the activities of Mark Antony D'Wolf, which predated the Revolution. When he

Table 2.4. Leading US slave traders in the Voyages
database, 1645–1820

Name	Voyages	Slaves	Port of departure
D'Wolf, James	36	3,414	Bristol
Gardner, Caleb	22	2,523	Newport
Vernon, William	16	2,375	Newport
D'Wolf, John	17	2,283	Bristol
D'Wolf, George	13	2,135	Bristol
D'Wolf, William	20	2,096	Bristol
Clarke, Peleg	9	2,057	Newport
Brown, Samuel	14	1,775	RI (unspecified)
Lopez, Aaron	13	1,580	Newport
Sterry, Cyprian	17	1,543	RI (unspecified)

Source: www.slavevoyages.org

entered the slave trade in the mid-eighteenth century, the business was an integral and legitimate part of trade in the British Empire. Born in Guadeloupe, the head of the D'Wolf family joined the world of seafaring, and ultimately the slave trade, through Simeon Potter, an important Rhode Island merchant. Mark Antony had thirteen children, and many of them became involved with the slave trade at some point in their lives. After Mark Antony's last slave voyage in 1774, the D'Wolfs halted participation in the trade until 1787. From that year to 1807, the family financed at least ninety-six voyages, bringing more than ten thousand slaves to the Americas. James D'Wolf, the main slave trader, financed in sole or joint adventures thirty-six voyages out of the ninety-six (see table 2.4).[23]

The Bristol–Anomabu/Cape Coast–Havana connection emerged as the trade route accounting for the bulk of the family's slave-trading business. It is possible to track the port of embarkation of about half of the 11,455 slaves carried off from Africa by the D'Wolfs. Of these captives, more than half were purchased on the Gold Coast. This resembled the broader pattern of the Rhode Island participation in the slave trade at this time. And just like other Rhode Islanders, the D'Wolfs adventured in ports beyond the Rhode Island–Gold Coast–Cuba connection. James D'Wolf's vessels *Punch* and *Ann* disembarked at least 189 slaves in Montevideo between 1800 and 1805. Their predominance in the business was also facilitated by their easy access to cheap rum, with James D'Wolf marrying the daughter of William Bradford, owner of one of the largest rum distilleries in Bristol.[24]

From Bristol, the D'Wolfs and their associates continued their trade with Cuba and successfully entered the Charleston slave market after 1803. The family sent to Charleston the son of William D'Wolf, Henry D'Wolf, to start a commission house responsible for the family cargoes. He partnered with a Charleston merchant, Charles Christian, and used newspaper advertisements to sell the slaves brought into the port by the D'Wolfs and other Rhode Islanders. During the year of 1807, the company advertised the arrivals of vessels bringing large numbers of "Prime Windward Coast Slaves."[25] Yet the main slave market for voyages organized by the D'Wolfs continued to be Havana. Of the 10,000 slaves introduced by D'Wolf vessels, 5,558 were disembarked in Cuba, 2,161 in Charleston, and smaller numbers in other ports. Here, too, the pattern of voyages financed by the D'Wolfs mirrored the slave trade of Rhode Island as a whole. Excluded from the British Caribbean, with slavery destroyed in Saint Domingue and with US markets officially closed (except for 1804–7), it is no surprise that Cuba emerged as the major destination for slaves carried on US ships. In light of this, just how important were Africa and Cuba to Bristol in this period?[26]

We can address this question by drawing on the insurance books of the Bristol Insurance Company, which give us a picture of all of Bristol's long-distance trade. Vessels departed from Bristol to many parts of the world, from China to Montevideo, indicating just how successful New Englanders were in the international long-distance maritime trade in the pre-steam era. If we examine the distribution of insured values by the destinations of the insured vessels, we can see the relative importance of the African trade, especially after the reopening of the South Carolina market in 1803 (table 2.5). In the two years after the company opened for business in 1800, the route from Rhode Island to Havana and back was the most important branch of trade, accounting for almost 40

Table 2.5. Amounts insured by the Bristol Insurance Company
by voyage itinerary

Voyage	1800–1801		1804–6	
	Total insured	Percentage	Total insured	Percentage
US–Cuba	130,030	37.1	162,875	33.9
Africa	51,280	14.6	156,344	32.6
Europe	57,718	16.4	73,700	15.4
Asia	14,000	4.0	32,000	6.7
Caribbean	88,930	25.3	49,190	10.2
South America	9,000	2.6	6,000	1.2
Total	350,958	100	480,109	100

Source: Bristol Insurance Company Books in Jay Coughtry, ed., *Papers of the American Slave Trade,*
Black Studies Research Sources (Bethesda, MD: University Publications of America, 1996)

percent of the value of all insured voyages. Voyages to Africa, in contrast, took up only 15 percent of insured values. The reopening of the South Carolina slave trade meant that the percentage of all voyages represented by round trips to Africa doubled the share of voyages insured in Bristol. For a time, nearly one third of all Bristol-insured long-distance trade consisted of slave voyages, and this ratio was probably higher than that of any other Atlantic port from which slave voyages set out.

This voluminous traffic did not take place in a vacuum, and the growth of Bristol as a slave-trading port was largely the product of growing abolitionist pressures within Rhode Island. When the D'Wolfs and other Rhode Island slave traders resumed their engagement with the traffic after the Revolution, it soon became clear that it was not business as usual. Most visibly, in 1791, Captain James D'Wolf was brought to trial in Newport for the murder of a slave woman during a voyage from the Gold Coast to Cuba. According to one of the sailors, the slave had fallen ill, most likely a victim of smallpox. After isolating her for two days, D'Wolf warned his sailors that if the woman stayed on board he risked losing the majority of his slaves. He then asked John Cranston— the sailor who testified—if he could do the job. Cranston refused, and

D'Wolf, with the help of another sailor, threw her into the sea. After being indicted for murder, he immediately left on a voyage to avoid the charges. The murder indictment dragged on for a few years until, in 1796, D'Wolf arranged for two members of the crew of the *Polly* to testify in Saint Thomas, a slave-trading port in the West Indies. They endorsed Cranston's account of the murder of the slave but emphasized the lack of choices left to Captain D'Wolf. The case was not pursued, but that a sailor had denounced his captain for the murder of a slave indicated the new environment in which Rhode Island slave traders were operating. This context of an expanding demand for slaves in the Americas along- side new attitudes to the traffic in the North Atlantic generated tensions that pervaded both public and private life in the state.[27]

These tensions were particularly marked in the history of the Brown family of Providence. Nicholas, Joseph, Moses, and John were partners in various trading ventures, including the trade in Africans in the years preceding the Revolution. It was also before the war that the Quakers of the Society of Friends in Rhode Island started to question not only the participation of their members in the slave trade but also the very issue of slave ownership. In 1773, the society officially urged its members to manumit their slaves and completely withdraw from the traffic. About this time Moses Brown joined the Quakers and followed that injunction. In the following years Moses became a militant abolitionist, writing and engaging in political debates over antislavery legislation. His brother John, on the other hand, continued to finance a few slave-trading ven- tures until the end of the century, becoming one of the most outspoken defenders of the business. Through the last quarter of the eighteenth century, Moses and John engaged in heated debates that assumed a pub- lic dimension in newspapers, political disputes, and legal cases.[28]

The trajectories of Thomas and Welcome Arnold in some ways resembled the story of the Browns, although lacking open conflicts. Like Moses Brown, the lawyer Thomas Arnold had been a Quaker and a key figure in the Providence Abolition Society. His brother, Welcome, a merchant who had organized a number of voyages with the Browns and co-owned a distillery at one point, had a more ambiguous take on slavery and the slave trade. In 1794, he organized at least one voyage to Africa with the *Rebecca,* which supposedly embarked 114 slaves on the

Gold Coast and disembarked the surviving 93 in the Caribbean. By 1797, however, Welcome Arnold apparently had abandoned the slave trade. This may have been a result of anti-slave-trade legislation and, more important, the use of these laws by Rhode Island abolitionists.[29]

On the federal level, as we have seen, US citizens had been prohibited from engaging in the slave trade to other countries since 1794, but it was on the state level that legislation forbidding all involvement in the slave trade first appeared. In 1779, during the Revolutionary War, Rhode Island prohibited the selling of slaves out of the state. In 1784, an act to gradually abolish slavery was also passed, and in 1787, the year of the Constitutional Convention, participation in the slave trade for citizens of Rhode Island was forbidden. The abolitionist Samuel Hopkins rejoiced that the state whose citizens had been the largest carriers of captives was also the first in the world to prohibit it. A penalty of one hundred pounds for every slave transported and one thousand pounds for every vessel involved in the trade was passed. Half of the money from fines would go to informers. The following year, as a result of the growing activism of Rhode Island abolitionists, Connecticut and Massachusetts also prohibited their citizens from participating in the slave trade. And it was in Massachusetts that the first prosecution against a slave trader took place. In 1789, the New Bedford abolitionist William Rotch started a suit against the *Hope,* a ship that had disembarked at least 283 captives in the Caribbean in three voyages between 1787 and 1789 under the command of John Stanton. The ship was the property of the Newport slave traders Caleb Gardner and Nathaniel Briggs and was indicted for its 1788 voyage, which had started at Boston. The defense argued that the owners were not citizens of Massachusetts and therefore not liable to be prosecuted under their laws, but to no avail. The prosecution ultimately won the case, though the penalties were small. Moses Brown himself had asked Rotch to drop the suggested fine of six thousand pounds at the beginning of the case. Many Quaker abolitionists strongly believed that if the mere existence of the laws did not dissuade slave traders from carrying the traffic, their counsels and letters on the issue would. The use of legislation, Brown argued when requesting Rotch to drop the fines, had the goal of showing the principles at stake. Brown was not completely wrong, since the law of 1787 apparently did have an immediate impact on Rhode Island merchants. In 1788, only four slave voyages departed Rhode Island for Africa, but thereafter, Rhode Island–based slave voyages increased significantly.[30]

Established at the heart of US slave trading, the Providence Abolition Society was able to use the legislation against violators of the law more effectively than its Pennsylvanian counterpart. The more idealistic approach of the Providence Abolition Society certainly did little to curb the number of Africans disembarked in the Americas, as historian Jay Coughtry emphasizes, but it did contribute to the broader shift in attitudes that would ultimately engulf the Rhode Island slave traders. And it did have some immediate impact on the forms of the trade and its main carriers. The act of 1794, for which Moses Brown had lobbied, further stimulated the activities of the Providence Abolition Society, especially because their pleas and letters to slave traders were not having the intended effect. Between 1794 and 1804 there were at least twenty-four legal prosecutions against Rhode Island slave traders (not all of them started by the Providence Abolition Society but most certainly depending on information provided by the society). The merchants Nicholas Brown and Thomas P. Ives of Providence quickly perceived that the law brought new pressures and, already in 1794, sent clear instructions to the master of their ship *Charlotte,* on a voyage to Africa, not to receive any slaves on board. The returning cargo should consist merely of rice, salt, hides, and goat shins. It seems likely that the company never really engaged in the slave trade, as its history in the legitimate commerce with Africa in the ensuing decades attests, but that the merchants had to warn their captain not to purchase any slaves indicates the changing environment in their hometown.[31]

The first cases were initiated in 1797 and involved Cyprian Sterry and John Brown for the financing of the voyages of, respectively, the *Ann* and the *Hope,* together responsible for the disembarkation of a total of 318 enslaved Africans in Cuba the previous year. Shortly after the Providence Abolition Society started the prosecutions, Sterry—the largest Providence slave trader—abandoned the business. The society promised to drop the case if Sterry made a written pledge to withdraw from the African slave trade, which he did. The case of John Brown was longer and more complicated. In 1797, Brown wrote to Welcome Arnold asking him to convince his brother Thomas that he had abandoned the "Guinea trade." Brown stressed that whereas he had been "concerned but in one voyage," other individuals and "several other towns have been concerned in many voyages." His main complaint was that while Thomas was prosecuting him and Cyprian Sterry, merchants in the neighboring towns of Bristol and Newport continued to be involved in much larger slave-trading operations. Welcome did write to his brother, only to receive complaints about the past behavior of John Brown. Thomas also argued that the case involving John Brown would be a good test of the effectiveness of the slave trade act of 1794. And indeed the district judge decreed the forfeiture of the vessel, but that was it. In a second trial Brown was acquitted.[32]

Pressures on Providence slave traders increased, and so did the role of Bristol. The D'Wolfs also had an abolitionist Quaker within the family, Levi D'Wolf, who had abandoned the trade in Africans after his first voyage and become a member of the Rhode Island Quaker Society. His conversion apparently did not generate tensions within the family until much later. Around 1800, pressure against the D'Wolfs' slave-trading activities came mostly from outside the family (and, by extension, Bristol). It grew with the efforts of a few federal officers, especially William Ellery. One of the signers of the Declaration of Independence, Ellery served as the first customs collector for Newport from the ratification of the Constitution until his death in 1820. In 1799, he denounced a slaver from Boston that arrived at Newport, leading to its subsequent forfeiture by the district judge. That same year he confiscated the slave schooner *Lucy*, property of Charles D'Wolf and, in a court-ordered auction, sent his deputy to bid on the vessel. Former owners had customarily been able to purchase their own forfeited vessels for low prices during these auctions, since no one else dared to bid against and thus upset the "Great Ones," as Ellery sarcastically called the slave traders. John Brown, Charles D'Wolf, and his brother James D'Wolf attempted to convince the deputy to abandon the auction and, after a negative answer, organized his kidnapping so that the schooner be returned to the D'Wolfs without problems. According to the deputy, "I was forcibly seized & carried on Board of a small sail Boat, lying close by the Street. [I] struggled, resisted & exclaimed for Help but in vain; there were sev-

eral people in sight at the Time, . . . but . . . afforded me no assistance."
Although Ellery and other abolitionists attempted to restrict the actions
of the slave-trading community of Rhode Island, individuals such as the
D'Wolfs managed to continue their activities within certain geographic
limits—more specifically, the limits of Bristol. In this case, as the letter
written by the deputy shows, the kidnapping took place under the eyes
of other individuals who did not attempt to interfere. The town truly
became a proslave trade refuge.[33]

In late 1800, a few months after the passage of the amendment to
the slave trade act of 1794, the secretary of the treasury sent a special
prosecutor, John Leonard, to act against the Rhode Island slave traders.
One of his first actions was to indict James D'Wolf for the voyage of the
Fanny, which had already been condemned by a vice-admiralty court in
the Bahamas. D'Wolf was sued for twenty thousand dollars but was rapidly acquitted in the district court. The ship's captain, Nathaniel Ingra-
ham, was not as lucky in a subsequent prosecution by Leonard. Ingra-
ham was sentenced to a heavy fine and a two-year jail term, becoming
the only Rhode Island slave trader to actually spend time in prison. The
actions of the special prosecutor generated a backlash from the Bristol slave traders, and in 1803, Leonard was physically assaulted. A New
Bedford newspaper told the story of the Bostonian who had "shown
himself inimical to the slave trade, by entering a complaint against a
vessel concerned in that nefarious commerce." After stopping at Bristol
on a return trip from Newport, "he was assaulted by a large company
of miscreants, taken from the public house, where he had put up, was
wounded by a knife, robbed of his pocket-book and papers, and otherwise inhumanly treated."[34]

The D'Wolfs' power increased within their town, but Rhode Island
was nevertheless going through important changes, as the actions by
Ellery and others demonstrated. For this, the most effective counter-
attack was the request made by James D'Wolf and Shearjashub Bourne
for a federal statute creating an independent customs collectorship for
Bristol, hitherto subject to the Newport office. This strategy might be
seen as a Rhode Island defense against the 1800 bill that put teeth into the
earlier prohibitions of the US foreign slave trade. But the request for the
statute, which passed in 1800, was only the first step. The officer appointed

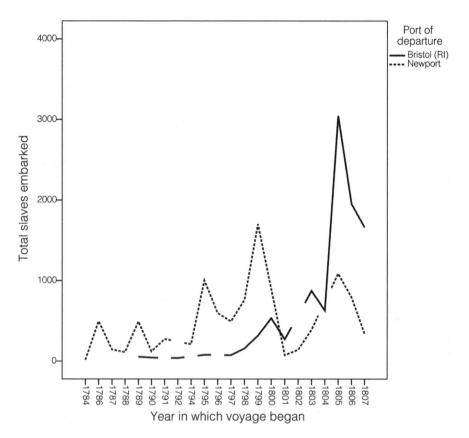

Fig. 1. Number of slaves disembarked in the Americas by vessels departing from Bristol and Newport (Source: www.slavevoyages.org)

to the new collectorship, Jonathan Russell, actually sought to enforce the legislation. Not until 1804 were the D'Wolfs able to obtain the position for their own nominee, Charles Collins. The appointment was nicely timed to coincide with the emergence of the booming slave markets of Cuba and South Carolina. According to historian Peter Coleman, so long as Collins—a slave trader himself—was in charge of the office, "DeWolf slavers fitted out in Bristol as if the trade were legal.... Collins, it seemed, was more the employee of the D'Wolfs than of the United States." The effectiveness of the strategy reflected on the unprecedented number of slave voyages outfitted at Bristol and the end of prosecutions against Rhode Island slave traders between 1804 and 1807.[35]

If Newport can still be considered the main slave-trading port in Rhode Island for the transatlantic slave trade, accounting for 54 percent of all voyages for which we know the port of departure, Bristol is not far behind. Bristol soon became the main port for the organization of slave-trading ventures in Rhode Island (fig. 1). Slave traders from neighboring towns transferred their activities to Bristol and made use of both the new insurance company and, from 1804, the compliant customs collector. Overall, sixty-nine voyages are recorded as clearing from Bristol. But the port's role expanded rapidly after 1804 with Collins as customs collector. By 1807, Bristol surpassed Newport as the main port of departure for slave vessels in Rhode Island. The Bristol Insurance Company, which the D'Wolfs founded in February 1800, grew rapidly in these years. The history of the Rhode Island slave trade became the history of Bristol, whose citizens developed effective strategies to protect their slave-trading business from the growing abolitionist environment of their state.[36]

From Saint Domingue to Cuba

As mentioned, one crucial element of the nascent US-Cuba connection on which Rhode Islanders thrived was the demise of Saint Domingue. In 1789, about eight hundred sugar plantations in the French colony were producing 143 million pounds of sugar, almost as much as the volume of sugar produced in all the islands of the British Caribbean combined. As Michel-Rolph Trouillot shows, coffee production went through an even more radical transformation in the second half of the eighteenth century, with many gens de couleur and poor whites taking advantage of the easier access to the industry (less capital and labor was required than in sugar cultivation). By 1790, more than three thousand coffee estates generated 77 million pounds in exports, supplying around 60 percent of all the coffee sold in the western hemisphere. This production depended completely on the labor of almost half a million slaves.[37]

Saint Domingue became a significant destination for US merchants after independence when British Caribbean ports closed to them. Not only was consumption of slave-grown products on the rise in the United States, but a significant reexport trade emerged in the 1780s. The

United States supplied essential articles for the plantation economy of Saint Domingue, including foodstuffs, lumber, and, on a few occasions, slaves. Although most documented cases of US slavers operating in the French Caribbean had Martinique as their final destination, a few of them, such as the *Elizabeth* and the *Betsey,* did go to Saint Domingue. Unlike the Spanish, however, the French had a very well established slave trade, and opportunities to US merchants in this part of the world continued to be relatively limited.[38]

The slave uprising in Saint Domingue was a fundamental moment of a reconfiguration of the Atlantic world that ultimately turned the US South, Brazil, and Cuba into the centers of New World slavery in the nineteenth century. Cuba benefited from the events in Saint Domingue not only because of the new spaces opened in the world market but also as a prime destination of French refugees, who arrived with all their knowledge in sugar and coffee production. From the beginning of the rebellion in August 1791, French refugees migrated to such places as Jamaica, Puerto Rico, and coastal cities in mainland North America, but by 1804, Cuban authorities estimated that almost twenty thousand of them had migrated to the island. They chose Cuba, Gabriel Debién argues, "primarily because they found there something better than shelter; they found a chance to build a new colonial homeland." The wealthiest refugees naturalized themselves as Spanish and became fully integrated into their new home; some worked as doctors, land surveyors, artisans, and technicians. Most of the migrants—especially those leaving in 1803, year of the Great Exodus, according to Debién—came from the lower ranks of Saint Domingue: gens de couleur, poor whites, and slaves. These migrants carried their expertise and, along with the Spanish and a few other foreign planters, including New Englanders, set a new system in motion in the Spanish colony.[39]

Coffee cultivation in Cuba was already seeing important developments before the 1790s, but the contribution of the French refugees to its expansion is undeniable. They contributed not only as coffee planters themselves but also through the transmission of their expertise. This was evident in the reception of the ideas developed by Pierre-Joseph Laborie in his influential work *The Coffee Planter of Saint Domingo,* published in the 1790s. A coffee planter in Saint Domingue before the Haitian Revolution, Laborie migrated to Jamaica, where he produced the final version of his manuscript. Translated excerpts of the book were published in Cuba in 1809 under the coordination of Pablo Boloix, an important figure within the Sociedad Económica de Amigos del País and the Real Consulado de la Habana, institutions organized by planters and authorities to stimulate coffee production in Cuba. Laborie's models and ideas, however, were already present in the previous writings of Boloix and in the organization of innumerable coffee plantations in Cuba before 1809, suggesting that the principles described by the Saint Dominguean planter had made their way there by word of mouth and with the direct participation of refugees in the establishment of new coffee plantations. In the late eighteenth century, coffee was produced on a very small scale in the island, and as late as 1790 no farm in the Havana region was designated as a *cafetal* (coffee plantation) yet. In 1800, eighty *cafetales* were operating in Havana and in the neighboring region of Santiago de las Vegas. Twenty-seven years later that area had 902 coffee plantations producing 1,687,631 arrobas of coffee (one arroba is about twenty-five pounds). Many French refugees, especially the wealthy, migrated to the western part of the island, but most established themselves in Santiago de Cuba, where land prices were a fraction of those in Havana. Whereas the region had only 8 coffee plantations operating in 1802, their number rose to 192 in five years, 160 of them French-owned.[40]

Sugar production in turn had been growing in the island since the British occupation of Havana in 1762, but it also saw a dramatic growth at the turn of the century, and with important contributions from the French refugees. The number of sugar mills in Cuba rose from 529 in 1792 to 1,000 in 1827. Some of the wealthiest French refugees, carrying the experience and capital accumulated with sugar cultivation in Saint Domingue, were able to reestablish themselves as sugar planters in their new home. Cuban authorities looked favorably on their arrival, and in 1791, Captain General Luis de Las Casas wrote to Madrid praising the refugees for having brought with them "their industriousness and their knowledge of cultivation." The desire to welcome French experts on sugar production led planters Francisco de Arango y Parreño, Nicolás Calvo, and the captain general himself to offer a plantation with slaves as a welcome gift to one of the refugees, the sugar engineer Estaban LaFayé.

Moreno Fraginals observes that Frenchmen were responsible for designing eight of the ten largest sugar mills in the island around 1804. Thus by 1807, not only had French refugees become the owners of a few hundred plantations across the island, but many collaborated with Cuban planters by selling their expertise on sugar and coffee production.[41]

These expanding sugar and coffee sectors in Cuba of course depended on large flows of enslaved Africans. A recurring complaint of French migrants was the lack of manpower, especially on the eastern side of the island. The supply of captives to the colony had been the monopoly of British merchants until 1789, when a royal *cédula* (decree) opened the slave trade to all nations. Leaving aside the British occupation of Havana in the 1760s, which led to the disembarkation of at least 7,000 captives (some reports talk of 10,000), the island had not been an important slave-trading port for most of the modern era. From European arrival in the sixteenth century to 1790, about 26,647 captives were disembarked in the colony. In the following seventeen years (1791–1807), that number rose to 86,991. A few French slave traders initially took advantage of the opportunities brought by the cédula, disembarking 4,798 captives in Cuba between 1790 and 1792. The beginning of the slave revolt in Saint Domingue and the further abolition of slavery by the French revolutionary government in 1794, however, temporarily suspended this French involvement in the slave trade to Cuba.[42]

The uprising in Saint Domingue started precisely when the royal cédula of 1789 was supposed to expire. Quickly realizing the opportunities for growth opened by the crisis in their French neighbor while also fearing that the revolt could lead to restrictions on the slave trade by the Spanish government, planters and authorities in Cuba hurried to defend the renewal of the decree that had opened the slave traffic to the island in 1789. The representative of Cuban planters in Madrid, Arango y Parreño, assured the Spanish king that, unlike in Saint Domingue, not only were free people of color in Cuba loyal to the Crown, but also the slaves were well treated by their masters and justly protected by Spanish laws. In his view, a large slave rebellion such as the one that had just been witnessed could never happen in Cuba. His proposal to extend the opening of the traffic to the island for six more years was accepted, and slave disembarkations continued unabated. Later in 1794, Captain

General Luis de Las Casas confirmed those arguments when, after being ordered to investigate rumors of a slave revolt with some alleged connection to Saint Domingue, he replied that they were all "vague and insubstantial."[43]

A few Creole (native-born Cubans of European descent) merchants in Cuba also took advantage of the opening up of the slave trade but, lacking strong connections to Africa, had to purchase most of their slaves in other Caribbean islands and, to a much smaller extent, in a few US ports. In August 1794, however, a hurricane destroyed a large part of the Spanish fleet in Cuba and led to the decline of Creole participation in the slave trade, as historian Sherry Johnson shows. The British blockade in late 1796 then combined with the capacity of US vessels to supply the Havana market as neutrals, turning the US slavers into the predominant force in the trade to Cuba. An important part of this shift was the Las Casas's reiteration in February 1796 of a *bando* (proclamation) against the importation of slaves not coming exclusively from Africa. As historian Manuel Barcia argues, although the captain general had earlier assured the Crown that Saint Domingue was not a threat, a revolt of seventeen slaves in Puerto Príncipe in 1795 led him to change his opinion. The bando established that a first offense could lead to a fine of one hundred pesos per slave, a second one to a fine of three hundred pesos, and a third one to the confiscation of property and expulsion from the island. Although the hurricane of 1794 diminished the output of Cuban slave traders, the prohibition of 1796 probably contributed to curtail their recovery at the turn of the century. These merchants were now prohibited from carrying slaves from their main sources of captives, the neighboring British and French Caribbean islands. The bando did not completely stop the entrance of Caribbean slaves or slave insurrections in Cuba, but by 1800, the captain general was reporting the imprisonment and conviction of several individuals trying to smuggle slaves not from Africa.[44]

With the French and the Spanish out of the business, the traffic to Cuba became almost the duopoly of British and US merchants before both countries passed slave trade laws in 1807. Between 1789 and 1807, US slave traders disembarked 39,794 captives, about 43 percent of all 92,381 enslaved Africans disembarked in Cuba during those years. Second came British merchants, responsible for the disembarkation of 29,759 captives. Together these traders accounted for more than four out of five slaves disembarked in the Spanish colony during that period. To Cuban planters the constant supply of captives by these foreign merchants proved fundamental. There were unsuccessful attempts from Cuban merchants to create companies in 1795 and 1803—respectively, the Sociedad Habanera del Africa and the Compañía Africana de la Havana—to establish a direct connection with Africa. The latter proposed to create "floating slave factories," Spanish ships that would stay anchored off the coast of Africa loaded with British merchandise to be used in the exchanges with African traders. The *Voyages* database has evidence of only five voyages disembarking slaves in Cuba between 1796 and 1808 under the Spanish flag, and it seems likely that these also had some form of US or British participation. Cuban-based merchants such as Santiago de la Cuesta y Manzanal, Juan Magín Tarafa, and Francisco Hernández sought to acquire the slave-trading skills and knowledge of foreign dealers.[45]

Even as a few Cuban merchants attempted to make their way into the transatlantic slave trade, a few Rhode Island slave traders worked their way into the very promising plantation business in Cuba. The positive prospects of crop production in the island had been inspiring Arango y Parreño to call for a combination of freer trade (especially with the United States), unrestricted access to African slaves, and the application of new scientific techniques in production processes. Whereas many French refugees were bringing their expertise on sugar and coffee plantation, US slave traders became the main suppliers of captives and, in a few cases, decided to participate more actively in that transformation by purchasing plantations themselves. It is unclear when Rhode Islanders started to purchase lands in Cuba, but by the very early 1800s, James D'Wolf was already using his properties in the island as a strategy to deal with eventual unfavorable circumstances in the Atlantic trade. "If the market at Havana slumped, and the Revenue Marine, as the Coast Guard was then called, made it risky to smuggle into American ports," George Howe argues, James D'Wolf "could afford to wait. He owned three

plantations in Cuba—the Mary Ann, the Mount Hope, and the Esperanza—where he could hold his stock until prices rose again, as they
always did, sooner or later."[46]

The combination of Cuban plantations, US slave-trading, and
French expertise becomes clear in the case of John Sabens, a slave captain from Bristol who operated with the D'Wolfs. In late 1806 he received a letter from his partner in Cuba: "Negroes are much cheaper
at Charleston than here, it would be well if you had a friend or correspondence in that place, that you authorize & give him your orders to
have the negroes purchased & remitted me immediately by some trusty
person." The partner was J. Catalogne, perhaps one of the many French
refugees who had been arriving in Cuba. "Should they arrive here as
the time mentioned," Catalogne continued, "I shall certainly be able to
plant next year from 40 to 50 thousand coffee trees, for which number
the land will then be prepared." While Sabens supplied the captives, Catalogne informed his associate that he had "already agreed with a very
intelligent frenchman to take care of & direct our plantation." French
knowledge on coffee cultivation also appears on a few 1818 plans of slave
plantations owned by James D'Wolf, all of them clearly inspired by the
models developed by Pierre-Joseph Laborie.[47]

The system was perfect, albeit short-lived. For those few refugees
fleeing Saint Domingue, US slave traders were an immediate solution
for the provision of African slaves and, in a few instances, capital. New
England slaveholders improved their investment opportunities in Cuba
by calling on French expertise in agricultural production and French
business networks. Cuban planters and merchants, for their part, took
advantage of the knowledge and skills related to crop production and
slave trading brought by these individuals in order to create one of the
wealthiest and most violent slave societies of the nineteenth century.

Abolition

The same scares that the Haitian Revolution had generated in Cuba
during the 1790s were experienced in various parts of the US South.
To David Brion Davis, the impact of the Haitian Revolution can be
compared to that of the Hiroshima Bomb, whose meaning could be ne-

glected but never forgotten. The uprising had contradictory effects in the United States. On the one hand, as in Cuba, it stimulated the expansion of crop production based on slave labor and led some planters to rationalize the event in ways that exonerated the transatlantic slave trade. The connection between the 1803 US purchase of Louisiana, which had been receiving many of the Saint Domingue refugees since the 1790s, and the reopening of the transatlantic slave trade to South Carolina is perhaps the best example of those dynamics. Unlike Cuba, however, a strong opposition to the traffic had emerged not only in the North but also in parts of the South itself. Planters of the Chesapeake, as we have seen, had opposed the transatlantic traffic since the Constitutional Convention for a combination of moral and material interests. Images of Saint Domingue provided a powerful tool to Northern and Southern opponents of the traffic and helped create the context for passing the slave trade act of 1807.[48]

Fear of slave insurrection in the South was not new: the region had seen revolts before. The largest of them, the Stono Rebellion of 1739—when approximately sixty armed slaves killed more than twenty whites as they marched toward Florida—pushed South Carolina to pass a slave code with new regulations for both blacks and whites and impose a prohibitive duty of one hundred pounds per captive) on the importation of enslaved Africans into the state. The duty was passed in 1740 and valid for only three years. By 1744, a few slave disembarkations took place in the state, but only by the 1750s would the numbers of disembarked Africans reach levels comparable to the 1730s. The same tensions between the fear of black majorities and the desire for laborers would be at work in the Deep South during the two decades after the Constitutional Convention, tensions that reached new heights after the outbreak of the Haitian Revolution in 1791. A large number of French refugees, many of them carrying their slaves, moved to North American cities such as Charleston, New Orleans, and Philadelphia during the 1790s and 1800s.[49]

The same South Carolinians who during the Constitutional Convention would defend the right of Southern states to import enslaved Africans—John Rutledge, Charles Pinckney, and Pierce Butler—had voted earlier that year in the state legislature for a three-year prohibition of the traffic. The suspension of the trade to South Carolina had been part of an act regulating the payment of debts in the state, but when the issue reemerged in 1792, South Carolina authorities were quick to renew the ban because of anxieties brought by the events in Saint Domingue. Two years later they prohibited the entrance of free blacks into the state. Georgia, the only state that officially still kept the slave trade open, prohibited the entrance of captives from "any of the West India, Windward, Leeward, or Bahama Islands, or from either of the adjacent provinces of East or West Florida" into the state in 1793. The act also established that any free blacks entering the state should visit the clerk office of their county within thirty days of their arrival in order to be enrolled. North Carolina, which had abolished slave traffic in 1786, reopened it in 1790 only to close it again in 1794. The following year the state passed a more specific act prohibiting any migrant from the West Indies, Bahama Islands, or French, Dutch, and Spanish settlements in the Americas from bringing their slaves into the state while regulating the entrance of free people of color in general.[50]

In 1800, Southern fears would be stoked by the slave conspiracy of Gabriel Prosser in Virginia, which in turn inspired two subsequent conspiracies in southern Virginia and North Carolina in the following two years. Authorities connected these cases to the events in Saint Domingue, and as large numbers of French refugees arrived in the United States during 1802 because of renewed conflicts in the French islands, anxieties were heightened. That year authorities in Norfolk complained that French ships had been sending rebellious blacks to the United States, an accusation later repeated by a Virginia newspaper. These rumors were renewed early in 1803 after residents from Wilmington, North Carolina, submitted a memorial to Congress denouncing what seemed to be the new policy of the French government in Guadeloupe: "to expel therefrom all negroes and mulattoes, to whom emancipation shall be accorded."[51]

On May 20, 1802, twenty days after becoming first consul of France, Napoléon Bonaparte revoked the law of 1794 abolishing slavery in all French colonies. Slavery was to be reestablished in all the colonies returned by the British in the Treaty of Amiens, such as Martinique. References to Guadeloupe and Saint Domingue in the law of 1802 were unclear, merely stating that a "healing system" should be established on those islands. Over the year it became increasingly clear that the healing should come through enslavement. Although Saint Domingue successfully resisted the attempt at reenslavement and ultimately became an independent nation, the former slaves of Guadeloupe saw the reversal of their fortune, with slavery in the island, as in other French possessions in the Caribbean, persisting until 1848. In addition to executing a large number of rebels, French authorities in Guadeloupe deported a number of individuals they considered dangerous. One was the free black Louis Jaquet, a former lieutenant in the French Revolution and later chief of brigade at Guadeloupe. According to Jaquet, after authorities confiscated his coffee plantation, they dragged him to a French cutter with two other prisoners. They were then transferred by force to a US vessel against the will of its captain. The US captain later said that the governor of Guadeloupe, Jean-Baptist Raymond de Lacrosse, had personally asked him to bring the three blacks to the United States, which he refused to do. The French general then recommended him "to take them, and throw them over board when at sea," which the captain also refused to do. Then, while at sea, the French cutter shot at his vessel and forced the embarkation of the three individuals. They were taken to Boston by the US captain, where authorities informed Secretary of State James Madison of the case. The memorialists from North Carolina also described a similar case around that same time, when the schooner *Fair Play* arrived in Wilmington from Guadeloupe with five blacks on board, "which the executive of that island compelled the captain of said schooner to bring away." According to their memorial, the United States had become "the dernier resort for enabling the French colonial governments to clear the islands of a species of population too obnoxious to be tolerated." Unless the US government acted quickly, "the peace and safety of the southern states of the Union will be greatly endangered."[52]

One month after the memorial was sent, Congress approved the "Act to Prevent the Importation of Certain Persons into Certain States, Where, by the Laws Thereof, Their Admission Is Prohibited." "Thus a government powerless to prevent the importation of slaves where states saw fit to permit it," historian Donald Robinson argues, "enjoined its agents 'vigilantly' to prevent the immigration of Negroes into states prohibiting their admission. Here was a law earnestly sanctioned by opinion in the South. It would be vigorously enforced there by federal officials." And indeed it was. Although a few vessels, such as the *Planters Adventure* and the *Ida,* had been forfeited in the South based on the amendment of 1800, most cases in Georgia, for example, were connected to the act of 1803. David B. Mitchell, later accused of participating in the smuggling of slaves into Georgia in the late 1810s, acted as state attorney in a number of cases related to the smuggling of captives from the Caribbean.[53]

Already in 1803 three vessels were forfeited in Georgia for violating the recently passed law, two of them from Santiago de Cuba, the region that had become home to thousands of French refugees. In the case of the *Amelia,* a US captain got permission from the US consul at Santiago de Cuba to sail the vessel with foreigners. The manifest showed fourteen passengers: one Danish couple coming from Saint Thomas and twelve French individuals from Saint Domingue. The group had brought at least five slaves with them. According to the captain, after arriving in Saint Simons, Georgia, the slaves were disembarked without his consent. When one of the individuals responsible for the deed returned, the captain asked about the captives. The reply was that "they were on some of the plantations & at that time picking cotton." In another case that year, the *Lady Nelson,* also coming from Santiago de Cuba, was forfeited after the slave of a Frenchman, "a passenger of respectability from St. Domingo," went on shore to purchase supplies. The customs officer in Savannah saw the slave girl on shore and ordered her back on board, warning the captain and mate not to let her disembark. The following day she went on shore followed by a slave boy who had been working as assistant to the cook, leading to their arrest and the ship's seizure. Although some of these actions may seem exaggerated to us today, they were in perfect consonance with the overwhelming reactions triggered by rumors of slave insurrection. In 1802, a militia was mobilized in Georgetown, Georgia, because of (unsubstantiated) rumors that an expeditionary force from the West Indies was on its way to organize a slave rebellion (which never happened) in the South. The mobilization took place after a black individual of alleged French background was spotted walking alone without a pass on a Saturday evening.[54]

Although it is true, as David Geggus argues, that the continuing importation of enslaved Africans after Saint Domingue should "make us skeptical that fear of insurrection brought the slave trade to the end," and the reopening of the traffic to South Carolina partially confirms this, the image of events in Saint Domingue were frequently employed by opponents of the transatlantic slave trade in the US South to create a consensus against the traffic throughout the region. They appeared a few times after South Carolina decided to reopen the slave trade to the state in 1803. Cotton planters in the South Carolina backcountry had been pressuring the legislature to reopen the transatlantic traffic, but the proposal was again rejected by a vote of 86 to 11 in 1802. The following year new interests emerged with the purchase of Louisiana—namely, supplying captives for planters in the vast western territory—and the legislature officially reopened the transatlantic slave trade to the state. A number of debates emerged, with positions against the reopening rang-ing from the economic devaluation of the existing slave population to considerations of domestic security. Just as Cuban planters had done in the 1790s, South Carolinians made a distinction between slaves from Africa and slaves from the Caribbean. The act that officially reopened the traffic specified in its second paragraph that "no negro, mulatto, mestizo, or other person of colour, whether bond or free," should enter the state from the Bahamas, West Indian islands, or South America. The section further stated that no "negro or person of colour, who heretofore hath been, or now is, or hereafter shall be resident in any of the French West-India islands, enter or be brought into this state." Last, lawmakers specified that the captives brought to South Carolina should be "persons of good character, and have not been concerned in any insurrection or rebellion."[55]

Federal debates in Congress were marked by an almost consen-sual disapproval of South Carolina's decision. Many called for the es-tablishment of the ten-dollar tax on each imported captive, one of the few powers the federal government had over the slave trade before 1808. Directly connected to South Carolina's decision was the issue of slav-ery in Louisiana. Many Northerners accepted the inevitability of slav-ery in the recently acquired territory but called for actions to prohibit the introduction of new slaves in order to curb the expansion of the institution. Mixed responses came from the Lower South, with James

Jackson from Georgia supporting the continuation of the transatlantic slave trade to his state while South Carolina senators defended that ban so that they could become the main suppliers of captives to the region. The reopening in South Carolina placed Upper South representatives in a delicate position. Whereas they would normally have supported a ban on the transatlantic slave trade in order to raise the value of the surplus captive population of their states, the direct access of South Carolinians to captives coming from Africa complicated things. The law passed in March 1804 attempted to find a middle ground between these distinct positions while punishing South Carolina for their resumption of the transatlantic traffic. The only captives allowed to enter Louisiana were those going with their masters, with the additional condition that they had been brought to the country before 1798.[56]

The ban in Louisiana almost led to a reversal of the act reopening the traffic in South Carolina. The state house in fact decided to close the trade again, but the senate ultimately upheld the act in a tight victory by one vote. The lure of profit had defeated the fear of slave insurrection, yet with the strong reaction of other states and, more important, the closing of Louisiana as a slave market, the decision increasingly appeared to have been a mistaken one. Fortunately for the proponents of the reopening, a much stronger reaction started in Louisiana itself, where French and US planters and merchants demonstrated their dissatisfaction with the ban on the slave trade from the beginning. During 1804 almost every report sent by Governor William C. C. Claiborne to Washington described the ban on the slave trade—foreign and domestic—as the residents' main complaint. Fear of slave insurrection, and there were indeed a few scares during that year, apparently did not inhibit potential importers. They needed slaves in large numbers and preferably from Africa. After mounting pressure, Congress quietly changed the legislation in December 1804 (though it took effect only in October 1805), allowing the importation of captives from other parts of the United States while maintaining the ban on the transatlantic branch of the traffic.[57]

The four years of uninterrupted traffic turned Charleston into the largest slave-trading port of the Americas, comparable to ports like Rio de Janeiro and Salvador. In 1807, however, Congress finally passed an act to abolish the traffic to the country on January 1, 1808. Although the final version of the law passed with a near unanimous vote in the House of Representatives, 113 to 5, some provisions in the previous bills led to steep disagreements, especially when they involved moral condemnations of the trade. When discussing the destiny of slaves found on board captured ships, for example, some Northerners opposed their confiscation by arguing that the idea that human beings could be property was false. Others called for the death penalty for convicted slave traders, defining their actions as a combination of "man-stealing" and murder.

Southerners immediately replied to these accusations. Soon it became clear that the alliance between New Englanders and Deep Southerners that had marked the Constitutional Convention, "the two ends of the union against the middle," in the words of Donald Robinson, gave way to stronger sectional fissures. Southerners did not openly defend the slave trade but worked to eliminate the moral dimension of the accusations coming from Northern congressmen. James Holland of North Carolina argued that the slave trade was simply the transference of captives from one master to another and that slaves in the South lived in better conditions than they had in Africa. Peter Early of Georgia in turn argued that Southerners would never work as informants and witnesses if the penalty for smugglers was the death penalty, famously concluding that "a large majority of people in the Southern states do not consider slavery as even an evil." The bill was stripped out of its most polemic clauses and approved, but it had shown, as Matthew Mason argues, that the constituents of Northern congressmen "were growing less eager to compromise on slavery, while Southerners like Early had proved themselves unwilling to accept much guilt about the peculiar institution."[58]

The ten sections of the law sought not only to stop the importation of Africans into US territories but also to eliminate most forms of US participation in the transatlantic slave trade. Citizens were prohibited from participating in the slave trade as owners, captains, or part of the crew, facing fines that of one to ten thousand dollars and imprisonment of five to ten years. The third section specifically condemned any person "building, fitting out, equipping, loading, or otherwise preparing or sending away, any ship or vessel, knowing or intending that the same shall be employed in such trade or business" to pay twenty thousand dollars. The necessity to show guilty knowledge in the courts would prove to be a problem in the following decades during judicial cases related to the slave trade, an issue faced by British authorities as well. The decision about the destiny of Africans found on board slave ships was left to every individual state, which was precisely what Southern congressmen had defended during the debates leading to the act of 1807.

Already in the summer of 1807 black and white abolitionists made preparations for celebrating the ban on the transatlantic slave trade. On January 1, 1808, hundreds of black Philadelphians marched to Saint Thomas's Church to hear the sermon delivered by rector Absalom Jones. After saying that Jehovah had "come down" into Britain and the United States when both countries passed laws abolishing the traffic, the rector continued: "Dear land of our ancestors! Thou shalt no more be stained with the blood of thy children, shed by British and American hands: the ocean shall no more afford a refuge to their bodies, from impending slavery: nor shall the shores of the British West India Islands, and of the United States, any more witness the anguish of families parted for ever by a publick sale." There was a sincere hope in his words that the abolition of the transatlantic slave trade had been the first step toward full emancipation of slaves in the nation. Despite the connections the rector made between the acts in the United States and Britain, the reception of both could not have been more distinct. "While other abolitionist acts prompted the most extravagant self-congratulation," Robin Blackburn argues in reference to the US act of 1807, "this was truly the Quiet Abolition." And indeed other than the celebrations of Northern free blacks in Philadelphia, New York, and Boston—which were fundamental in their own right—most people remained silent. Black communities later also abandoned celebrations, possibly because it became increasingly clear to them that their original hopes regarding that date had been frustrated. Perhaps to his own luck, Absalom Jones did not live long enough to see the heyday of public sales of slaves—this time from the Chesapeake, not Africa—in his own country.[59]

Conclusion

Absalom Jones traveled to many parts of the United States to deliver sermons during 1807. In August, a Providence newspaper reported that "the black clergyman from Philadelphia, performed divine service with much propriety at St. John's Church, in this town." The note observed that Jones considered visiting the neighboring town of Bristol to preach against the slave trade. "But he cannot prevent the traffic in human flesh," the article concluded, "and is advised, should he go there, not to descant on that *very delicate subject*, if he wishes to escape 'tar and feath-ers,' or a worse fate." On the eve of abolition, Rhode Island slave traders were entrenched in the small town of Bristol, remaining attached to the business that had made some of the greatest fortunes of New England. To these individuals, attacks on the slave trade were attacks on a pillar of their economy. As John Brown of Providence argued in the debates on the slave trade amendment of 1800, "the very idea of making a law against this trade which all nations enjoyed, and which was allowed to be very profitable, was ill policy." Its profits, the congressman defended, could be used to pay the national debt while stimulating the rum indus-try in New England.[60]

The period between the American Revolution and the slave trade act of 1807 was marked by the participation of US slave traders to an extent that was unparalleled in US history and, in some ways, distinct from other branches of the trade. In an imaginary continuum of na-tional branches of the transatlantic slave trade, the United States would perhaps lie at one end and Spain at the other. The Spanish were the first to enter the slave trade and the last to abolish it. Despite this early entrance, Spanish slave traders generally operated within the domin-ions of their empire. Although examples of slave traders selling captives beyond the frontiers of their empires abound—British slavers in the French Caribbean in the second half of the eighteenth century or French dealers in eastern Cuba in the 1820s—Spanish dealers rarely ventured into non-Spanish territories. US slave traders were not only latecomers (although carrying slave-trading experience from the colonial era) but also more strongly connected to foreign markets than was the case for any other national flag in the transatlantic slave trade.

This was a symptom of the world of freer trade that US mer-chants—including slave traders—helped create. The calls for the liber-alization of trade made by Adam Smith and other political economists had a practical example of their effectiveness in the activities of US slave traders, who made their way into monopolized markets in Africa and the Americas and helped to destroy the mercantilist system that had been the basis of colonial slavery in the New World. Despite this unmatched connection to foreign ports, US involvement in the transatlantic slave trade was perhaps the last example of a truly national slave trade (as opposed to the highly internationalized contraband slave trade of the mid-nineteenth century). The years between US independence and the slave trade act of 1807 witnessed the growth of a genuine US branch of the traffic: US financiers employed mainly US captains and US crews on voyages with US-built vessels loaded with US rum that were insured by US insurance companies. The main foreign element in those voyages were the individuals being sold, since cultural constraints and concepts of otherness assured that Africans and their descendants would be the people eligible for enslavement instead of their European counterparts.

This profitable trade produced its defenders during the early Republic, but the persuasiveness of their arguments quickly changed. When John Brown defended the slave trade in Congress in 1800, he was one of five congressmen to vote against the amendment and, more important, the only Northerner. Attitudes to the slave trade had shifted since the Constitutional Convention, when the alliance between New Englanders and Deep Southerners protected the slave trade from federal intervention until 1808. Although the issue had not yet been settled in the South, as the reopening of the traffic to South Carolina three years later would show, Rhode Islanders became increasingly isolated in their defense of the slave trade in the North. Rhode Island slave traders in turn became increasingly isolated within their state, as abolitionists and federal agents used the anti-slave-trade legislation against them. The impact of these actions on the numbers of captives carried to the Americas was certainly limited, if not nonexistent. The main consequence of their actions was to isolate Rhode Island slave traders within the city of Bristol by the early 1800s, and that may actually have empowered the D'Wolf family as slave traders from other parts of the state increasingly relied on them to continue their operations. By the early nineteenth century the D'Wolfs and their associates had set up a sophisticated structure connecting Northern credit, rum and cotton production, long-distance maritime trade (including its slave variant), and slave plantations in Cuba producing sugar and coffee for the world market.

Yet the activities of Rhode Island abolitionists—as those of the Pennsylvania Abolition Society or the New York Manumission Society —were part of a broader shift in attitudes that became evident in 1807, when Northern congressmen had to position themselves against the traffic owing to the expectations of their constituents. These expectations continued to exist in the ensuing decades, albeit somewhat dormant, as issues related to US participation in the transatlantic slave trade disappeared from the political sphere. Their disappearance largely reflects the disappearance of some of the main forms of US participation in the traffic. Together with its British counterpart, the slave trade act of 1807 was the first step of a radical transformation of the transatlantic slave trade to the Americas.

Transitions, 1808–1820

I
n a charge delivered to grand juries in Boston and Providence in 1819, Justice Joseph Story denounced the persisting involvement of US citizens in the transatlantic slave trade after abolition. By the late 1810s, they were still "steeped up to their very mouths (I scarcely use too bold a figure) in this stream of iniquity." According to Story, US slave traders continued to profit from the traffic under the flags of Spain and Portugal. "I wish I could say that New England and New Englandmen were free from this deep pollution," he continued, "but there is some reason to believe that they who drive a loathsome traffic, 'and buy the muscles and the bones of men,' are to be found here also." The reasons that specifically led Story to believe this are unclear, but in the following two years he would see some of his accusations confirmed after the US Navy seized nine suspected slave ships off the coast of Africa. The captures were publicized in numerous newspapers, and Story himself worked as circuit justice in many of the trials. A careful look at these nine seizures shows how much the traffic had changed since 1807.[1]

In his 1819 charge, Story noted that although the number of US citizens involved in the traffic were likely few in number, "our cheeks may well burn with shame while a solitary case is permitted to go unpunished." Some of the vessels captured off the coast of Africa had a number of US citizens aboard, but indeed their numbers were not large. The first batch of captured slavers—the *Endymion,* the *Esperanza,* the *Plattsburg,* and the *Science*—resulted in the arrest of eighteen individuals, some of them US citizens. The *Endymion,* for example, had a captain, a mate, and five other crew members from the United States, one a Rhode Islander (which bolstered Story's previous accusations against New Englanders). More remarkable, however, was the diversity of the group. Among those identified, there were two Frenchmen, one German, one Swede, one Prussian, one Indian, two natives of Manila, and two blacks (one of them "born at sea on board an English vessel"). "The prisoners appeared to be principally foreigners," said a newspaper article, "of almost all nations, and shades of complexion." The four vessels had Spanish colors, papers, and, at least nominally, captains. "The Americans found on board, and detained as the real commanders," another article described, "insist that they were only passengers, and in no way connected with the voyage." The judge nonetheless condemned Captains Joseph Findlay Smith of the *Plattsburg* and Adolphe La Coste (a Frenchman resident in New York) of the *Science* to pay three thousand dollars in fines and serve five years in prison each. The vessels had been outfitted, respectively, in Baltimore and New York.[2]

The other sailors arrested claimed not to know the true objective of their voyages and were released. One newspaper called for better instructions to US sailors in order to raise their awareness of the slave trade legislation. This should end the "complaints made that the punishment of this class of offences should fall upon the ignorant agents, instead of the more guilty contrivers and instigators of the crime," a complaint that resurfaced many times as other US captains and crews were arrested on board slave ships in later decades. The main problem was that, by 1820, US ownership of slave voyages not only had been dramatically reduced but had become hardly distinguishable from its Spanish and Portuguese counterparts. The *Science,* for example, was apparently the property of foreign slave traders, namely the French merchant Eugene Malibran. According to instructions found on board the vessel, the captain should take the US vessel to Cuba, where it would be transferred to his brother Pedro Malibran (who had become a naturalized Spanish citizen) and put under Spanish colors.[3]

The *Plattsburg* was condemned as a US vessel but was later claimed as the property of Juan Marino, a Cuban merchant. The ship had previously been the property of the Baltimore merchants Thomas Sheppard, John D'Arcy, and Henry Didier. The last two had successfully employed a number of privateers in the War of 1812 and in the wars of Spanish American independence. It seems likely that this was not the first US vessel that they had sold to Spanish slave traders, but in this case the intermediary role of George Stark, an agent who offered to sell the vessel in Santiago de Cuba for $12,500, made the entire process suspicious. The vessel was sold and turned into a Spanish slaver, with the original crew discharged. The original captain, two mates, and eight of the sailors, however, remained on board and accompanied Stark to Africa, where the vessel was then seized by the *Cyane* before the embarkation of slaves. The judge ultimately considered that the first forfeiture had been legitimate. In his view, Spanish owners would be acting against their own interests by having US citizens on board their ships (because that directly contravene US laws). Since 1808, however, that was precisely what Spanish slave traders had been doing. US captains and crews played an important role in the transference of slave-trading expertise to Spanish slave traders in the 1810s. It is hard to assess the true ownership of the vessel today because both George Stark and Juan Marino are obscure figures who do not appear in other slave trade documents.[4]

In the other cases of 1820, the issue of ownership was even murkier, but there were good reasons for Joseph Story to suspect that US citizens were still financing slave voyages. The *Endymion,* as we have seen, had at least seven people on board who were US citizens, including the captain, a former navy midshipman. The ownership of the vessel was never disclosed during the case, and no Spanish or Portuguese merchants apparently ever claimed to be the real owners. That was also the case for the *Esperanza.* According to a British commodore who had previously boarded the ship, a US citizen named C. Radcliff owned the vessel. When the ship was seized, Radcliff was reportedly six miles into the interior of the Gallinas River, Sierra Leone, with a group of native slave dealers, thus avoiding arrest. Nothing else is known about him, but it is also possible that Radcliff was working as an agent for bigger Spanish slave traders, as other US citizens had done in the past decade.

That also seemed to be the case of a Mr. Lightburn, agent of the *Alexander*. The ship was the fifth vessel seized by the US Navy off the coast of Africa, only a few months after the first four captures. The vessel had left Havana allegedly for a legal voyage to Africa. The captain proceeded directly to the Rio Pongo, in Upper Guinea (home to a creolized merchant community that included a few US citizens), and landed Lightburn. The vessel then sailed to the Cape Verde Islands, where it was to wait until the agent had purchased enough slaves. On learning of this, however, the crew refused to heave anchor to proceed back to Rio Pongo. When the US ship *Hornet* arrived at the port, the crew denounced the true intent of the *Alexander*'s voyage, and the vessel was seized. Earlier that year the United States had just passed its final slave trade legislation, turning slave traffic into a crime of piracy and, consequently, punishable by death. No Spanish or Portuguese merchant ever claimed ownership of this vessel either.[5]

The following year the US ship *Alligator* seized four other vessels off the coast of Africa—the *Jeune Eugenie,* the *Mathilde,* the *Daphne,* and the *Eliza.* Unlike the seizures of 1820, these vessels were more clearly foreign-owned, generating diplomatic tensions between France and the United States. Before arriving in the United States, all vessels but the *Jeune Eugenie* had been retaken by their crews and sailed to French dominions. Lieutenant Robert F. Stockton of the *Alligator* was, nonetheless, proud of his actions. According to him, slave traders had transformed their operations into "a science, and heretofore in the disguise of Frenchmen, . . . have made certain calculations with regard to their success, laughing at the exertions of all Christendom to put an end to it." Having to explain himself to Secretary of State John Adams (after an aggressive reaction from the French minister to the United States), Stockton argued that, in the case of the *Daphne,* he "was satisfied from the external appearance of this vessel, that she was an American bottom, and of that description of vessels called, by way of distinction, Baltimore built vessels." The ship also carried a set of Dutch papers, despite having a French flag, and a number of other irregular documents. Similar circumstances led him to believe that the *Jeune Eugenie* was also a US ship, since no clear proof of the transference of the vessel, which had been built in the United States, could be found. The *Mathilde* in turn had "only three persons of her whole crew, including officers, [who] were subjects of the French government." The main problem was that, by 1821, multinational crews and US-built vessels were becoming two key features of the transatlantic slave trade as a whole. Neither was a reliable indicator of the nationality of a vessel. The world of sovereign nation-states regulated by international law that emerged in the wake of the Napoleonic Wars seemed unprepared for the transnational nature of the emerging contraband slave trade.[6]

Although the South Atlantic traffic to Brazil remained largely untouched by the rise of abolitionism until 1831, when the country formally abolished it, its North Atlantic counterpart went through radical transformations. The first steps of these changes were brought by the slave trade acts of 1807 in the United States and Britain. Between that year and 1820, other developments would guarantee that, by the early 1820s, the forms of British and US participation in the transatlantic slave trade would be very different from those before 1808. The clearest US element in all nine cases discussed above was that most vessels had been built in the United States, but as the number of US-built vessels used in the traffic expanded, the number of citizens directly financing slave voyages decreased. By 1820, their participation was restricted mainly to the small but resilient slave-trading community of Bristol. Other forms of US participation in the traffic had developed in the wake of abolition, including the participation of US captains and crews in slave voyages to Cuba and the smuggling of slaves into the United States. At times these different forms intersected, but in general they remained largely separate from each other over the period in question. In this chapter I clarify the dynamics of this transitional period and isolate those forms of US participation that survived the 1820 US act making slave trading piracy.

US Merchants and the Growth of the Spanish Slave Trade to Cuba

Many abolitionists and authorities in the United States and Britain believed that citizens and subjects from both nations continued to engage in the slave trade under the protection of other flags after 1807. Despite some exaggerations—some believed that all the traffic under the Spanish flag was actually British and American—their accusations had some truth. Dozens of cases adjudicated in the British vice-admiralty courts had a US or British connection, most of them using the Portuguese and Spanish flags to cover their operations. The *Esperanza*, captured in 1810, was a US vessel owned by merchants from New York and Boston with Spanish papers on board. The vessels *Nueva Constitución* and *Juan*, captured, respectively, in 1812 and 1813, also proved to be US property. Many others were believed to be US or British, or perhaps even more common, US *and* British. That was the case, for example, of the *Pepe*, the *Dolores*, and the *Nueva Paz*.[7]

The case of the US ship *Amelia* (formerly the *Agent*) was highly publicized by the African Institution in the early 1810s because the documents found on board contained detailed slave-trading strategies. In instructions to the British captain, the owners recommended that the ship be taken to Bahia to become Portuguese, providing the names of the people who would "procure for you some honest merchant, who, for a small sum, shall undertake all that is necessary for owners to do." One such individual was Patrick Toole, US vice-consul at Salvador, perhaps the first of a series of US diplomatic representatives who established shady connections with slave traders in Cuba and Brazil in the ensuing decades. "As you shall have to grant a bill of sale for the brig, when she is apparently sold," the letter stated, "you must be very cautious to take a counter bill of sale; and again, as collateral security, a bottomry bond on the vessel for 10,000 dollars, with a power of attorney from the sham owner to you, to sell and dispose of her in any manner you shall think proper." The letter also recommended that the captain request a declaration from the buyer, with attesting witnesses, showing that the sale was fictitious and that the vessel continued to be his property. These strategies would become a common feature of US involvement in the traffic.[8]

It is difficult, as it was for contemporary authorities, for us to assess the ownership of slavers with some form of US connection. These ventures could have been completely financed by US citizens, part of joint ventures involving US, Spanish, and British merchants, or simply the product of Spanish slave traders employing US expertise (buying US-built vessels and hiring US captains, mates, supercargoes, and crews). The *Carlota Teresa*, a US-built vessel that completed four voyages to Af-

rica and disembarked 832 captives in Havana between 1809 and 1812, had
a large number of US citizens as both sailors and owners. After being
seized by the Royal Navy and taken to New Providence in the Bahamas
for adjudication in 1811, the vessel was restored because no evidence of
British ownership could be found. Although documents showed that
the owner was Francisco Antonio de Comas of Havana, the depositions
implicated at least three US citizens in financing one of the ventures: a
Mr. Fawn of Norfolk, Thomas Martin and Co. of Charleston, and Zac-
cheus Atkins, supercargo of the voyage, who would receive 10 percent of
the slave sales. In this case, Antonio Comas seems to have worked as a
middleman, providing the Spanish flag to US slave traders.[9]

In other cases, certainly more often than the other way around,
US citizens operated as intermediaries for Spanish slave traders, as the
Spanish became increasingly interested in purchasing US-built vessels
and other US resources. This was a direct consequence of the Spanish
domination of the slave trade to Cuba shortly after 1808. Before that
year, as we have seen, US slave traders had dominated the traffic to the
Spanish island. Estimates from the *Voyages* database are that 104,730
slaves were embarked in vessels bound for Cuba between 1790 and
1809. Of these, 46,571, or 45 percent, were carried by US slave traders.
Spanish slave traders, on the other hand, were responsible for the embarkation of 5,234 captives during that period, approximately 5 percent
of the total (these numbers do not taken into account the intraisland
traffic to Cuba). In the years between 1810 and 1820, this distribution
went through a radical shift, with vessels under the Spanish flag carrying
117,739 captives, the equivalent of approximately 88 percent of a total of
134,450 embarked slaves. The US flag during those same years, according to *Voyages*, embarked 773 captives, or 0.6 percent of the total. These
distributions, especially the ones related to the Spanish flag, are not far
from the numbers offered by the classic work of Josep Maria Fradera,
more recently discussed by Martín Rodrigo y Alharilla. According to
these historians, the Spanish share of the slave trade to Cuba rose from
13 percent in 1790–1809 to 92 percent in 1810–20. Although all of these
works are undoubtedly correct in emphasizing the massive entrance of
Spanish slave traders into the business after 1808, the actual percentage
of Spanish participation was certainly a little lower because of a small

but persistent British and US traffic carried on under the Spanish flag after the slave trade acts of 1807. Thus the estimates from *Voyages* for the British and, especially, US slave trades are based on data that exclude British- and US-owned slave ventures under the Spanish flag, a problem, I suspect, also present in the numbers given by Fradera and Rodrigo y Alharilla (which incorporate US and British voyages under the Spanish flag as if Spanish slave traders had organized them).[10]

There is no easy way to assess the size of US and British participation, given the scarcity of sources, but the records of vessels seized by the Royal Navy and condemned in the vice-admiralty courts can give us a better sense of their role in the traffic to Cuba. In the early 1810s, the Royal Navy seized suspected vessels of all nationalities, a situation that changed only after the Napoleonic Wars. We can divide the period 1808–19 into three phases (table 3.1). The years between 1808 and 1811 saw the largest percentage of slave ventures organized by US citizens in the post-1807 traffic to Cuba. Slave ships owned by US citizens carried 5,514 captives to the Spanish colony, 30 percent of the number of slaves embarked during that period. They were surpassed only by Spanish slave traders, responsible for about 57 percent of the total. This initial US and British participation in the traffic to Cuba seems to have been, to a large extent, a residue of the reopening of the slave trade to Charleston between 1804 and 1807. Of twenty-nine slave voyages that started in the United States between 1808 and 1812, fifteen departed from Charleston. Second to Charleston were Rhode Island ports, especially Bristol, which accounted for six voyages.[11]

The impact of abolition on the US slave trade becomes clear when we consider this participation against the backdrop of the transatlantic slave trade to the Americas as a whole. Present estimates point to the embarkation of 840,754 captives in Africa between 1808 and 1820. Portuguese merchants alone embarked 648,595 enslaved Africans, 77 percent of all slaves embarked during this period. Portuguese slave traders continued their activities unabated, since none of the treaties signed with Britain during the 1810s affected the South Atlantic connections that had been the heart of the traffic to Brazil. French slave traders in turn stayed out of the business during the Napoleonic Wars, a situation that immediately changed after their end. Vessels flying French colors carried

38,821 captives to the Americas between 1814 and 1820, about 4.6 percent of the total. Of these captives, 4,766 were disembarked in Cuba (table 3.1).

Estimates from *Voyages* are that US slave traders embarked about 10,478 captives in the period 1808–20, of which only 2,573 were destined for Cuba. It is important to note, however, that most disembarkations in North America in the 1810s, which appear under the US flag in *Voyages*, were in fact a product of privateering (at times involving US citizens) against Spanish slave traders, as discussed later in this chapter. They were not the result of US slaving ventures to Africa. Thus even though the *Voyages* estimates for the US flag in the slave trade to Cuba are too low, as a comparison shows, the number of US vessels estimated to have carried slaves into the United States is probably too high (see table 3.1). Yet even if we add the estimates of *Voyages* for captives disembarked in the United States to those of table 3.1 to Cuba, all of them under the US flag, the total does not exceed 20,000 captives. This is equivalent to 2.4 percent of all Africans embarked in ships destined to the Americas between 1808 and 1820. The impact of abolition is indisputable when we consider that US slave traders had carried 130,829 captives to the Americas in the thirteen years before abolition, a volume at least six times larger than in the thirteen years after abolition.[12]

The British and US acts of 1807 also affected regional sources of slaves in Africa. The Gold Coast, which had been the main source of captives for Rhode Island slave traders, became a much less significant region for the embarkation of slaves. The effect was immediate. Although estimates for 1807 are that 10,389 enslaved Africans were embarked on slave ships destined to the Americas, the following year saw the embarkation of 2,215 captives. The year 1809 saw the lowest number of embarkations since the seventeenth century: 209 captives. Embarkations would pick up in the following decades, but in much smaller numbers compared to the pre-1808 era. The US merchants who had become part of a creolized merchant community in Upper Guinea also felt the effects of abolition, increasingly operating as middlemen for the Portuguese and the growing Spanish slave-trading community. The Spanish *Eugenia* and the Portuguese *Juana* were both said to have bought slaves from US and British merchants at the Rio Pongo in 1816. The change also reflected the growing importance of the Spanish language in the

Table 3.1. Estimated number of Cuban-bound vessels and the slaves they embarked in Africa by flag of vessel, 1808–19

	Spain	Portugal	Britain	United States	France	Totals
1808–11						
Voyages	50	8	3	26	0	86
Percentage	57.8	9.3	3.0	30.4	0.0	100.5
Slaves	10,476	1,686	551	5,514	0	18,227
1812–15						
Voyages	55	4	3	16	2	81
Percentage	67.7	5.5	3.4	20.3	2.8	100
Slaves	12,152	978	608	3,646	500	17,882
1816–20						
Voyages	278	4	0	5	15	302
Percentage	92.1	1.3	0	1.7	5.0	100
Slaves	81,578	1,069	0	1,301	4,267	88,215
Totals						
Voyages	370	16	14	52	17	469
Percentage	78.9	3.4	3.0	11	3.6	100
Slaves	100,305	3,733	3,760	11,761	4,766	124,325

Note: Two voyages were included as US owned in 1808–11 that were described as having had insufficient Spanish papers, the *Santiago* (voyageid 7553) and the *Mariana* (7556). For 1812–15, one voyage, the *Pepe* (7571), was included as British when in fact it had British and US owners. I added the present estimates from the Voyages database for the Spanish and US flags for each period and distributed the sum according to the percentages of each flag in the total number of vessels captured and condemned by the British between 1808 and 1815 (57 voyages). Some vessels in my voyage sample are not yet included in the current Voyages database. For 1816–20 I included the voyages of the *Empresa* (14653, 14730) and *Enrique* (14690), vessels that I believe were US owned, as discussed later. The other two voyages were those of the *Abaellino,* a vessel owned by Charles D'Wolf that was bound for Cuba but had to stop and sell the slaves in Martinique, and the *Malvina,* a vessel partly owned by the Rhode Island slave trader Jacob Babbitt. The following link gives direct access to the sample used for 1808–15: http:// slavevoyages.org/tast/database/search.faces?yearFrom=1808&yearTo=1816&natinimp=3.7.9& fate=27.28.29.30.102.104.106.108.110.112.114.118.120.122.124.126.128.130.132.134.136.138.141.142.144.148.202. *Source:* www.slavevoyages.org

region. Around 1811, the Upper Guinea merchant John Pearce, a descendant of a Yani woman and a US slave trader, was sending his sons to schools in Matanzas, Cuba, to learn Spanish. The growing importance of the language gave some advantages to factories whose dealers could communicate with the visiting Spanish captains and supercargoes.[13]

The changes spawned by the British and US slave trade acts were also rapidly perceived by Francisco de Arango and other Cuban planters. Arango, as we have seen, had been defending the liberalization of international trade as a strategy to increase the supply of African labor to the island by foreign slave traders since the 1780s. Over time he became increasingly interested in the establishment of a Spanish slave trade to the island, calling, after the Haitian Revolution, for an alliance with the French against the British. The cooperation could open the French market for Cuban sugar while putting the slave trade to the island under Franco-Spanish control. Such an alliance never occurred, and the early 1800s were marked by the failed attempts of Spanish merchants to enter the traffic. The slave trade acts in Britain and US were the turning point. By the end of the decade Arango observed that foreign slave traders were unable to fulfill the growing demand for slaves in Cuba.[14]

This time Spanish merchants seized the opportunity and engaged more consistently in the transatlantic slave trade, with a few US citizens taking advantage of that shift by offering their services and selling their vessels to Spaniards. One of them, Joseph Pritchard, sold the *P. D. Experiment*—a vessel built in Charleston in 1805—to the Havana slave trader Juan Magín Tarafa in 1809. Magín Tarafa, along with other Spanish slave traders such as Santiago de la Cuesta y Manzanal and Francisco Hernández, were key figures in transferring the traffic to the island to Spanish hands. That same year they started to send vessels to London with instructions to purchase British merchandise to be exchanged for captives on the African coast. They were interested, however, not only in US-built vessels but also in US slave-trading expertise. After selling the vessel, which then became the *Fama*, Pritchard worked as its captain in a voyage to Africa that embarked 104 captives. It is also possible that Magín Tarafa merely provided his name for the US merchant, because the vessel was actually captured around Spanish Florida, but the central role of the Spanish slave trader in the traffic around that time seems to indicate that Pritchard was working as an agent for the Spanish.[15]

The ship was captured in early 1810 on the frontier of Spanish Florida and Georgia, apparently carrying 97 enslaved Africans that had survived the Middle Passage (it is unclear in the documents whether the slaves were on board at the time of the seizure). Perhaps they were disembarked on Amelia Island, off the northeast Florida coast, and smuggled into Georgia before the vessel was captured, but even if they had been seized with the vessel, their destiny would still have been slavery in Southern plantations. The slave trade act of 1807, as we have seen, left to individual states the question of what should happen to captured slaves. In the case of Georgia, as in other Southern states, Africans captured from slave ships were to be sold in local auctions organized by the state government. Surprisingly, in light of many similar cases of the 1840s and 1850s, the fact that a US citizen, Joseph Pritchard, was the captain of the *Fama* was enough for the district judge of Georgia to decree the forfeiture of the vessel based on the laws of 1800 and 1807. Margín Tarafa provided documents proving that the vessel had been legally transferred to him, but the judge ignored his claims.[16]

Abolition thus forced US slave traders to develop new strategies, the outcome of which was that Spanish slave traders drew on US and British expertise. That same year in the case of the *Amedie,* a US vessel captured by the Royal Navy in December 1807 with 103 slaves on board, the master of the rolls, Sir William Grant, decided in favor of the British captors. Following the logic of the *Somerset* case, he concluded that once Parliament declared the trade in Africans to be against the principles of justice and humanity, the slave trade could not have "a legitimate existence" in British courts. The navy was given the green light to detain slave vessels of other nations except from those that officially allowed the trade to continue. Because the trade had been outlawed in the United States in 1808, the Royal Navy could legally seize slave ships flying the US flag, further stimulating the use of the Spanish flag by US slave traders. This view was rapidly confirmed by Sir William Scott, judge of the High Court of Admiralty, in the decision of the *Fortuna,* another US slave ship captured by the British in 1810.[17]

The Royal Navy, however, also searched and detained Spanish, Portuguese, or French slave ships that had had contact with British ports, merchants, insurers, or investors under the assumption that these circumstances were sufficient for their conviction. This view received support from the courts in the *Donna Mariana* case of 1812. As a result, a considerable number of foreign vessels were condemned at the Sierra Leone vice-admiralty court during the 1810s. Between 1809 and 1819, at least forty-three Spanish slave ships were detained and condemned in British courts. Many Portuguese vessels were also seized, leading to complaints from the Portuguese government and the subsequent payment of three hundred thousand pounds in compensation by the British in early 1815. The aftermath of the Napoleonic Wars saw a new round of seizures and new indemnifications for mistaken detentions. In 1817, the British government recognized the illegality of Spanish seizures and paid four hundred thousand pounds to the Spanish government. Instead of paying the owners of the ships illegally captured, the Spanish crown spent the money purchasing warships from Russia to be used against its rebelling colonies.[18]

The growing British pressure stimulated the demand for US-built vessels among slave traders across the Atlantic. According to historians Lance Davis, Robert Gallman, and Karin Gleiter, the tradition of fast sailing vessels in the United States was "formed during the disputes with England of the late eighteenth and early nineteenth centuries. Merchantmen were built to elude British men-of-war." With multiple seizures and convictions in British courts, these vessels strongly appealed to slave traders. The combination of this demand and the impact of the slave trade act of 1807 explains the discrepancy between the number of vessels flying the US flag and the number of US-built vessels employed in the slave trade after 1807, as would become clear in later decades. Whereas the number of US slave traders directly financing voyages decreased after abolition in 1808, the number of US-built vessels employed in the business increased. In Chapter 2, we saw that the number of slaves carried on vessels flying the US flag and vessels built in the United States in 1795–1807 were almost equivalent (see tables 2.1 and 2.2). Unfortunately, the data for place of ship construction are not sufficient to build estimates for 1808–20, but it seems likely that this is where the growing divergence between US-built and US-flagged vessels started. Men such as Magín Tarafa and the Santander merchant Juan de Carredano bought a number of US-built vessels to conduct commerce under the Spanish flag. Carredano, for example, financed at least four slave voyages, two with vessels built in the United States, the *Mulata* and the *Segundo Campeador*. Based on the port city of Santander, Spain, the starting point of all four voyages, Carredano disembarked about a thousand slaves in Cuba.[19]

A few US slave traders, nonetheless, financed slave voyages during the 1810s, even in the context of the War of 1812 (table 3.1). Between 1812 and 1815, about one in five of all slaves carried off from Africa to Cuba were on board US-owned vessels. The decrease in US participation was probably connected to the turn to privateering by slave traders such as James D'Wolf, who became the principal owner of four privateers, the *Water Witch*, the *Blockade*, the *Macdonough*, and, the most successful of them all, the *Yankee* (partly owned by the Bristolian John A. Smith). The *Yankee* captured forty vessels during the war, yielding James D'Wolf a profit of $1.5 million. It was rumored, nevertheless, that James D'Wolf continued to carry slaves during the war, and British authorities accused one of his vessels of having embarked four hundred captives in the Gambia under the Spanish flag in early 1814.[20]

British and US slave trading resumed after the War of 1812. When, in 1817, authorities at Sierra Leone provided a list of eighteen slave-trading cases of recent years, all of them allegedly proved in courts of justice, seven had a US connection. Most of these were former US privateers that had been turned into slavers, such as the *Rosa* (formerly the *Commodore Perry*), the *Dolores* (formerly the *Commodore McDonough*), the *Nueva Paz* (formerly the *Argus*), and the *Triumphante* (formerly the *Criterion*). Other accusations of US involvement were directed against the *Saucy Jack* during the War of 1812, the *Dorset*, a schooner from Baltimore, and the *Paz*, a vessel flying the US flag that managed to escape after killing several British sailors. One year earlier, the African Institution in London had argued that most slave-trading ships "have come from the United States, having first obtained a Spanish disguise at Havana. They have consisted chiefly of vessels which had been employed as American privateers during the war, and which sail uncommonly fast." Indeed, US and British slave traders seem to have financed some of them. The *Rosa*, for example, had been outfitted in the United States, manned by US citizens, and was "supposed to be the property of an Englishman." The *Dolores* was also "said to belong to an English house in the Havana," and the *Nueva Paz* was "supposed in part to be British property."[21]

These several instances of US and British ownership of slaving ventures occurred mainly before 1816. Only after 1815, however, did the volume of enslaved Africans embarked on vessels destined for Cuba reach unprecedented levels. The year 1817 alone saw the embarkation of 27,752 captives, a number higher than all the embarkations between 1808 and 1814 combined. Between 1816 and 1819, vessels bound to Cuba embarked 88,215 captives (table 3.1). About 88 percent of these were carried by Spanish slave traders—an estimate that is no doubt subject to some upward bias. The numbers for US participation, by contrast, underrepresent the true figure. The estimates for US participation for 1808–19 are based on the few US-owned voyages that I have been able to track. Bristol slave traders remained active in the traffic until 1820, as I will discuss below, and the 1,301 captives embarked by US-owned ships should be considered a lower-bound estimate of the US contribution to the Cuban slave trade. It seems likely that these US slave traders disembarked at least as many if not more than the 5,000 captives carried in the four years before the War of 1812, given that the overall traffic to Cuba increased so much in the later 1810s. It is important to note, however, that although a number of US slave traders resumed their dealings after the War of 1812, there is no evidence that the US slave-trading community expanded after 1815.

The main point is that even after allowing some room for US participation during the second half of the 1810s, Spanish presence was massive. Precisely when the business reached unprecedented levels, it came to be controlled by Spanish slave traders. Historian Manuel Moreno Fraginals has tracked the names of seventy-six Spanish individuals and companies prominent in the traffic to Cuba by the late 1810s. Prodigious slave traders such as Joaquín Madan González and Martín Madan Brown of Matanzas and the Spanish slave trade pioneer Santiago de la Cuesta y Manzanal amassed great fortunes from the slave trade to the Spanish colony. By 1836, Santiago de la Cuesta y Manzanal had the third largest fortune in Cuba. Even the nephew of Francisco de Arango y Parreño, Rafael de Arango, organized a few successful slave voyages in the second half of the 1810s. Some of these major figures also appear on the *Voyages* database. The Zangronis family, for example, was responsible for at least five slave voyages and the disembarkation of 2,124 captives in Cuba between 1816 and 1818, and there is evidence of another five voyages organized by the family after 1820. Juan José Zangronis moved to Ouidah, in modern-day Benin, in the 1830s to act as the direct supplier of slaves to his father and brother in Cuba. According to a British missionary, Zangronis became the second largest slave trader in the region, second only to the slave trader Francisco Felix de Souza, the Chachá de Ajudá (of whom he became an associate).[22]

The predominance of Spanish slave traders in the traffic to Cuba is also reflected in the ownership of vessels seized by privateers operating along the Gulf Coast during the second half of the 1810s. The *Montserrat,* a vessel seized by a privateer and taken to Amelia Island with 256 captives on board, had Pedro Blanco as its captain and owner. Blanco would later become one of the main slave traders of the contraband era (especially famous among historians because of his role in the case of the *Amistad*), organizing at least twenty-six slave voyages that disembarked almost eight thousand captives in Cuba. Another prominent Spanish slave trader who suffered losses from the attacks of privateers was Juan Madrazo. In 1816, he was part of a junta established at Havana to discuss more effective methods against the privateering activities that had been disrupting Cuban commerce since the early 1810s. The following year one of Madrazo's slave ships was captured by a privateer, which then took the vessel to Amelia Island and smuggled the slaves into Georgia (this is discussed in more detail below). The famous *Antelope,* seized by a privateer off the coast of Africa and taken to Florida, where a US revenue cutter then captured it, was originally owned by Cuesta, Manzanal & Hermanos (the company of Santiago de la Cuesta y Manzanal). The ship had been built in the United States in 1802 but had subsequently become the property of Spanish slave traders. Though some US slave traders remained in the business, the main form of US participation was now the provision of ships, and many Spanish merchants purchased the increasingly famous fast ships of Baltimore. Whether we look at the ownership of the prizes of privateers or the ownership of the vessels seized by the British in the second half of the 1810s, it is clear that by then the slave trade to Cuba had become mainly Spanish.[23]

The Slave Trading Enclave after Abolition

Like the Liverpool slave traders, who redeployed their fleet to such fields such as the palm oil trade (a key lubricant in the early Industrial Revolution) after 1807, the vast majority of their Rhode Island counterparts withdrew from the traffic and redirected their efforts to other areas, including the nascent domestic slave trade between the Chesapeake and the expanding West. The partners Henry D'Wolf and Charles Christian, for example, tried to shift their focus to the domestic slave trade immediately after 1807, redeploying their vessels in the route connecting Charleston to New Orleans. Without the success of the transatlantic slave-trading days, Henry D'Wolf returned to Rhode Island in 1808. The Newport slave-trading company of Gardner & Dean also decided to abandon the business and instructed its agent in South Carolina to sell its vessel immediately after the completion of its last African voyage in 1807. They ordered him to separate items like casks, irons, and chains for a separate sale, which certainly found their way into the developing domestic trade in slaves. Despite all the problems of enforcement faced by the US government, the new law did alter the environment in which slave traders operated. In early 1808, the Rhode Island slave trader Nathaniel Wardwell had his vessel seized by US authorities in Georgia on suspicion of having disembarked slaves at Cumberland Island. The *Columbia* had been to Africa, but other sources show that the vessel had in fact disembarked its 94 captives at Havana. The district judge of Georgia ultimately discharged the vessel for lack of evidence, but the case showed that new pressures were at work already in 1808.[24]

According to historian Peter Coleman, Bristol avoided the economic impact of abolition by investing in the contraband of British goods from Canada, transfers of vessels to Spanish merchants, voyages to repatriate Americans stuck in foreign ports, and legitimate coastal ventures. The slave-trading elite of the town, nevertheless, decided to avoid the impact of abolition by simply ignoring it. The D'Wolf family organized slave voyages to Cuba throughout the 1810s, developing new strategies to circumvent the pressures brought by the shifting environment. In the *Bristol Insurance Company Book* of 1810–12 (William D'Wolf was then the company president), the Spanish ship *Francisco de Assis* was insured for its voyage from Norfolk to Africa and thence to Havana. The insurance covered "the danger of the seas, of fire, enemies," but had "mortality of slaves excepted." Another case appears in receipts sent to John D'Wolf by his agents in Cuba in 1812 describing his share of the sales of the cargo of the ship *Arrogancia Castellana.* What exactly constituted the cargo was not mentioned, but very likely the *Arrogancia Castellana* was the vessel that disembarked 255 slaves in Havana that same year under the name *Arrogancia.* Captain Munro was probably John or William Munro, both of whom were from Bristol and had experience in the pre-1808 slave trade. Other such voyages probably exist in the *Voyages* database, but the North American connection is now lost. It is also important to note that one of the agents selling the slaves brought by John D'Wolf was Chaviteau, apparently another French refugee who became connected to the D'Wolfs in Cuba. The strength of those early ties between US slave traders and French refugees persisted well into the nineteenth century. Many of the captives disembarked by Rhode Island slave traders were likely bound for the US-owned plantations in Cuba that had been set up with the help of French refugees, some of them owned by the slave traders themselves.[25]

There are indications that Charles D'Wolf continued to organize slave-trading operations during the 1810s. In December 1818, he received a letter from J. Buch in Martinique about his vessel *Abaellino.* The captain of the ship approached Buch for assistance because not only he but his crew and cargo of enslaved Africans had been afflicted with smallpox during the Middle Passage. To complicate things, they had lost the boiler used to prepare the food. The ship could not proceed to the port of intended destination (probably Cuba) under those conditions, the author of the letter argued, it was "forbidden both by humanity and interests." Buch decided to disembark the 230 surviving captives in the French island and organize a quick sale to avoid the spread of the disease. One merchant offered to buy the entire cargo at $150 per slave. Buch argued that the slaves had been very well selected and in normal conditions could be sold for $250 each, but their present condition had lowered their value. The Martinique planter offered to pay $8,000 in cash and the rest in molasses or in three cash installments spread over the following year.[26]

Rumors that James D'Wolf also continued to engage in the slave trade in the aftermath of the War of 1812 continued to emerge, but unlike his brother Charles or his nephew George, the evidence of his participation is much thinner by the second half of the 1810s. Some of the rumors were closely investigated by William Ellery, the Newport customs collector who had been fighting the illegal slave trade in Newport since the late eighteenth century. "The Hermaphrodite Brig formerly called the McDonnough of Bristol was made a Spanish Bottom," Ellery wrote to the secretary of state in 1815, "but was still the property of certain merchants of that town, and would soon sail for the coast of Africa with an intention to purchase slaves there." He described the investigation and a conversation with the surveyor of the Bristol port, who said that "three or four vessels had sailed from that port and that he had heard that the smallest of them had arrived at Havana with upwards of two hundred slaves, that as no complaint had been made he had taken no bonds." The main figure behind the operation, according to the officer, was James D'Wolf.[27]

There are indications that James, however, had already sold the *MacDonough* to his nephew George D'Wolf at the time Ellery was investigating the case. In fact, George D'Wolf, often referred in the sources as "the General," became the main figure of the slave-trading network of Bristol. On the Cuban side of that network, the key individuals that helped turn the *McDonough* into a Spanish vessel were Joseph Oliver Wilson and the Havana firm Disdier & Morphy. Captain of the *Yankee* during the War of 1812, Wilson moved to Cuba after the war, becoming a plantation owner and changing his name to Don José Wilson. The captain continued to engage in the slave trade to Cuba and, in the specific case of the *McDonough,* acted as the attorney of George D'Wolf in the Spanish island. The historian of Bristol, George Howe, mentions a statement made by Enrique Disdier, supposedly deposited with the town clerk of Bristol, which confirmed that Wilson had passed a bill of sale merely to use Spanish colors and that although "the said Brigantine now appears to be the property of said Disdier & Morphy, she is still the property of said Wilson, as attorney." The strategy here resembles the one employed by the captain of the *Amelia* in Brazil, who acquired Portuguese colors before his voyage to Africa.[28]

According to Howe, the *MacDonough* carried 400 captives out of Africa already in 1816. The historian also says that the ship soon had its name changed to *Enrique,* in reference to Enrique Disdier. Thus, it is unclear under which name the vessel carried the slaves, but more than one source shows that voyages certainly happened. Later documents of another agent of the D'Wolfs in Cuba, Edward Spalding, make reference to at least two voyages of the *McDonough* with the participation of Oliver Wilson. There is also evidence of two voyages of vessels named *Enrique* in 1816, although the dates of disembarkation are very close to each other. The first disembarked 187 captives in May, and the second disembarked 210 in July. Both had nominal Spanish captains, but it seems likely that at least one of them was the *McDonough.* In 1817, after being chased by a British man-of-war, the vessel would famously strike a reef off the coast of Matanzas with the loss of all the slaves on board.[29]

Other documents show that the Spanish company had been working closely with other Bristol merchants in slave-trading cases. In a letter of December 1815 to John A. Smith, co-owner with Wilson of a plantation at Camarioca, in Matanzas, the Spanish merchants announced that the *Fortuna* had safely arrived on the south side of the island, indicating that Smith had some interest in the voyage. The letter also referred to a previous communication from Smith and a Mr. Morice, suggesting that both had some interest in a schooner that was then fitting out for a second voyage. Smith's partner was probably Daniel N. Morice, another French refugee from Saint Domingue who became associated with Bristol slave traders. Unlike most other refugees, however, Morice moved to Bristol after a short stay in Cuba, from where he established multiple commercial ties with the Spanish colony. Disdier & Morphy assured the Bristol merchants that their "interest shall not be interfered with or suffer in any shape while under our management." The letter concluded by saying that the "empreza" had arrived that morning with a cargo of 390 slaves. Although the authors do not mention the word "slave" (using instead a cryptic word that resembles "hogsheads"), this was the vessel *Empresa,* which disembarked 390 captives in Havana in January 1816 under the command of a Captain Oliver. The letter also does not refer to the ownership of the vessel, but it seems likely that Joseph Oliver Wilson was the captain of the ship, indicating possible Bristol ownership here, too. The following year, also under Oliver's command, the vessel disembarked 290 captives in Havana.[30]

These associations between US slave traders and Cuban merchants also offered great opportunities for the Cubans. In the case of the *Mac-Donough,* Disdier & Morphy would receive ten slaves and 5 percent of all the profits of the voyage. Disdier's role in the traffic rapidly increased, and in 1817, he offered King Ferdinand VII of Spain twelve thousand rifles and a thousand pairs of pistols obtained from his transactions with slave traders. (Thus slave-trading operations strengthened not only the colonial regime in Cuba but also—through the sales of weapons to royalists—the efforts to maintain the fragile Spanish presence in neighboring regions undergoing wars of independence.) Half of the arms were sent to the Vice-Royalty of New Spain, the other half to Puerto Rico and Costa-Firme (Venezuela). By the 1820s Disdier had become the owner—along with his associate Guillermo C. Gowen, another US citizen—of at least three coffee plantations in Matanzas. One of them, the San Patricio, had 260 slaves in 1825, making it one of the largest coffee plantations on the island at the time. Like Disdier and other Cuban slave traders, George D'Wolf also used the profits from his slave-trading activities to purchase a Cuban plantation, the Arca de Noé.[31]

It is impressive how Bristol slave traders managed to protect their operations from the wider changing environment for so long. Many of the pressures that had shaped the traffic since the late eighteenth century remained. Anti-slave-trade militants such as Ellery continued to pressure the Bristol slave traders and, after 1816, found an ally in the city's postmaster, Barnabas Bates. According to Howe, nine Bristol slavers were condemned in the second half of the 1810s, eight of them owned by George D'Wolf. In a letter to Obadiah Brown of Providence, Bates described in detail the illicit activities conducted by traders in Bristol. The description fits the strategy pursued by George D'Wolf in the *Mac-Donough* case: "Cargoes suited to the African market are procured here & taken on board vessels suited to the business and cleared for Havana

[sic]. The Master there effects a nominal sale of vessel & cargo to a Spaniard, taken on board a Spanish nominal Master & proceeds to Africa. A power of Attorney to effect the sale is always prepared here before sailing." He also denounced the owner of the *General Peace,* which had been outfitted as Spanish and had just been sold to George D'Wolf.

After stressing that some of the individuals involved in those operations were actually his friends (the D'Wolfs had recommended Bates for the position), the postmaster concluded the letter by urging Brown to "write & talk more on the subject, to advertise a determination to prosecute, & thus at least evince your knowledge of the existence of facts." His call was an attempt to revive the pressure that Obadiah's father, Moses Brown, and other members of the Providence Abolition Society had put on the slave-trading community of Providence a few years earlier. After all, they had practically eliminated the traffic from the city even before the federal prohibition of 1807 was passed. But Bristol was different. As the letter shows, the D'Wolfs continued to exert power within the city. Having to ask for help from outside the town, Bates asked that his identity remain anonymous because "such is the depraved judgment of the multitude, that to tell of crimes is almost as odious as to commit them." Although dramatically reduced since 1808, the illegal operations at Bristol continued to be protected by local authorities, including the collector of customs Charles Collins, and by large swaths of the population.[32]

Outside the slave-trading enclave of Bristol things continued to change, changes that were felt by James D'Wolf. These shifting sensibilities allowed his adversaries to use his history in the transatlantic slave trade against him. In 1817, with the chartering of the Second Bank of the United States, James D'Wolf campaigned for the establishment of the Rhode Island branch of the bank in Bristol. Providence merchants such as Nicholas Brown and Thomas P. Ives pressured for the branch to be opened in their city and sent an agent to meet with the board of directors in Philadelphia. When a member of the board asked the agent about the origins of James D'Wolf's fortune, he answered, "Mr. D.W. had been successful in privateering during the war, but that their principal traffic has hitherto been in the African trade, from that source alone I believed, they had drawn the principal trust of their wealth. That Mr. D.W. in defiance of the laws of his country & of humanity, still pursues that trade in an *indirect manner* even to this day." The agent's denunciation was obviously connected more to their immediate economic interests than to any opposition to the slave trade. After the branch was established in Providence, George D'Wolf became one of its directors without opposition from Brown and Ives. The company had indeed been dealing with many of the major Bristol slave traders for years. Yet that James D'Wolf's involvement in the traffic could be used against him indicates how entrenched the general condemnation of the commerce in human beings had become throughout the North.[33]

These shifting sensibilities were also reflected in the public sphere, as the growth of British anti-slave-trade activism and subsequent denunciations of US involvement in the traffic brought the issue back to debate. In 1819, an anonymous letter published in several newspapers denounced the participation of US citizens in the slave trade, making a number of references to James D'Wolf without citing his name. The author, signing as Philanthropos, argued that it was a well-known fact that the crews and commanders operating in the slave trade to Cuba were Americans. After describing those strategies, he described a case that, according to him, had occurred some time ago but could still be in the memory of many. It involved "the great mammoth slave drover, who lives not fifty miles from Bristol in Rhode Island." The author then described in detail the famous prosecution against James D'Wolf in the 1790s. "It happened that a negro woman caught the small pox—he caused her to be hoisted up to the main-top of the ship, and there he kept her some days—finding she did not die, this *fiend* in human shape threw her overboard ALIVE." Philanthropos then described the mock trial in the West Indies that allowed him to return to his hometown. According to the author, the slave trader continued to engage in the traffic afterward, mentioning that a certain schooner *Yankey* had been carrying hundreds of slaves in several voyages.[34]

Leaving aside the suspicions of William Ellery and these general accusations against James D'Wolf, there is little evidence that he, in fact, continued to engage in the illicit commerce in the second half of the 1810s, at least not with the same intensity of his nephew George. He certainly still had dealings in Africa by 1817, but nothing indicates that these involved the buying and selling of enslaved Africans. He had some interest in the *Charlotte,* a vessel that was also connected to Ives & Brown. In 1818, his brother Charles D'Wolf and another Bristol slave trader, Jacob Babbitt, asked for the captain of the *Richard* (a vessel owned by Ives & Brown that had been engaging in legitimate commerce with Africa) to collect a debt with a Dutchman at the Elmina Castle on the Gold Coast. The debt was related to a previous voyage of the *Charlotte,* whose captain died in 1816. There is no evidence that the *Charlotte* had gone to Africa for slaves, and the participation of Ives & Brown seems to indicate that it had not. By 1818, James D'Wolf had passed the debt to his brother Charles and Jacob Babbitt, who expected to be paid in "gold dust, prime ivory, Spanish dollars or English government bills of exchange." That James D'Wolf had passed the debt to others may indicate that he was in the process of abandoning trade with Africa altogether. Ives & Brown had reached that conclusion that same year because of their losses with the voyage of the *Charlotte.* "Unless more favourable exchanges can be made," the company wrote in a letter to a merchant in the Îsles de Los, off the Guinea coast, "it appears to us that trading voyages between this Country & Africa on an extended scale must be relinquished." The voyages of the *Richard* were, in fact, the last ones that the company organized to Africa.[35]

The slave-trading enclave of Bristol, nevertheless, continued to operate until 1820. We have already met some of the key figures involved in the traffic in the second half of the 1810s: George D'Wolf, Charles D'Wolf, Joseph Oliver Wilson, John A. Smith, and Edward Spalding. A number of cases in the late 1810s revealed other major players in the last years of the Rhode Island slave trade: Jacob Babbitt, James Dooley, John William Baker, Allen Munro, P. C. Greene, and a few Spanish and Portuguese partners that became fundamental for covering their operations under foreign flags. Jacob Babbitt was a traditional slave trader from Bristol who had financed at least two voyages between 1799 and 1806, both disembarking the Africans in Cuba. He established a number of commercial ties with Cuban planters, supplying food, machinery, and credit while shipping sugar to other parts of the world in the ensuing decades. As late as 1820, some of his voyages were still disembarking captives in the Spanish colony. Implicated with him in these ventures was the Baltimore captain James Dooley. Captain of a privateer during the

War of 1812, Dooley worked as the master of vessels trading sugar between Matanzas and New York in the late 1810s, when he established ties with Rhode Island and Cuban merchants. Based in Maryland, Dooley was probably the main conduit for Baltimore-built vessels.[36]

The main agent of both Dooley and Babbitt in Cuba was Edward Spalding, who was, as we have seen, the main representative of many other Bristol merchants, including the D'Wolfs. It is in the documents left by Spalding that one can see the ramifications of the networks connecting the United States, Cuba, and Africa in the 1810s. Going through his financial records, one does wonder if some of the horses and hogsheads delivered to Cuban planters by Jacob Babbitt and George D'Wolf were not in fact enslaved Africans. On the Cuban side of these networks were the planters and other slave traders, many of them US citizens who had been migrating to the Spanish colony since the turn of the century. One of them was John William Baker, a US citizen from Philadelphia who had moved to Cuba in the early 1800s. Like Joseph Oliver Wilson, he became a naturalized Spanish citizen, changing his name to Juan Guillermo Bequer. And as with many other slave traders in Cuba, he became a wealthy plantation owner. When the British abolitionist David Turnbull toured Cuba in the second half of the 1830s, he cited Baker as an example of the harshness of US and Spanish planters in the island. According to Turnbull, Baker had established himself "on an estate where he has congregated no less than 700 male negroes, to the exclusion of a single female, locking up the men, during the short period allowed for needful rest, in a building called a barracoon, which is in fact, to all intents and purposes, a prison."[37]

On the African side of these operations there were not only native and creolized merchants who supplied the captives but also the captains and supercargoes who supervised and organized the transactions. Two key figures among these, in the late 1810s, were P. C. Greene and Allen Munro, both from Bristol. More than one witness would spot these figures and their vessels on the coast of Africa between 1819 and 1820. In January 1820, the sailors of the *Arraganta* (the privateer that famously seized the *Antelope*) claimed to have seen two Bristol vessels—the *Exchange* and the *Rambler*—off the coast of Africa. They confessed that they had stolen twenty-five captives from the first, which was then operating as a tender for the second. The *Exchange* was owned by William Richmond of Bristol. One of the sailors of the privateer also identified the *Rambler* as a Bristol slaver, despite its Spanish flag. The ship was indeed owned by George D'Wolf. According to George Howe, the ship had been the property of James D'Wolf until 1809, when he sold it along with two other vessels to his nephew George. He allegedly had five other slavers by the late 1810s, the *Bello Corunes,* the *John Smith,* the *Jacquard Packet,* the *Rolla,* and the *Lisboa.*

Some of these other slave ships were also seen in Africa at the time. In June 1820, a number of US newspapers publicized the capture of three Bristol slavers with slaves on board off the coast of Africa by the Royal Navy, one of them being the *Rambler.* One month later, an extract of a letter by the US consul at Cape Verde was also published, describing in more detail the cases of the three Bristol slavers and a few other cases of US involvement in the traffic. The letter said that the three captured vessels were the *Rambler,* the *Jacquemel Packet* (probably the *Jacquard Packet* of George D'Wolf), and an unnamed ship but that all three managed to escape with their cargoes before reaching Sierra Leone. The unnamed ship was probably the *Lisboa,* also owned by D'Wolf. The consul mentions the case of a Captain Robert F. Green of Providence, late commander of the schooner *Lisbon.* According to the consul, the captain had been caught by the British while embarking slaves but was already "at Cape Mount [in present-day Liberia] with 500 slaves, waiting an opportunity to ship them to Havanna, or to have a vessel sent out for them."[38]

The *Lisbon* was probably the *Lisboa,* the last slaver to leave Bristol according to George Howe. The ship, owned by George D'Wolf, was denounced by Ellery to the secretary of the treasury (after receiving information from Barnabas Bates) not only for having false Portuguese colors, but also for being loaded with irons, chains, and a cargo suited for the African slave trade. The vessel was ultimately able to depart Bristol with the help of customs collector Charles Collins, the same individual who had been covering the slave-trading operations of the D'Wolfs since 1804. According to Howe, the entire crew of the *Lisboa* died in Africa, "and were buried by the very slaves they had intended to buy." The only survivor was a Clark Green of Bristol, who boarded as supercargo but was actually the master. It seems that Robert F. Green, Clark Green, and P. C. Greene may have been the same person. In the end, even the one captain from Providence seems to have actually been from Bristol.[39]

The letter from the US consul also mentioned the seizure of two vessels owned by James Dooley (although wrongly assuming that he was from Bristol) by the Royal Navy. These were probably the *Cintra,* seized in November 1819, and the *Saint Salvador,* seized in January 1820. Documents found on board both ships and the depositions of the captains reveal the connections among these various individuals. A letter by P. C. Greene found on board the *Saint Salvador* had been written from Cape Mount, Windward Coast, a region that would later become Liberia. The letter, addressed to the mate of the *Saint Salvador,* instructed him to go meet Charles Gomez, a slave dealer at the Manna River, also on the Windward Coast (where the vessel was seized). "Should Gomez ask anything about my slaves at Cape Mount," Greene wrote, "tell him I have one hundred, and am likely to get the whole to bring down with me in three or four days." In conclusion, he stressed that he was well, "but found a very long walk to this town, which fatigued me very much." It seems likely that the long walk had been a consequence of British seizure of the *Lisboa.* The *Saint Salvador* was then one of the vessels for which Greene had been waiting while at Cape Mount, as the US consul had noted in his letter. His plans were temporarily frustrated, because the Royal Navy also seized the *Saint Salvador* before the embarkation of slaves.[40]

Captain Antonio José Alvarez described his activities in detail, saying that he had bought the vessel at Baltimore and loaded it with a cargo at Bristol. The British captor noted that the crew consisted of six Portuguese, ten American, and sixteen French and Italian sailors, which made him suspicious of the legality of the voyage (according to Portuguese law, two-thirds of the crews of Portuguese vessels were required to be natives of Portugal). The British captors also found an African slave, Popo, being carried on a boat from the *Saint Salvador.* During an interrogatory Popo said that Charles Gomez made him a slave for owing him three iron bars. "Gomez said he had waited too long, and he would sell him; he sold him for one hundred bars; Gomez took the hundred bars in rum, powder, and tobacco." The vessel was ultimately restored to its owners because the commissioner of arbitration argued that the British could not seize a Portuguese vessel without slaves on board, and the only African found was on a boat already off the vessel. But all the evidence indicates, in fact, that Bristol slave traders owned the vessel.[41]

The other ship seized by the British at the time, this one clearly involving James Dooley, was the *Cintra*. According to its captain, a French citizen based on Trinidad de Cuba, the vessel had been loaded and boarded by most of its crew—two Spanish, eight French, and ten American sailors—at Bristol. The supercargo of the venture was Allen Munro, another traditional Bristol slave trader who had financed at least four slave voyages between 1799 and 1807. A British ship seized the vessel in October with twenty-six captives on board. This time the two judges of the Anglo-Portuguese Mixed Commission agreed on the illegality of the voyage and condemned the vessel. Despite its Portuguese colors, the captain confessed that he believed the vessel to be owned by James Dooley, who had appointed him the captain, and by John W. Baker of Trinidad de Cuba.[42]

Despite the continuous problems posed by British and US naval action on the African coast, by mid-1820 these slave traders finally managed to get at least one of their cargoes—perhaps the captives that P. C. Greene had kept with him at Cape Mount—delivered to Cuba. In a letter of August 1820 addressed to a T. W. Payton of Matanzas, Greene asked the consignee to follow the instructions of James Dooley for the net proceeds of the sale of 194 captives brought by the *Malvina* in June. The letter from Dooley explained that Jacob Babbitt should receive $19,294, John A. Grace should receive $11,097, and Antonio Jose Alvarez, who had been the captain of the *Saint Salvador* and had probably worked as captain again, should be paid $2,900. It is clear in this case that the major investor was Babbitt. Dooley appears in the role of agent, a role that had been enlarged by the growing demand for Baltimore-built vessels.[43]

In some ways the slave-trading context of the late 1810s in Cuba was an inversion of the US-Spanish relations of the pre-1808 era. If Spanish slaveholders depended on the supply from North American slave traders at the turn of the century, the US slavers could not conduct their business without some form of Spanish participation by the late 1810s. The *Francisco,* seized by the British with sixty-nine captives on the Rio Pongo and condemned at Sierra Leone in early 1820, had allegedly been outfitted at Matanzas by two US citizens, Madden and Simpson. Of the twenty-three crew members, eleven were US citizens, including the supercargo. The financial records of Edward Spalding show that Baker, or, to be more precise, Juan Guillermo Bequer, was the main owner of the cargo loaded at Matanzas. Valued at $14,117, it consisted of thirty-six hogsheads of tobacco, fifteen boxes with three hundred muskets, two hundred powder kegs, and a few other items. The owner described as a US citizen by the British officers, Madden, was in fact the great Matanzas planter and slave trader Joaquín Madan, who managed the entire operation. Another document shows that Jacob Babbitt had some interest on the voyage, since a fourth part of the net proceeds of the *Francisco* was to go to him.[44]

Despite the success of a very active slave-trading network based on Bristol—or perhaps because of it—broader changes would finally bring those operations to an end in 1820. In April, President James Monroe did not reappoint Charles Collins to the post of collector, instead assigning Barnabas Bates to the position. The following month Congress passed a law turning the slave trade into a crime of piracy. Although direct involvement fell away, Bristol merchants continued to profit from the business in innumerable ways. In 1821, for example, Charles D'Wolf wrote to Spalding about a shipment of powder and four hundred muskets. The buyers in Cuba were "the General" (George D'Wolf) and Captain Smith. These items certainly found their way into the Spanish slave trade. But the role of Bristol as a slave-trading port had come to an end. Bristol slave traders thereafter would have to either profit in less direct ways or relocate to the Spanish colony. There are no records of slave voyages outfitted at Bristol—or Rhode Island as a whole—after 1820.[45]

The extent of Bristol's involvement in the transatlantic slave trade during the 1810s is certainly larger than what appears in the historical record. According to George Howe, Charles Collins burned all the slave-trading records before leaving his position in 1820; John D'Wolf, who had been in charge of all family records, destroyed those connected to the traffic; and George D'Wolf allegedly buried all his ledgers in the garden of his mansion, documents that have never been found. It seems unlikely, however, that the unearthing of these documents or the discovery of new ones would change the general picture of the slave trade to

Cuba as outlined above. Spanish slave traders rapidly occupied the space left by US slave traders after abolition and, often with US-built vessels, captains, and crews, legally conducted their slave-trading activities according to Spanish laws during the 1810s. To Bristol slave traders—many of them owners of plantations in Cuba—remaining in the business was obviously attractive. Even former captains such as Joseph Oliver Wilson and John Sabens accumulated sufficient capital to purchase their own plantations. The structure built in the early years of the nineteenth century with the help of Saint Domingue refugees endured and expanded during the ensuing decades, supplied over the 1810s by captives carried in their own slave-trading voyages. The importance of the traffic to Bristol is evident. But from the perspective of Cuban slaveholders, US citizens in the role of slave carriers became increasingly dispensable.[46]

Slave Smuggling in the South

With the shift toward Cuba brought by abolition in 1808, slave smuggling into the United States became dependent on the activities of a few new adventurers. Most historians have recognized that the act of 1807 had a stronger impact on slave importations into the United States than on the participation of US citizens in the traffic to non-US territories. Slave smuggling through Georgia and Louisiana continued mostly as a consequence of privateering, not of slave voyages to Africa organized by US slave traders in the United States. The *Voyages* database presently contains twenty-one records of voyages that disembarked, or intended to disembark, slaves in North America, only five having US ports as their point of departure. Of these, four were voyages that had started in 1807 and could not be completed before the enactment of the slave trade act in January 1808. The slave trader William Boyd of South Carolina, for example, instructed the captain of his ship *Africa* to arrive by "every means possible" before January 1, when "the act prohibiting the importation of slaves goes into operation." After realizing that he would not arrive in the United States on time, the captain attempted to change his destination to Cuba and the vessel was seized by the Royal Navy. After 1808 the preferred destination for all voyages outfitted in the United States became Cuba.[47]

Leaving aside the entrance of more than three thousand slaves in Louisiana with their French masters and other refugees fleeing Cuba in 1809 (to whom Congress decided not to apply the penalties for violating the act of 1807), most slaves who disembarked in the United States immediately after abolition came through the smuggling operations of figures such as the Lafitte brothers at Barataria Bay, Louisiana. A few may also have been smuggled through Amelia Island, in Spanish Florida (a smuggling point since the eighteenth century), as the voyage of the *P. D. Experiment,* discussed earlier, seems to indicate. But it was really the smuggling activities of Jean and Pierre Laffite that attracted the attention of US authorities in the early 1810s. The two brothers established a number of depots in the area to smuggle the cargoes of ships captured by privateers, including slaves. The Napoleonic Wars and the War of 1812 provided the initial context for widespread privateering along the Gulf Coast. The Laffite brothers worked as intermediaries connecting privateers (many of them French in the first half of the 1810s) and buyers in Louisiana. Between 1809 and 1812, they sold at least 142 slaves. After 1812, the brothers also became the owners of a few vessels themselves and business expanded for a while. In 1814, they smuggled 415 captives with one single sale, but in that same year the federal government finally shut down their operations.[48]

After 1815, however, the return of peace dramatically expanded smuggling into the United States. A message of 1810 by President James Madison referred exclusively to the involvement of US citizens in the slave trade to non-US territories, yet another message of 1816 indicated that slave smuggling into the United States was the more serious issue. In a list of thirty cases of privateers that disembarked captives in North America or were seized by US authorities between 1810 and 1820, twenty-one took place during the five last years. Privateers, says historian David Head, supplied between 70 and 75 percent of all slaves disembarked in North America over the 1810s, becoming the main source of slave smuggling in the country. This was a direct result of the growth of Spanish American privateering after the Napoleonic Wars. The restoration of King Ferdinand VII in 1814 (with conservative policies that abolished Spain's Constitution of 1812) and the fall of Napoleon in 1815 (which eliminated the common enemy that had united Spanish subjects in the Iberian Peninsula and in the Americas) led to a period of insurgence that culminated in the foundation of multiple republics throughout what had once been Spanish America. The collapse of Spanish rule stimulated the competition between North Atlantic powers and produced, as historian Rafe Blaufarb argues, "a vacuum in which opportunities for unorthodox, adventurous, and piratical action flourished." Thus began a few years marked by the multiple seizures of slave ships and the sale of their cargoes on the US-Spanish border, especially through the islands of Galveston, Texas, and Amelia, Florida.[49]

The growing demand for slaves on the US cotton frontier had been solved in part by the flow of captives carried in the incipient domestic slave trade from the Chesapeake. Some planters, nonetheless, bought Africans who had been smuggled into the country whenever they got the chance. Although no one had openly defended the slave trade in the debates leading to the act of 1807, the position of Southern congressmen—that many Southerners did not consider slavery an evil or would not help authorities if slave traders were to receive capital punishment—indicated that many planters still held ambiguous views toward the traffic. When a vessel was libeled in 1815 for allegedly bringing two slaves from Cuba to be sold in Savannah, the district judge of Georgia called the case "unpleasant." What bothered him, however, was not exactly smuggling. "This is an unpleasant case that has arisen from the theoretical philanthropy of those modern philosophers, as well in Europe as in this country," the judge argued before delivering his decision, "who are advocates for abolishing the slave trade, and which they have effected at the price of much blood." Had the trade been allowed to continue, the judge concluded, "the prisoners would have found their way to the Southern States, where altho slaves, without crime, they would meet humane treatment." Public calls for a reopening of the slave trade would occur only in the 1850s, but such reasoning helped create an environment in which some planters in Georgia and Louisiana were emboldened to purchase smuggled slaves after 1808.[50]

On the Cuban side, the 1817 treaty between Spain and Britain, which set 1820 as the expiration date of the transatlantic slave trade to Spanish dominions, stimulated a dramatic upsurge in the import of Africans to the island (the same would happen in Brazil in the following decade when a treaty with Britain set the abolition of the trade in 1830). Some of the most valuable cargoes being carried on board Spanish vessels by the late 1810s were, therefore, enslaved Africans. With most traditional US slave traders either out of the business or operating in the traffic to Cuba, figures such as Louis-Michel Aury, Gregor MacGregor, and the Lafitte brothers took risks and made large profits by illegally redirecting those captives from Spanish vessels to North America.[51]

A French privateer who had fought under the command of Simon Bolívar, Louis-Michel Aury parted ways with his commander in 1816 and joined the struggle for the independence of Mexico. Under the authority of a member of the Mexican congress, Aury established his headquarters at Galveston Island that same year. During his short stay of less than one year, he granted commissions to approximately twenty privateers. These ships would bring their prizes to be judged in the admiralty court he had set up and sell the seized goods, including enslaved Africans, in Louisiana. The collector at New Orleans, Beverly Chew, classified their activities as "the most shameful violations of the slave act, as well as our revenue laws," defining those individuals as a "motly mixture of freebooters and smugglers." They re-created the smuggling operations of Barataria, the collector argued, in a place where they could protect themselves from US authorities. In close connection to New Orleans, "an active system of plunder was commenced on the high seas, chiefly of Spanish property, but often without much concern as to the national character."[52]

The following year the Scotsman Gregor MacGregor, another former member of Bolívar's army, launched an expedition to conquer Florida from the Spanish. After occupying Amelia Island, MacGregor issued a few commissions to privateers, but his rule lasted for less than three months. When MacGregor left, however, Aury transferred his operations to Amelia Island and issued an even larger number of commissions to privateers. The commander of the US ship *John Adams* observed that slaves seized from Spanish vessels by privateers could readily be "smuggled into Georgia, as many of the inhabitants are too much inclined to afford every facility to this species of illicit trade." According to contemporary reports, Aury's crew smuggled about half a million dollars in contraband, most of it made of enslaved Africans captured from Spanish ships (if this contraband consisted entirely of slaves, that would mean the smuggling of between 1,500 and 2,000 captives).[53]

Several cases show the details of these smuggling operations. In 1817, one of Aury's commissioned privateers seized the *Isabelita* and smuggled its cargo of slaves, originally owned by the Cuban-based slave trader Juan Madrazo, into the United States. The Africans on board the Portuguese slave ship *Jesus Nazareno* met a similar fate after the ship was seized and taken to Amelia Island. On the US side, the smuggling of all these captives had the participation of an agent sent by Savannah planters, William Bowden and, according to some reports, the former governor of Georgia, David Brydie Mitchell. The federal government had appointed Mitchell a Creek Indian agent, and it was precisely through Creek territories that these captives were supposedly entering the country. More than one witness would later describe conversations implicating Mitchell in slave-smuggling operations. When Major John Loving, for example, expressed interest in purchasing slaves at Amelia Island, Mitchell replied "that he had been thinking of such purchase himself, and that Loving might bring any Africans, which he might purchase, through the Indian country with safety, to the agency, where he, the agent, would protect them." Mitchell later denied the accusations, but Attorney General William Wirt, a slaveholder from Virginia, was appointed to prepare a report on the case. After evaluating all the evidence in his fifty-page report of 1820, Wirt famously concluded that "Mitchell is guilty of having prostituted his power, as agent for Indian affairs at the Creek agency, to the purpose of aiding and assisting in a conscious breach of the act of Congress of 1807, in prohibition of the slave trade, and this from mercenary motives."[54]

Shortly after Aury left Galveston for Amelia, Jean Lafitte, who had been operating with his brother in New Orleans, relocated to the abandoned island. The Lafitte brothers quickly built a new scheme for slave-smuggling operations by establishing slave barracks on the Texas side of the Sabine River. Unlike the Barataria years, however, they made Louisiana purchasers come after them. Whenever they had captives ready for sale they would send cryptic messages through privateers carrying legal goods to New Orleans. Interested buyers would then have to meet them outside US borders and deal with the problems of smuggling the captives into the country. Their clients included the legendary Jim Bowie and his brothers. One of them described their slave-smuggling operations in an interview that was later published in the pages of the *DeBow Review*. After purchasing the slaves from Lafitte at the often quoted "rate of one dollar per pound," they acted as informers and delivered the slavers to the customs house. An amendment to the act of 1807 passed in 1818 (discussed in detail below) rewarded informers with the equivalent of half the value of the captured slaves, who were then sold locally in public auctions. By using the money they received as informers, the Bowie brothers reacquired the slaves and became legally entitled to sell them within US territory, making on the whole a profit of sixty-five thousand dollars. US authorities acknowledged the difficulties of stopping the smugglers. The captain of the US frigate *Congress* complained to the secretary of the navy that while the larger and less valuable goods carried to Galveston entered the United States regularly through the customs house, more valuable items such as slaves were "smuggled in through the numerous inlets to the westward, where the people are but too much disposed to render them every possible assistance. Several hundred slaves are now at Galveston, and persons have gone from New Orleans to purchase them."[55]

As historian Robert May observes, US citizens were involved in privateering and filibustering operations ranging from the revolutionary governments of Aury and McGregor to the filibustering activities of James Long in Texas a few years later. George D'Wolf and other Rhode Islanders also took advantage of the privateering fever. A few of them redeployed old slavers and privateers of the War of 1812 for use in this new context. The *Brutus*, a privateer owned by James D'Wolf and William Gray of Salem during the War of 1812, became the *McGregor* (in reference to the Scotsman who had taken over Fernandina, a Spanish port on Amelia Island) under the ownership of Gray. The privateer *General Paez* once was the *General Peace*, the same ship that Barnabas Bates had denounced as a slaver in 1818. George D'Wolf in turn owned the *General Padilla*, a privateer that operated under Colombian colors and seized Spanish prizes in the early 1820s. There is no evidence, however, that the privateering adventures of George D'Wolf led to the smuggling

of enslaved Africans in the US South. For the most part, the US participants in privateering and smuggling operations in the South seem to
have been largely disconnected from the old slave-trading community
of Rhode Island.[56]

We can now turn to the numbers of captives illegally introduced
into the United States between 1808 and 1820. Present estimates from
Voyages are that 6,548 captives were disembarked in North America
(which included Spanish territories) during those years. Given the scarcity of records for that period, however, the authors of *Voyages* assumed
that around 500 slaves were embarked and 410 disembarked every year
(except for 1808, 1810, and 1817–18, when disembarkations are actually
documented). Research on privateering by David Head has shown that
a number of privateers that are not in *Voyages* attempted to disembark
between 2,476 and 2,592 captives in the United States between 1810 and
1820. If we add these numbers, as well as the voyage of the *P. D. Experiment,* to the present estimates, as Head has suggested, the number of
disembarked slaves would range somewhere between 9,024 and 9,140.
Some smuggling may have taken place from elsewhere in the Caribbean,
but the volume of this traffic was likely insignificant.[57]

The Legislation of 1818–1820

The end of the Napoleonic Wars marked a turning point in the international relations history of the transatlantic slave trade, represented
in the United States by the passing of new legislation against the slave
trade between 1818 and 1820. With the defeat of Napoleon in 1814, French
planters and merchants with colonial interests quickly exerted pressure
over the restored Bourbon monarch. Even before the negotiations for
a peace settlement between Britain and France had started, rumors
abounded that the French would not agree to anything involving the
abolition of the slave trade to their possessions. Some even had expectations that Haiti could become Saint Domingue again. The compromise
embodied in the Treaty of Paris of 1814 allowed the French to keep the
slave trade open for five more years. News of the treaty triggered one of
the most impressive abolitionist campaigns in history. In Britain, an
unprecedented number of anti-slave-trade petitions were submitted to

Parliament, with signatures ranging somewhere between 750,000 and 1,375,000. The popular reaction pushed both houses of Parliament to pass addresses calling for a reopening of the negotiations with France for the extinction of the traffic and the pursuit of anti-slave-trade measures in the forthcoming Congress of Vienna. Anti-slave-trade pressure as a central feature of British foreign policy was born.[58]

Instructed to convince the Congress of Vienna to accept a plan for the concerted action of European powers against the traffic, Lord Castlereagh, Britain's foreign secretary, met with the opposition of plenipotentiaries from Portugal, Spain, and France, who insisted that the traffic could only be ended gradually. The final treaty of the congress, nonetheless, stated in act 15 that the commerce, "known by the name of 'the Slave Trade,' has been considered, by just and enlightened men of all ages, as repugnant to the principles of humanity and universal morality." Although many abolitionists were frustrated with the outcome, and the slave trade continued for more four decades, the declaration was an important step in setting the standards against which nation-states could be measured. In a presidential message of 1816, Madison praised the advances made by other nations for the "general suppression of so great an evil." In the following years the United States would engage in what historian Matthew Mason has properly called "the battle of slaveholding liberators." Planters such as John C. Calhoun—classically described as the "Marx of the master class"—eagerly joined Northerners in priding themselves that the United States had been the first nation to abolish the slave trade (deliberately ignoring the case of Haiti, of course). In a discussion with other government officials in 1820, Calhoun declared that by cooperating with Britain, "we appear to the world as the satellite and she the primary planet—a position the more disparaging to us, because in point of fact she was merely following our lead," in reference to the slave trade acts passed by both countries in 1807.[59]

With the failure to establish a multinational plan for the suppression of the traffic, and without the context of war that justified several captures of suspected slavers in previous years, the British government entered into an era of diplomatic efforts that accompanied its global economic and political expansion. These efforts were reflected in the establishment of a treaty system encompassing states ranging from slave-trading empires such as Portugal and Spain to African chiefdoms and Arab potentates in the Persian Gulf. The forms of these treaties varied. The Netherlands, Portugal, and Spain all signed treaties with Britain in 1817 that included mechanisms for international enforcement in the form of mutual right of search and mixed commissions to judge vessels suspected of engaging in the slave trade. The Netherlands had already agreed to stop the trade in 1814, with the treaty of 1817 only adding these enforcement instruments. Portugal and Spain agreed to prohibit the business north of the Equator, but Spain also committed to abolish the business entirely in three years after the signing of the treaty, that is, May 20, 1820.[60]

From the beginning, however, other states looked suspiciously at British intentions, as reflected more clearly in the French and US refusals to establish treaties containing the mutual right of search or the establishment of mixed commission courts. Acceding to that would be similar to assenting to British global domination. In article 10 of the Treaty of Ghent, established after the War of 1812, the United States and Britain had agreed on continuing their efforts to abolish the slave trade. But British proposals of a mutual right of search touched on delicate issues that had been at the center of that war, namely Royal Navy's practice of impressing US sailors (which had also played an important role in the Embargo Act of 1807 and the Non-Intercourse Act of 1809). During the war, John Quincy Adams compared the right of search to the transatlantic slave trade and concluded that, in some contexts, the right of search was actually worse.[61]

During the Congress of Aix-la-Chapelle in 1818, Castlereagh proposed that a limited right of search among the Great Powers (the Austrian Empire, France, Prussia, Russia, and the United Kingdom) should be established to suppress the traffic. The main opponents to the proposal were the French, who argued that given the historical rivalry between France and Britain, it was "too probable that the mutual exercise of the right of visit at sea would furnish it with new excitements." The congress also rejected Castlereagh's suggestion of a joint declaration defining the slave trade as piracy. The new pressures brought by the growing anti-slave-trade activism of the British government had already led the French government to pass legislation abolishing the traffic in 1817 and 1818, but both were problematic. The first act prohibited only the importation of slaves into French territories. The second expanded the legislation to include the involvement of French citizens to foreign territories, but punishment was remarkably weak: in case of convictions, vessels and cargoes would be confiscated and French captains prohibited from commanding other vessels. Conventions with the British allowing the mutual right of search and the seizure of vessels equipped for the slave trade were passed only in, respectively, 1831 and 1833. In the meantime, French participation in the slave trade resumed, with vessels under French colors disembarking an estimated 166,805 enslaved Africans in the Americas between 1814 and 1831. Almost 40 percent of these were taken to Cuba, especially Santiago de Cuba, a privileged destination for French refugees since the early nineteenth century.[62]

Despite the French and US refusals to establish the right of search with Britain, the new context of peace inhibited the Royal Navy's seizure of foreign vessels in the second half of the 1810s. In 1817, Sir William Scott, the same judge who had decided in favor of the British captors in the *Fortuna* and *Donna Mariana* cases, ruled that the *Louis* (7567), a French slave ship seized by the British the previous year, should be restored with the slaves to its original French owners. The case established the general view that, first, the Royal Navy could not search foreign vessels in peacetime and, second, British courts could adjudicate only British vessels (unless other nations had conceded appropriate rights). This interpretation would have a great influence on US jurists and various US administrations, where a similar view became the norm in slave-trading cases involving other nations. As we will see in the following chapters, a large number of captured slave ships that had some form of US involvement were acquitted under very similar reasoning. Proving US ownership of vessels—precisely the aspect of the slave trade that had been most affected by the act of 1807—became a fundamental requirement for condemnation in US courts.[63]

Although the United States refused to comply with the terms of a possible Anglo-American cooperation against the traffic, the events at Amelia and Galveston Islands would turn the issue into a renewed object of debate in Congress. The growing moral condemnation of the trade provided the context for US actions on its shared frontiers with Spain, regions in which the country had clear geopolitical and economic interests. The Spanish territories in North America had long been desired by successive US administrations, a dream that only increased with the purchase of Louisiana from France in 1803 (since some Mississippi and Alabama rivers actually flowed through the Spanish colony). The acquisition of Florida started during the Madison administration, which took advantage of Spanish fragility during the Napoleonic Wars and acquired a few parts of the territory. It was also during this period, more precisely in 1811, that Congress secretly passed the No-Transfer Resolution. Offered by Secretary of State James Monroe, the resolution allowed the United States to employ military forces to prevent any parts of Spanish Florida from passing "into the hands of any foreign power."[64]

Florida had been a problem for US planters and authorities since the eighteenth century, above all because it became a refuge for fugitive slaves from southeastern plantations and indigenous peoples pushed aside by the expansion of the cotton frontier. A widespread fear that these groups could be employed by foreign powers against the United States was partially confirmed during the War of 1812, when British forces occupied portions of the Spanish territory and established alliances with free blacks and indigenous groups. These war alliances had consequences that persisted after the end of the war, most famously in the case of the Negro Fort, a former British base at the Apalachicola River. Largely supplied with guns, the fort was left by the British officers after the end of war to their black allies. The place became one of the largest maroon communities in North America, sheltering about 500 people for most of its history. Many southeastern slaveholders believed that its mere existence would stimulate their slaves to escape or, even worse, rise up in rebellion. US forces literally blew up the fort in the summer of 1816 (a lucky shot hit the powder magazine) and killed 270 people. Yet Southern anxieties persisted. Since the defeat of the Red Stick at Horseshoe Bend in 1814, many Creeks had also been taking refuge in towns that included fugitive slaves and Seminoles in the Spanish territory. These groups retaliated against US settlements, leading to conflicts that culminated in the First Seminole War.[65]

The growth of privateering operations under commissions issued by Gregor MacGregor and Louis-Michel Aury at Amelia Island certainly heightened these tensions, especially because many of the individuals involved in these expeditions were coming from the West Indies (Aury was famously accompanied by an army of Haitians). "Considering that the restless and adventurous of all nations, and especially of the island of St. Domingo, have ranged themselves under the banners of the different leaders, by sea and land, who are engaged in the civil war now raging between Spain and her colonies," the secretary of the navy wrote in July 1817, "apprehensions are justly entertained by the citizens of the southern section of the state of Georgia, that their peace and tranquility will be disturbed, and their rights infringed." Moreover, it had become clear during the War of 1812 that Florida was a fundamental strategic point for the safety of New Orleans (which in turn had a central role in the commercial circuits of the expanding western territories). And although this western expansion had been one important element for the success of all the Spanish American privateering along the Gulf Coast, a large number of complaints from US merchants to the federal government indicates that those activities had been disrupting US trade.[66]

The consolidation of a stronger opposition to the transatlantic slave trade by the late 1810s was also connected to the regularization of the domestic slave trade, which expanded on an unprecedented scale. States such as Maryland, Delaware, and Virginia had been selling slaves in an internal market since the 1790s, with the Carolinas and Kentucky becoming additional suppliers of captives as demand rose on the cotton frontier after the Napoleonic Wars. The crucial decade, as historian John Craig Hammond has argued, was the 1810s. Whereas about 5,000 slaves were sold or carried with their migrating owners from the Chesapeake to the states of the Lower Mississippi Valley between 1790 and 1810, this number shot up to 120,000 during the years 1811–20. The dramatic rise of this domestic trade led to connections between western territories and eastern slave states that reshaped national politics and generated a confluence of economic and moral reasoning among planters in the supplying and receiving states. They shared common interests in the regularization of the US coastal trade—and consequently the Baltimore–New Orleans route that was at the center of the domestic slave trade—and supported new measures for the suppression of all the piracy and privateering (and, consequently, the slave-smuggling operations that became attached to them) that had been disrupting commerce.[67]

Under the argument that Amelia Island had been occupied by a piratical government, thus violating the No-Transfer Resolution of 1811, and transformed into a base for slave smuggling, the US government authorized its occupation in December 1817. The following year Andrew Jackson entered East Florida with his army to eliminate the threat posed by the Seminoles and free blacks, occupying the Spanish fort of Saint Marks and executing two British subjects in the process. He was helped by the Creek leader William McIntosh, who, ironically, was later accused along with David B. Mitchell of being involved in the smuggling of slaves into Georgia. Ignoring all the violations of international law that had just been committed by his own country, Secretary of State John Quincy Adams blamed the Spanish for the recent events and stressed their lack of control over their own territory. Pressures mounted, and in 1819, Adams signed the Transcontinental Treaty with the Spanish foreign minister to the United States, Luis de Onís, also known as the Adam-Onís Treaty. The treaty settled new western borders between both nations in North America and finally ceded the entire state of Florida to the United States.[68]

The combination of these multiple developments—the growth of British anti-slave-trade pressure, the denunciations of former US privateers in the African slave trade, and the events on Amelia Island—revived the slave trade as a public issue in the country. In December 1817, memorials submitted to Congress by the recently founded American Colonization Society and the Society of Friends at Baltimore called for changes in the law to curb the participation of US citizens in the traffic. The petition from Baltimore also called for an inquiry into possible concerted actions with other nations against the traffic, automatically leading to a few debates in January 1818 about a resolution based on the petition. Senator James Barbour of Virginia observed that the United States "took the lead in the humane effort to exterminate this horrible traffic. He rejoiced to see that the great nations of Europe had adopted her precepts, and were imitating her enlightened and philanthropic example." He did agree, therefore, with the first part of the resolution, on amending the nation's laws to end US involvement in the traffic. The second part—exploring the expediency of concerted measures with other nations—he rejected, as did other congressmen. The resolution

passed in its entirety, but many congressmen such as Rufus King believed that joint action against the traffic did not include the mutual
right of search.[69]

Also in January 1818, a congressional committee established to assess the state of the slave trade in the United States and the events at
Amelia Island concluded that the occupation had been timely and justified by the resolution of 1811. "The course pursued on this occasion
will strongly mark the feelings and intentions of our government upon
the great question of the slave trade," the report explained, "which is
so justly considered by most civilized nations, as repugnant to justice
and humanity, and which, in our particular case, is not less so to all the
dictates of a sound policy." The report concluded by noting that new
regulations against the traffic were necessary, especially because the act
of 1807 did not stipulate any rewards for informants. On April 20, 1818,
Congress passed a bill to change the act of 1807, reducing the fines and
jail time for condemned individuals while shifting the burden of proof
to the defendant. This new legislation also condemned the building of
vessels to the slave trade, although the presence of US-built vessels in
the illicit commerce had not yet become an issue in the political sphere.
Individuals convicted of intentionally building vessels for the slave trade
or of participating in slave voyages as masters or investors could receive
fines ranging from a thousand to five thousand dollars and three to
seven years in prison. The amendment also established that half of the
value accrued from the forfeitures would go to the informers.[70]

Despite the new legislation, which clearly had numerous problems
(one just needs to remember how the Bowie brothers denounced the
smuggling of slaves that they had brought to the country themselves),
the traffic continued to be condemned in newspapers, as in the anonymous attacks against James D'Wolf, and in a number of petitions submitted to Congress between late 1818 and early 1819. One complaint was
the persistence of the clause that left to individual states the decision
regarding the destiny of slaves found aboard slave ships or being smuggled into the country. Memorials from the American Colonization Society argued that the best way to stop the trade was by acting directly
in Africa. The Philadelphia Abolition Society, as historian J. R. Oldfield
shows, submitted a memorial in December connecting the persistence

of the transatlantic slave trade to issues of national honor and pride: "While the unhappy African . . . will hail with delight the flag of Europe, which restores him to freedom, he will tremble at the approach of the American banner which transfers him from one set of masters to another." The response was quick, and in March 1819, Congress passed another act against the slave trade. This time the law authorized US armed vessels to be employed on the coast of Africa (the beginning of what would become the Africa Squadron) and established that seized slaves should be sent to Africa. The American Colonization Society received one hundred thousand dollars from Congress to help establish a colony for rescued Africans in West Africa, which came to be Liberia.[71]

Less than a month before the passing of this legislation, however, Congressman John Tallmadge Jr. tried to pass an amendment to the bill for the admission of the Missouri Territory into the Union and sparked a two-year debate about slavery and, by extension, the slave trade in Congress. The amendment prohibited the introduction of slaves into the new state and established that slavery should be gradually abolished there. Many argued that Missouri's incorporation as a slave state would not only change the political balance of the Union but also lead to the inevitable growth of the domestic slave trade. Tallmadge was followed by Timothy Fuller in the House and the sexagenarian Rufus King in the Senate, with both arguing that the slave trade act of 1807 provided the necessary power for the federal government to control the internal commerce in captives. King gave some stringent antislavery speeches in the Senate and argued that it was hard to believe that "the condition of slaves is made better by the breaking up, and separation of their families, nor by their removal from the old states to the new ones."[72]

Some Northerners connected the Missouri issue with the transatlantic slave trade. A petition from Newport, Rhode Island, of January 1820 stated that no penalty would be severe enough to stop the transatlantic slave trade "if an immense market is to be opened in the Territories of the west for the unhappy victims of this traffic." The new territories would "increase the temptations to introduce them illegally, already too great, and fatal to the morals and industry of your constituents." In April 1820, soon after the Missouri Compromise, a Vermont newspaper published an article with abstracts from a British newspaper basically confirming what the petitioners of Newport had said a few months earlier. The article listed multiple cases of US involvement in recent slave-trading cases, to which the Vermont publication invited "the attention of the northern gentlemen who voted in favor of the Missouri Question." The article reproduced short notes from the British newspaper praising the British officers who had recently seized a number of vessels in Africa, along with a detailed description of the voyage of the *Cintra,* one of the US vessels seized, as we have seen, by the British in 1820. After leaving Cuba with a French master and an American crew, according to the British newspaper, the ship sailed to Bristol, where, "under the protection of *free Americans*," the ship was loaded with its slave-trading cargo. The note also observed that the owners of the vessel were the US citizens James Doody of Baltimore (Dooley) and William Baker of Trinidad de Cuba, "who prove to the world their devotion to liberty by enslaving their fellow-creatures."[73]

Southerners reacted to the accusations in Congress by minimizing the role of a domestic market in slaves and arguing that most planters migrated with their captives. They also showed an unprecedented support for harsher penalties for US citizens involved in the transatlantic slave trade, something they had vehemently opposed in the debates of 1807. In just thirteen years the international status of the traffic had undergone a radical transformation. The new initiatives would also be an important step toward isolating US slavery from the transatlantic slave trade and, consequently, from the reach of British abolitionists. Thus, on May 15, 1820—about two months after the Missouri Compromise— the final US legislation against the transatlantic slave trade was passed: a statute charging US citizens involved in the transatlantic slave trade with the crime of piracy. The new law was, as its long name indicates, an amendment to an act passed the previous year. Any condemned US citizens—or foreigners found aboard US slave ships—could, therefore, face the death penalty. The law was initially to be in force for two years, but Congress made it permanent in 1823. Informants would receive fifty dollars for every slave found on board; crews of the US Navy responsible for seizures would receive twenty-five dollars per slave. Thus, as historian Paul Finkelman observes, an informant who denounced a ship with a hundred captives on board could make five thousand dollars with one action.[74]

These harsh penalties certainly dissuaded many US citizens from directly financing the business. The impact of the new legislation was also reinforced by the federal crackdown on pirates and privateers operating under questionable authority (such as those of the Laffite brothers) that had started in 1819. As David Head has shown, in the second half of 1819 alone, twenty-two individuals out of twenty-three were convicted for their involvement in piracy, an extremely high rate compared to the thirteen men indicted and no convictions of the period between 1815 and the first half of 1819. One of the most publicized cases of 1819 led to the execution of Captain Jean Desfarges of the *Le Brave,* a privateer owned by Jean Laffite. The government continued to strike hard at other pirates during the first half of the 1820s, with a few other executions. Between October 1821 and September 1822, authorities claimed to have seized or destroyed twenty-nine pirate vessels in Cuban and Puerto Rican waters. These actions consequently destroyed the main sources of smuggled slaves into the United States. By 1821, the Laffite brothers had abandoned Galveston, and the federal government subsequently de-populated the island. Some smuggling through Texas continued to take place, but under the increasing pressure of US authorities. That same year six men in Louisiana were fined $115,000 for the transportation of about ninety enslaved Africans. The Monroe administration removed the Indian agent David B. Mitchell after the report of Attorney General William Wirt. The combination of this new legislation with the presence of the US Navy on the coast of Africa, despite all its problems, certainly contributed to the withdrawal of many US citizens from the slave trade to other countries as well.[75]

Conclusion

In 1821, when James D'Wolf started his term at the Senate, the Missouri Debates had been raging for two years. Reacting to critiques of slavery from the North, Senator William Smith of South Carolina delivered a re-markably racist speech that concluded with references to James D'Wolf (who had not even started his term yet). After observing that Rhode Islanders had not only been critical of slaveholders but had opposed to the acceptance of Missouri unless slavery was restricted there, the senator argued that this "could not have been the opinion or temper of the majority" of that state. After all, its people had just recently elected James D'Wolf, "and this gentleman had accumulated an immense fortune by the African slave trade." Smith revealed a list of 202 vessels that had carried slaves to Charleston during the reopening period—an invaluable resource for present-day historians—to show that James D'Wolf had financed at least ten of them. Smith stressed that he was not criticizing D'Wolf's past actions, since the trade had been legal according to the laws of the United States at the time. Using a classical rhetorical device, Smith also promised to "say nothing about the African trade which he had been engaged in since it was prohibited by law, because that would very deservedly subject him to a criminal prosecution." His ultimate goal was merely to show how the North promoted and profited from the slave trade. "Those people who most deprecate the evils of slavery and traffic in human flesh," Smith concluded, "when a profitable market can be found, can sell human flesh with as easy a conscience as they sell other articles." He could, of course, have added the several Cuban slave plantations owned by James D'Wolf and many other New Englanders, but that would have led to a critique of slavery itself, something most Southerners were struggling to separate from the slave trade.[76]

It is a mistake to believe, as Senator William Smith did, that the election of James D'Wolf and his slave-trading activities took place in an environment of complacency and cynicism. In 1821, James D'Wolf wrote to his brother John that "brother Levi's Quaker policy I do not think will do him any good." The same tensions that had marked the history of the Brown family in the late eighteenth century were finally affecting the D'Wolfs. Concerned with accusations made by a Providence Quaker, James D'Wolf made clear that "his election to the Senate speaks the popular feeling of R.I. [Rhode Island]," even though, he continued, "the quakers & abolition society made use of any means & exaction in their power to prevent my election." That slave traders in Bristol were able to engage successfully in the transatlantic slave trade until 1820 speaks more to the ability of those dealers to circumvent the law than to any consensual support of the traffic within the state. Perhaps because they were just a few miles away from Bristol, Newport petitioners could more clearly connect the opening of new western territories for slavery and the persistence of the transatlantic slave trade during the Missouri Debates.[77]

The final bargain embodied in the Missouri Compromise and the subsequent 1820 crackdown on the slave trade solved some of the tensions between slavery and the transatlantic traffic that had survived abolition in 1808. The year 1820 also marked the conclusion of a deep transformation in the forms of US involvement that had been set in motion by the slave trade act of 1807. Between those two years, the US branch of the transatlantic slave trade characteristic of the pre-1808 era was dismantled, giving way to multiple forms of US participation. These forms at first coexisted, but by 1820 some were becoming predominant while others had nearly disappeared. We can set these different forms into four groups. First, a persisting group of US merchants—mainly entrenched in Bristol—continued to finance slave voyages to Africa until 1820, all of them having Cuba as their intended final destination. They were the best examples of a surviving genuine US slave trade, but by the late 1810s the Spanish component of their slave-trading operations had significantly increased. Second, a larger group of US merchants profited from the sales of US-built vessels to the growing Spanish slave-trading community, establishing a divergence between the number of captives carried aboard US-built vessels and those carried by US slave traders themselves. Third, and closely connected to the sales of vessels, was the large number of US captains and agents who established shady connections with the main Spanish slave traders over those years by selling their slave-trading expertise. Last, the smuggling of slaves into the United States after January 1, 1808, became the product of a network of adventurers—largely disconnected from the traditional Rhode Island merchants—involved in the wars of Spanish American independence.

The legislation of 1820 had a great impact on the first and last forms of US involvement described above. The first had already been dramatically reduced since 1807. The first four years (perhaps the first year alone, in fact) after the enactment of the slave trade act of 1807 saw the massive withdrawal of US merchants as investors in slave-trading ventures. As in Britain, this was a key impact of the act of 1807. The changes of 1820 ensured that even the slave-trading enclave of Bristol would end, with the appointment of Barnabas Bates—who had been denouncing its slave-trading activities for years—to the position of customs collector. Slave smuggling in the South revived as a result of abolition in 1808, and a certain ambiguity among Southern planters regarding the traffic was part of this, but by 1820 both seemed to have come to an end, at least temporarily. The main smuggling spots were closed by naval action, and Southerners as a whole supported the new legislation in order to regulate western expansion. Not surprisingly, the Virginian Charles Fenton Mercer was hailed as the "American Wilberforce" for his crucial role in passing the 1820 act.[78]

The growth of other forms of US participation—sales of US-built vessels and the direct participation of US captains, supercargoes, and sailors—were in turn directly connected to the emergence of a stronger Spanish branch of the transatlantic slave trade. Historian Manuel Moreno Fraginals also establishes the year of 1807 as a turning point in the Cuban shift. Abolition in Britain led British slave traders to sell the structures they had built and the knowledge they had accumulated in previous decades to Spanish Cuban slave traders. According to the historian, the voyages of the *Ciudad de Zaragoza* and the *Junta Central* in 1810 offer two great examples of crews that were a mixture of British sailors experienced in the traffic and young Spaniards willing to learn its specifics. As we have seen in this chapter, however, US slave-trading expertise was probably more important than the British contribution to the Cuban traffic. US captains and crews would be found aboard a large number of Spanish vessels in the 1810s. The transition was not smooth, and as Moreno observes, the combination of abolitionist pressure and inexperience in the traffic led to particularly high rates of mortality in the Middle Passage during the initial moments of this shift.[79]

As the Newport petitioners of 1820 well knew, even the suppression of the transatlantic slave trade could not stop the growth of slavery if new western territories were incorporated into the Union as slave states. "The slave population in the Atlantic States must of necessity rise with the demand for labor and the means of life," the Rhode Islanders argued, "and the event would be, as your memorialists can confidently predict, that the number of persons of this unhappy description in the United States would be a thousandfold greater than if the slaves were confined, as your memorialists would advise, to the States now holding them." And so it went, with the number of slaves in the nation reaching four million by 1860. Slavery also expanded in Brazil and Cuba, but under the auspices of a massive contraband transatlantic slave trade. Throughout the Atlantic world, including abolitionist Britain and the Northern United States, consumers, financiers, governments, and industrialists continued to benefit from the persistence of slavery and the transatlantic slave trade. Despite being an outspoken critic of the Atlantic slave trade, Moses Brown owned a cotton mill in Rhode Island, and like most most mill owners in the United States, he depended on the cotton grown by African slaves in the South. Similar examples abound.

Still, the US branch of the transatlantic slave trade had come to an end. Evidence of US citizens financing slave voyages almost disappears after 1820. Moreover, the legislation of 1820 was an important step for the consolidation of an opposition to the transatlantic slave trade in the United States, an opposition that later proved to be an insurmountable obstacle for possible alliances among the three main slave powers of the Americas in the mid-nineteenth century. The transformations of the US involvement in the slave trade over the 1810s were largely a product of the same dynamics—now supported by a federal law against the trade—that had been narrowing the spaces for slave-trading activities in New England since the late eighteenth century. These shifting attitudes to the traffic coexisted with the persistence of racism and slavery in the Atlantic World, but for the slave-trading community of Rhode Island, they ultimately prevailed.

The Consolidation of the Contraband
Slave Trade, 1820–1850

"Commerce is sometimes an adroit metaphysician—but a bad moralist!" When the former slave trader Théophilus Conneau published these words in 1854, he showed how some Western powers continued to be deeply involved in the slave trade despite their public condemnation of the business. England, for example, "with all her philanthropy, sends, under the cross of St. George, to convenient magazines of lawful commerce on the coast, her Birmingham muskets, Manchester cottons, and Liverpool lead," which were then exchanged on the coast of Africa for Spanish and Brazilian bills on London. "Yet, what British merchant does not know the traffic on which those bills are founded, and for whose support his wares are purchased?" France, "with her *bonnet rouge* and fraternity," also sent goods to the coast of Africa, from Rouen cottons to Marseille brandies. Even "philosophic Germany" dispatched "looking-glasses and beads." The United States obviously did not lag behind. Although slave traders could be hanged as pirates in that nation, US merchants did not hesitate to supply them with tobacco, cotton, rum, and other goods. "It is the temptation of these things," he concluded, "that feeds the slave-making wars of Africa, and forms the human basis of those admirable bills of exchange."[1]

The use of "admirable bills of exchange" had been, along with the growth of specialized merchant banks and the rise of the stock exchange, part of the financial revolution that had transformed Britain since the creation of the national debt and the foundation of the Bank of England in the 1690s. Before its dramatic industrial growth in the nineteenth century—turning it into, according to some observers, the "workshop of the world"—Britain had already become, as noted by Alexander Hamilton in 1795, the "creditor of the world." The effects of this transformation became clear during the Napoleonic Wars, as the British offered subsidies to its allies and efficiently financed the war through public debt while France had to rely mainly on the heavy taxation of its citizens. This period was also marked by the migration of refugee bankers to England and the dramatic decline of the Amsterdam capital market, turning the City of London into the financial center of the world. Confirming its naval supremacy, Britain emerged as the greatest world power in 1815, entering a new phase of unprecedented industrial, commercial, and financial expansion. This growth was accompanied by an intellectual and political movement toward free trade. "Free trade also benefited the City by transforming London into a great entrepôt for world trade in foodstuffs and raw materials," P. J. Cain and A. G. Hopkins argue, "thus boosting shipping services, marine insurance, specialized commodity exchanges, and wholesaling and commission agents." Not surprisingly, the banker Alexander Baring was responsible for introducing the famous Merchants' Petition for Free Trade—organized by Thomas Tooke, David Ricardo, Thomas Malthus, and other members of the Political Economy Club—in the House of Commons. These calls for free trade were shared by different groups around the world, from US slaveholders to Prussian Junkers, as they became connected to the capitalist world economy through the production of primary products such as cotton and wool. Slaveholding elites in independent Brazil, Alfredo Bosi argues, were perhaps more faithful to free trade principles than British and Yankee economists. Laissez faire and slavery became a hallmark of Brazil, Cuba, and the US South.[2]

The unprecedented economic growth of Britain was also reflected in the expansion of the United States, which had emerged from the War of 1812 with strong economic prospects. "The Royal Navy provided the shield that enabled the United States to expand across the continent untroubled by foreign predators, while the City of London supplied the capital that made expansion possible," Hopkins argues. "Other settlers on other frontiers were beginning a similar process of clearance and acquisition with the same support. There was nothing exceptional about the destiny of the United States or about Britain's role in helping it to become manifest." Britain became not only the main financer of US enterprises but also the main consumer of all the cotton exported by the South. The growth of the United States in turn made the nation the main consumer of all the coffee and sugar exported by, respectively, Brazil and Cuba. The growing demand for these products consequently led to the growth of slavery in Cuba, Brazil, and the United States. Whereas the United States relied on the natural growth of its slave population, however, Brazil and Cuba depended on the continuous inflow of enslaved Africans to their coffee and sugar plantations. Between 1820 and 1867, more than two million captives were embarked on vessels destined to both countries despite the anti-slave-trade treaties and legislation passed in both Spain and Brazil.[3]

The connection between the industrial, financial, and commercial expansion of the North Atlantic, on the one hand, and the growth of slavery and the contraband slave trade, on the other, was not limited to the consumption of slave-grown produce in Britain and the United States. The same Alexander Baring opposed a bill of 1815 prohibiting British subjects from lending capital to individuals in countries where the slave trade was still allowed. He was ready to support any measures "to crush this odious traffick," even implementing the death penalty if necessary, but British citizens should not be prohibited from extending their credit to individuals in slave-trading nations. "This unqualified sweep would at once extinguish the trade which existed between this country and the Spanish settlements; for it was impossible to carry on this trade without that species of credit, which would be made criminal by this Act." And, indeed, British credit became a fundamental part of nineteenth-century slave economies. British commercial houses advanced manufactured goods and cash to Brazilian merchants and planters. In return, they received plantation produce in an interval that could take up to two years. A few British companies, in fact, directly employed slaves in their enterprises in Brazil, such as the mining companies of Minas Gerais.

The Saint John d'el Rey mining company became the largest individual slaveholder in the state by the 1860s, employing around 1,400 captives in almost every aspect of its operations.[4]

In one specific area of the contraband slave trade, however, the United States became unquestionably predominant: the provision of ships. This was mainly the result of a combination of abundant supplies of cheap lumber and improvements in the US shipbuilding industry, which saw advances in vessel design theory, contributions from specific shipbuilders based in the United States such as William H. Webb, and the abandonment of legal constraints to vessel designs. By the mid-nineteenth century, US shipbuilders were seen as the top-notch con-structors of wooden sailing vessels, driving numerous British shipbuild-ers to bankruptcy during the 1840s. This became clear in the whaling industry, with British merchants being completely driven out of the business during the first half of the nineteenth century.[5]

British preeminence in Brazil was indisputable, but bilateral re-lationships between Brazil and the United States did improve during the first half of the nineteenth century (the selling and chartering of US-built vessels to merchants based in Brazil played an important role in this). Cuba, by contrast, was perhaps the only place where a US pres-ence competed more closely with the British, with the Spanish colony becoming a key commercial partner of the United States. The island imported lumber, foodstuffs, and manufactured products, reaching the position of third most important trading partner of the United States by the 1830s (with the total value of exports and imports exceeded only by Britain and France). The strengthening of these ties led to the entrench-ment of US merchants in different sectors of the Cuban economy. The Cuban Center of Statistics reported 1,256 US citizens living in the island around 1846 and, again, 2,500 in 1862. The US presence in Cuba, ar-gues Louis A. Perez Jr., was numerically small but significant in strategic points of the economy. North American commercial houses in the main Cuban ports worked as trading establishments purchasing sugar, selling manufactured imports, and providing credit for local planters. US cit-izens also invested in mining, imported machinery into the island, and developed a network of boardinghouses along the Cuban north coast. The Havana-Güines line, the first Latin American railroad, was developed by US engineers and depended on North American supplies and equipment. Some North Americans also invested in slave plantations on the island and became part of the two ends of the trading ties between the United States and Cuba. In 1823, there were at least fifty plantations valued at three million dollars owned by US citizens in Matanzas. The South Carolinian George W. Williams observed during his trip to Cuba in the 1850s that he found "quite a number of planters from the United States residing here, and they nearly all hail from the Northern States." When New Englander Mary Gardner Lowell traveled to Cuba in 1831, she visited Nathaniel Fellows, the nephew of the deceased Boston merchant, who inherited the merchant's estate. By the time of Lowell's visit, Fellows owned three plantations and rented a fourth, with 406 slaves distributed across them. The precursors of these US plantations in Cuba were the Rhode Island slave traders, who had been establishing them with the help of French refugees since the turn of the century. As we have seen, not only the D'Wolfs but also former captains such as Joseph Oliver Wilson and John Sabens had been able to purchase estates on the island. These individuals had been supplying captives to their own plantations over the 1810s, but after 1820 it seems that most of them had abandoned the slave-trading business to become purchasers only.[6]

All American and European nations had either formally outlawed or had signed treaties against the African slave trade by 1830. The contraband slave trade that emerged had some specific characteristics that distinguished it from the business carried by mercantilist empires in previous centuries. First, the context of illegality raised the costs of slave-trading expeditions and, as a result, made concentration of ownership more pronounced. It also led slave traders to organize themselves in joint stock companies as a strategy to spread the costs and losses that became an integral part of the business. Second, the growth of the contraband slave trade took place in the context of rapid industrial growth in Britain, the United States, and other European countries. Besides the growth in demand for slave-grown products, this new situation meant that the manufactured goods (and credit) that flooded international markets would also find their way into the contraband slave trade, as made clear in the words of Captain Conneau. Slave trading became more internationalized than ever before. Last, the illegal business grew within the post-1815 world of nation-states supposedly regulated by the law of nations. Failure to establish a multilateral agreement against the trans-atlantic slave trade during the Congress of Vienna, as we have seen, led the British government to develop a treaty system centered on bilateral agreements with different nations. This treaty system certainly had an impact on the organization of the business, as I will discuss in the following chapters, but proved incapable of eliminating the illegal traffic altogether. Despite formal abolition of the trade in Brazil and Cuba, political arrangements within both countries ensured that African labor would continue to supply their plantations. In this chapter I explore the national and international contexts that permitted the flourishing of a contraband slave trade to the Americas and the nature of US participation in it.

The Slave Trade Domesticated: The United States

Slavery continued its inexorable march westward in the United States. Though the Panic of 1819 arrested the boom of the second half of the 1810s, indebted farmers and planters continued to expand their cotton enterprises during the 1820s. In 1820, cotton exports from the country reached a total value of approximately $22 million. Ten years later their value rose to almost $30 million, and in 1840, they passed the mark of $60 million. Unlike Brazil and Cuba, however, the labor force used in the expanding frontier could no longer be supplied by Africa. The passing of anti-slave-trade legislation during the first two decades of the century and the military interventions that closed the points of slave smuggling at Amelia Island and along the Gulf Coast in the late 1810s effectively shut the doors for the importation of captives directly from Africa. Evidence of slave smuggling into the United States is scarce for the years after 1820. Estimates are that fewer than a thousand slaves were carried directly from Africa to the United States between 1820 and the Civil War. The larger numbers offered by Philip Curtin—one thousand disembarkations per year—he has described as a "shot in the dark," given the scarcity of data. Some smuggling of captives from other parts of the Americas may have taken place after 1820, but evidence is scarce here as well. Robert W. Fogel and Stanley L. Engerman suggested based on census data that a thousand slaves were disembarked in the country by year between 1808 and 1860. Fogel later revised these numbers and suggested that perhaps the number of slaves smuggled into the country between 1810 and 1860 was not different from the number of cases actually detected and prosecuted by US authorities. His argument is based on studies showing that not a single African-born individual appeared in the samples of black regiments of the Union Army or among the two thousand narratives of former slaves used by them. It seems likely that slave smuggling to the country—whether from Africa or the Caribbean—was minimal after 1820.[7]

The laborers exploited in the expansion of the cotton frontier essentially came from within the United States, after the consolidation of what historian Adam Rothman has called the "domestication of the slave trade." Between 1820 and 1860, more than 875,000 slaves were carried by land and by sea between the slave-exporting regions and the southwestern frontier, most of them sold in a flourishing domestic market. These commercial circuits had the obvious potential to undermine the ideologies of paternalism that became an integral part of proslavery thought in the South, a contradiction that abolitionists explored to the fullest. A number of Southerners tried to minimize the existence of slave markets and color them with benevolent tones. According to their arguments, indebted planters sold their slaves only under extremely adverse conditions, being emotionally devastated for doing so. In this context, the status of slave traders responsible for supplying most of the labor in the cotton frontier became highly ambivalent. John Archibald Campbell of Alabama argued, for example, that respectable slaveholders had condemned slave traders in all epochs, citing the advice of the Roman playwright Plautus "to place no trust in those fellows."[8]

After the Missouri Compromise the separation between the transatlantic slave trade and Southern slavery (including the internal trade that kept it alive) appeared immediately in a number of speeches, laws, and legal decisions. In 1822, Mississippi passed an act "to reduce into one, the several acts, concerning slaves, free negroes, and mulattoes." The act permitted the introduction of slaves born and resident in the United States that were not criminals while prohibiting the entrance of captives born or resident outside the United States under a penalty of a thousand dollars per slave. That same year Supreme Court Justice Joseph Story acknowledged that slavery had a legitimate existence in certain countries, including the United States, before arguing in a court decision that the transatlantic slave trade was a violation of international law. Abolitionists, in contrast, continued to connect the domestic slave trade to its international variant, a practice that increased with the growth of Northern abolitionism in the 1830s. An extensive report prepared by the New England Anti-Slavery Society, for example, denounced the horrors in the sales of African Americans in the South, arguing that it "involved the crimes of murder, kidnapping and robbery, and is equally worthy with the foreign to be denounced and treated by human laws and tribunals as piracy, and those who carry it on as enemies of the human race." In response, Southerners followed the strategy of William Smith during the Missouri Debates: defend the benevolent nature of the institution while blaming Northerners for their participation in the transatlantic slave trade. Thomas C. Thornton, for example, started his proslavery treatise by stressing that "the people of the north who had from the commencement, united trade and traffic with their agricultural operations for a living, engaged *heartily* in this work of *importing* and exporting slaves." According to the reverend, resistance to the transatlantic slave trade was more widespread in the slaveholding states than in the North.[9]

Before the 1850s, therefore, proslavery arguments went hand in hand with opposition to the transatlantic slave trade. Thomas R. Dew's *Review of the Debate in the Virginia Legislature on the Abolition of Slavery,* considered by some historians to be the first fully developed defense of slavery in the United States, begins with a historical overview of the slave trade. In his account, the commerce in human beings had a negative impact on Africa, causing "a violation of the principles of humanity" and giving "rise to much suffering and to considerable destruction of human life. Judging by its effects, we must condemn it, and consequently agree that slavery in our hemisphere was based upon injustice in the first instance." Citing Robert Walsh's *Appeal,* however, he argues that the United States had its "hands unpolluted with the original sin" and asks, "Did we not wash them clean of the contagion the moment our independent existence was established? Where is the stain that rests upon our escutcheon? There is none!" William Brown Hodgson, a Savannah planter who owned 450 slaves in 1850, praised Thomas Fowell Buxton a few years earlier for his condemnation of the transatlantic slave trade. "It is a proud reflection for these United States, that they were the first among the nations of the Earth, to denounce this trade as piracy," Hodgson argued. "Nor will the effort to suppress the slave trade, by operating upon the mind of Africa, and substituting a legitimate commerce, which addresses itself to the interests of the African be deemed adverse to the treaty engagements of this government." Southern planters were attuned to British anti-slave-trade writings, and many incorporated the arguments of the British anticoercionists of the 1840s, who believed that the actions of the Royal Navy had merely heightened the mortality and suffering of those captives carried across the Atlantic. When James Henry Hammond wrote his famous letters to Thomas Clarkson to defend slavery in 1846, he started by joining him in the condemnation of the transatlantic slave trade but noted that British suppression policies were worsening the conditions of Africans in the Middle Passage. Endorsing the abolition of the slave trade, David Brion Davis has argued, "enabled the more scrupulous planters to build a mental wall separating them from the violence of African 'slave-making' and from the publicized horrors of the Middle Passage."[10]

Despite widespread opposition to the traffic in the United States, nationalist resistance to the mutual right of search in peacetime continued to hinder joint efforts with Great Britain. The Missouri Debates heightened the antislavery sensibilities of John Quincy Adams but did not change his opinions on the right of search, as it became evident in his famous declaration of 1822 that the only thing more despicable than the African slave trade would be granting the right of search to other powers. That would be "making slaves of ourselves." Rufus King also pressured the Monroe administration not to concede to Britain on this issue. The call for the establishment of international agreements to suppress the slave trade was nonetheless discussed almost annually in Congress during the early 1820s. The main figure offering these resolutions was the Virginian Charles Fenton Mercer, founder of the American Colonization Society and author of the bill that turned the slave trade into piracy in 1820. The persistence of Mercer was an extension of his earlier anti-slave-trade efforts that sought to transform the illegal business into piracy under the law of nations. In the early 1820s this seemed plausible, as it became clear in the views of Justice Joseph Story during the case of the *Jeune Eugenie,* one of the four suspected French slavers captured by the US Navy off the coast of Africa in 1821. The French consul asked for the vessel to be restored to its original owners, but Story argued that the ship was clearly US-built and had defective documents of its new nationality. More important in his view, however, was the fact that the transatlantic slave trade was not only illegal in France but also "repugnant to the general principles of justice and humanity" and, therefore, contrary to the law of nations. Story was actually rejecting the previous British interpretation in the similar *Le Louis* case, when the admiralty judge Sir William Scott had established—also based on the law of nations—that a British court had no power over a French ship in peacetime. The federal government, however, did not support Story's novel interpretation, with Secretary of State John Quincy Adams and President Monroe pressuring the court to return the vessel to the French government. The only protest came from Attorney General William Wirt, who argued that the government had "taken the safe side" in surrendering the vessel to France. After all, that "vessels are in the constant habit of using the flags of all nations to cover their illicit operation is familiarly and universally understood."[11]

John Quincy Adams and the British representative Stratford Canning met regularly in the early 1820s in attempts to establish a treaty, with the right of search issue persistently reappearing as an obstacle in the negotiations. A treaty between the United States and Britain got very close to being passed in 1824. Adams wrote a convention establishing that, once Britain declared the traffic to be piracy, the mutual right of search could be granted for circumscribed areas. Captured vessels would be tried at the country of origin of the vessel, eliminating the necessity of mixed courts, which many in the United States saw as conflicting with the Constitution. The British government signed the agreement, but it failed to pass the Senate in its original form. US senators added a number of amendments, the most important of which excluded the coast of North America as one of the areas where suspected slavers could be captured by either nation. The mutual right of search, in the new version, should be limited to the coast of Africa and the Caribbean. The British rejected the changes, and negotiations ceased.

The failure paved the way for the Supreme Court decision in the case of the *Antelope* in 1825, the Spanish ship that, as we have seen, was seized by a privateer and subsequently taken into custody with about 280 slaves aboard. The opinion of the Court, which included Joseph Story among its constituents, was that countries as distinct as Russia and Geneva had equal rights under the law of nations and that, since no nation had the power to prescribe rules for another, the law of nations could not be unilaterally transformed. While the traffic remained lawful for some countries, it was "neither repugnant to the law of nations, nor piracy." The court concluded, therefore, that vessels seized in time of peace by the US Navy—as had been the case with the *Antelope*—should be restored to their original owners. When the same Joseph Story delivered the opinion of the court in the *Amistad* case sixteen years later, it was clear that this had become the established view. The Senate had unanimously approved a resolution by John C. Calhoun stating that only Spain had jurisdiction over the ship. The key difference here was that the Africans had been illegally enslaved according to the laws of Spain itself.[12]

After the failed attempt to establish an anti-slave-trade treaty with Britain, John Quincy Adams noted that a number of senators suspected and feared that these joint efforts could be connected to British designs for the abolition of slavery itself. Those fears had been connecting the growth of abolitionism in Britain to the prevalence of slave uprisings in Barbados (1816) and Demerara (1823) (which in turn had an antecedent in the connections made by white Southerners between the actions of the abolitionist Société des Amis des Noirs and the Haitian Revolution). The relation between abolitionism and slave revolts reappeared in the alleged conspiracy of Denmark Vesey in 1822, which, according to some observers, was related to the antislavery indictments made by Rufus King during the Missouri Debates.[13]

These tensions reflected in the emergence of the Second Party System in 1828, which led to a complete silence over the issue of slavery. The election of the Democrat candidate Andrew Jackson that year, James

Oakes notes, led to a concerted effort to suppress slavery as a political issue that was continued by successive administrations for more than a decade, including those presided by Whigs. Both parties managed to keep slavery—and consequently the transatlantic slave trade issue—off the radar. These efforts were reinforced by, on the one hand, the growth of abolitionism in the North and, on the other, the persistence of slave rebellions in the South and in the Caribbean. The year 1831 saw both the foundation of William Lloyd Garrison's abolitionist newspaper the *Liberator* and Nat Turner's slave rebellion in Virginia, in which sixty whites were killed. That same year a slave uprising shook Jamaica, with the US consul in the island sending graphic descriptions to Secretary of State John Forsyth of supposed rapes and brutal violations perpetrated against the wives and daughters of white planters (even though, as David Brion Davis has observed, uprisings in the British Caribbean had been distinctly nonviolent). The beginning of the emancipation process in the British Empire and the foundation of the American Anti-Slavery Society in Philadelphia in 1833 heightened Southern suspicions. Consequently, when British foreign secretary Lord Palmerston offered to accept a treaty with the United States in 1834 that would leave the North American coast out of the designated right of search areas, the same Forsyth replied that the government was resolved not to make "a party to any convention on the subject." In domestic politics the key measure was the establishment of the gag rule in Congress, prohibiting the acceptance of petitions related to slavery. Between 1826 and 1838 the transatlantic slave trade was not mentioned in a single annual presidential message.[14]

The silence, however, was also due to the significant decrease in US participation in the transatlantic slave trade after 1820. Although the number of US-built vessels employed in the business probably increased during those years, the US flag had nearly disappeared. The *Voyages* database presently has evidence of seven voyages under the US flag between 1821 and 1835. Three of them had captains with names that indicate a possible US origin—Brown, West, and Hill, respectively the captains of the *Esencia, Ceylon,* and *William Gardner*—but the other four have no information regarding their ownership. The only two for which there is such information, the same *William Gardner* and the *Atrevido,* were in fact owned, respectively, by the Spaniard Campo Labierreta y Martinez and the notorious slave trader Francisco Felix de Souza. The British consul at Cadiz warned in 1830 that a few vessels, including the *William Gardner,* had arrived in the city under US colors but had been purchased by Spaniards. The *Atrevido,* also built in the United States, was purchased by a British captain after being condemned for piracy a few years earlier. The captain then exchanged the vessel for slaves (which he disembarked at Havana) with Francisco Felix de Souza, who in turn employed the ship in the slave trade to Bahia under the command of João Garcia. The role of US captains and agents would increase again by the late 1830s, but it seems that the years between 1820 and 1835 saw the lowest levels of US participation in the traffic since independence.[15]

The Birth of the Contraband Slave Trade in Brazil

Brazilian independence in 1822 led British authorities to act quickly. From the beginning, recognition of independence by the British was coupled with a commitment to abolish the slave trade. The British made similar agreements with most other recently independent Latin American countries, but the Brazilian case was more complicated. The commerce in human beings carried to Brazil had no counterpart in terms of strength and longevity, leading abolitionist William Wilberforce to refer to the country as the "slave trade personified." If the early treaties between Britain and Portugal abolishing the slave trade left the South Atlantic branch untouched—Portuguese slave traders were allowed to carry on their business below the equator and between Portuguese possessions in Africa—British abolitionists took Brazilian independence as an opportunity to intervene more effectively, a move that had been cut short by the Portuguese during the previous decade. A treaty was signed and ratified between late 1826 and early 1827, with Brazil agreeing to abolish the trade within three years after ratification. The treaty was passed without participation of the Chamber of Deputies, which added to the dissatisfaction of sectors of Brazilian elites, increasingly suspicious of the extreme centralization of power around the emperor. The chamber had been debating proposals for gradual abolition during

1826, all of them proposing periods longer than three years for the end of the trade. Most deputies, including abolitionists, saw the established date as synonymous with economic disaster. The establishment of an expiration date for the slave trade led to a dramatic rise in slave importations. About 61,000 Africans were disembarked in Brazil in 1826, an increase of 41 percent from the previous year. Three years later an all-time peak in the history of the slave trade to Brazil was reached, with the disembarkation of almost 73,000 Africans. The year 1829, in fact, saw the largest number of slave embarkations in the history of the transatlantic slave trade: present estimates point to 117,644 individuals being carried on slave vessels out of Africa. The other main destination besides Brazil was Cuba, which received almost 20,000 captives that year.[16]

In 1830, Dom Pedro officially decreed the abolition of the slave trade to Brazil. The three-man regency that replaced him—Dom Pedro abdicated the throne in 1831—agreed on the necessity of a national law regulating the slave trade. National sovereignty should be reaffirmed in response to a treaty that many saw as a foreign imposition. The law that came to be passed in 1831 was actually more radical than the terms of the treaty of 1826. Its first article declared that all slaves illegally carried to Brazil should be declared free. Other articles identified and condemned a range of participants in the trade, from crews of slave ships to planters buying illegally imported Africans. Those arrested could face three to nine years of incarceration, corporal punishment, a fine of two hundred *milreis* for every African illegally disembarked, and dealing with the expenses of returning the liberated Africans to their continent. None of these penalties could be exacted in a mixed commission court. In 1831, the number of importations decreased dramatically, with 6,178 enslaved Africans disembarked. Between 1831 and 1834, estimates are that 46,192 Africans were disembarked in Brazil, less than the number of slaves disembarked in 1830 alone (figure 2). According to Leslie Bethell, the decrease was the product of a glut in the market, oversupplied in the wake of abolition. The early years after the 1831 law, however, saw some serious efforts from Brazilian authorities to curb the contraband slave trade, with a large number of speeches in Parliament denouncing its persistence. In the aftermath of the 1835 Malê Revolt, the foreign minis-

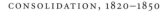

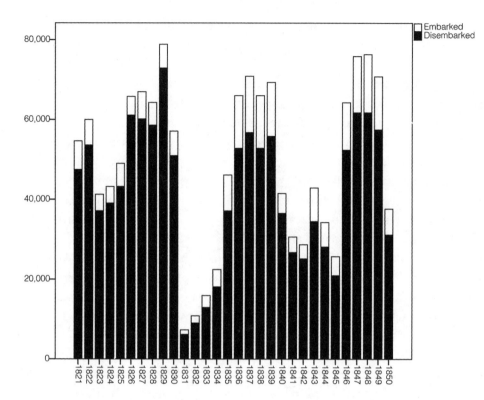

Fig. 2. Number of captives embarked and disembarked by year in Brazil, 1821–
50 (Source: www.slavevoyages.org)

ter signed additional articles to the treaty of 1826, facilitating the seizure
of vessels suspected of engaging in the slave trade based on their equipment.[17]

The first signs of change came in 1834, when the municipal chamber of Bananal, in the state of São Paulo, sent a representation to Parliament asking for the revocation of the 1831 law. The following year
Bernardo Pereira de Vasconcelos also suggested that the law should be
revoked. Vasconcelos was one of the main founders of the Regresso, a
forerunner of the Brazilian Conservative Party. Honório Carneiro Leão,
Joaquim José Rodrigues Torres, and Paulino José Soares de Souza were
other central members of the group that also came to be known as
saquaremas. Vasconcelos and other Regresso politicians continued to
criticize the anti-slave-trade legislation and to call for the official pro-

tection of the property in slaves illegally introduced after 1831. Although conservatives continued to speak out against the law in Parliament and in newspapers, petitions calling for its revocation also came from the municipal chambers of the cities of Valença, Mangaratiba, Bananal, Barra Mansa, Paraíba do Sul, and Vassouras. The unifying element was coffee. As demand for coffee rose in the international market, plantations spread throughout the Zona da Mata in Minas Gerais and the Vale do Paraíba, an area stretching from the province of Rio de Janeiro to northern São Paulo. Except for Valença, founded in 1823, the cities just mentioned were founded between 1831 and 1833. As coffee production in the area developed, demand for labor rose. In the three decades after 1821, as David Eltis points out, more slaves arrived on the Brazilian south-central coast than in the rest of the Americas combined. Present estimates point to the disembarkation of 579,591 slaves in the region. Some sugar plantations established earlier in the century also persisted in the state of São Paulo and were certainly responsible for part of the demand for slave labor. Not all of the illegally imported slaves were employed directly in coffee and sugar production; many were directed to auxiliary sectors such as the production of foodstuffs. An estimated 743,793 enslaved Africans were disembarked in Brazil between 1831 and 1851.[18]

Bahia continued to produce sugar during the period of the contraband slave trade, receiving about a hundred thousand of all the slaves disembarked in Brazil between 1831 and 1851. Exports from the traditional sugar-producing region of Pernambuco continued, with the province receiving relatively high numbers of Africans compared to Bahia in the 1830s. In the 1840s, the number of disembarkations decreased dramatically despite the rising volume of sugar being produced, as a greater number of free-wage laborers, seasonal workers, and squatters were employed. The economic divergence between the Northeast and the south-central regions nonetheless continued to increase. "Whatever is sold at Rio de Janeiro, whether chains of gold or iron, the flesh of a man or beast, its equivalent may be received in cash," the British consul at Pernambuco explained in one of his reports, "whilst at Pernambuco, the cash payments are impracticable; how much more so must they be in other less productive parts of the country? It is this which makes Rio de Janeiro the desired resort, the *el dorado* of the slave trader; he lands his slaves, receives his dollars, and returns to the African coast for more victims." Actually, some members of the conservative party would later proudly remember the years of the contraband slave trade to Southeast Brazil. "When, Mr. President," the *regressista* Paulino Soares asked in 1858, "were these large agricultural plantations established, formed or reinforced with arms acquired between 1837 and 1851, that until today produce the large exports with which we pay for imports?"[19]

The main consumer of the coffee produced in these plantations was the United States. By 1844, US consumption of coffee had expanded dramatically. In the century after 1783, per capita consumption of coffee went from less than an ounce to nine pounds. Combined with the fifteenfold growth of the population, it meant an increase of 2,400 percent in the importation of coffee. Saint Domingue, Jamaica, Cuba, and Java supplied this coffee at different moments between the late eighteenth and early nineteenth centuries, but by the 1830s, Brazil had surpassed all of them as the main coffee producer in the world. One consequence was the radical transformation of the Vale do Paraíba, which, from a peripheral region in the early 1800s, became the center of the Brazilian slave economy. More coffee consumption in the United States, therefore, meant larger numbers of slaves illegally carried from Africa to Brazil and more environmental devastation caused by the expansion of the coffee frontier. US distributors and consumers, on the other hand, rarely thought of the coercive origins of their coffee, with the product becoming, in the words of two historians, "geographically sanitized."[20]

The Birth of the Contraband Slave Trade in Cuba

The growth of sugar consumption in the United States during the first half of the nineteenth century had similar effects in Cuba. According to Manuel Moreno Fraginals, sugar produced in Louisiana met some of this demand, but beginning in 1832, shifts in tariff policies favored competition from Cuba. Sugar exports from the island increased from fourteen thousand tons in 1832 to thirty-eight thousand tons in 1838. As we have seen, the United States had been the chief customer for Cuban sugar since the 1790s. Britain and France became important consumers after the 1810s, and although the share of Cuban exports to the United

States decreased during the 1830s and 1840s, the country continued to be the chief importer of Cuban products. Moreover, even though the US share of Cuban sugar production declined during this period, the US consumption of Cuban molasses reached new levels, rising from four million gallons in 1816 to sixteen million gallons in 1839. Coffee was another important Cuban export to the United States, although the island was increasingly unable to meet the growing demand (which came to be supplied, as we have seen, mainly by Brazil). Despite the colonial status of Cuba, its integration into the less regulated market of the nineteenth century led to a dramatic growth of the transatlantic trade in slaves to Cuba. An estimated 387,966 enslaved Africans were disembarked on the Spanish island between 1820 and 1850. The number of slaves carried to the island decreased only during the 1840s, when a series of hurricanes destroyed coffee production in the island, sugar prices declined, and Captain General Jerônimo Valdés (1841–43) tried to more actively curb the trade in contraband to the island (figure 3).[21]

The second Spanish constitutional period—the Trienio Liberal of the early 1820s—revived political tensions related to slavery that had been part of discussions in the Cádiz Cortes during the early 1810s. In 1821, José María Queípo de Llano, the Count of Toreno, who seems to have met British abolitionists during his exile in London, called for the creation of a committee to elaborate new slave trade laws to fulfill the treaty of 1817. Shortly after the draft of a new law was read in a plenary session, Juan Bernardo O'Gavan—a Cuban deputy excluded from the Cortes in Madrid—published a proslavery manifesto that exposed the position of Cuban slaveholding interests. After replicating classic tropes of proslavery thought (for example, Africans fared better in the Americas than in Africa), O'Gavan argued that the transatlantic slave trade was necessary to keep Cuba under Spanish dominion. If new efforts to cut the inflow of enslaved Africans were established, seen by many Cubans as attacks on their prosperity, Cuba would seek independence or annexation by the United States. The Cortes at Madrid rejected the proposals for new anti-slave-trade legislation, and the issue remained unsettled through the end of the Liberal Triennium.[22]

A fundamental step for the reopening of the slave trade to the Spanish island was the establishment of the *régimen de las facultades*

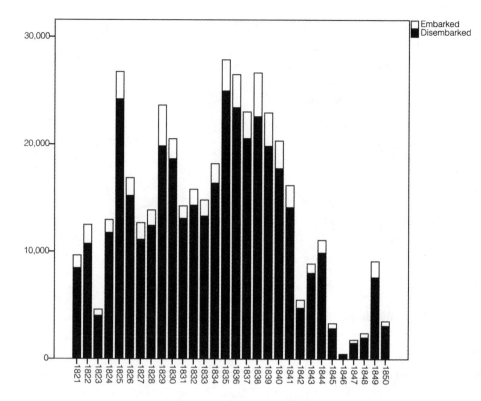

Fig. 3. Number of captives embarked and disembarked by year in Cuba, 1821–50
(Source: www.slavevoyages.org)

omnímodas. This measure gave absolute powers to the captains general
of the island, a transformation that also had its origins in the Liberal
Triennium. In 1823, Joaquín Gómez, one of the main slave traders in
Cuba, presented a proposal to strengthening the powers of the captain
general to ssure that Cuba would remain within the Spanish Empire.
Gómez and the Deputación Provincial de la Havana (a group represent-
ing planters from the rural districts) argued that this was necessary to
curb social disruptions caused by conspirators seeking independence
as well as threats of slave rebellion. The empire's defeat at the Battle of
Ayacucho, marking the independence of Peru and the end of Spanish
colonial rule in the mainland of the Americas, stimulated the approval
of the new measures to strengthen colonial ties with Cuba. The regimen
was approved in 1825 and, among other things, ceded control over the

contraband slave trade to the captain general. This limited the opportunities of the British government to pressure Spain, since only captains general could decide which measures coming from Madrid should be applied in Cuba. Captain General Francisco Dionisio Vives y Piñón, for example, refused to publish in Cuba a communication sent by the Spanish government stating that Africans illegally introduced into Cuba had the right to freedom. José Antonio Saco, who had been publicly condemning the traffic since 1832 as a crucial step for "whitening" Cuba, was deported, and a general silence over the contraband slave trade was imposed until the 1860s. Reinforcing this silence was the exclusion of Cuba from the new Spanish constitutional phase that started in 1837. Cuba's marginalization protected the island from Spain's electoral processes and from the circulation of ideas against slavery and the slave trade. Therefore, the concession of absolute powers to the captain general and the exclusion of the island from the areas contemplated by the Spanish constitution of 1837, historian José Antonio Piqueras argues, were the key instruments in silencing critical voices. Contrary to the common view that these measures were attacks on Cuban society, slave-trading and slave-holding elites in the island actually supported them, considering them a lesser evil. While Cuba continued to be governed from Madrid, it collaborated with the slaveholding interests of the island.[23]

In provisions to the treaty added in 1835, Spain committed itself to pass legislation abolishing the slave trade, a law that was passed only ten years later. In 1845, after increasing British pressure and the conspiracy of La Escalera, a series of slave rebellions that culminated in the violent repression of a large number of slaves and free blacks during 1844, the Cortes passed a penal law criminalizing the slave trade. Two amendments, however, mandated that Cuban officials could only seize vessels coming directly from Africa and protected plantations from being searched for illegally disembarked captives. The penal law of 1845 thus had the effect of protecting the property of the slaveholders who kept the transatlantic slave trade alive. In the 1860s, Captain General Domingo Dulce y Garay (1862–66) frequently complained that the law was an obstacle to curtailing the slave trade to the island. The legislation did , however, eliminate the open tolerance with which Cuban officials had been treating the illegal traffic and, consequently, raised distribution costs (namely bribing). As mentioned, the mid-1840s saw a decline in the number of slaves transported to the island, in part a result of anti-slave-trade efforts by Captain General Gerónimo Valdés since 1842, in part because of the falling prices of sugar around that same year. A recovery in sugar prices in the late 1840s, however, did not automatically lead to more importations, indicating the possible impact of the penal law of 1845.[24]

Some historians estimate that by the late 1820s a fourth of Cuban slaves were employed in the sugar sector, a fourth in the coffee sector, another fourth in the cities, and the final fourth in such other activities as food crops, cattle ranches, and small-scale tobacco production, which persisted into the 1840s. Sugar and coffee production grew dynamically throughout most of this period, with the volume of investments in both sectors being almost the same in the late 1830s. In the 1840s, however, a series of hurricanes that devastated the coffee zones, combined with Brazilian competition, led to a specialization in sugar production. The number of sugar mills in Cuba, which had increased from 529 in 1792 to 1,000 in 1827, reached 1,439 in 1846. The appearance of almost 500 new mills between 1827 and 1846 was accompanied by an increase in their productive capacities. Output per mill rose from 72 tons in 1830 to 120 tons in 1841. By 1860, each sugar mill averaged 316 tons. While in 1820 Cuba produced 54,906 tons of sugar, in 1840 this production reached 161,248 tons. In late 1837 the first railroad on the island was inaugurated, and within the following twenty-five years four hundred miles of railway were completed as the sugar frontier continued its march westward. Mills increasingly converted to steam power, iron rollers and vacuum boilers were introduced, and the sugar sector became among the most technologically advanced in the mid-nineteenth-century world. As in Brazil, this expansion had a deep ecological impact, leading to the radical deforestation of vast areas and transforming Cuba into one of the main importers of US lumber.[25]

The Resurgence of US Involvement in the Traffic to Cuba

The sale and chartering of US-built vessels were important features of the growth of trade relations between the United States and Latin America.

The success of the US shipbuilding industry during the US "golden age of sail" had an impact on the transatlantic slave trade, with slave traders increasingly employing US-built ships in the contraband to Cuba and Brazil. In 1826 the US consul at Bahia mentioned the large number of US vessels sold in Salvador. According to him, "The greater part of the vessels employed in said slave trade, at and from this port are built in the United States, are regularly sold here, and the crews discharged. . . . It is common for American vessels to take freight and proceed to Africa from this port, and commonly return in ballast." He asserted, however, that US citizens had withdrawn from the business as investors, since he had "never been able to ascertain that any citizens of the United States have, directly or indirectly, any interest whatever in said slave trade. I am well acquainted with the concern of those Americans who live here, and do not believe they have any interest in said trade." In Rio de Janeiro, companies such as Maxwell, Wright & Co. and Birckhead & Co. had also been taking advantage of the sale of US vessels (as well as slave-trading equipment) since the 1820s. Foreign merchant houses frequently announced US-built vessels and slave-trading equipment in the classifieds section of the *Jornal do Commercio,* one of the main newspapers in the city. In a series of advertisements for the US brigantine *Seaman* in 1828, Maxwell, Wright & Co. described the vessel as well fit for the slave trade ("bem adoptado para o commercio de escravatura").[26]

Unfortunately, it is impossible to estimate how many of the US vessels sold by US companies in Rio de Janeiro entered the slave trade during the 1820s. The *Voyages* website contains the place of construction for 168 slave voyages for that decade, but France is extremely overrepresented in the sample, since the data for 159 of the slave expeditions came mostly from the work of Serge Daget. The remaining nine voyages nonetheless indicate the existence for a growing demand for US-built vessels in the country. Only one expedition during those years used a vessel built in England. All others had been constructed in such US ports as Baltimore and Philadelphia. In 1825, the prominent slave trader Francisco Felix de Souza ordered one of these vessels built in the United States. Ten years later he bought the *Florida* from the New York merchants J. A. Gordon and Pexcel Fowler, with the vessel being delivered at Whydah, in West Africa, in November 1835.[27]

The year 1835 had, in fact, marked a turning point in the history of US participation in the transatlantic slave trade. A treaty between England and Spain that permitted the capture of vessels equipped for the slave trade after that year led to the development of new strategies that involved non-Spanish merchants on a whole new level. The 1839 Palmerston Act unilaterally extended the practice of seizing suspected slavers based on their equipment to the Portuguese flag. In April 1840, the British chargé in Rio, W. G. Ouseley, warned Palmerston that "the flag of the United States is now likely to be made use of by the Portuguese slave traders, and in a manner that will render it difficult to interfere effectually to prevent at once the evil consequences of the assistance thus afforded to them." Also starting in 1839, British commissioners in the Mixed Commissions of Rio de Janeiro and Sierra Leone reinterpreted the existing treaties between Brazil and Britain in such a way that captures of vessels equipped for the slave trade became possible for the first time. In 1845, tensions between Britain and Brazil would reach a new level with the passing of the so-called Aberdeen Act, which empowered British courts to adjudicate Brazilian vessels captured by the Royal Navy. "Palmerston's aggressive diplomacy," argues Don Fehrenbacher, "tightened the screws on the other maritime nations and drove slavers increasingly to the protection of the American flag."[28]

Before 1835 the vessels that carried slave-trading equipment and goods used in the exchange for slaves in Africa were usually the same ones that transported human cargoes back to the Americas. The first consequence of the treaty of 1835 was the division of slave-trading operations into two parts, with vessels of other nationalities—especially from the United States—carrying the slave-trading equipment and goods to Africa in the first leg of the voyages. These vessels were then sold on the African coast (or, in many cases, sold in Cuba but deliverable in Africa) and returned to Cuba with captives generally under another flag. Others maintained their original nationality and returned in ballast after delivering the cargo in Africa. This strategy was also put into practice in the Brazilian slave trade during the first half of the 1840s, as vessels flying the Portuguese and Brazilian flags were increasingly captured before the embarkation of enslaved Africans. "Portuguese slave dealers have been endeavouring to induce English vessels to take the slave trading articles as freight to the Coast of Africa," Ouseley noted, "until it was made known by Her Majesty's Consul, that such a speculation would be likely to entail serious and unpleasant consequences on all the parties concerned." Prominent slave traders of the 1840s such as Manoel Pinto da Fonseca, José Bernardino de Sá, and Joaquim Pereira Marinho frequently employed US vessels as auxiliaries to the slave trade for years before turning them into slavers under new flags (see Chapter 5).[29]

This new context opened up opportunities for foreign merchants and individuals willing to operate in this shady area connecting legitimate commerce and the transatlantic slave trade. How far these merchants could go without breaking the law remained open to interpretation. Whereas some merely sold vessels and took all the precautions necessary for the legal transference of the vessel, others acted in clear contravention of the law by lending their names to the ownership of vessels that in fact had Spanish and Portuguese slave traders as their real proprietors. Maxwell, Wright & Co. in Rio de Janeiro, for example, considered the chartering as well as the sale of vessels to slave traders as perfectly normal business under the laws of the United States as long as these ships did not return with enslaved Africans on board or had their nationality switched once their ownership changed hands. In this they were supported by the US minister to Brazil, William Hunter, who had in fact written to the US secretary of state in 1838 urging the abolition of certain legal restrictions regarding the sales of US vessels overseas. "In practice," he argued, "no sales are made to citizens of long residence— that is, to houses of the highest and longest standing, who are best able to be purchasers."[30]

The sales of US vessels thrived during the 1830s, being used in 1,070 voyages, the equivalent of 63 percent of all 1,697 slave voyages estimated for the years 1831 to 1840 (table 4.1). These US-built vessels were responsible for the embarkation of 432,453 enslaved Africans during this period. Next came vessels built in Europe (mainly Spain, followed by Portugal and France), with 384 voyages (22.6 percent) embarking 155,119 enslaved Africans. The predominance of US-built vessels did not mean that all of them had entered illegally into the slave trade or that all of them had been used as auxiliaries to slavers. Present evidence on the use of the US flag (the strategy that needed US intermediaries willing to break

Table 4.1. Estimated number of vessels and the slaves they
embarked by country of ship construction, 1831–40

Ship construction	Voyages	Percentage	Slaves
Europe	384	22.6	155,119
United States	1,070	63.0	432,453
Caribbean	105	6.2	42,305
Brazil	116	6.8	47,006
Africa	23	1.4	9,401
Total	1,697	100	686,284

Source: www.slavevoyages.org

the law more openly) shows that only a small fraction of these vessels
retained their nationality in the slave trade to the Americas during the
1830s. For Cuba, specifically, the existing evidence points to only a few
voyages under the US flag between 1836 and 1840. Vessels flying the Stars
and Stripes in this five-year period embarked 7,645 enslaved Africans,
approximately 7 percent of the 110,023 captives embarked on slave expeditions that had Cuban ports as their final destination. Vessels flying the
Spanish and Portuguese flags carried most enslaved Africans during this
period, respectively 27 and 65 percent of the total. During the 1840s, the
US flag practically disappeared from the slave trade to Cuba, and in fact,
the flow of captives to the island significantly diminished overall.

Merchants and shipbuilders from Baltimore, who had been at the
forefront of the shipbuilding industry with their notoriously fast clippers, were probably the first to take advantage of the new context. The
high demand for Baltimore schooners and brigantines led to the efflo-
rescence of the local shipbuilding industry in the late 1830s, precisely
when the rest of the United States faced an economic depression. Their
connection to the transatlantic slave trade became increasingly evident,
with rumors that some vessels had been specifically designed for the
illicit commerce in human beings to Cuba. In 1835, a British commissioner at Sierra Leone complained that it would make no difference if
the British government increased the number of men-of-war in Africa

or sent their fastest cruisers since "the shipbuilders of Baltimore will out-match them in the sailing qualities of their clippers." Based on information provided by a slave captain, he argued that "the vessels now building at Baltimore for the slave trade . . . [were] of the fastest-sailing models which their skill and ingenuity could devise." The increasing perception that US shipbuilders and merchants had been intentionally aiding the transatlantic slave trade was stimulated by comments such as that made by John Chase, responsible for the selling of a US schooner to slave traders in Bahia. According to a British lieutenant, Chase "told me he had on the stocks a vessel to be called the 'Mariana,' nearly ready, built expressly for the Slave Trade; and that, by God! he would build as long as he could find purchasers."[31]

In October 1836, the British commissioners in Cuba, Edward W. H. Schenley and R. R. Madden, described to the Foreign Office the new context brought by the Anglo-Spanish treaty of 1835. Four US vessels arrived in the Spanish colony that year, the *Emanuel* and *Dolores* from New York and the *Anaconda* and *Viper* from Baltimore. The four vessels had been built in Baltimore. The first two were sold to Spanish slave traders and sailed under Spanish colors to Africa. The other two, however, sailed fully equipped for the slave trade under US colors, although their cargo was really owned by Pedro Forcade, a Frenchman involved in the Cuban traffic. According to the British commissioners, the presence of those US vessels was a direct consequence of the declaration given by Secretary of State John Forsyth two years earlier, that the United States was not willing to establish any convention with Britain on the slave trade. "The expression of the above determination by the head of a free Government," they argued, "has been the means of inducing American citizens to build and fit in their own ports vessels only calculated for piracy or the Slave Trade, to enter this harbor, and in concert with the Havana slave-traders, take on board a prohibited cargo, manacles, &c., and proceed openly . . . under the shelter of their national flag."[32]

Schenley and Madden also wrote to the French and US consuls in Cuba to denounce the cases. The message to the French consul was brief, as was the reply they received: "that our united efforts may succeed in putting a stop *to these odious undertakings*." By now, both governments had established conventions that allowed the seizure of French

or British vessels equipped for the trade by the navies of both countries. The message to the US consul was a little longer. After describing
the arrival of the four US vessels and their use in the traffic, the British
commissioners concluded by noting that it was the absence of a convention between Britain and the United States that had allowed the emergence of such cases. A short reply came from the vice-consul stating
that the consul, Nicholas Trist, was on a voyage to the United States and
that he should take their message into consideration on his return. The
vice-consul was John A. Smith, probably the same individual involved
in slave-trading voyages with other Rhode Island merchants during the
1810s. He already owned a plantation Cuba and would relocate there
after 1825, when the bankruptcy of George D'Wolf devastated the economy of Bristol. Smith was one of the most heavily affected, seeing all his
fortune (made with the privateer *Yankee* during the War of 1812 and in
subsequent slave-trading ventures) vanish.[33]

On his return in 1836, Trist replied to the British consulate. The
reply was short and centered on Schenley and Madden's comments
about the absence of a treaty between US and Britain. Trist stressed
that the British minister in Washington had recently called for such a
convention but that "the Government of the United States in a manner
[had indicated] the most decided disinclination to become a party to
even any discussion whatever of the subject." The British government
continued to raise the issue in the following years, especially because
many of the documents authenticating the voyages were frequently found
aboard captured slavers with the signatures of Nicholas Trist and John A.
Smith. Trist had, in fact, also been signing documents for slave ships in his
position of consul for Portugal in Cuba. By the late 1830s the denunciations at last generated heated reactions in Britain and the United States,
with abolitionists from both countries attacking Trist. The *Emancipator*
published a note in 1839 arguing that Trist's aggressive reaction to the
British commissioners was because "they were interfering with his voca-
tion and no doubt with his profits." That same year the Irish abolitionist Richard R. Madden, one of the two British commissioners who had
been pressuring Trist since 1836, came to the United States to testify in the
case of the *Amistad*. While waiting for the trial, he prepared an open letter to William Ellery Channing detailing slave-trading strategies in Cuba

and Trist's active role in them. The letter was published in Boston and widely circulated in the country. The US abolitionist Lewis Tappan later promised to send a copy of the pamphlet to Joseph Sturge, founder of the British and Foreign Anti-Slavery Society, noting that it was "a severe thing, but justly deserved, & will, I hope, do much good."[34]

Trist had always been open about his views on the role of US representatives overseas, and the foreign merchant community in Havana agreed with him. Among these merchants was Edward Spalding, who had worked as an agent of Rhode Island slave traders over the 1810s (on more than one occasion Trist would ask Spalding to testify on his behalf). According to Trist, the sales of US vessels should meet no interference. If Britain intended to act against this commerce, they should first prohibit their own factories from producing the bolts and shackles used aboard slavers. The growing attacks led him to produce extremely long responses. Trist agreed that US-built vessels were present in the slave trade to Cuba but concluded that the small number of English ships was because Britain had no tradition of building fast merchant vessels. "But for this circumstance," he argued, "Great Britain would just as well supply the slave traders here with ships, as she does with muskets, gunpowder, manufactures and other articles." Trist must have rejoiced at the appearance of British-built steamers in the last years of the traffic.[35]

President Martin Van Buren acknowledged in a message of December 1839 that "the provisions in our existing laws which relate to the sale and transfer of American vessels while abroad are extremely defective," calling for their revision. He also sent Alexander Everett to investigate the accusations against Trist in Cuba and directed two warships to the coast of Africa to stop the illegal use of the US flag (thereby eliminating any need for the Royal Navy to board US vessels). Starting in 1839, as the British navy was bringing suspected slavers into US ports, federal officers arrested a number of shipowners and merchants in Baltimore. At least seven vessels were detained and seven individuals taken to the courts during 1839–40. Of the accused, Robert W. Allen, John Henderson, and Francis T. Montell were acquitted and Joshua W. Littig and Frederick A. Peterson forfeited their bail. Albert Sleter and Isaac Morris, however, were sentenced to two years in prison and a two-thousand-dollar fine (although Morris managed to escape before going to prison). John F.

Strohm, who had been responsible for the building of the *Ann,* appealed to the Supreme Court after his vessel was confiscated only to hear from Justice Roger B. Taney that "it was very clear that the Anne was built for the slave trade, and that Strohm & Co knew it." Although proving guilty knowledge continued to be extremely difficult, US judges occasionally considered the evidence compelling enough for condemnation. This first round of slave trade cases apparently had some impact on the business. Even though Baltimore clippers continued to be employed in the slave trade in following years, the direct connection between Baltimore shipbuilders and slave traders in Cuba had been cut.[36]

Trist also developed a theory that the British struggle against the Cuban slave trade was aimed at favoring Brazilian cotton production (which had British capital) to the detriment of its US counterpart. As US and French merchants struggled to compete vis-à-vis their British competitors, the increase of British abolitionist pressure after emancipation in the British West Indies gave rise to multiple conspiracy theories. The indictments of British hypocrisy continued with US representatives in Brazil and Cuba in the following decades and influenced successive US administrations. Trist remained in his position as consul until 1841, when he was removed, apparently for political reasons. The reappearance of the US flag in the slave trade in the second half of the 1830s had nonetheless drawn attention to the issue of indirect participation in the transatlantic slave trade, generating debates that brought to the forefront the extension of US, French, and British involvement in the illegal business. Despite the conspiratorial tone of Trist's accusations, his observations that the British were as immersed in the slave trade as the Americans definitely had some truth to it. This was precisely one of the main complaints of the British abolitionist David Turnbull. "I believe it is perfectly understood, that every foreign merchant at the Havana, and at the other sea-ports of the island, has an interest more or less direct in the maintenance of the slave trade," he wrote, "as if striving to prove how nearly they could approach the limit of the law without an actual infringement of it: *Quam prope ad crimen sine crimine.*"[37]

British legislators had been trying to curb the indirect participation of British subjects since the early nineteenth century to no effect. In 1806, Parliament had already prohibited the advance of credit to foreign slave traders within British territories in the form of goods or cash, and in 1824, a new act removed the geographic limitations of this law. The main loophole in the law, however, was proving intentionality. Accused individuals had to have proven prior knowledge of the destiny of their goods to be condemned, a task that proved to be nearly impossible for accusers to accomplish. British merchants, therefore, continued to provide a large part of the goods used by slave traders in Cuba and Brazil, and in fact, merchants in Sierra Leone recycled ships condemned by courts of mixed commission and sold them back to slave traders. The controversies around the indirect participation of US citizens in the illegal business soared in the late 1830s and generated a backlash against the indirect involvement of British merchants. Parliament appointed a select committee to investigate the issue. Some abolitionists certainly considered that this indirect participation should be suppressed despite the costs, and Henry Brougham tried to pass new legislation in 1843 to that end. However, as had been the case earlier in the century, the strands of British abolitionism more attuned to the precepts of laissez faire had the last word. Brougham's efforts in Parliament were rejected while, that same year, Pedro de Zulueta, cofounder of a British company accused of supplying goods to slave traders, was acquitted by the British courts.[38]

French merchant houses also sold merchandise and, occasionally, vessels to slave traders in Brazil during the 1840s, generating similar debates in France. Foreign Minister François Guizot argued that, as in Britain, "no disposition of the law covers commerce with slave stations, as long as there is no actual purchase or sale of slaves' taking place." When, in 1849, Palmerston pressured the Sardinian government to take measures against the indirect participation of its merchants in the slave trade, he received a reply along similar lines. The Sardinian minister for foreign affairs argued that if Sardinia was forced to stop its vessels from carrying provisions and articles used in the trade for slaves by Brazilian merchants, that exclusion should apply to ships of all nations. And although Sardinian vessels could be used by slave traders in Brazil, "as these vessels are generally of excellent construction," if their sales were executed using the established forms and according to prescribed consular acts, passing into third hands in a legal manner, "the sellers cannot reasonably be called to account for the use which the purchasers might make of them under a foreign flag."[39]

Conclusion

"Is there any reason to apprehend that the contraband trade may become extensive in time of peace," Foreign Secretary Viscount Castlereagh asked authorities at Sierra Leone in 1817, "if some decisive measures are not adopted by the powers conjointly to repress the same?" Their answer was emphatic: "Of this no doubt can exist. It will be carried on more extensively and more ferociously than ever." The assertion may have been slightly exaggerated (estimates of embarked slaves are a little higher for the thirty-five years before 1815 than for the thirty years after), yet it certainly contained some truth. Although the number of supplying and receiving regions declined after 1815, the numbers of embarkations and disembarkations per year many times surpassed those of the pre-1815 era. The largest number of embarked slaves in the history of the transatlantic slave trade occurred in 1829 (117,644 captives). Estimates are that, between 1820 and 1866, over 2 million slaves were disembarked in the Americas (2,092,442 captives), the equivalent of around 20 percent of all disembarkations between 1501 and 1867.[40]

The growth of free trade led to an unprecedented internationalization of this traffic. The contraband slave trade became symbiotically connected to the manufactured products, credit, and resources that came from the North Atlantic. The hub of nineteenth-century financial, commercial, and industrial development, Great Britain, generally hesitated to act against the indirect participation of its subjects in the illegal business. The widespread view within different British administrations was that interfering in this aspect of the business would lead to the destruction of legitimate commerce with Africa as a whole. "As long as the slave trade existed anywhere and as long as the British remained dedicated to the goals of laissez-faire and civilizing the world through trade," David Eltis argues, "it was impossible to prevent British involvement."[41] As we have seen, these limits were shared by other Western governments such as France and the United States, which had been able to virtually eliminate the direct financing of slaving expeditions by most of its citizens but failed to curb their participation as aiders and abettors of the illegal business. After 1835 the issue of indirect participation in the slave trade became increasingly politicized, as Britain pressured other governments to curb the indirect involvement of their citizens even as it proved incapable of controlling the contribution of its own subjects.

The enforcement of anti-slave-trade legislation and treaties met real limits set by laissez-faire ideals and the liberalization of trade, whether one looks to the British, French, Sardinian, or US cases. From this broader perspective, the reasons for the hesitation of the US government to control the indirect participation of its citizens in the slave trade appears to have been more complex than a simple result of slaveholding interests dominating the federal government. The accusations of US involvement in the slave trade, in fact, broke the national silence on the subject (in part because US participation itself had grown). David Ericson estimates that while the US Navy spent around $20,000 per year between 1819 and 1842 for the suppression of the slave trade, these expenses rose to $385,000 per year for the fiscal years between 1843 and 1859.[42] The shift was directly connected to the passing of the Webster-Ashburton Treaty of 1842, as discussed in the following chapter, which marked the beginning of a new era of Anglo-American tensions.

Thus, efforts to suppress the transatlantic slave trade in the long period of peace that started after 1815 found two fundamental, interrelated obstacles: the world of nation-states regulated by international law and the emergence of a world economy increasingly based on free trade principles. The barrier that the first imposed to suppression was already clear in the 1810s, as countries such as Portugal and Spain postponed negotiations for the abolition of the slave trade for as long as they could. Eliga Gould has noted that the situation of opponents of the slave trade was similar to that of abolitionists in the United States, "with the sovereignty that nations enjoyed on the high seas supplying an obstacle to the trade's complete suppression that was as insurmountable as the sovereign rights of slave states within the American union."[43] Therefore, despite formal abolition of the traffic through treaties with Britain and national laws, Cuba and Brazil were able to develop internal arrangements that permitted the continuous inflow of captives from Africa. The United States, in contrast, developed internal arrangements that stopped the transatlantic slave trade but refused to establish a treaty with Britain similar to those of Brazil and Cuba. It was becoming increasingly clear to many across the Atlantic what was the only power capable of opposing the designs of the British abolitionist empire. Slave traders were, perhaps, the first to realize the opportunities offered by this new configuration, exploiting these international tensions to the fullest.

F · I · V · E

The United States and the Contraband
Slave Trade to Brazil, 1831–1856

T he most outspoken and active opponent of the participation
of US citizens in the transatlantic slave trade to Brazil was,
strange though it may seem, a slaveholder from Virginia.
Governor of the state at the time of abolitionist John Brown's
hanging, Henry A. Wise had been the US minister to Brazil from 1844
to 1847. Brazil had already enacted a law prohibiting the introduction
of African slaves in the country by that time, but large numbers of disembarkations continued year after year. The US minister learned all the
details of the involvement of his fellow citizens in the business shortly
after his arrival in Brazil and was impressed by its highly internationalized nature. The enslaved Africans carried to Brazil, he argued, were
"captives of African wars, inflamed by Brazilian cachaça, shackled with
British iron, armed with British muskets, supplied with British goods,
transported in vessels of the United States."[1] That most of those vessels
came from the northern part of the United States roused his indignation
even more. He exposed it in a letter to Maxwell, Wright & Co., one of
the merchant houses responsible for chartering and selling US vessels to
slave traders in Brazil:

> I find the same old interest at work here, and now, to fasten
> American slavery on Brazil, which, in our early history, fas-

tened its condition of a slave State on Virginia: vessels and
capital from precisely the same quarter bring the slaves to
this country in this age, which carried them to that country in times past. The very lands in the *old and new worlds,*
where "world's conventions" are held, and whence abolition
petitions flow, are the lands where there are manufacturers
of goods "fit for the coast," and where there are owners of
vessels to be "chartered and sold, deliverable on the coast of
Africa," who "will not eat slave sugar!"[2]

The renewed Jeffersonian interpretation that Wise applied to the
involvement of New Englanders and the British in the Brazilian slave
trade reveals the variety of forms that complicity with the transatlantic
slave trade could assume. His observation that these were the same individuals who refused to eat slave-grown sugar (he also seemed to enjoy
mentioning the case of the owner of an abolitionist newspaper whose
ship was sold to slave traders) represent one end of a long spectrum of
complicity in the slave trade. On the other end of this spectrum were
individuals who directly financed and organized voyages to the coast
of Africa for slaves. Many US citizens could be found between these
extremes—merchants, captains, crews, shipbuilders, and brokers. They
profited from the exportation and shipping of slave-grown produce
in Brazil, the selling of US-built vessels to slave traders on the African
coast, and the production, transportation, and selling of goods used in
slave-trading transactions, and a few of them, in fact, had some interest
in slave voyages organized by Portuguese, Brazilian, and Spanish slave
traders operating in Brazil.

Wise's anti-slave-trade activities reverberated in the United States,
as had, a few years earlier, the Nicholas Trist controversy in Cuba. Along
with the official congressional publication of Wise's correspondence,
newspapers and abolitionist groups published accounts of slave-trading
cases involving the US flag (many of them based on Wise's letters).
"Wise's passion for notoriety and his mountebank abhorrence of the
African slave-trade have drawn him into a position from which it will
be curious to see how he will extricate himself," John Quincy Adams
commented after reading the correspondence published in 1845. "The

slave-trade piracy is carried on from Brazil," he continued, "as it was and is from the Havannah. Instead of falling in with and aiding and abetting it for a share of the plunder, as Trist did at the Havannah, Wise sallies forth like a knight of the sad face against it. He moralizes and heroizes with the British Minister Hamilton and with the slave-mongers of Rio, till he takes a lover's leap from the sublime to the ridiculous."[3]

Although the participation of US citizens in the Brazilian slave trade occasionally made it into the pages of congressional and parliamentary documents in the United States and Britain, the Brazilian government remained silent about the issue. The contraband slave trade in fact rarely generated discussion within the Brazilian government, despite its large numbers between the second half of the 1830s and 1850. This silence was, as we have seen, a product of the entrenchment of south-central slaveholding interests in the Brazilian state-building process through the actions of Brazilian conservative politicians; the saquarema era, as classically characterized by historian Ilmar Rohloff de Mattos.[4] Internal opposition to the slave trade during these years consisted of a few isolated voices, nothing comparable to the environment marked by tensions that marked abolitionist processes in the North Atlantic. The absence of significant opposition was not restricted to the political sphere; it also appeared, for example, in the words of priest Leandro Rabelo de Castro, author of an essay aimed at ending slave-trade debates among theologians. According to his biographer, the work argued not only that slavery was based on natural rights but also that "it was acceptable to bring African slaves to Brazil despite the recently passed law, arguing that, considering the Brazilian circumstances, stopping the traffic would mean the complete subversion of the country."[5]

The participation of US citizens in the Brazilian slave trade has roused the interest of historians of slavery and abolition, but few have explored it deeply. Warren Howard and Don Fehrenbacher have, respectively, outlined the organizational aspects of that participation and explained its political and diplomatic consequences.[6] More recently, Gerald Horne and Dale Graden have offered detailed studies.[7] Most works reproduce the statement of David Tod, US minister to Brazil in 1850, that half of all Africans disembarked in the country were "introduced through the facilities directly and indirectly afforded by the American flag." Based on these reports, Seymour Drescher concludes that in the 1840s, "more African slaves were moved from the Old World to the New under the American flag . . . than were moved from the old exporting South to the importing South within the United States." The main problem with this perspective is that it conflates radically different forms of US participation, ranging from the legal sale and transference of vessels by merchant houses to US captains aiding in the embarkation of slaves on the African coast. Whereas the latter took place in clear contravention of anti-slave-trade laws, many other cases happened in the shady area connecting legitimate commerce and the slave trade. These generated tensions that, as we have seen in the previous chapter, pervaded the governments of the United States, Britain, and France.[8]

In this chapter I analyze the impact of anti-slave-trade pressure by assessing the size of US participation in the Brazilian slave trade and its varied forms. This pressure came not only from the British government but also from US ministers and consuls appointed to Brazil during the 1840s who sought to interpret and enforce US anti-slave-trade legislation. If the British were responsible for catalyzing the suppression of the traffic in 1850, these US officials had some effect on how US citizens profited from the slave trade, with the predominance of certain forms of US participation over time. Last, the scholarship occasionally displays some confusion regarding the role of US citizens in the Brazilian slave trade. Two historians argue, for example, that "North American merchantmen carried some of the greatest annual slave importations Brazil had known—until the Atlantic slave trade was terminated by the British navy in 1850."[9] Gerald Horne goes further, arguing that "U.S. nationals were leaders in fomenting the illicit slave trade and, as a result, permanently transformed Brazil for all time."[10] Such an argument is possible only by conflating different periods of US participation in the slave trade, since the evidence of US ownership shares in slave voyages to Brazil, as discussed below, is extremely scarce. Below I show how the Brazilian slave trade remained firmly under the control of Portuguese and Brazilian individuals and explore the strategic use of the American flag as one among many tactics employed by slave traders.

Table 5.1. Estimated number of vessels and the slaves they embarked to Brazil by country of ship construction, 1831–50

Ship construction	Voyages	Percentage	Slaves
Brazil	275	15.4	113,569
Portugal	138	7.7	56,784
United States	1,042	58.2	429,939
France	39	2.2	16,224
Spain	157	8.8	64,897
Others	138	7.7	56,784
Total	1,789	100	738,198

Note: Many of the voyages for which I was able to track place of construction were from captured vessels taken to mixed commissions before arriving at the intended port of disembarkation. It is safe to assume that most of these voyages had Brazil as their main destination for the period under consideration, so I used all the existing data for place of construction for voyages that appear in the database as having Brazil and Africa as the main ports of disembarkation. *Source:* www.slavevoyages.org

The Numbers of US Participation in the Brazilian Slave Trade

Besides the consumption of slave-grown sugar and coffee, the largest US contribution to the Brazilian slave trade—or the entire nineteenth-century slave trade for that matter—was in the form of ships. US-built vessels carried more than four hundred thousand slaves to Brazil during the contraband slave trade, a less often mentioned result of the golden era of the North American shipbuilding industry. In fact, US-built vessels accounted for about 1,000 voyages, or 58.2 percent of all 1,789 slave voyages estimated for this period (table 5.1). This percentage is similar to those offered by David Tod and other US ministers in Brazil, who said that at least half of all slave disembarkations in Brazil took place with some form of US participation. Other leading producers of slave vessels during these years were Brazil (15.4 percent), Portugal (7.7 percent), and Spain (8.8 percent).

As discussed in the previous chapter, pressure from British authorities against the traffic to Cuba and Brazil increased in the second half of the 1830s as a result of new agreements and interpretations of existing laws that allowed the seizure of vessels equipped for the slave trade under the Spanish, Portuguese, and Brazilian flags. As a consequence, US-built vessels retaining their original nationality became highly valued items for Portuguese and Brazilian slave traders, who used them as auxiliaries to slavers or, to a smaller extent, as slavers themselves. Ninety-two percent of all slave disembarkations in Brazil between 1840 and 1849 took place in Southeast Brazil and Bahia (table 5.2). An estimated 373,875 enslaved Africans landed in Southeast Brazil and Bahia, 72 percent of all Africans carried to the Americas in that decade. Bahia slave traders rarely used the US flag on slavers: only two voyages, disembarking fewer than 800 slaves, arrived under the US flag during the 1840s. The Brazilian flag continued to dominate the number of slave voyages organized in Bahia.[11]

The numbers of the US contribution in the more indirect role of tenders and auxiliaries to slavers are more complicated to estimate. One possible strategy is to look at the voyages between Brazil and Africa that were registered by British consuls in Bahia and Rio de Janeiro. It is impossible to distinguish between slavers and auxiliaries among the custom records used in the British reports. As every British minister made clear before sending his data back to the foreign office, these numbers say little about the flow of slaves. Vessels departed for other ports such as Montevideo before going to Africa. Slavers disembarked captives in surrounding natural ports before arriving at the main ports of Rio de Janeiro. Therefore, since the custom office returns include slavers and vessels assisting them, they provide an upper-bound estimate conflating direct and indirect US flag contributions to the Brazilian slave trade.

If we look at African-related departures and arrivals in both provinces, we see again that more US vessels operated in Southeast Brazil than in Bahia, where Sardinian vessels predominated (table 5.3). Of 502 voyages that departed from Bahia to Africa, 121, or 24 percent, were Sardinian. Departures and arrivals of US vessels, in contrast, were about 10 percent of the total. Most of these vessels carried cachaça, tobacco, textiles, and other goods traded for slaves on the coast of Africa and

Table 5.2. Estimates of voyages and slaves disembarked in
Rio de Janeiro and Bahia by flag, 1840–49

Southeast Brazil	Portugal	Brazil	United States	France	Other*	Total
1840–44						
Voyages	106	139	19	2	7	274
Slaves	42,994	56,146	7,847	884	2,653	110,524
Ratio	38.9	50.8	7.1	0.8	2.4	100
1845–49						
Voyages	33	287	60	17	10	408
Slaves	16,851	144,877	30,414	8,425	4,932	205,499
Ratio	8.2	70.5	14.8	4.1	2.4	100
Bahia						
1840–44						
Voyages	13	39	1	2	1	56
Slaves	4,226	12,659	348	695	348	18,293
Ratio	23.1	69.2	1.9	3.8	1.9	100
1845–49						
Voyages	3	87	1	2	4	98
Slaves	1,345	35,128	435	870	1,780	39,559
Ratio	3.4	88.8	1.1	2.2	5	100

* Spain, Sardinia, Denmark, and Hanse Towns

Source: www.slavevoyages.org

returned to Brazil in ballast. US vessels were also less important than
Brazilian and French vessels in the aiding of the slave trade to Bahia.

The Brazilian flag was also the most frequently used during the
1840s in Southeast Brazil, always responsible for at least half of all disembarkations. During the first years of the decade, especially in 1840,
the Portuguese flag continued to be widely used. By 1843, however, the
Portuguese flag had nearly disappeared from the business as a consequence of the abolition of the slave trade in Portugal in 1842, although

Table 5.3. Departures and arrivals to and from Africa by flag, 1840–49

	Portugal	Brazil	United States	France	Sardinia	Other	Total
Rio de Janeiro							
Departures							
1840–44	27 (21.3)	53 (41.7%)	28 (22.0%)	6 (4.7%)	—	13 (10.2%)	127
1845–49	28 (12.9)	74 (34.1%)	66 (30.4%)	22 (10.1%)	17 (8%)	10 (4.6%)	217
Total	55 (16)	127 (36.9%)	94 (27.3%)	28 (8.1%)	17 (5%)	23 (6.7%)	344
Arrivals							
1840–44	27 (34.6%)	15 (19.2%)	24 (30.8%)	5 (6.4%)	—	7 (9.0%)	78
1845–49	25 (19.1%)	28 (21.4%)	49 (37.4%)	15 (11.5%)	6 (4.6%)	8 (6.1%)	131
Total	52 (24.9%)	43 (20.6%)	73 (34.9%)	20 (9.6%)	6 (2.9%)	15 (7.2%)	209
Bahia							
Departures							
1840–44	18 (11.4%)	75 (47.5%)	15 (9.5%)	23 (14.6%)	18 (11.4%)	9 (5.7%)	158
1845–49	8 (2.3%)	138 (40.1%)	34 (9.9%)	50 (14.5%)	103 (29.9%)	11 (3.2%)	344
Total	26 (5.2%)	213 (42.3%)	49 (9.7%)	73 (14.5%)	121 (24.1%)	20 (4.0%)	502
Arrivals							
1840–44	10 (9.1%)	40 (36.4%)	15 (13.6%)	18 (16.4%)	10 (9.1%)	17 (15.5%)	110
1845–49	7 (2.4%)	104 (36.2%)	28 (9.8%)	45 (15.7%)	84 (29.3%)	19 (6.6%)	287
Total	17 (4.3%)	144 (36.3%)	43 (10.8%)	63 (15.9%)	94 (23.7%)	36 (9.1%)	397

Sources: Quarterly returns in consular reports from Rio de Janeiro and Bahia in British Parliamentary Papers between 1840 and 1849

it continued to be sporadically used until the contraband traffic to Brazil was finally suppressed in the 1850s. The use of the French flag, in contrast, increased over time. If estimates are that only two French vessels disembarked slaves in the region between 1840 and 1844, the following period saw the disembarkation of more than eight thousand slaves by seventeen vessels under French colors. The ratio increased fivefold.[12]

The participation of vessels flying the US flag in Southeast Brazil was much larger than in Bahia. During that decade, vessels under the US flag disembarked 38,261 enslaved Africans, approximately 12 percent of all 316,023 captives illegally landed in the region. In the first half of the 1840s, about 7 percent of all slaves were disembarked under the US flag. By the second half of the 1840s, mounting British pressure contributed to a twofold increase in the US flag ratio, corresponding to almost 15 percent of all disembarkations in the region. This is the most direct use of US vessels in the slave trade, which became increasingly dependent on the role of US captains and brokers over the decade, as I discuss below.

In Southeast Brazil the involvement of US vessels in slave-trading operations was more significant. Fewer departures to Africa occurred under the US than the Brazilian flag, but by the second half of the decade their numbers were very close. Between 1845 and 1849, 74 Brazilian vessels departed for Africa from Rio in comparison to 66 North American ones. US vessels accounted for the largest number of arrivals from Africa, But this figure attests to the much more important role of US vessels as auxiliaries, not actual slave ships. Far more Brazilian- than American-flagged vessels sailed to Africa without ever appearing later in the lists of arrivals at Rio de Janeiro ports. During the 1840s, 127 vessels departed for Africa under Brazilian colors while only 43 returned. In contrast, 94 vessels departed Rio de Janeiro under the US flag and 73 arrived. Most of the US vessels that never returned sailed in the second half of the decade.

North American Merchants and Slave Trading
Networks in Brazil

The slave-trading community operating in Rio de Janeiro underwent significant transformations in the aftermath of the 1831 law. The main slave traders of the first quarter of the nineteenth century had diversi-

fied their investments and abandoned the business by the late 1820s. Part
of their investments actually went to the coffee plantations that radically
transformed the Vale do Paraíba in the following decades. When the demand for African labor on those plantations increased in the 1830s, a renewed slave-trading community emerged. Although some of these slave
traders can be found in slave-trade documents before 1831, the leading
figures emerged after that date. Moreover, the dominance of José Bernardino de Sá and Manoel Pinto da Fonseca, the chief slave traders of
the contraband era, occurred in a context of increasing concentration
in the ownership of slave voyages, another consequence of abolitionist pressure. Between 1838 and 1844, the four leading firms controlled
60 percent of slave-trading operations, with Bernardino de Sá at the
top. In the following seven years this percentage rose to 67 percent, with
Manoel Pinto da Fonseca ascending to the top of the slave-trading community, being responsible for 36 percent of all voyages (Bernardino de
Sá organized 22 percent of the voyages of the previous period). A similar process took place in Cuba. Whereas seventy-six firms within five
major groupings controlled the business before 1820, a dominant single
business became the norm after that year, with its owners and partners
changing over time.[13]

The organization of the trade also changed, with joint-stock companies replacing the individual and family operations that characterized
the pre-1820 slave-trading communities around the Atlantic. Despite the
increasing concentration at the top, smaller merchants were able to acquire shares of these companies, thereby participating more directly in
the slave trade during this period. This participation was nevertheless
minimal, with the traffic to Brazil staying under the control and direction of Portuguese and naturalized Brazilian slave traders. There was no
counterpart of the D'Wolf family by the mid-nineteenth century. Most
slave voyages to Brazil associated with the US flag in which ownership
interest can be tracked down had a major Portuguese or Brazilian slave
trader behind them. José Bernardino de Sá, Manoel Pinto da Fonseca,
and Tomás da Costa Ramos (also known as the Maneta) were the main
slave traders in Rio de Janeiro employing US individuals as agents, brokers, and captains in the access to the American flag. The Spanish slave
trader Francisco Rovirosa also appears connected to a few voyages orga-

nized with the help of the American flag. The Bahia slave trade likewise saw concentration of ownership, despite the fact that, unlike in Rio, the slave-trading community in the province remained basically the same before and after 1831. One of the few exceptions was Joaquim Pereira Marinho, who entered the business in its illegal period and became a leading slave trader. Marinho had an interest in over one fourth of all slave voyages organized between 1842 and 1851. Some of the evidence connecting American vessels and flag to the slave trade in the province directly leads to him. The British consul at Bahia described how the American vessel *Eleanor*, having been sold in 1846 to "a noted slave-dealer of this place, J. P. Marinho, a native of Portugal naturalized in Brazil," continued to carry cargoes to Africa under the US flag. In 1847 the vessel would change its name to *Theodozia* (3616) and hoist the Brazilian flag before being seized by the Royal Navy. Not surprisingly another US vessel, the *Kimpton,* continued to perform the same activities as the *Eleanor* throughout 1848. Consigned to Pereira Marinho, the American vessel under the command of E. P. Stanhope took cachaça and other goods— including textiles from New York—to Ambriz and Onim on the African coast and returned to Brazil in ballast.[14]

But it was in Rio de Janeiro that most slave voyages of the contraband era were organized and, consequently, where the US flag appeared more frequently. According to the Alcoforado report, a description of the Brazilian contraband slave trade written in 1853 by a former slave trader, Joaquim de Paula Guedes Alcoforado, the main individual behind the use of the US flag during the 1840s had been the Portuguese Manoel Pinto da Fonseca. Described by the Brazilian foreign minister as "the great slave trader *par excellence* of Rio," Fonseca dominated, as we have seen, the last years of the illegal slave trade. From his beginnings as a clerk in a merchant house in Rio, Fonseca started to organize slave voyages in the second half of the 1830s. The first for which we have evidence was the *Especulador* (46260) in 1837. It was in the 1840s, however, that Fonseca, with the help of his brothers, ascended to his prominent position within the Brazilian slave-trading community. There is evidence of at least forty-three slave voyages organized by Fonseca and his brother Joaquim: nine under the US flag, eleven under the Brazilian flag, two under the Portuguese flag, and the rest with no flag. Of all slave voyages organized under the US flag between 1831 and 1867 where evidence of ownership is available, Fonseca is the most frequent name to appear. He was followed by Manoel Basílio da Cunha Reis, one of the main Portuguese slave traders established in New York in the 1850s and responsible for the organization of at least seven slave voyages to Cuba under the American flag. In Brazil, Fonseca seems to have been indeed the main figure behind the use of the US flag in the slave trade.[15]

Fonseca's criminal activities did not attract the attention of the Brazilian police. On the contrary, as the Brazilian foreign minister observed, "[Manoel Pinto da Fonseca] and scores of minor slave dealers go to the Court—sit at the tables of the wealthiest and most respectable citizens—have seats in the Chamber as our Representatives and have a voice even in the Council of State." If we take Alcoforado's words seriously, the voice at the Council of State was that of the lawyer João Manoel Pereira da Silva. According to Alcoforado, Fonseca operated in conjunction with J. M. Pereira da Silva and two US brokers in his strategies involving the US flag. After studying law in Paris, Pereira da Silva returned to Brazil in 1838, rapidly establishing himself as a lawyer and becoming associated with the Regresso group. Like many of his peers, he was extremely critical of Brazilian anti-slave-trade legislation and British abolitionist policies. One year after his arrival he was already defending slave traders in the mixed commission court at Rio de Janeiro. As the main lawyer in the case of the *Diligente* (1801), a vessel captured with 302 Africans on board in 1838, Pereira da Silva presented an *embargo* (a legal recourse in Brazilian law) based on a judicial disagreement regarding the vessel's nationality. The mixed commission quickly rejected the embargo, based on recent instructions sent by Palmerston. To the British minister the embargoes were directly opposed to the regulations of the treaties, which prohibited appeals to mixed commission decisions. Moreover, embargos generated delays that frequently resulted in sentences missing the stipulated twenty-day deadline after a vessel's capture. In a newspaper petition calling for the acceptance of embargoes, Pereira da Silva publicized his view that Brazil could maintain its autonomy only through the use of the embargo. Pereira da Silva's actions in the courts and in Parliament were becoming increasingly popular. In 1840, when a Brazilian schooner-of-war captured a launch with 47 Africans and took it to the mixed commission, a number of protests appeared demanding the case to be judged by Brazilian courts. An anonymous article criticized members of the Brazilian government who ignored that "the entire population of the country calls for the repeal of the law of November 7, 1831." They ignored, with their "*Anglicized* wishes," that "the whole nation, the honourable class of landed proprietors, applaud with *vivas* the praiseworthy efforts of those deputies who, like Dr. Pereira da Silva, have combated so strongly to put an end to a law so fatal and pernicious to the agriculture of Brazil."[16]

The interweaving of national honor and defense of the slave trade would reappear many other times in Pereira da Silva's speeches and writings. In 1841, along with a petition from the legislative assembly of Minas Gerais, he called for the complete revocation of the law of 1831 in Parliament. Planters who had acquired African slaves after abolition should be amnestied and the illegally imported Africans prohibited from using the law to gain their freedom. The British commissioner in Rio de Janeiro quickly sent a copy of the speech to Palmerston, adding that Pereira da Silva was "an advocate of this city, and who has, on several occasions, been employed in defending slave causes before this Court." The following year Pereira da Silva expounded on British hypocrisy at the mixed commission court itself. In his defense of the *Acaraty*, he argued that the crew of the suspected vessel had escaped because of the actions of the Brazilian commander, who hoisted a British flag before approaching the ship. According to him, the lieutenant should have known that the whole merchant community was terrified by the British violations and would naturally try to escape. Moreover, his act was morally reprehensible. "That English cruisers should avail themselves of treachery, of unworthy snares, condemned by public morality, in order to capture ships which they suspect," argued Pereira da Silva, "is not surprising, as their interest, that of their possessions in Asia, obliges them to have recourse to all means for reducing and bring to decay the agriculture of Brazil and Cuba, which gives them so much anxiety and terror by the daily progressive and rapid development of those countries." The mast of the Brazilian ship should keep the "glorious and honoured" flag of his Imperial Majesty. The defense was also published in the *Jornal do Commercio,* one of the main newspapers in the city, generating an angry response from British commissioners.[17]

One of his most aggressive attacks came in 1845 in a series of articles that were compiled and published with the title *Inglaterra e Brasil —Tráfico de Escravos.* Under the pseudonym "a deputy," Pereira da Silva wrote in reaction to an article published by the *Times* of London associating Brazilian slave traders and pirates. It was another opportunity to list the many cases of British hypocrisy, violations, and attacks on Brazilian sovereignty that culminated with the passing of the Aberdeen act that same year. The author echoed many of the popular arguments that dominated President John Tyler's administration in the United States. Emancipation in the British West Indies had failed. Former slaves refused to work, agricultural production declined, and the British government attempted to remedy the situation by imposing tariffs on slave-grown products from Brazil and Cuba. He cited the message of 1845 from the US president accusing the British of redirecting the Africans freed by the mixed commissions to their colonies under conditions similar to slavery. Britain's ultimate goals were to control the seas, eliminate the competition of other agricultural nations (this repeated an argument he had made before the mixed commission court in 1841), and, in the case of Brazil, to destroy all legitimate trade carried out with Africa. The United States, in contrast, constantly appeared as the shining example of how to resist British pressure.[18]

The book also contains references to a large number of Brazilian vessels captured by the British navy, some of them owned by Manoel Pinto da Fonseca. Even more outrageous to the author, however, was the destruction of a factory owned by Fonseca on the coast of Cabinda (in present-day Angola). Starting with the demolition of eight barracoons (slave-holding structures) at Gallinas in 1841—described by the main officer in charge of it as "the most severe blow ever struck at the slave trade"—British naval officers were instructed to repeat the strategy in other parts of Africa with the support of Palmerston and the colonial secretary, John Russell. The men-of-war *Waterwitch* and the *Madagascar* destroyed eight barracoons at Cabinda, including Fonseca's. The following year Lord Aberdeen, now replacing Palmerston at the head of the

Foreign Office, sent a letter to the Admiralty prohibiting the destruction of buildings on the African coast by British officers. In his view, the law of nations or any of the existing treaties did not sanction these acts. Slave traders immediately reacted after the letter was published in the Parliamentary Papers. One Señor Buron sued a Captain Denman for £180,000 for his losses at Gallinas, and Fonseca, perhaps under the orientation of Pereira da Silva, did the same with the British officers responsible for the destruction of his factory at Cabinda.[19]

To prove the size of his losses, Fonseca sent documents of all the goods transported aboard the *John A. Robb,* a US vessel consigned to him by Maxwell, Wright & Co. and James Birckhead, two well-known American merchant houses in Rio de Janeiro. The *John A. Robb* performed the same activities that other US vessels had been doing in Cuba a few years earlier. Goods and equipment for the slave trade were carried to the coast of Africa under the protection of the American flag. After boarding the *John A. Robb,* the lieutenant of the *Waterwitch* would later recall, he noticed that many of the crew were Spaniards or Portuguese and that the master, a native of Germany, spoke English imperfectly. His suspicions became stronger when the captain presented him a manifest written entirely in Portuguese and lacking the signature of the US consul among the documents that supposedly proved the vessel's American nationality. After receiving information from the crew that the ship was equipped for the slave trade, Lieutenant H. J. Matson continued to keep an eye on it. On boarding the vessel again, he received another message from one of the crew

offering to point out where the cases of slave-irons, &c., were stowed, but of which I took no notice. I had a long conversation with the master, who spoke very frankly and unreservedly respecting the Slave Trade, when the Portuguese cabin passengers landed; he said that as the cargo belonged to Manoel Pinto, every person must know that it was intended to purchase slaves; he believed that American vessels were allowed to carry what they chose excepting slaves; that it was possible the "*John A. Robb*" might eventually take off slaves, but it would not be when under his command.[20]

Matson concluded that the vessel had been sold to Portuguese slave traders but had not yet been paid for, staying under the protection of the US flag while discharging its cargo. "I was perfectly aware that even had she been full of slaves I could not interfere," Matson argued, "unless I could prove that she was not entitled to the protection of the flag of the United States."[21]

James Birckhead and Maxwell, Wright & Co., the two houses responsible for consigning the *John A. Robb* to Manoel Pinto da Fonseca, had been taking advantage of the growth in slave-trading activities since the late 1820s. Around that time James Birckhead was the most active US commercial house in Rio de Janeiro and closely associated with Maxwell, Wright & Co. Both houses made large profits from the sale of US vessels in the province. The ties between Manoel Pinto da Fonseca and these foreign merchants in Rio de Janeiro were already evident in 1840. A petition published in the *Jornal do Commercio* attesting to Fonseca's integrity was signed by a long list of merchants from Rio de Janeiro, among them some British and American houses such as Maxwell, Wright & Co., Forbes, Valentino & Co., and James Birckhead (signing as Diogo Birckhead). When in 1843 the US consul in Rio de Janeiro, George W. Slacum, listed US vessels suspected of being directly or indirectly involved in the slave trade to Brazil, the three companies were the consignees of all seventeen ships in the list. The consul noted that the "American vessels engaged in the trade between this port and Africa are invariably chartered to slave dealers; and I have no doubt many of them are the property of those dealers, sailing with the American flag and register, under a charter-party." That same year he would make a similar accusation to the new secretary of state, Abel P. Upshur.[22] His successor as US consul in Rio, George William Gordon, tabulated eighty US-registered vessels sold in the city between 1840 and early 1846. Forty-four of these vessels, according to him, were used in the slave trade: five sold by James Birckhead and seventeen by Maxwell, Wright & Co. The latter, in fact an Anglo-American house, was especially important, for it combined better than anyone else two commercial activities that ended up being strictly connected in the two decades of the contraband slave trade: the selling and chartering of vessels to slave traders and the exportation of coffee. By consigning and selling ships to Manuel Pinto da Fonseca and other slave traders, Maxwell, Wright & Co. facilitated the transportation of goods and slave-trading equipment in outbound trips under the US flag, contributing to the success of illegal slave-trading voyages in a context of increasing British pressure. As we have seen, disembarked slaves were often taken to the Vale do Paraíba coffee plantations or related sectors. Most of the coffee produced by these slaves was afterward exported to the United States by the same Maxwell, Wright & Co., which, by the mid-1840s, had become Brazil's main coffee exporters.[23]

The Brazilian Slave Trade Enters the US Political Sphere

One of the earliest cases involving US vessels and Maxwell, Wright & Co. was the that of the *Sophia*. Consigned to the company, the vessel disembarked 750 slaves in Rio de Janeiro in 1841 after being turned into a slaver and adopting the Uruguayan flag. The US consul in Rio, George W. Slacum, denounced the case on learning that the captain had abandoned the American crew on the African coast once the sale was concluded, resulting in their deaths. The sole survivor returned to Rio, where he deposed against the captain and revealed that the *Sophia* was turned into the *Bella União*. Slacum believed that the vessel had been destroyed after the Africans were disembarked, but it is possible that this was the ship of the same name captured by British authorities with 664 slaves the following year under the ownership of Manoel Pinto da Fonseca. What became increasingly clear from the investigations of Slacum and other consuls was that African slaves were frequently taken on board with the connivance of American captains and under the protection of the US flag. Once the vessel was ready to return to Brazil, the transfer would be completed, and only then would the American captain leave the ship. Although not all US merchants accepted the offers from slave traders, for much of the US merchant community in Rio, selling vessels to slave traders or carrying goods to be used in the slave trade on the African coast was a lawful business. Slacum described a conversation with one of these merchants.

> It is but a few days since the question was asked me by an American merchant of high standing, "what is your opinion

of the legality of a sale of an American vessel here, deliverable on the coast?" My answer was, "Could I ascertain the fact of such a sale, I would seize her at all hazards." He replied, "The question is yet an unsettled one." This may be so, but it is settled in my mind. No man could convince me of his ignorance on the object of the purchaser or the innocence of his own intentions.[24]

Despite the consul's indignation, the question remained unsettled until the definitive suppression of the transatlantic slave trade following the Civil War. It had already been the object of controversy a few years earlier, during the Nicholas Trist affair in Cuba, which had not resulted in any official policy or instructions to US consuls regarding the indirect participation of US citizens in the slave trade. "I much fear that a repetition of the scenes at Havana will be attempted here," Slacum wrote to Secretary of State Daniel Webster. As a solution, the consul proposed that all trade carried on US vessels to Africa from foreign ports be prohibited, limiting the trade with Africa to vessels leaving US ports. In addition, he suggested that it should be made a felony for anyone to sell US vessels on the African coast or deliverable there. It was highly unlikely, however, that measures such as these could be passed in the context of expanding commerce and laissez-faire ideals that characterized the era. These tensions became clear in the controversy between Slacum and William Hunter, the US minister to Brazil. Hunter did not see any problem in US-built vessels being sold to slave traders and, in fact, had already asked for changes in the law regulating the sales of US vessels overseas. "I think, had Mr. Hunter taken the same view of the matter that I did," a frustrated Slacum complained, "a stop would have been put to these secret sales and open charter-parties; and that our flag would no longer be prostituted to the interests of foreigners."[25]

The increasing presence of US vessels in the Brazilian slave trade, however, did not go unchallenged. The actions of the Royal Navy had been intensifying existing tensions with the United States (over issues such as territorial disputes over the Canadian and Pacific Northwestern borders, the annexation of Texas, and the cases of the *Caroline* and the *Creole*). In 1842, the British minister Alexander Ashburton went to the

United States with full powers to sign a treaty to end those tensions, including slave trade-related ones. The result was the Webster-Ashburton Treaty, whose eighth article established that the two nations should have squadrons on the coast of Africa adequately prepared for the suppression of the slave trade and allowed for the cooperation between them when necessary. Article 9 observed that so long as slave markets in the Americas remained open the end of the trade would be delayed. Both countries therefore agreed that "they will unite in all becoming representations and remonstrances, with any and all Powers within whose dominions such markets are allowed to exist; and that they will urge upon all such Powers the propriety and duty of closing such markets effectually at once and forever."[26]

The treaty generated mixed responses on both sides of the Atlantic. Lewis Cass, US minister to France, protested to the US secretary of state about the absence of a formal British renunciation of the right to board US vessels in the Webster-Ashburton Treaty. Despite not having the right of search over US vessels, British commanders in fact continued to operate as they had done before the treaty, approaching suspected vessels to ascertain their nationality. The previous year Cass had already argued that British intentions behind the Quintuple Treaty—a convention signed by England, France, Austria, Russia, and Prussia in December 1841 agreeing on the mutual right of search for the suppression of the slave trade—were to strengthen its maritime power and gain some commercial advantage by disrupting the trade carried by other nations.[27]

In Britain, Palmerston criticized the treaty as an abandonment of the right of search efforts. John C. Calhoun agreed that Britain had renounced the right of search. In a speech justifying his vote in favor of ratification, Calhoun argued that he considered only the ninth article problematic because of his aversion against interfering with other powers. He nonetheless endorsed the efforts to close markets for imported Africans in the Americas as "right and expedient in every view." Brazil and Cuba already had enough slaves, and it was in the American interest to have the slave trade to those countries closed. The fraudulent use of the US flag would not be an issue anymore, and US cruisers on the African coast would have the sole purpose of protecting US commerce in the region. Last, Cuba and Brazil were rivals on the production of many articles, especially cotton. "Brazil possesses the greatest advantages for its production, and is already a large grower of the article," continues the report of Calhoun's speech, "towards the production of which the continuance of the market for imported slaves from Africa would contribute much."[28]

Historians have stressed not only the proslavery nature of American foreign policy but also how a conspiratorial view of British motives became entrenched in the State Department through figures such as Abel P. Upshur and John C. Calhoun during the presidency of John Tyler. The failure of emancipation in the British West Indies led some Southerners to connect it directly to British efforts to destroy slavery in the Americas. This interpretation pervaded the instructions sent by the secretary of state, Abel P. Upshur, to the US minister to Brazil, George Proffit. "That England is endeavoring to abolish the institution of domestic slavery throughout the American continent, no longer admits of doubt," Upshur wrote. "It is difficult to imagine what motive she can have for this," he continued, "except to destroy the competition of slave labour with that of certain of her colonies in the articles of sugar, cotton and rice. So great a measure of policy on the part of so great a nation can scarcely be attributed to a mere movement of humanity or philanthropy." One of Proffit's missions was to keep the American government informed about all British actions regarding Brazilian slavery. The secretary of state feared that British attempts to destroy the institution in Brazil would stimulate individuals fighting slavery in the United States. "How far we should have the right or feel the inclination to resist such an attempt in Brazil," Upshur concluded, "I do not undertake to say."[29]

Despite the fears regarding British actions toward slavery in the Americas, US officials continued to condemn US participation in the transatlantic slave trade. The issue was finding a balance between anti-slave-trade actions and respect for Brazilian sovereignty, as Calhoun made clear in his speech of 1842. Upshur concluded his instructions to the Brazilian minister by commenting on article 9 of the Webster-Ashburton Treaty. Although the United States and England committed themselves to urge the countries that still imported African slaves to close those markets, no particular mode of pursuing such goal had been established. It was a "matter of great delicacy in itself, for a government that did not feel that it was fairly liable to the suspicion of allowing the sale of slaves, would be justly offended at such a gratuitous remonstrance on the part of other governments." Proffit should be ready to unite with the British minister in "representations and remonstrances" to the Brazilian government but would proceed with extreme caution, "upon proper grounds and in a becoming manner." There was no contradiction, therefore, between the efforts to eliminate the US flag from the Brazilian slave trade and the Anglophobic view that became entrenched in the State Department. As Slacum assured Upshur in a letter denouncing the use of American vessels by slave traders, "I hope you will not misunderstand me, sir, and think I can for a moment entertain the idea of surrendering the right of 'visit and search.' No, sir; upon that point, no man can be more firm than myself." On the contrary, his suggestions targeted British merchants and foreign slave traders, the main individuals profiting from that state of things in his view.[30]

John C. Calhoun replaced Upshur as secretary of state and Henry Wise replaced Proffit as minister to Brazil in 1844. In his instructions to Wise, Calhoun noted that "there is a strict identity of interests on almost all subjects, without conflict, or even competition, on scarcely one" between Brazil and the United States. Wise should explain to the Brazilian government, which he did later that year with these exact words, that it was an American policy not to interfere with the internal affairs of any other nations and to forbid any other of doing the same to them.[31]

The 1840s proslavery critique of British hypocrisy—a product, to a large extent, of the descriptions and denunciations of US officials working in Cuba and Brazil—culminated with the controversial message from President John Tyler in 1845, which, as we have seen, was almost immediately used by J. M. Pereira da Silva in Brazil. The president described the complicity of US merchants in the transatlantic slave trade to Brazil but also stressed the aid of "English brokers and capitalists." After praising Wise for his actions, "whose judicious and zealous efforts in the matter cannot be too highly commended," he concluded the message by observing that British anti-slave-trade policies seemed "calculated rather to perpetuate than to suppress the trade, by enlisting very large interests in its favor." Tyler listed these interests—merchants and capitalists provided manufactures to be traded in Africa, slaves found aboard captured vessels were taken to the British West Indies to work, and Royal Navy officers received bounties based on the number of slaves found aboard captured vessels—and concluded that it would be nearly impossible to suppress the "nefarious traffic" in face of that situation.[32]

The US Compromise against the Traffic in Brazil

The appointment of Henry A. Wise as US minister to Brazil in 1844 led to a radical transformation in the relationship between US participants in the African trade and the US consulates of Rio de Janeiro and Bahia. Whereas George W. Slacum faced the direct opposition of Hunter, the next US consul in Rio de Janeiro, George William Gordon, found in Henry Wise a resolute ally in his efforts to eliminate the American flag from the contraband slave trade. The two US agents put into practice more effective actions to stop what they considered to be an offense to the flag of their nation. One of their first targets was the US consul in Bahia, Alexander Tyler, suspected of connivance with local slave traders. When British authorities seized and brought the *Sooy* to Rio de Janeiro, Gordon immediately wrote Tyler asking for any information about the ship, which had apparently been sold in Salvador. Tyler wrote back with details about the ship, but Wise asked for further clarifications. The investigation led to an apology from the consul, who had in fact been employed as a clerk at the house of John Gilmer, a US merchant involved in the selling and chartering of vessels to slave traders. Wise would ultimately recommend the maintenance of Tyler at the Bahia consulate after he resigned from his position as a clerk for Gilmer, believing that the consul was then prepared to stop the use of the US flag by slave traders. The protests from the American merchant community at Bahia against Tyler seem to indicate that his actions had some effect there.[33]

If Wise and Gordon were not able to arrest American citizens in the *Sooy* case, it was not long before they sent the first individuals accused of involvement in the Brazilian slave trade to be tried in US courts. The last prosecutions related to the transatlantic slave trade in US courts had taken place in 1839–40 during the Nicholas Trist affair, when Baltimore shipbuilders were tried for aiding and abetting the slave trade (see Chapter

4). Not until 1844 would US courts again see slave trade-related cases, all of them directly connected to the growth of the illegal slave trade in Brazil. In one of his last letters to Secretary of State Upshur, written in February 1844, Slacum provided evidence that led to the arrest of Cornelius E. Driscoll, master of the *Hope*. This course of action was followed by Wise, who, together with Gordon, contributed to the detention of a large number of captains suspected of aiding and abetting the slave trade to Brazil. During 1844 and 1845, Captains Jason S. Pendleton, Cornelius E. Driscoll, Hiram Gray, Thomas Duling, Joshua M. Clapp, Peter Flowery, and Cyrus Libby, as well as the crews of the *Cacique* and the *Pons,* were taken to US courts for their participation in the slave trade. Around the same time at Bahia, the US consul Alexander Tyler, under the instructions of Gordon, ordered the detention and imprisonment of Jacob Woodberry, captain of the *Albert.*[34]

The trial of the captain and mate of the *Montevideo,* Jason S. Pendleton and Robert Baker, resulted in their conviction in 1844: one year of jail and a one-thousand-dollar fine for the captain, six months of jail and a five-hundred-dollar fine for the mate. This positive outcome motivated Wise and Gordon to continue their actions. "The slave trade still goes on," Wise told Secretary of State James Buchanan in May 1845, "although my action here, and the message of the President to Congress communicating my despatches, which has just been received, have produced undoubtedly a great and good effect." Wise also described with enthusiasm to the British minister in Rio the series of captures and convictions taking place.[35] A conversation between two American captains at Cabinda (in modern-day Angola) made clear that Wise and Gordon's course of action was having some impact on the US citizens connected to the slave trade. According to Captain Gilbert Smith of the *Sea Eagle,* the

> deponent informed him [Captain Lovett of the *Sterling*] of the minds of Mr. Gordon, consul of the United States at Rio de Janeiro, and Mr. Wise, minister at said place, and of the American merchants residing there, respecting selling and chartering vessels for the coast of Africa; and deponent spoke with him about everything connected with the same that he could then think of, and, as a friend, advised him not to sell

his vessel on the coast of Africa at any price whatever, as, after the knowledge deponent had given him, he would lay himself and owners liable to the severest laws of the United States; and not only that, but, in deponent's opinion, it would throw a stigma on his character, and those for whom he was doing business, that they would not easily shake off; that, in reply, Captain Lovett assured deponent that he should not sell his vessel on the coast.[36]

Portuguese slave traders seemed to be less worried. Captain Smith described a conversation he had with Cunha, an agent of Manoel Pinto da Fonseca, at Cabinda, before advising Lovett. "I told the said Cunha that Captain Pendleton was in irons, by order of the minister and consul of the United States," Smith wrote in his private journal. Cunha "seemed to ridicule the laws of the United States relative to the slave trade. He said M. Pinto de Fonseca could do as he pleased with the Brazilians and Americans." In fact, though Captain Pendleton and the mate of the *Montevideo* were convicted, most of the captains who were sent to US courts in the 1840s were acquitted. In early 1845, Wise wrote back to Calhoun after learning that Cornelius Driscoll, captain of the *Hope,* got bail and went back to Brazil. Driscoll's return to Brazil, according to Wise, had a very negative impact on their efforts against the participation of US citizens in the Brazilian slave trade. "The moment he [Driscoll] came," Wise argued, "the slave-traders exulted openly in a triumph over the U. States' law & those who were trying to execute them faithfully." Driscoll told friends in a barroom in Rio de Janeiro that they did not have to worry with trials in New York since he could save anyone for a thousand dollars. He then described how he sold the *Hope* at Cabinda and how, while taking his crew to the *Porpoise,* six hundred Africans were taken aboard the sold vessel. When a British cruiser approached, he returned to the ship with his papers to protect it. "Made myself a pirate, they say. Some of my scurvy seamen informed on me afterwards," continued Driscoll, "and the marshal caught up with me in New York and put me in jail. Pretty soon they had me up before old Betts and were talking of hanging me. But here I am. And I'll never go back."[37]

The case of the *Porpoise,* mentioned by Driscoll as responsible for returning the US crew from a vessel sold in Africa, marked the end of that moment of intense anti-slave-trade actions by the two US officers. Consigned to Maxwell, Wright & Co., the vessel had been employed by Manoel Pinto da Fonseca as a tender to slavers such as the *Senator* and the *Kentucky*.[38] Gordon and Wise prepared for the vessel to be seized in Brazilian territorial waters, generating a diplomatic controversy that raised the tension between both countries. As tensions escalated, Wise had an informal meeting with Holanda Cavalcanti, the Brazilian marine minister. Cavalcanti told Wise that the only reason for the unpopularity of England in Brazil was that "she opposed and interrupted the African slave trade; that if the United States prevented their flag and citizens from engaging in it, they too would become unpopular, and there could not be friendly relations with Brazil." Wise answered that the United States would not accept the foreign slave trade to be carried on by American citizens unmolested and that the country would assume any responsibility in the process of eliminating their flag from the trade. The Brazilian minister exploited Anglo-American tensions by simply observing that "England would rejoice at this." Wise's final reply combined anti-slave-trade actions, proslavery ideology, and an Anglophobic perspective:

> I replied I knew Great Britain would rejoice, and, therefore, Brazil and the United States ought to aid each other to arrest the further prosecution of the African slave trade, and ought effectually to punish their own citizens engaged in it, in order to strip England of all pretext for visit and search on the high seas and on the coast; that the best defence of the lawful slavery already existing in Brazil and the United States, would be for both those powers to enforce, sternly and strictly, their own laws for the suppression of the contraband slave trade, and for them to aid each other in this high and humane duty.[39]

Already out of the Department of State by that time, Calhoun did not receive the *Porpoise* case positively. He feared that Wise could be "pursuing an injudicious course in reference to the Slave trade. My

instructions to him were full and pointed on the necessity of preserv-
ing the most friendly relations with Brazil in every respect." The issue,
however, had less to do with the participation of US nationals in the
Brazilian slave trade than with the maintenance of harmonic diplomatic relations between both countries. Former president John Quincy
Adams also thought that Wise had gone too far. "I said I highly approved
Mr. Wise's exposure of the scandalous slave-trade carried on by Americans and English from Brazil," Adams told Secretary of State Buchanan,
"but I was apprehensive he had carried out the spurious doctrine, that
the flag carries territorial jurisdiction with it all round the world, to an
untenable extent; and I hoped the President would not assume it, for it
could not be maintained." Buchanan wrote back to Wise in September
1845 commenting on the whole *Porpoise* affair. Although the president
could not approve Wise's proceeding in that case, Buchanan explained,
he had no doubt of his noble motives. The secretary of state then explained issues of sovereignty and the law of nations that had not been
respected in the case. He concluded by calling Wise's attention to the
article 9 of the Webster-Ashburton Treaty, instructing the minister to,
when appropriate, "urge upon the authorities of Brazil such representations and remonstrances as, without giving offence, will be best calculated to accomplish the humane and important object provided for by
the Treaty and which the Government and people of the United States
have so much at heart."[40]

In 1846, President James Polk officially pardoned Cyrus Libby, captain of the *Porpoise,* as well as James Pendleton and Robert Baker, captain and mate of the *Montevideo.* Other individuals convicted for their
participation in the slave trade were granted presidential pardons in the
following years. Many others were tried and acquitted. These cases have
led some historians to interpret anti-slave-trade laws as "dead letters,"
minimizing the conflicts and tensions that pervaded and shaped US
participation in the slave trade. This perspective generally ignores actual
convictions and how anti-slave-trade legislation continued to influence
the behaviors of slave traders and their networks. Moreover, some of
these acquittals generated angry reactions. In an article published in the
New York Journal of Commerce in 1846, the authors noted the recent pardons granted to Pendleton of the *Montevideo* and Cyrus Libby of the

Porpoise and argued that the "slave trade is no subject for concealment or disguise. If American ship owners or American captains will become allies of the notorious slave traders of Brazil . . . they should be exposed to public indignation." After detailing the activities of Consul Gordon in Rio, the article concluded that "we would hope a pardon has not been extended to Capt. Pendleton without some good cause. The crime for which he was condemned is not one entitled to special clemency." The author of a short note on the *Oberlin Evangelist* was more radical: "Polk and Pendleton are, in fact, brothers and partner in trade—the one holds stolen Africans as his property—the other was engaged in stealing Africans to make them property."[41]

Wise considered captains like Driscoll the tip of the iceberg. He had written to Secretary of State Calhoun calling for amendments to the laws against the slave trade, stressing "the crying injustice of punishing the poor ignorant officers and crews of merchant ships for high misdemeanors and felonies, when the shipowners in the United States, and their American consignees, factors, and agents abroad are left almost entirely untouched by penalties for sending the sailors on voyages notoriously for the purposes of the slave trade." Not surprisingly, in the same letter complaining about Captain Driscoll, Wise named Maxwell, Wright & Co. and James Birckhead as the main consignees of vessels sold and chartered to Brazilian slave traders. As the British navy captured more and more slave vessels, documents implicating American merchant houses increasingly became public. Maxwell, Wright & Co. asked Wise for his opinion on the sale of vessels deliverable on the African coast or the chartering of vessels to carry cargoes to those places. The US minister did not miss the chance and replied with a long letter detailing the US anti-slave-trade legislation and a summary of the most important cases related to the subject. "Neither the charters nor the sales of vessels deliverable on the coast of Africa, are acts in themselves unlawful," Wise wrote, "but these acts, and many others, innocent in themselves, if coupled with an unlawful intent, are criminal offences, punishable under the statutes of the United States against the foreign slave trade." The problem was that there was no trade between Brazil and the African coast "but what partakes directly or indirectly of the nature, and of the profits or losses, of the slave-trade. The slave-trade is the main, the staple business; and all other trades, with the slightest exception, is accessory or auxiliary to it." To Wise, although the act of chartering or delivering a vessel on the African coast was lawful in itself and had been considered to be so in Brazil until then, the intent of aiding and abetting the slave trade that he saw dominating these transactions made all of them illegal. It was simply ignorance of all these facts (the strategies of slave traders involving US flag) in the United States that made them lawful. "Neither Congress nor the country have been informed until the correspondence of Mr. Slacum was published; and that, as yet, has not reached the public mind. This will no longer be the case." In the final pages of his letter, Wise made it clear that he would continue his efforts against the involvement of US citizens in the slave trade and, "in all cases, if probable grounds, I will advise and aid arrests by all the means and influence I can exert, without respect to persons." In addition to the threats, Wise asked for the help of the American merchant community in Rio to change the state of things, concluding the letter by observing that his objective was "preventing crime for the future, without looking at all to the punishment of the past."[42]

Maxwell, Wright & Co. withdrew from any trade related to Africa as a consequence of the tensions generated by the actions of US officers in Rio de Janeiro. According to Wise, the company had completely abandoned the chartering and selling of vessels for the coast of Africa after his long letter of December 1844.[43] In 1847, when Captain Joshua M. Clapp applied for a sea letter at the US consulate in Rio, the consul asked him a few questions to ascertain his purposes. When asked if Maxwell, Wright & Co. had chartered the *Panther* to the coast of Africa, Clapp, who had been tried for aiding and abetting the slave trade, answered that they had not, "they, before that time, had abandoned the trade to the coast of Africa. I myself chartered the ship to Manuel Pinto da Fonseca." The company had definitely abandoned the chartering and selling of vessels to Fonseca. Their names disappeared among the consignees of vessels departing to Africa in the second half of the 1840s, with the company concentrating its efforts on the much safer business of exporting coffee.[44]

If American houses such as Maxwell, Wright & Co. and James Birckhead had been the main consignees of the vessels chartered and sold to slave traders, the chief broker intermediating the transactions between the American merchants and Manoel Pinto da Fonseca, according to Wise, had been a British subject resident in Rio de Janeiro: Carter Thomas Weetman, of the firm Hobkirk, Weetman & Co. In a letter to the British commissioner in Rio, Wise accused Weetman of acting as a broker in most recent cases of US vessels sold and chartered to Fonseca. The minister highlighted the case of the *Agnes*, which went to Liverpool for "coast goods" before sailing to Africa by way of Rio de Janeiro. His conclusion—that the British had an active role in the persistence of the transatlantic slave trade to the Americas—made its way into the official message from the US president in 1845.[45]

That letter generated an investigation from the Foreign Office regarding the two instances in which British subjects were accused of being implicated in the slave trade. The answer from the Liverpool merchants was that once those goods left their deposits they could not have any control over their use. As we saw in the previous chapter, the laws against the aiding and abetting the slave trade in Britain and in the United States were built around the knowledge or intent of the accused. The situation of the British broker was more complicated, but Weetman argued that he had already consulted the British authorities regarding the legality of his business and had received a positive answer from the attorney general. Palmerston would later confirm that Weetman had broken no laws because his activities predated an 1843 act making it illegal for British subjects residing anywhere to be implicated in the slave trade or slavery. The British minister in Rio de Janeiro released a circular note warning British subjects to respect the act of 1843, which Weetman had supposedly ignored. Wise wrote Hamilton Hamilton again accusing the British broker of negotiating the charter-parties of the *Pons, Kentucky,* and the *Enterprise* with Manoel Pinto da Fonseca after the issuance of the circular note. Unlike Aberdeen, who charged Wise with having poor evidence of the role played by British brokers, Palmerston took the accusations more seriously when in charge of the Foreign Office after 1846. "The mere fact of a British subject at Rio negotiating charter-parties for vessels about to be engaged in voyages to the coast of Africa, or being otherwise conversant with or engaged in such transactions is no breach of British law in cases where no guilty knowledge exists," Palmerston wrote to the British minister to Brazil in 1847. The problem in this case was that these charter-parties had been negotiated with "a person well known to be one of the greatest slave-traders of Rio de Janeiro, and notoriously employed almost exclusively in that illegal traffic," being almost impossible for the agent to prove his ignorance of the use to which those vessels would be put to.[46] This was precisely the explanation Wise had given to Maxwell, Wright & Co. of what constituted aiding and abetting the slave trade. Weetman publicly denied the accusations in 1848, arguing that his company negotiated the last charter before the reception of the circular note in 1845. Moreover, even before the issuing of the circular, "on discovering that Her Majesty's Consul considered such charters of a questionable nature . . . , resolved rather than run the slightest risk of having our names compromised, we would negotiate no further charters to the coast of Africa."[47]

The Go-Betweens of Man-Stealers

By 1845, Maxwell, Wright & Co. and Hobkirk, Weetman & Co. had abandoned any African-related trade. It is clear from the depositions of crews and documents found aboard the vessels seized throughout 1844 that both companies were central to the US flag scheme developed by Manoel Pinto da Fonseca. Their withdrawal from the business, however, did not mean the disappearance of the US flag from the slave trade. On the contrary, it opened opportunities to individuals willing to operate in the gray area connecting legitimate commerce and the slave trade, favored by the growing demand for slaves in the second half of the 1840s. A few US nationals quickly occupied this space, most of them captains and ex-captains. Compared to Maxwell, Wright & Co. and other merchants of the first half of the 1840s, these individuals established even closer connections to slave traders. As the consul replacing Gordon in Rio de Janeiro complained, since the acquittal of Captain Libby of the *Porpoise,* "the persons incidentally concerned in the trade are much more open than they were before."[48]

The more active position occupied by a few American captains became clear in a number of interrogations made by Parks before granting sea letters, a temporary register issued by consuls to purchasers of vessels. Most captains were using money advanced from charter-parties contracted with slave traders from Rio de Janeiro. As Parks made clear, "The vessels which sail under these letters are in most cases owned by Brazilians, who pay the applicant for the sea letter about five hundred milreis each vessel, for passing the examination before Mr. Tod and myself, and covering the property." Captain Charles Rauch, for example, received money in advance from Nicolau Ventura Fortuna to buy the *C. H. Rogers* in 1848. Rauch, starting "before the mast" around 1826, had been commanding a vessel for the past eleven or twelve years. He bought the *C. H. Rogers* with a four-month payment in advance of the charter-party he had with Fortuna. Another vessel owned by Fortuna, the *Safira*, had already been captured that same year before embarking slaves. The following year, Brazilian authorities seized his vessel *Tolerante*, probably the same vessel condemned that year under the ownership of Manoel Pinto da Fonseca.[49]

Captain David C. Bevans explained the system in more detail. When buying the *Brazil*, a vessel that completed at least two voyages to Africa, Bevans got the money from Jenkins & Co. and hypothecated the vessel to the company. After the time specified he had to pay back that amount or give the vessel to the company, sailing the ship in return for wages. According to the US consul, "Nearly the whole of the slave trade in American bottoms is transacted by this house of Jenkins and company, either as principals or factors." The company consisted of Jenkins from New York, an Englishman named Russell, and a Portuguese named Guimarães. When asked if the money borrowed from Jenkins & Co. came from the company itself or someone else, Bevans answered that there was a third party. It came from the notorious José Bernardino de Sá, a slave dealer, in the words of Parks, "who ranks second only to Manoel Pinto da Fonseca in this country, and perhaps the world." After Bevans failed to pay the value of the vessel, the company, probably under Bernardino de Sá's instructions, transferred its ownership to Louis Francis Desireé Krafft, a naturalized American from France who had been involved in the African trade since the early 1840s and was closely associated with the Portuguese slave trader.[50]

Around this period American slave traders were mentioned for the first time in the lists of individuals suspected of involvement in the slave trade prepared by British and Brazilian authorities. Their number and role should not be overestimated. In a period characterized by the concentration of ownership, these individuals were not autonomous slave traders but simply associated with figures such as Manoel Pinto da Fonseca and José Bernardino de Sá. In his report of the African slave trade to Brazil during 1849, the British consul to Rio de Janeiro enclosed a list with the names of slave merchants residing in the city and their respective nationalities. Among the thirty-eight names, only two Americans appeared: Jenkins and Clapp. After Brazil employed new strategies to suppress the slave trade in the 1850s, the police compiled several lists of suspects engaging in the contraband traffic. Of almost four hundred names, only one is clearly American: George Marsden. There were probably other US citizens operating in the Brazilian slave trade, as US diplomatic documents in Brazil indicate, but Jenkins, Clapp, and Marsden seem to have played a central role in the incorporation of US vessels and the US flag by slave traders in Brazil.[51]

Whereas Jenkins was connected to José Bernardino de Sá, Clapp and Marsden often appeared associated with Manoel Pinto da Fonseca. According to the Alcoforado report, which does not provide dates, two American brokers had key roles, along with the lawyer J. M. Pereira da Silva, in the US flag strategy put forward by Fonseca. The report does not name the brokers, noting only that one of them was in prison at the time the report was being written in 1853. This was probably George Marsden, arrested earlier that year for his involvement in the case of the *Camargo*. During the 1830s, Marsden had captained the *Louisiana,* an American vessel consigned to Maxwell, Wright & Co. that frequently carried coffee cargoes to New York. By the second half of the 1840s, Marsden had abandoned his work as a captain, becoming officially associated with H. F. Whittle in the brokerage business, a partnership that lasted until 1850. Described by the British commissioner in Rio as a "notorious slave-trader," Marsden had been "on various occasions warned by the Ministers of the United States resident here, and on one occasion, one of them, I believe Mr. Wise, was on the point of sending him to the United States on a charge of slave-dealing." In 1853, the British, maybe unaware of Marsden's detention, warned the Brazilian government that the "agents of the slave-traders are still in a state of activity." With Marsden's help, a vessel had been sold to the bookkeeper of Antonio Pinto and Joaquim Pinto da Fonseca, brothers of the notorious Manoel Pinto da Fonseca, already living in Portugal after his deportation.[52]

The second broker mentioned by Alcoforado was probably Joshua M. Clapp, who, by the second half of that decade, seems to have been Fonseca's main link to US vessels and the US flag. "During my residence at this court," the US minister to Brazil David Tod wrote to the secretary of state in 1851, "all interested in maintaining our laws for the suppression of the use of our flag in the infamous slave traffic, have been thwarted and annoyed more by Joshua M. Clapp and Frank Smith, (both citizens of the United States,) than by all other persons put together." Their role had been so central that "but for their agency in the business," Tod continued, "at least so far as this port is concerned, our flag would have been free from the foul stigma that has rested upon it." Connections between Clapp and Fonseca appear frequently in the documents. According to the British commissioner James Hudson, the *Flora* had been fraudulently sold to Fonseca through Clapp's agency. The vessel would soon arrive in Montevideo, he warned the British commissioner, from whence it would depart to the African coast, probably under Brazilian colors. Clapp's connection to Fonseca also appeared among the documents found on board the *Ann D. Richardson,* seized by the US Navy in 1848. In a letter to the ship captain, Clapp recommended that the captain could sell the bark on the African coast "taking a bill of exchange, drawn against Manuel Pinto da Fonseca, payable to my order, for 15,000 Spanish dollars."[53]

Joshua Clapp started his career as a common sailor on a whaling voyage. Shortly after his first voyage, he entered the "merchant service" and in 1841 became the commander of a New York schooner. In a deposition to the US consul, a US citizen resident in Rio said that he met Captain Joshua M. Clapp around 1843, "then and since largely engaged in purchasing and chartering American vessels for the slave trade." The deponent said that he "assisted in fitting and rigging quite a number of vessels for the said Clapp, which were sent to the coast of Africa for slaves." Clapp's first voyage to Africa was in 1844 aboard the *Gannicliffe,* a vessel sold to Manoel Pinto da Fonseca on the African coast that subsequently disembarked 420 enslaved Africans in Cabo Frio, Rio de Janeiro. The following year, Clapp captained another American vessel to the African coast, the *Panther,* originally consigned to Maxwell, Wright & Co., but chartered to Manoel Pinto da Fonseca by Clapp himself. The vessel was captured by the US squadron at Cabinda before the embarkation of slaves and taken to the Circuit Court of Charleston, South Carolina, where Clapp was tried and acquitted in 1846 (despite the forfeiture of the vessel). The following year he was again the captain of an American vessel leaving Rio de Janeiro to Africa, the *Don Juan.* "The fact that the flag of the United States affords in every way the greatest protection to the Slave Trade," the British consul to Rio complained in his annual report, "has lately been but too clearly proved by the numerous cases that have occurred of American vessels being sold to well-known slave-dealers without changing colours; and there are now in this harbour two brigs, the '*Brazil*' and '*Don Juan,*' wearing American colours, while they are well known to belong to notorious slave-traders."[54]

In 1848, Clapp started to advertise the selling and chartering of US vessels in the *Jornal do Commercio.* In a list of seventeen American vessels sold in Rio de Janeiro and, according to the US consul, directly connected to the slave trade, Joshua M. Clapp appears as the purchaser of nine. Other purchasers are also US captains, some of them with a long experience in the African trade, such as Charles Lovett, who as we have seen was advised by another captain a few years earlier to not sell his vessel on the African coast. The ownership of these vessels, like those of the other captains described before, was possible through the money advanced by local slave traders. Clapp mentions the money advanced by a Spaniard named Don Francisco—a slave trader according to the US consul (perhaps Francisco Rovirosa)—and the Rio merchants Barbozo and Castro for three of his vessels. These individuals advanced Clapp between fifteen and sixteen thousand dollars. Similar schemes were certainly put into practice for other ships owned by Clapp; Clapp's *Frederica,* chartered to Fonseca, was probably one of them.[55]

Captain Frank Smith, who had become an associate of Joshua Clapp in 1848, appears in the list purchasing two other vessels. Their close relationship and organizational role in slave-trading voyages are detailed in a deposition to the US consul about the *Quincey* case. According to the mate of the vessel, Clapp and Smith organized various aspects of the voyage, including his hiring. In 1849, the *Quincey* disembarked 742 Africans in a plantation at Campos, Rio de Janeiro. Smith supervised the whole process of fitting and equipping the vessel for the voyage and considered going as a supercargo. Clapp and Smith "were to have, as I understood them, a given sum per head. Smith afterward told me that he would or had made from twenty-four to thirty cents de rees (twelve to fifteen thousand dollars). Smith and Clapp both told me that they would allow me about five thousand dollars." The identity of the slave traders financing these voyages (the deponent also mentions the successful slave voyage of the *Snow*) does not appear in the source, but it is unlikely that Clapp and Smith were operating autonomously. As the deponent notes, "The blacks brought out in the '*Quincey*' were for account of a house in Rio, but I do not know the terms upon which they were brought."[56]

Clapp and Smith had in fact been working with other slave traders besides Fonseca. Smith appeared as the consignee of a large number of vessels flying the US flag with forged documents that were seized by the Royal Navy in 1849. According to a British agent, it was Captain Smith's duty "to obtain masters, crew, flag, and papers, and he gets his per centage on all slaves landed from vessels that have worn the United States' flag," matching the description given by the mate of the *Quincey*. According to the lieutenant, their owner was "the celebrated Don Juan Minetta, a one-armed man, and esteemed the richest in the Brazils," who owned "seven or eight vessels under the American flag, which he has bought at Rio, and whose papers are all forgeries." Don Juan Minetta was probably the one-armed slave trader Tomás da Costa Ramos, whose nickname, "Maneta," was a reference to his disability. In 1844, Ramos was a factor at Lagos sending slaves to Cuba on freight. The following year the *Isabel,* a US-built vessel owned by the slave trader, was seized, indicating that Ramos had already established himself at Bahia. The Portuguese slave trader was the first to employ steamers in his activities, according to the Alcoforado report, something confirmed in the denunciations of the British minister in Rio, who described the activities of Ramos' steamer *Providencia,* operating since 1846. Ramos continued to engage in the slave trade to Brazil after the law of 1850 abolished the slave trade to the country for a second time. After being deported, he established himself in Lisbon and, with a few other slave traders, re-directed his exports to Cuba (see Chapter 6). His access to US vessels continued into the 1850s.[57]

Clapp, Smith, and other captains purchased vessels with the money advanced by Portuguese, Brazilian, and Spanish slave traders, but who sold the ships to these intermediaries? There were obviously many sources for US vessels, but the traditional American merchant houses apparently continued to be constant suppliers. Clapp bought the *Whig* from James Birckhead and the *Zenobia* from Maxwell, Wright & Co. Maxwell, Wright & Co. had abandoned the trade with Africa but not the business of selling vessels. If Wise had difficulties in bringing these merchants under US anti-slave-trade laws when they were dealing directly with Fonseca in the first half of the 1840s, interdiction under these circumstances would be virtually impossible. The central role played by intermediaries such as Joshua Clapp—the "go-between of the man-stealers of Rio de Janeiro," as so well defined by British consul—made the work of American authorities both simpler and more complicated. It was easier because these individuals clearly broke the law, as the deposition of the mate of the *Quincey* made clear, facilitating the process of proving guilty knowledge in the courts. On the other hand, capturing them became much harder since, unlike traditional merchant houses, they specialized in the aiding and abetting of business, being capable of moving according to the circumstances. Moreover, these captains turned ship-owners had strong ties to the Brazilian slave-trading community, which made the task of raising enough evidence complicated as long as the slave trade to Brazil was protected by local elites. The US minister to Brazil described Joshua Clapp and Frank Smith as "shrewd, intelligent men, with an unlimited amount of money at their command, and therefore difficult to cope with; so long as they were upon the spot, it was impossible to find legal testimony sufficient to convict them before a court and jury." Tod was writing in 1851, when these ties were already being dismantled. "All were morally convinced, yet no one could be found to testify of his own knowledge to their guilt. They have now, however, left the country, and the truth is now coming to light, and I have at last found evidence abundantly sufficient to convict them."[58]

Despite the difficulties, ministers and consuls persisted in their efforts to stop US participation in the Brazilian slave trade. Their denunciations continued, vessels were seized and tried in US courts, sea letters were occasionally denied, and a number of suggestions were made to the State Department to eliminate the US flag from the commerce in human beings. Although the Stars and Stripes continued to be used by slave traders in the second half of the 1840s, references to forged documents also seem to have increased, indicating some success in the actions of the American consuls in Brazil. Consul Gorham Parks wrote back to the US secretary of state explaining that he had "required the strictest proof as to every qualification required by the law—such as citizenship, reality of purchase on account of applicant, and not for other persons." In the same letter, Parks complained about the acquittals of individuals suspected of engaging in the slave trade in US courts. He added that the recent case of the *Laurens,* a vessel captured by American authorities based on information he furnished, was based on strong evidence of the intent to violate the anti-slave-trade legislation. The evidence was "so strong that, if she gets clear, it will be useless to capture another." The US minister David Tod reinforced Parks's words. "The immense value of the prize, as well as the vast importance of her acquittal to the future operations of the slave merchants of this city," Tod argued, "will induce her owners to make powerful exertions to extricate the vessel and cargo. I hope you will cause them to be met at every step in the progress of the case. No exertions should be spared to bring the case before the court upon its true merits." The *Laurens* had been captured in January 1848 after sailing from Rio with an unusual number of water casks on board and a foreign crew. This indirect evidence was enough for Judge Betts. The combination of a charter-party whose value was twice the rate for legitimate similar voyages and a crew made up mainly by foreigners when US sailors were available ("the act must be regarded as denoting an intent to put the vessel to an use which the Americans could not be made to subserve") led the judge to decree the forfeiture of the vessel and its cargo.[59]

The sentence apparently had some effect on the slave-trading community. According to Tod, "Since the seizure of the *Laurens,* the bare presence of a vessel of the United States in the harbor, capable of following them to sea, will do much towards arresting the use of our flag." British representatives in Rio de Janeiro also informed the Foreign Office of the impact of the case. The condemnation of the *Laurens,* "not on account of slave equipment, but in consequence of the evident Slave Trade intention of the voyage," Robert Hesketh wrote, "has occasioned much distrust amongst these lawless adventurers in their various devices to profit by the use of the American flag." Minister Hudson confirmed Hesketh: "The judgment given by Judge Betts in the United States in the case of the 'Laurens' has produced a sensible effect amongst the American Slave Dealers here,—many of them are withdrawing from the trade of selling ships for slave trade." Slave traders adapted to new pressures, and the US flag continued to be used occasionally by slave traders in Brazil, but efforts to limit its use were not without effect.[60]

The Suppression of the Transatlantic Slave Trade to Brazil

If the Aberdeen Act increased the tensions between Brazil and Britain, as we have seen in the angry protests of J. M. Pereira da Silva, Lord Palmerston's second term at the head of the Foreign Office beginning in 1846 would take these tensions to a new level. To Palmerston and the prime minister, Lord John Russell, the Royal Navy had every right to seize vessels on the Brazilian coast based on the Brazilian government's failure to comply with the terms of the 1826 treaty. The Foreign Office issued new orders authorizing the capture of vessels equipped for the slave trade in Brazilian waters. With the end of hostilities at Rio de la Plata, British vessels were redirected to Brazil and a series of captures and destruction of vessels on the Brazilian coast took place, culminating with a firefight with Brazilian authorities at the fort of Paranaguá. On the brink of war with Britain, the Brazilian government could not see any alternative to suppressing the slave trade. Senator Francisco de Paula Sousa had considered resisting British pressure by establishing an alliance with the United States under the argument that the was violating the Monroe Doctrine, but isolation seemed certain in case of war. In fact, Prime Minister Russell threatened Brazil with a potential alliance involving Britain, France, and the United States. The Brazilian agent in England commented: "It is unique that lord John Russell included the American Union in this alliance ... at the moment that the latter gives

an spectacle to the civilized world of a dispute that threatens the stability of its institution and that has its origins in the slavery issue itself. . . .
Unfortunately, this uniqueness does not exclude the possibility of this
fact." After passing the chamber of deputies and senate, a bill abolishing
the slave trade presented by the minister of justice Eusébio de Queiroz
officially became law on September 4, 1850. The largest branch of the
slave trade in Atlantic history was coming to an end.[61]

Slave traders operating in Brazil did not abandon the business
immediately after the law of 1850. The year 1851 was marked by several
successful disembarkations and a few captures by British and Brazilian authorities. Two slave voyages were completed successfully in 1852.
The US minister to Brazil Robert C. Schenck reported to the secretary
of state that, because of the actions of British cruisers and Brazilian
ministers of state, the slave trade to the country seemed to have been
nearly, if not completely, suppressed. The US minister, however, did not
discard the possibility of new slave disembarkations. As he explained,
"The first panic of the slave dealers that remain being passed, they have
had time to look around them, to see and devise means for entering
with more security into their old business." Moreover, the barriers inter-
posed on the commerce of slaves between Africa and Brazil made their
prices double in the local markets. "A single cargo successfully landed
and sold now would make the fortune of the adventurer," Schenck concluded. His speculations seemed to be well founded when, in April 1852,
the *Palmeira* disembarked hundreds of African slaves in the state of Rio
Grande do Sul. Brazilian authorities were quick to frustrate the slave
traders' plan of transporting the disembarked Africans to São Paulo on
small vessels through Santa Catarina.[62]

One month later, the British minister to Brazil, Henry Southern,
wrote to the Foreign Office about indications that the US vessels *Mary
Adeline* and *Camargo* were being prepared to engage in the slave trade.
"Mr. Marsden, a broker in Rio, a citizen of the United States," continued
Southern, "is the party who is actively interested in getting up and aiding these speculations." The US consul in Rio also wrote to the US secretary of state about the suspicious circumstances of both vessels. Later
that year the British minister informed the Foreign Office that he had
learned from Brazilian authorities that slave traders were prepared to re-

sume the traffic to Brazil, "only awaiting a change in the Government, or some relaxation of its present rigorous system of persecution, in order to set their plans in motion. Such is the price of a Slave at present, and such the demand for labour, that there is no doubt that the slave-dealers hold in their hands the means of inundating the country with raw Africans on the shortest notice." In December, one month after the note, the *Camargo* disembarked five hundred slaves at Bracuhy, south of Rio de Janeiro. As Southern had predicted, the main figure providing the access to US vessels was George Marsden, still operating with slave traders despite the law of 1850.[63]

But this time things were different. Under the coordination of Justice Minister Eusébio de Queiroz, the Brazilian police had put into practice effective tactics to suppress the slave trade. The *Camargo* landed its African cargo successfully, and many of the enslaved were taken to the coffee plantations of Bananal. For the first time, however, the government ordered a police search inside the plantations for the Africans illegally disembarked, a difficult task in face of the great power of local planters such as Joaquim José de Souza Breves. Thirty-eight Africans were found and rescued. Breves was charged with illegally importing slaves but was acquitted. Despite rumors that Joaquim Breves and his brother were organizing disembarkations in the following years, the arrival of the *Camargo* seems to have been the last successful slave voyage to Brazil. Four members of the crew–two Americans, a Spaniard, and an Englishman—were arrested. The captain, Nathaniel Gordon, who was hanged in New York ten years later for his participation in the slave trade, disappeared after the destruction of the vessel. The case was still under investigation when the Rio de Janeiro police arrested George Marsden on January 4, 1853. A few days earlier, the US consul, Robert C. Schenck, had asked the Brazilian minister of foreign affairs for details of the US part in the disembarkation, regretting that the "success of those engaged in the infamous Traffic, has been accomplished under the flag of the United States." After learning of the imprisonment of Marsden and two sailors, Schenck wrote to the US secretary of state suggesting that he could "obtain testimony upon which these villains can be prosecuted at home; or may, possibly, make an arrangement with the Imperial authorities, for sending two of the guilty seamen in person, to be used as State's evidence in our court, for the indictment and conviction of Gordon."[64]

Still in jail four months later, Marsden wrote to the US consul for help. After all, he explained, according to the law of 1850, the authorities had eight days to make their case against him or he was entitled to his liberty. In the meantime, "at Bananal, three wealthy Brazilians, proprietors of estates (fazendeiros,) suspected of having an interest in this same cargo of Africans, were tried by jury . . . and were then acquitted. The judge did not appeal, and they of course are at liberty, if they ever were made prisoners." Unlike those planters, Marsden claimed to have had no interest in the vessel, owned, at least in part, by Captain Gordon. "I had no control over him [Captain Gordon] while at this port, much less after leaving here, and if he engaged in any unlawful act afterwards, it would be strange law that could make me responsible." The consul and the chargé d'affaires, Ferdinand Coxe, contacted the Brazilian secretary of state, Paulino de Souza, for clarification. The issue was not whether Marsden was guilty but why he had not had a fair trial after almost five months of his imprisonment. In July, Marsden was finally released on the condition of leaving the country. In his reply to the US legation, the Brazilian minister attached a copy of an 1850 contract made between Francisco Rovirosa y Urgelles and George Marsden for Marsden's delivery of the US schooner *Volusia* on the coast of Africa. Marsden would also pay the expenses of the crew, with an interest in the business of seven contos, five hundred mil reis (7,500$000), the same amount Rovirosa was to receive after the voyage was completed. The profit was to be divided according to the proportion invested by each one. To the chargé d'affaires, Marsden may have engaged in the slave trade in the past, as the contract of 1850 showed, and Brazil had the right to deport the individual based on the evidence, but what remained to be explained was his imprisonment for almost five months without a trial. In one of his final exchanges on the subject with Paulino de Souza, Coxe argued that the fact that Marsden was the consignee of the *Camargo* did not automatically show his culpability. Such a circumstance "might have happened to any of the most respectable commercial houses in Brazil; which could not be held responsible for acts of illegality committed by vessels, of which they had accidentally been the consignees many months before

the commission of such acts." Had Coxe been the US minister in the mid-
1840s, the transactions involving Maxwell, Wright & Co. and the local
slave-trading community may well have continued undisturbed.[65]

The question of what constituted the aiding and abetting of the
slave trade was settled in the minds of Henry Wise and George Gordon
in the mid-1840s, yet this was certainly not the case for other US citizens,
as became clear in a congressional debate in early 1851. A petition presented by Henry Clay and signed by important Rhode Islanders asked
for more effective measures to suppress the African slave trade. Clay
later submitted a resolution asking for the Committee on Commerce to
consider the possibility of more effective legislation and summarized the
schemes involving the US flag in the Brazilian slave trade as described in
the correspondence of US diplomats in Brazil. Jefferson Davis of Mississippi, future leader of the Confederacy, argued that although US laws
made participation in the slave trade piracy, it should not be denied
"that the owner of an American ship may sell it in a foreign port if he
pleases. And whilst the latter right remains, ships of American construction will probably be found in the slave trade." Moreover, one could not
assume that there was no trade between Africa and Brazil other than the
slave trade: "It is certainly offensive to assume that such is the only trade
for which vessels are fitted out in the ports of a friendly nation. What
would we say if any other country should take such position towards
the United States?" Senator Andrew Butler of South Carolina endorsed
this position, adding that "the intimation that this is a monopoly, and a
monopoly of a piratical character, is altogether against my notions of a
liberal charity, at least towards commercial relations between any people
whatever." As in Britain and France, policy makers in the United States
faced the contradictions of fighting the transatlantic slave trade in an
environment marked by ideals of laissez-faire capitalism. Most senators,
however, agreed that something should be done to curb the participation of US vessels and citizens in the slave trade, and the resolution was
approved by forty-five votes to nine.[66]

The timing of the debate almost made it irrelevant since the Brazilian government had already put into practice measures to suppress
the slave trade to the country, including that carried on US vessels. After
many year in the illegal business, top slave traders such as Manoel Pinto

da Fonseca, José Bernardino de Sá, Tomas da Costa Ramos, and Francisco Rovirosa y Urgelles were deported. But the traffic in human beings would regain its force, this time to a location much closer to the United States and with a much more pervasive presence of the US flag. Many of the main slave traders had actually carried immense fortunes with them. Lord Palmerston argued that 140 slave traders had returned to Portugal from Brazil, generating the deposit of £1.2 million in a Lisbon bank. The sugar plantations of Cuba and Puerto Rico increasingly demanded labor, expanding opportunities for deported slave traders. Some continued their slave-trading activities from Lisbon while waiting for a possible reopening of the business to Brazil. "The Brazilian Government complains, with much bitterness, of the Slave Trade which is permitted to be carried on from Portugal to the Havana, by parties either belonging to Brazil or in connexion with houses established at Rio de Janeiro," the British minister wrote in a note to the Foreign Office. "Every packet is said to bring news of successful enterprises of this kind," he continued, "which both Senhor Paulino and the Minister of Justice allege keeps alive the hopes of the slave-dealers of Brazil, and moreover enables them successfully to employ their capital and their agents, while waiting for better times at home." With no indication that the Brazilian slave trade would reopen and increasing pressures from British representatives in Portugal, some slave traders withdrew from the business.[67]

A more successful group of Portuguese slave traders involved in the traffic to Cuba operated from New York. The Portuguese Company, as the group came to be known, organized a large part of all slave-trading ventures out of New York. This reorganization of the business was noted by the Brazilian minister of external affairs José Maria da Silva Paranhos in 1856, when he reported that the "imperial government has been searching for intelligence information through its agents in countries where we can fear the action of speculators, specially in the United States, Brazil, Spain and its possessions, where it seems certain that smugglers have established the main basis of their operations." After being deported from Brazil, George Marsden became involved with the Portuguese company in New York, organizing the voyage of the *Grey Eagle*. Captured by the British, the *Grey Eagle* was taken before

the circuit court of Philadelphia, with Marsden leaving the country before a possible conviction could take place (see Chapter 6). Although
Cuba was the main destination for their voyages, the New York group
still hoped for a reopening of the slave trade to Brazil. In 1856, the frustrated attempt to disembark the slaves carried aboard the US vessel
Mary E. Smith attested to the effectiveness of abolitionist policies in
Brazil since the law of 1850. The captain, Vicente Daniel Cranatich, was
arrested by the Brazilian police, and Manoel Basílio da Cunha Reis, part
owner of the voyage according to documents found on board the ship,
was indicted but released on bail in Boston. It became clear to Portuguese and Spanish slave traders, along with their networks involving US
citizens (some of them petty slave traders), that they should concentrate
on Cuba.[68]

Conclusion

The suppression of the Brazilian slave trade brought to an end the
schemes of a few US nationals who specialized in the provision of US
vessels and papers to slave traders in Brazil. As had been the case with many
of their employers—the Portuguese slave traders who were deported or
left Brazil for Portugal—most of the US citizens involved in the traffic
left Brazil or were deported after abolition. Joshua M. Clapp and Frank
Smith had already left the country by 1851, precisely when the US consul
wrote back to the secretary of state providing evidence that implicated
them in the traffic to Brazil. George Marsden was deported after spend-
ing five months in jail. The larger American merchant houses in Rio,
having disassociated themselves from the slave-trading community long
before 1850, continued to profit from the exportation of slave-grown
coffee. In 1859, three years after the last frustrated attempt to disembark
slaves on the Brazilian coast, an anonymous member of the company
Maxwell, Wright & Co. observed with a certain nostalgia, "Better have
good Negroes from the African coast, for our happiness and theirs, notwithstanding the Briton, with his morbid philanthropy, which makes
him forget his own home and allows his poor white brother to die from
hunger, a slave without a master to pity him; the hypocritical and stupid

Briton, who weeps over the destiny of our happy slave and thus exposes himself to the ridicule of true philanthropy."[69]

How would the transatlantic slave trade to Brazil have changed had the United States and Britain agreed on a treaty establishing the mutual right of search in 1842 instead of 1862? Citizens of the United States rarely had an interest in slave voyages to Brazil, and the business remained under the complete control of Portuguese and Brazilian slave traders. Perhaps Joshua M. Clapp or George Marsden would have been convicted, but the number of enslaved Africans illegally transported to Brazilian plantations would have changed very little. As we have seen, slave traders constantly switched to other flags in face of abolitionist pressure. The use of the US flag was one among many strategies employed in the illegal business, with the Sardinian and French flags playing important roles in Bahia and Rio de Janeiro, respectively. Moreover, an increasing number of vessels simply abandoned flags and documents altogether throughout the 1840s and 1850s. In the end, the United States had little influence over the regulation or the business of slave trading in Brazil. So long as coffee production demanded enslaved Africans and the Brazilian political situation favored their illegal introduction into the country, the slave trade would continue.

Joint actions from the US and British government could certainly take the US flag out of the business along with US shipping agents and captains, but it is doubtful that US-built vessels or British merchandise could have been stopped from entering the illegal business in the free-enterprise environment in which all transatlantic trade operated at this time. Neither the United States nor Britain could control the ultimate end to which these items were put. Although the two countries followed almost opposite trajectories regarding slavery, they faced very similar problems regarding the abolition of the transatlantic slave trade. The key issue was how to enforce anti-slave-trade legislation in a free market environment. Not surprisingly, most of the few steamships that appeared in the final years of the slave trade were built in Britain or using British technology despite Britain's efforts to suppress the traffic.[70]

Even after the suppression of the Brazilian slave trade, US-built vessels continued to be used in the Brazilian coastal trade that, after

1850, increasingly transported slaves from the Northeast to the South-east in a nascent domestic slave trade. Brazilian authorities even considered officially using the US flag to protect the domestic trade after the British captured and emancipated the slaves of the *Piratinim,* a Brazilian vessel carrying captives from Bahia to São Paulo. Secretary of State John J. Crittenden reacted favorably to the possibility, arguing that "the superior safety of their property in our vessels would not arise solely from its being protected by our flag from aggression by other powers, but from the excellence in the build of United States vessels and the skill with which they are navigated." That Brazilian elites considered using the US flag as a protection against the British after the suppression of the Brazilian slave trade is another sign of how widespread was the perception of the United States as the only powerful opponent to expanding British designs. In this sense, the refusal to establish a mutual right of search with Britain in 1842 was important, since it reinforced the general perception that the northern neighbor would not submit to British projects. When the British attacks in the late 1840s exposed Brazilian fragility, slave traders reconstituted and expanded their networks to include the United States. The usefulness of the slave-holding republic to the transatlantic slave-trading community would be tested again, but this time in the context of Cuba.[71]

Slave Trading in the Slaveholding Republic, 1851–1858

"It is some years ago since I took an opportunity to say," an anonymous author complained in 1856 in the *Charleston Mercury*, "that the relation of Brazil to the slave trade was a question of more direct and vital interest to the future of the South, than most of the factious folly of Northern Abolitionists." According to the author, the issue should be reconsidered because Brazil was "the only large slaveholding Empire that belongs to Christendom; sympathizing naturally, from institution, neighborhood and interest, with the South." The author described how Britain, who "arrogates to herself God's prerogative in the distribution of national fortunes, and forbids the natural development of an independent society," had pressured Brazil for the suppression of the slave trade. The Brazilian example should be taken as a warning to all Southerners of possible similar intrusions in the Gulf of Mexico and the Caribbean Sea, which are "intended to be, and, with a Southern Confederacy would be, one great slaveholding Mediterranean." The countries around these waters had the climate, production, and habit of slave states. "These States are destined to form," the author continued, "and but for the European character of the North, would long since have formed, a political system of their own. Their development must be mutual, and any such arrogant interference with one, is a direct injury to all the others. If there is an European balance of power, so is there an American balance of power."[1]

The complaints published in the *Charleston Mercury* point to the more complex geopolitical position occupied by Cuba in the mid-nineteenth century. The long dream of incorporating the island into the United States had been shared throughout the century by figures as diverse as Thomas Jefferson and John Quincy Adams. By the 1850s, however, the desire to incorporate the island became strongly attached to slavery expansionism (which, in some cases, led to Southern visions of a slaveholding empire involving the US South and multiple Caribbean and Central American regions, as in the letter published by the *Charleston Mercury*). This longing for Cuba culminated in the Ostend Manifesto, a document prepared by Pierre Soulé, James Buchanan, and John Y. Mason—US ministers to, respectively, Spain, Great Britain, and France—arguing that Cuba should be sold to the United States or incorporated through war. At the same time, some slaveholders in the island considered annexation as the best way to protect slavery against British abolitionism and slave rebellion (issues that came to be seen as completely interconnected after the Escalera conspiracy). Many Cuban exiles also supported annexation and, at times, the filibustering epidemic of the 1850s. As a consequence, British pressure to abolish the Cuban slave trade never took the aggressive and open form that it had taken in Brazil. British authorities were fully aware that a more violent action would be received as an assault on the "American balance of power"—a perception that had already been clearly stated in President Monroe's 1823 speech to Congress—and provide the necessary pretext for the US annexation of Cuba. Geopolitical tensions involving Britain, Spain, and the United States, therefore, protected the island from any stronger anti-slave-trade measure.[2]

It was under the protection offered by these international tensions that the slave trade to the island significantly rose in the 1850s. Although the first half of the nineteenth century was marked by a trend downward in the prices for cotton, coffee, and sugar (which as we have seen did not obstruct the profits of plantations in the United States, Brazil, or Cuba), the prices of all three products, especially sugar, rose suddenly in the 1850s. In 1839, Cuba was responsible for the production of

130,200 tons of sugar, or 16 percent of the total 820,318 tons produced for the world market. This rose to 30 percent in 1860, with the island producing 749,000 of 2.5 million tons. In a period of more rapid growth of the world economy and with sugar prices on the rise, the expanding and highly modernized sugar industry in Cuba demanded an increasing number of laborers, absorbing almost every slave illegally disembarked on the island between 1851 and 1867. This pressing need for labor was also reflected in experiments with Chinese immigrants and the eventual disembarkation of more than four hundred kidnapped Yucatán Indians in a concerted plan involving Cuban slave traders and the president of Mexico Antonio López de Santa Anna. The main consumer of Cuban sugar, as had been the case with Brazilian coffee, was the United States, which accounted for about half of all exports (followed 15 to 20 percent for Britain).[3]

In this context, the US contribution to the transatlantic slave trade reached a new level, expanding in the interstices of Anglo-American tensions. Slave traders, who skillfully intermeshed legitimate commerce with the transatlantic slave trade, exploited these international frictions and contributed to their persistence throughout the 1850s. The US flag, ships, captains, and seamen were much more pervasive in the final era of the Cuban slave trade than in its Brazilian counterpart of the 1840s. And slave traders did not merely repeat the strategies of the Brazilian trade. One important innovation of this final period was the transformation of US ports into bases for the organization of slave-trading voyages. After the dismantling of slave-trading networks in Brazil, some traffickers moved to the country that had been offering the most stringent resistance to the actions of the British navy. New York, especially, became famous as the center of transatlantic slave trading in the late 1850s.

Slave traders in the slaveholding republic, however, also faced internal pressures, with conflicts between US authorities and slave-trading networks punctuating the decade. The persistence of an entrenched opposition to the illegal business stimulated district attorneys, marshals, and other authorities to act, forcing slave traders to adapt constantly to new pressures. But tensions between slave traders and local authorities now became chiefly a Northern phenomenon. The absence of any condemnation of the slave trade in the complaints of the *Charleston Mercury* indicates the end of a Southern consensus against the traffic. Much attention has been paid to the movement to reopen the transatlantic slave trade to the United States and to instances of slaves entering the country on voyages organized by Southerners by the end of the decade. As in Brazil during the previous decade, however, the main figures behind the slave trade in its final phase—including the many voyages organized from US ports—were Portuguese and Spanish. Understanding these transformations of the traffic is a fundamental part of a broader comprehension of the relation of the transatlantic slave trade to US politics and its contribution to the mounting crisis of the 1850s.

The Reconfiguration of Slave-Trading Networks

Later in the 1850s, when the transatlantic slave trade became a renewed subject of debates in the public sphere, denunciations of US citizens making fortunes out of the illegal business filled the papers. These ignored the fact—well known to British and US authorities—that the business was generally financed and carried by foreigners, a view that occasionally made into the newspapers but had much less political appeal. As we will see in Chapter 7, there were a few US individuals at the center of slave-trading operations, such as Charles Lamar and Timothy Meaher. Like James D'Wolf in the early 1800s, Lamar and Meaher were the main figures behind the financing and organization of a few expeditions that disembarked slaves in the South. From a broader perspective, however, their cases were exceptions in all respects. Evidence of US ownership of slave voyages in the last phase of the transatlantic slave trade, as earlier with Brazil, is nearly absent. In Cuba, where the system of joint-stock companies became the norm, the British consul believed that "American capitalists" had bought shares of one of these expeditions through agents from Boston and New Orleans.[4] The consul did not furnish any names, and we should not discard the possibility that US investors were shareholders. The existing evidence, however, indicates that the vast majority of voyages and shares remained under the control of Spanish Cuban and Portuguese slave traders. The issue of ownership is especially complicated in this final era (as US courts found out) because of the common slave-trading strategy of placing the own-ership of the vessel under the name of the US captain or other obscure US citizens. The British consul in New York perfectly summed up the situation:

> Excepting as shipmasters to navigate ships from hence to the coast of Africa, and as brokers and agents in facilitating the operations of principals, very few if any native American citizens in the northern states are engaged in this traffic. I know the names of some ten or twelve of the principal trad-ers residing here. All are Spaniards, Cubans or Portuguese by birth; and several have accumulated great wealth from this nefarious traffic. In the South there are, doubtless, some Native Americans interested; but I question if, besides the Wanderers cargo, more than one, or at most two other car-goes have been landed in Florida. The newspaper accounts of arrivals of such cargoes are due to political motives, and a design to make capital of these rumors at the approaching presidential election.[5]

Authorities in the United States generally shared similar views about the slave trade carried under the US flag and from US ports. "It appears as far as I can know that in the majority of cases in which our flag is used in this traffic," the commodore of the Africa Squadron ob-served in 1857, "that it is by vessels sailing from the port of New York, owned by Portuguese and other foreigners, who obtain the right to carry it by a short residence in our country and that in most if not all cases said vessels are manned not by Americans, but by foreigners."[6]

Many of these foreigners were the same slave traders and associ-ates that had been driven out of the traffic to Brazil by the authorities in the early 1850s. In the immediate aftermath of Brazilian abolition it seemed that many of them had abandoned the illegal business. Many Portuguese slave traders returned to Portugal with significant capital, a process that had actually started during the 1840s as a consequence of British abolitionist pressure. The British consul in Lisbon believed that between three hundred and four hundred Portuguese nationals involved in the slave trade had voluntarily left Brazil between March 1850 and March 1851 carrying about £400,000 with them. Excited by the apparent end of the slave trade to Brazil, Lord Palmerston stated in the House of Commons that he had been informed by the British consuls at Lisbon and Porto "that 140 traders who had been settled in Brazil had fled over to Portugal, and had invested their gains in lands and houses." Another proof of the end of the slave trade to Brazil, he continued, was that "a large floating capital of £1,200,000 has recently been withdrawn from these pursuits, and has been invested in setting up a bank of discount at Lisbon." Manoel Pinto da Fonseca, in fact, described in his last will and testament that most of his fortune was in banks and companies' shares. Tomás da Costa Ramos, João Pedro da Costa Coimbra, and Antônio Gomes Brandão all allegedly invested their capital in the construction of a railroad in southern Portugal.[7]

Many individuals, however, redirected their activities to the growing slave trade to Cuba while maintaining the hope for a reopening of the traffic to Brazil. The Spanish, as we have seen, had formally prohibited the slave trade to the island through a treaty with Britain in 1817. In 1845, a penal law was passed abolishing the traffic. Most captains general in the 1850s would not enforce the law to the point where Cuban planters could be economically damaged. In 1851, a British commissioner wrote that the recently appointed captain general, José Gutiérrez de la Concha (1850–52), had said that if he could convince himself that no further importations of slaves were necessary for the agricultural wealth of the island, he would enforce the law. Should he "not come to this conclusion, he will be disposed more or less to wink at a farther importation of blacks." The people who supplied this information to the British official still believed that few slaves, if any, would be illegally disembarked on Cuba.[8]

All the optimism was misplaced as rising prices of sugar led to a dramatic increase in the number of slave disembarkations during the 1850s. Present estimates indicate that the slave trade to the island nearly doubled from the 1840s to the 1850s, as the disembarkation of 68,950 slaves between 1840 and 1849 rose to 111,661 in the following decade. It is important to note, however, that in the absence of the penal law, which inflated the price of slaves (the lieutenant-governor of Trinidad, for ex-

ample, allegedly received fifty-one thousand dollars in bribes for allowing one disembarkation in 1860), this volume could have been two or
three times larger. It was precisely because some authorities refused to
cooperate that bribes became so essential to the Cuban slave trade, with
officials occasionally trying to enforce the law within the limits imposed
by the geopolitical tensions among the United States, Britain, and Spain.
Officials had to find a balance between showing the will to extinguish
the illegal trade (in order to maintain the strategic support of Britain
against external threats) and keeping the support of Cuban slaveholders
(who occasionally called for US annexation as a way of protecting slavery
in the island). A number of criminal prosecutions took place during the
decade, and even the influential Julián Zulueta, perhaps the wealthiest
sugar planter and slave trader in Cuba, spent a few months in jail. The
government of Captain General Juan de la Pezuela (1853–54) was particularly marked by conflicts with Cuban planters because of his stronger efforts against the slave trade to the island. Pezuela established in
his first decree that governors and lieutenant-governors who connived
with the illegal disembarkation of slaves in their provinces would be removed from office, as actually happened in Trinidad and Santo Spiritus.
Afterward he tried to modify the 1845 law with a registration scheme
for all slaves in Cuba so that authorities could identify illegally introduced captives. José Gutiérrez de la Concha (1854–59) assumed the post
of captain general for a second time and immediately canceled Pezuela's
decree, assuring planters that his officials would not enter their plantations. Concha's main concern was maintaining the stability of slavery
and gaining the support of Cuban planters, politics that were continued
by his successor, Francisco Serrano (1859–62). The context demanded
a public attitude against the slave trade and occasional actions to curb
the illegal business were occasionally taken by Concha and Serrano, but
both were careful not to cut off the flow of enslaved Africans to the plantations or stimulate the dissatisfaction of Cuban planters.[9]

It was in this turbulent context that, with the abolition of the Brazilian slave trade, some of the deported slave traders attempted to transfer their operations to Cuba, an effort that Cuban authorities quickly cut
short. Antonio Severino de Avellar, a Portuguese trader from the Brazilian traffic who was, he said, just passing through Havana on his way to

the United States, told the Brazilian police that he was given twelve days to leave the island by the captain general. The failure of Portuguese slave traders to establish themselves in Cuba was a consequence of the new requirements of the business in its final phase. With the penal law and the increased bribes, only such well-connected individuals as Julián Zulueta, Francisco Feliciano Ibañez, José Luis Baró, Mariano Borrell, Francisco Martí, and Nicolás Martínez de Valdiviso, most of whom owned estates and had strong connections to local authorities, had the ability to safely organize the disembarkation of slaves on Cuba. Captain General Francisco Serrano—who, according to British authorities, facilitated the illegal disembarkation of enslaved Africans on the island—was a relative of Borrell.[10]

The leading slave traders in the last phase of the transatlantic slave trade according to the *Voyages* database are shown in table 6.1. A central problem for historians is that the period was marked by a multitude of nominal owners as the organization of the business changed and new strategies to circumvent the law emerged. Moreover, the predominance of figures such as Julián Zulueta and other Spaniards over the slave trade to the island is underrepresented here. Historian José G. Cayuela Fernández estimates that between 1854 and 1859, Zulueta was responsible for the introduction of sixteen thousand enslaved Africans. He was followed by Feliciano Ibáñez, who introduced between ten thousand and eleven thousand captives, Francisco Martí, responsible for the disembarkation eight thousand captives, and the Count of Cañongo, with five thousand captives. By 1860, Zulueta probably owned more slaves than anyone else in Cuba, the result of his multiple roles in slave-trading operations to the island. Well-connected to captains general and maintaining the reputation of a great respectable merchant, Zulueta even visited Spain in 1848 to lobby for easier regulations on the slave trade. "After allowing for the fact that many ventures are linked with individuals who were merely nominal owners," David Eltis argues, "it seems likely that only a minority of successful ventures sold their cargo in this period without Zulueta's involvement in some capacity."[11]

With Brazil and Cuba practically closed to Portuguese slave traders, most of those willing to continue in the illegal business established their bases of operations in Lisbon and New York during the early 1850s.

Table 6.1. Leading slave traders in the Voyages database, 1851 and 1866

Name	Voyages	Slaves disembarked
Zulueta, Julian de	14	7,891
Oliveira Botelho, Antonio Augusto de	11	4,835
Cunha Reis, Manoel Basílio da	9	2,931
Drinkwater, Frederick	5	637

Source: www.slavevoyages.org

After receiving denunciations and intercepting letters written from Lisbon by Francisco Rovirosa y Urgelles—the Spanish slave trader involved in the disembarkation of the *Camargo* (see Chapter 5)—the Brazilian police started an investigation that culminated in his interrogation and imprisonment in May 1853. When asked if it was true that he had continued to engage in the commerce of enslaved Africans, Rovirosa answered, "It was true that he had traded in said slaves but that he had not sent them to the Brazilian empire, having, on the contrary, sent them to the island of Cuba." Not only did he openly confess his involvement, but he named others who continued to engage in the illegal business. According to him, Tomás da Costa Ramos, Manoel Pinto da Fonseca, and João Pedro da Costa Coimbra in Portugal, as well as Antonio Augusto de Oliveira Botelho (who appears in second place in table 6.1) in the United States, were the main figures sending slaves to Cuba at the time.[12]

Oliveira Botelho had already been denounced for organizing slave voyages to Cuba in 1851. According to intelligence received by the British minister to Rio, he had sent at least four vessels from the United States. These ports, especially New York, became increasingly important for the outfitting of slave voyages over the decade, surpassing their Cuban counterparts after the mid-1850s. The key figures in this transformation were the Portuguese slave traders, at times referred as the Portuguese Company, who turned New York into a major slave-trading port. Although usually lumped by a few historians into a single large group, the Portuguese Company apparently was composed of many companies and partnerships formed throughout the 1850s. Besides Antonio Augusto de Oliveira Botelho, other main Portuguese slave traders in New York were Manuel Fortunato de Oliveira Botelho (Antonio Augusto's brother), Joaquim Teixeira Miranda, John Albert Machado, Gaspar José da Motta, J. Lima Vianna, the members of Abranches, Almeida & Co., José Lucas Henriques da Costa, and, perhaps the best known of them all, Manoel Basílio da Cunha Reis, who appears in third place on table 6.1.

Portuguese slave traders in Brazil during the 1840s were tightly connected to the African end of their networks. Cuban importers of the 1850s, by contrast, generally had no control over slave establishments in Africa. As we have seen, that had been a persistent problem of the Spanish slave trade since the eighteenth century. In 1820, a British commissioner in Cuba described how Spanish slavers had to go to Mozambique because "the Portuguese will not give them any good negroes at their installments" in West Africa. Some Spanish slave traders managed to enter into the African side of the operations, but never to a degree comparable to the massive Portuguese presence in central supplying regions. Slave factories were either independently owned or held by the Portuguese slave traders of New York. The prominent role of the New York traders was especially true for West Central Africa (by far the main exporting region during the final years of the trade). Many of this group had previously been in charge of slave factories owned by Brazilian companies during the 1840s but had gone on to become owners of slave expeditions. In 1845, the British commissary judge at Sierra Leone complained that John Albert Machado, despite having been a supercargo for condemned slavers and an agent for Brazilian slave traders, was allowed to reside in the colony "and carry on in my opinion a very suspicious trade in Freetown." The African experience of these slave traders certainly helped them when they began to organize their own expeditions. By the late 1850s, a British commander pointed to the company of Cunha Reis as "the greatest slave-dealers on the Coast; they have factories at Punta Lenha, Embonma, Londono, Snake's Head, Moanda, Killongo, and Black Point."[13]

José da Silva Maia Ferreira—considered the father of Angolan literature—was also among the group of migrants that moved from Africa to New York in the aftermath of the Brazilian suppression of the transatlantic slave trade. The years of Maia Ferreira in the city are generally associated with his work for the Figanière brothers and his nomination as Portuguese vice-consul to New York in 1856. Before that date, however, Maia Ferreira was part of the slave-trading network of Portuguese residents of New York, being listed with a few others by Benguela authorities in 1855 for his involvement in the transatlantic slave trade. In a letter written from New York to the slave trader Antonio Severino de Avellar, Maia Ferreira stated that ships in New York were "very, very cheap." In another letter to Avellar, he said that Cunha Reis "will go there, and he can inform you better of all the losses that the authorities from here, especially from Customs, are causing to all vessels dispatched to the homeland of Othelo!"[14]

In one of the many letters found aboard the *Mary E. Smith,* captured in 1856, one of the Portuguese merchants on the African side of operations, Guilherme José da Silva Correa, described some of the characteristics of the traffic in the 1850s. Addressed to João José Vianna, one of the Portuguese New Yorkers, the letter revealed the persistent hopes that the traffic to Brazil could be reopened, which also attests to the much more costly environment that marked the slave trade to Cuba. "By virtue of accounts received from Rio, I learn that some business is on the point of being done for that place." Correa then instructed Vianna to buy a vessel "to carry 400 packages," observing that with forty-five to fifty pipes of water they could carry between 450 and 500 packages, which clearly meant slaves. "Baltimore is the best place for cheap vessels," he noted, and "the vessel is to come with the American flag." In a second letter, Correa instructed Vianna, who apparently was on board a slave vessel, to hand over the proceeds of his packages to Zulueta. Without Brazil, Portuguese slave traders would have to get used to Cuban planters being a fundamental part of their operations.[15]

With the relocation of Portuguese slave-trading networks in the United States, contrabandists had direct access to US vessels and depended less on US intermediaries. Some of these migrants became naturalized US citizens, owning and employing US vessels in slave expeditions. They played multiple roles, organizing their own voyages and acting as brokers or other intermediate functions to Spanish slave traders interested in using the US flag to cover their operations. The suspicious vessel *Atlantic,* for example, initially appeared as the property of Abranches but was in fact owned by the Spanish company of Pla, Franganelle and San Miguel of Havana. By playing the role of interme-diary themselves, the Portuguese slave-trading community came to see George Marsden—one of the key figures facilitating the use of the US flag in the Brazilian slave trade in the 1840s—as superfluous. After his arrest and deportation from Brazil in 1853, Marsden relocated to New York, where he continued to engage in slave-trading operations. One of the first cases involving the American was the *Grey Eagle,* a US vessel that disembarked 584 slaves in Cuba in 1854. British authorities found the vessel afterward and took it to the Philadelphia Circuit Court. The case led to arrests, including that of the Portuguese New Yorker John Albert Machado. He confirmed that he had advanced money to Mars-den, but on account of a Spaniard named Don Leoncio Riveiro. After Machado paid a three-thousand-dollar bail, Marsden escaped to Can-ada. Shortly after the case, the Cuban who owned the vessel wrote to Machado asking for another ship, offering sixteen thousand pesos. But the Portuguese apparently did not want to participate in another ven-ture after what had just happened. Machado had to deal with Marsden, who "unceremoniously" asked for money from Canada while preparing to move to Lisbon. A few months later, another slave trader wrote from Lisbon complaining about Marsden's arrival and describing him as a "headache."[16]

Another key aspect of the reorganization of Portuguese slave-trading networks in New York was the opportunity offered by the exist-ing legitimate trade (especially in palm oil) between the United States and Africa. Like other Portuguese New Yorkers, Machado skillfully equipped his vessels for the legal produce trade to cover his unlawful operations. According to an article published in the 1860s, when the il-legal dimension of his activities came to the forefront, "it is said that he has been for some fifteen years engaged in legitimate and illegitimate trade with the Coast, making his ventures in palm oil, ivory, and ne-groes, with impartial zeal and varying profits."[17] Machados's "operations in the slave-trading business were conducted with a cunning & secrecy," a US authority reported, "to which his compatriots and colleagues, J Lima Viana, Botelho, Abranches Almeida & Co, Figaniere, &c did not think it worthwhile to resort." He fitted out his vessels at different ports and used the name of his wife to cover his operations. "By liberal bribery during the period when slave-trading had not yet become unpopular in New York," the report continued, "he contrived to escape notice & detection for a long time." Only after 1860 would Machado's name surface in the many slave-trading cases that US newspapers denounced and publicized.[18]

The Portuguese resident in New York also took advantage of the temporary protection offered by the Portuguese consulate. Unlike Proffitt, Wise, Tod, Gordon, and other US diplomats in Brazil, Portuguese representatives in the United States rarely mentioned any of the conflicts involving slave traders in their dispatches of the first half of the 1850s. The main figures of the so-called Portuguese Company actually maintained the status of respectable merchants. At a meeting of Portuguese residents in New York organized in 1856, a committee was appointed to raise funds for the people of the Cape Verde Islands, who had been experiencing food shortages. One of the five figures of the committee was Manoel Basílio da Cunha Reis. The group immediately raised more than two thousand dollars, with Cunha Reis and Antonio Augusto de Oliveira Botelho appearing as the largest contributors. The poet José da Silva Maia Ferreira also made a contribution. The reputable status of the main Portuguese slave traders probably explains their close relationship with Portuguese consulates in the United States during the 1850s. In Lisbon itself, historian João Pedro Marques has shown how, despite the official abolition of the slave trade and the frequent denunciations of the business by authorities and the press, individual slave traders were rarely the object of criticism. Indeed, many of the major figures deported from Brazil in the early 1850s became fully integrated into Portuguese society on their return. José Bernardino de Sá was ennobled as Baron of Vila Nova do Minho, while Manoel Pinto da Fonseca would be remembered shortly after his death in 1855 as a great man who had "applied his capital in useful works for the nation."[19]

The main Portuguese diplomats in the United States during the 1850s were Joaquim César de Figanière e Mourão and his son, César Henrique Stuart de la Figanière. Joaquim had been part of a mixed commission in Sierra Leone in 1820. In the following decades he occupied other positions within the Portuguese government, including minister

to Brazil around 1839, when he constantly complained of irregular captures of Portuguese vessels by the British navy. During most of the 1850s,
he worked in Washington as Portuguese minister to the United States
while his son, César Henrique Stuart de la Figanière, worked as the Portuguese consul general at New York. His other son, Guilherme (William) de la Figanière, a naturalized US citizen, worked together with his
brother as a merchant, allegedly dealing mainly with wine importation.[20]

One of the tasks of César Figanière as consul general in New York
was to defend the interests of Portuguese merchants. Therefore, when
the government of Haiti captured the Portuguese vessel *Ceres* as a suspected slaver, César Figanière immediately wrote to the French consul
in the island asking him to protect Portuguese property in case "Haitian authorities had proceeded arbitrarily and without proof against
them." If the French consul confirmed that the vessel was a slaver, César
Figanière declared that he would immediately stop acting on behalf of
the arrested individuals. The consul, however, provided passports and
documents to some well-known slave traders who bought vessels in the
United States, including Manoel Antonio Teixeira Barboza from Benguela (whose sponsor was John Albert Machado) and Antonio Augusto
de Oliveira Botelho. Suspicions that César de la Figanière connived with
slave traders significantly increased, however, after documents found on
board a seized slaver implicated Manoel Basílio da Cunha Reis in the
illegal business. Cunha Reis had been a member of Figanière, Reis &
Co., a company involving himself and the brothers César and Guilherme
Figanière. In a few cases, Cunha Reis appeared to be taking advantage
of the reputation of his partners to advance his interests. When a company in Rio de Janeiro stated that it would not deal with a slave trader,
he assured them that his partners were engaging solely in "legitimate
commerce."[21]

The advantages offered by the strong connections of the Portuguese on the African coast and in New York were counterpoised by their
continuing dependence on Cuban networks to sell the slaves. Many of
the documents of transactions involving the Portuguese New Yorkers
specify major Cuban merchants such as Julián Zulueta, Salvador de Castro, and others as financers at the Cuban end. There is some evidence
that the voyage of the *Echo*—the famous case used by pro-slave-trade

agitators in the South to promote their views—had Manoel Basílio da Cunha Reis as one of its main organizers (despite the district attorney's attempts to prove that the vessel was owned by the captain). According to the British consul at Charleston, the crew of the *Echo* was "plentifully supplied with money for their defense and their wants, drafts to a large amount having been forwarded to them from the Havannah."[22]

Dependence on Cuban capital and intermediaries also led to many conflicts in transactions within the Spanish island, involving occasional frauds and other problems. In a series of letters intercepted by the Brazilian police, slave traders in New York complained throughout 1854 of payment problems in Cuba. In one case, Don Salvador de Castro, another important Cuban financer of slave voyages, kept apologizing for not paying for recent deliveries while Portuguese slave traders discussed among themselves the best strategy to ensure payment. In October 1854, the Portuguese slave trader Gaspar José da Motta wrote to his partner Antonio Severino de Avellar of a failed attempt from a third person to settle the account with Don Salvador "because General Concha believed that it shouldn't be through these means that the services should be paid." Unfortunately, there are no details of how the issue was settled, but according to Motta, another slave trader had just written that in order to retaliate against individuals in Trinidad, "he will deliver to the English consul all the documents he has." Although these letters do not give a complete picture of the issues at stake, they do show the conflicts that marked the interactions between Portuguese and Cuban slave-trading networks as well as the presence of the captain general in the transaction. In the case of the *Pierre Soulé,* a joint-stock venture with twenty-eight owners, the director of the operation, José Lucas Henriques da Costa, described the difficulties he faced after disembarking the 479 slaves (referred throughout his letters as "volumes") in Cuba. Most of the owners lived in Benguela, although a few of the Portuguese New Yorkers, such as the poet José da Silva Maia Ferreira and José Lucas himself, also had slaves on board. After postponing the payment many times under "frivolous excuses," the Cuban buyers finally refused to pay for the slaves under the excuse that most of them were too small. Only after soliciting the support of other Havana merchants was Lucas able to receive partial payment of $85,000. With losses amounting to

$48,000, Lucas remarked that he had at least completed the voyage even though Cunha Reis was in jail and an order for his own imprisonment had been issued. The more autonomous African traders in West Africa also had problems in Cuba. The British consul at Lagos wrote in 1857 that since 1854 the Cuban dealers "have rendered the most unsatisfactory returns to the shippers here of their consignments." A vessel dispatched by some well-known Havana dealers to Africa for slaves was returned without anyone on board because no one would "be shipped on freight and consignment from hence unless the vessel is sent by some firm in the Havana on whom every reliance can be placed for fair dealing."[23]

Cuban slave traders had alternative sources of US vessels and flag, since they had their own connections to Spanish companies established both in New York and in New Orleans, the second main slave-trading port in the United States. One of the New Orleans intermediaries was the house of Golden, Shaw, and Lespanna, which, according to a British naval officer, received the "principal shareholders, or an accredited agent provided with funds" from Havana every time slave expeditions were organized in Cuba. The British consul in New Orleans replied to the denunciation saying that the company in question did business as brokers and agents for vessels trading between New Orleans, Havana, and Veracruz. "It is possible that they may be employed by parties for the purchase of vessels, which are afterwards destined for the Slave Trade," the consul continued, "but I should doubt very much the accuracy of the statement that they find the funds or have any interest in the venture." This is probably the same kind of services that other Spanish companies in the United States such as Prats, Pujol & Co., Jiménez, Martínez & Lafitte, Gregorio Tejedor & Cia, and Justo Mazorra & Co. provided to Cuban slave traders. These companies, however, were not as well connected to the African end of the business as the Portuguese New Yorkers, which explains the pervasive presence of the Portuguese Company in slave-trading operations throughout the 1850s.[24]

The Numbers of US Participation in the Cuban Slave Trade

In an analysis of the period between 1820 and 1850, W. E. B. Du Bois argued that the rise in slave prices caused by the combination of industrial development and anti-slave-trade legislation in the United States, Brazil, and Cuba attracted US capital and enterprise to the illegal business. According to him, "The American slave-trade finally came to be carried principally by United States capital, in United States ships, officered by United States citizens, and under the United States flag." If we add the transformation of US ports into slave-trading headquarters during the 1850s, his statement offers a baseline against which to evaluate the evidence on all these forms of US participation in the final era of the transatlantic slave trade.[25]

Of all the types of US involvement described by Du Bois, the predominance of US-built vessels in the transatlantic slave trade was certainly the most prominent. These vessels were more preponderant in Cuba during the last phase of the transatlantic slave trade (table 6.2) than in Brazil during the previous decade (see table 5.1). Estimates are that 192,452 enslaved Africans were carried on vessels built in the United States, the equivalent to almost 90 percent of all slaves disembarked in the Americas between 1851 and 1866. It is important to note, however, that, first, these vessels did not necessarily fly the US flag (see table 6.3) and, second, US-built vessels became predominant in all phases of long-distance commerce during this era, not only in the slave trade.

Second to the United States came England, whose steamers such as the *Quevedo* and the *Cicerón* were increasingly used by slave traders (table 6.2). Estimates are that at least twelve voyages were organized with British-built vessels, responsible for the disembarkation of more than seven thousand captives in Cuba during the final era of the slave trade. A few voyages were also organized with vessels built in Africa. This was a reflection of increasing abolitionist pressure in the later phase of the transatlantic slave trade, when factors on the African coast increasingly accumulated functions that had until then been spread across the Atlantic (a process that gave some leverage to the Portuguese New Yorkers in their interactions with Cuban slave traders). As the seizures of vessels based on slave-trading equipment increased, manacles and slave decks were manufactured locally with iron and other local materials. This process culminated in the construction of a few vessels with local woods in Africa, most of them along the Congo River.[26]

Du Bois was also correct to point out the pervasive presence of

Table 6.2. Estimated number of vessels and the slaves they
embarked by country of ship construction, 1851–66

Ship construction	Voyages	Percentage	Slaves
Spain	20	6	12,180
Portugal	4	1	2,436
England	12	3	7,308
United States	313	89	192,452
Central Africa	4	1	2,436
Total	353	100	216,813

Note: Brazil was excluded as a destination for these estimates. This table is based
on a sample of 89 voyages with a known country of construction. To construct
the estimates I used the total number of embarked slaves from the estimates page
in the Voyages database between 1851 and 1866 for all destinations except Brazil
(216,797 captives). I divided this number by the average of embarked slaves by
vessel for the same period (614.2) to derive the total number of voyages for the
period in question (353 voyages). Row 1 distributes these voyages according to
breakdown of the sample of 89 with known country of construction. Row 2 is
row 1 multiplied by the average number of slaves embarked. The discrepancy
between the total number of embarked slaves on the table and in Voyages is due
to rounding.
Source: www.slavevoyages.org

the US flag in the business, although it is important to note that US colors only became predominant in the second half of the 1850s and that
many vessels actually abandoned the flag and documentation altogether
in inbound voyages as anti-slave-trade pressure increased. The Spanish flag was the most used between 1851 and 1854, responsible for the
embarkation of 59.3 percent of all enslaved Africans during the period
(table 6.3). There is no evidence of the US flag being used in 1851, but
in the following three years vessels flying the Stars and Stripes would
embark 10,528 enslaved Africans. The years 1854 and 1855 saw a dramatic
decrease in the use of the Spanish flag, a possible reflection of the anti-
slave-trade actions of Captain General Pezuela. After being arrested in
the United States, Captain James Smith of the slaver *Julia Moulton* said
in an interview that Pezuela had seized his latest cargo to Cuba, worth

Table 6.3. Estimated number of vessels and the slaves they embarked by flag flown at point of departure from the Americas to Africa, 1851–58

	1851–54			1855–58		
	Voyages	Slaves	Percentage	Voyages	Slaves	Percentage
Spain	57	30,626	59.3	25	13,895	28.3
Portugal	20	10,528	20.4	4	2,138	4.3
United States	20	10,528	20.4	61	33,134	67.4
Total	97	51,682	100	90	49,167	100

Note: This table is based on a sample of 100 voyages for which data on the flag are available. For the methodology employed, see table 5.2. Discrepancy in totals is due to rounding.

Source: www.slavevoyages.org

$220,000. "He did more to break up the slave trade than any one else. If he had remained in office he would have stopped it altogether. But now Concha is back again, and it goes on as flourishing as ever."[27]

In 1854, the number of slaves embarked under the US flag (2,679 captives) surpassed the number of those carried under Spanish colors (1,743 captives). The role of the US flag increased over the decade, although the Spanish flag continued to be used. Between 1854 and 1856, the difference between the numbers of slaves embarked under each flag was not great. In 1857, however, there is evidence of the embarkation of 6,438 enslaved Africans under the US flag against 1,798 under the Spanish. The following year, this difference increased dramatically as a consequence of the retreat of the British navy (see Chapter 7). That year at least 11,070 enslaved Africans were embarked under the US flag against 1,653 under the Spanish. By using these data to estimate the number of slaves carried under each flag, we see that the US flag was responsible for the embarkation of 33,134 enslaved Africans between 1855 and 1858, or 67.4 percent of the total. Most other captives were embarked on vessels flying the Spanish flag (28.3 percent).[28]

A central problem in the interpretation of Du Bois's work is his description of the pervasive presence of US capital in the transatlantic slave trade, especially if we consider US capital in the more strict sense of direct financing (the area most affected by the anti-slave-trade legislation passed in the first two decades of the nineteenth century). As David Eltis argues, "The locus of control and the source of the capital for the Cuban trade was Cuba itself." The foremost owners of ventures during the final period of the slave trade were Portuguese or Spanish (see table 6.1). The Portuguese resident in New York both acted as intermediaries for others and organized their own voyages, drawing on their strong connections on the African end of the trade. Spanish companies in both the United States and Cuba were direct owners of slaving ventures but relied on Portuguese intermediaries, especially on the African coast.

Frederick Drinkwater (the only non-Iberian name to appear on table 6.1) does not seem to have been a participant in the same ways that Botelho, Cunha Reis, and Zulueta were. He was part of the group of captains and former captains who had been offering their services to Portuguese, Brazilian, and Spanish slave traders since at least 1835. Described by the US vice-consul in Cuba as a "well-known American shipmaster from Portland," Drinkwater appeared as the owner of five vessels that disembarked slaves in Cuba between 1857 and 1858. The same vice-consul would later note that at the time Drinkwater purchased the five vessels, he "was in the employ of, or in some way connected in business with, Mr. Antonio Cabarga," a well-known Spanish slave trader.[29]

Figures such as Frederick Drinkwater became a common feature of the transatlantic slave trade in its final era, partially confirming Du Bois's assertion that US captains became predominant in the business. Down to the Civil War many US citizens captained slave voyages while acting as dummy owners for slave traders in Cuba. The only slave trader ever to be hanged under the 1820 US law, Nathaniel Gordon, falls into this category, as does Drinkwater. However, it is important to note, first, that it is hard to estimate how many US captains actually captained the inbound voyages of slave expeditions. Many simply sold their vessel on the coast of Africa (or in Cuba, but deliverable in Africa) and returned to the United States as passengers, being able, in this way, to escape conviction in US courts. Second, a large number of them were naturalized US citizens. According to a report on the role of a Spanish company from New Orleans, its initial action was choosing a master, "and for this a naturalized citizen is always preferred to a native-born American. . . . The master selects a vessel, and, being provided with money by the agent or owner, buys her and registers her in his own name as master and sole owner. The vessel is then fitted out with the assistance of the firm above named [Golden, Shaw, and Lespanna]." As in Brazil, then, these individuals operated with money advanced by the big slave traders of Cuba.[30]

The pervasive presence of naturalized US captains was part of wider transformations in the US seafaring world during the first half of the century. The intensification of long-distance commerce after the Napoleonic Wars went hand-in-hand with tighter discipline and less autonomy aboard the vessels, which led young Americans to avoid working as seamen in favor of commercial pursuits on land. The result was an increase in the number of foreign sailors in the US merchant force and a subsequent easing by the US government of the naturalization process of non-US sailors. In 1843, Congress abolished the requirement for seamen to purchase citizenship certificates and, in 1847, officially reduced the residency clause of an 1813 law (five continuous years of residence) for those awaiting citizenship. It was in this context that a number of foreigners became naturalized US slave captains. The preference for naturalized citizens in slave-trading operations was an important strategy to elude the authorities in the event of a capture or a trial. Many court cases ended without convictions because of the problems in establishing not only the ownership of the vessel but also the citizenship of arrested captains. Louis Krafft and Charles Rauch, captains who had already been involved in the slave trade to Brazil during the 1840s (see Chapter 5), continued their activities with Cuban slave traders. The first was a Frenchmen and the second an Austrian, both naturalized US citizens.[31]

One important element missing in Du Bois's assessment is the important role played by US ports as points of departure of slave voyages during the 1850s (table 6.4). The organization of slave expeditions in US ports had nearly disappeared in the three decades that followed the anti-slave-trade law of 1820. By the 1840s, a few slave voyages departed from the United States, but only by the 1850s did such US ports as New Orleans and New York become central for slave-trading operations. The

Table 6.4. Estimated number of vessels and the slaves they embarked by broad region of departure from the Americas to Africa, 1851–58

	1851–54			1855–58		
	Voyages	Slaves	Percentage	Voyages	Slaves	Percentage
Europe	4	1,988	3.8	—	—	—
United States	30	15,902	30.8	51	27,656	56.3
Caribbean	56	19,816	57.7	39	21,511	43.8
Brazil	7	3,976	7.7	—	—	—
Total	97	51,682	100	90	49,167	100

Note: This table is based on a sample of 58 voyages. For methodology, see table 5.2.
Source: www.slavevoyages.org

years 1851–54 reflect the transition between the Brazilian and the Cuban slave trade, with some voyages still being organized in Brazil and Europe. Most of them (57.7 percent) were nevertheless organized in Cuba itself, a situation that shifted during the decade. Brazilian and European ports disappeared in the years 1855–58 and US ports surpassed their Cuban counterparts. In these years at least 27,656 enslaved Africans are estimated to have embarked on vessels that departed from the United States, especially New York. The decrease in the participation of Cuban ports may also have been a direct effect of the anti-slave-trade efforts put into practice by Captain General Pezuela in 1854. Evidence of slave voyages starting at Havana and other Cuban ports reappeared only by 1857.

Despite the historiographic emphasis on the connections between US and Brazil during the 1840s, it was undoubtedly Cuba that allowed the US connection to flourish. The participation of the United States in the transatlantic slave trade increased over the 1850s, whether we look at the use of the US flag, the number of voyages organized in US ports, or the percentages of US-built vessels in the illegal business. The second half of the decade was, therefore, the period that best fits Du Bois's assessment. One key feature of his interpretation, however—the presence

of US capital—needs to be radically revised. Despite the pervasive presence of the US flag, ships, and ports, the slave-trading networks continued to be controlled mainly by Portuguese and Spanish slave traders,
who took advantage of the spaces opened by the tensions between the
North American slaveholding republic and the British Empire.

Tensions and Strategies

The challenges faced by US representatives in Cuba were in many respects similar to those faced by their counterparts in Brazil during the
1840s. As Henry Wise and others had done in Rio de Janeiro during the
previous decade, figures such as Andrew K. Blythe, Thomas Savage, and
Charles Helm, denounced and tried to curb the use of US vessels and
the US flag in the slave trade to Cuba. Although there is evidence of a
few slave voyages under the US flag departing from Cuba in the first
half of the 1850s, it was in 1857 that their number significantly increased,
with the disembarkation of almost four thousand enslaved Africans in
the island under the US flag. That year consul Blythe wrote to the US
secretary of state to inform the government of what he saw as a defect in
the law of 1803 regulating the sales of vessels, a loophole that allowed US
vessels to be employed in the transatlantic slave trade. The complaint
was very similar to those made by US consuls in Brazil. Sea letters conceded by consuls in these transactions allowed slave traders to maintain
the US character of vessels in their voyages to Africa. Blythe also wrote
to the secretary of state to ask about how much evidence was needed for
him to arrest people suspected of engaging in the slave trade and send
them for trial in the United States. The question was forwarded to the
attorney general, who answered that although consuls were not judges,
they could detain individuals involved in crimes committed on board
US ships—whether they were on the high seas or in foreign ports—and
remit them to the United States.[32]

Thomas Savage, vice-consul at Havana, also made similar complaints, constantly providing information of US vessels sold at Havana
that became suspected slavers and refusing the clearance of some of
them. "My efforts in detecting and putting a stop, in this place, to the
prostitution of the American flag for purposes of slave trading," Sav-

age wrote, "have created a considerable excitement and hostility to me among a certain class of persons here." More than once, Savage asked for instructions regarding his powers to refuse the documents for suspected slavers. With his investigations and denunciations, the vice-consul made possible the condemnation of at least two vessels, the *Lyra* and the *Charles Perkins.* He also refused clearance for other suspected vessels, getting into a conflict with the captain of the *Ardennes,* who did not accept the condition imposed by Savage that the ship should go directly to Key West before proceeding to Africa. As Henry Wise had argued for 1840s Brazil, Savage believed that there was no lawful trade between Cuba and Africa. "The truth is," the US consul argued, "all this talk about lawful trade amounts to nothing at all. The parties concerned deem it safer to fit out their expeditions in ports of Cuba, and, unfortunately, always find American citizens willing to lend their names and their services to enable such parties to have the use of the American flag to cover their iniquities."[33]

The case of the *Nancy* may be the best example of the challenges faced by the consul. Spanish authorities seized the New Orleans vessel for being equipped for the slave trade before its departure from Havana. As in most cases of US vessels outfitted for the slave trade in the island, it could be traced back to a Cuban slave trader, in this case an individual named Don Ramón de Guerediaga. The captain general of Havana contacted the US consulate to ask for the documents of the vessel and the consul's help in investigating the case. The consul saw himself in a complex position: although he was fighting US involvement in the slave trade, he had to guarantee that the American captain and members of the crew received a fair trial in Cuba. The captain wrote many letters to Savage from prison to convince him that the voyage to Africa was legal. After his release from prison, the captain accused the consul of inducing the crew to give false testimony about the vessel to justify its seizure. According to Savage, the captain had received help in the production of these letters from the surveyor general of New Orleans, Francis D. Newcomb, but especially from Cuban slave traders such as Antonio Cabarga. Captain Williams became "the instrument of a certain set of slave traders in this city, who have been, for some time past, making use of our flag for their nefarious purposes, and whose exponent and abettor is

Don Antonio Cabarga, a shipcandler." According to the consul, Cabarga had been involved in the transactions not only of the *Nancy* but also of the *Lydia Gibbs* and the *Cortez*. This is the same individual who appears connected to the US captain Frederick Drinkwater, emerging as a key figure in the schemes involving the selling of US vessels in Cuba for slave-trading purposes.[34]

Whereas US representatives in Cuba faced institutional limits to their actions and the opposition of a large part of the public opinion, authorities in the United States acted in a very different environment. The district attorneys of Massachusetts and of Southern New York, respectively B. F. Hallett and John McKeon, repeatedly tried to condemn slavers and stop the departure of slave vessels from their states. In June 1856, the State Department wrote to McKeon about denunciations sent from Africa that the slave trade was still being carried on by vessels sailing from his state. The department hoped that this information, combined with that possessed by McKeon, could bring to justice those individuals in New York who still engaged in the transatlantic slave trade.[35]

John McKeon had been trying to dismantle the slave-trading networks of Portuguese New Yorkers since at least 1854, when the *Julia Moulton* (4191), a US vessel that departed from New York, embarked 660 slaves south of the Congo River and disembarked them in Cuba for the consignee Don Salvador de Castro. In September 1854, McKeon, who had "been actively engaged for some weeks past in ferreting out certain parties charged with fitting out vessels in New York for the purpose of trafficking in slaves," ordered the arrest of the captain of the vessel. Captain Smith was condemned to two years in jail and fined a thousand dollars. The arguments in the first phase of the trial revolved around the issue of his citizenship, whose true nationality, his lawyer argued, was German and his true name Schmidt. In a second phase, the issue of ownership emerged, with the jury investigating whether there was evidence of US ownership of the vessel. Smith's attorney suggested that the real owner of the vessel was a Portuguese named Lemos. A number of Portuguese residents in New York, including César Henrique de la Figanière, were called to depose about the slave trader. In his deposition, the consul said that he had some business transactions with Lemos but declined to describe their nature (one of his secretaries supposedly accompanied Captain Smith to Boston and paid for the vessel). The district attorney also asked whether he had transactions with Don Salvador de Castro, the consignee of the slaves disembarked by the *Julia Moulton,* and whether it was true that he had sent two barrels of rum and two barrels of wine aboard said vessel. The consul general refused to answer both questions. The case immediately made it into the newspapers, one describing the consul general's silence as indicating "that there are slave traffickers among us, bearing the seals of a foreign power."[36]

After reading a summary of the *Julia Moulton* case, the Portuguese minister of foreign affairs wrote to the Portuguese minister to the United States, Joaquim César de Figanière e Morão, asking about the consul general's refusal to answer the questions. The minister immediately wrote to his son for clarification. César Figanière answered that José Antunes Lopes Lemos had in fact appeared at the consulate in January 1853 but that their sole transaction was a deposit Lemos made to his house, Figanière Irmãos. (Other documents do, however, point to connections between Lemos and such New York slave traders as J. Lima Vianna.) As for the accusations that he sent a secretary to Boston to pay for the vessel or that he sent wine or liquor aboard the *Julia Moulton,* Figanière simply stated that these were false. After this answer, his father still found it necessary to warn César that he should not receive or give favors when performing his official duties and that he should restrict his consular acts to those in his official instructions.[37]

In early 1855, District Attorney McKeon again requested César Figanière's presence, this time in the case *US vs. Bartholomew Blanco.* Figanière refused to go, arguing that his position of consul general gave him the right not to participate. A subsequent series of exchanges between the district attorney and the consul general led to discussions between the US secretary of state and the Portuguese minister to the United States. In February, Figanière finally appeared in court to depose. According to him, his house had bought vessels for "transient persons," including Don Salvador de Castro, who used to come to his store. The consul made it clear, however, that "neither directly nor indirectly have I had anything to do with the slave business, nor never had any conversation with any of those parties in relation to the slave trade."[38]

As vessels implicating Manoel Basílio da Cunha Reis in the slave trade were captured, attacks and suspicions against the Portuguese consul in New York increased. In the case of the *Altiva* (formerly the *Onward*), a vessel suspected of being outfitted for the slave trade and owned by Cunha Reis, César Figanière was again called to depose. The consul said he was surprised to find out that the *Altiva* and other vessels cleared from New York were engaging in the slave trade. He denied any participation in the illegal business and argued that his government had in fact instructed him to refuse clearing to vessels employed in the slave trade. He also said that Cunha Reis had been on the coast of Africa for fifteen years and that "it was the habit of Consulate officers to receive money on deposit, &c., for various parties without inquiry." More evidence implicating the house of Figanière, Reis & Co. in the slave trade, however, continued to appear. Letters found aboard the *Mary E. Smith* by Brazilian authorities in 1856 showed Cunha Reis to be one of the owners of the venture. In a letter to the merchant house of Carvalho and Rocha from Rio de Janeiro, Cunha Reis discussed options for his payment "in the event of this vessel [the *Mary E. Smith*] being fortunate." If the vessel arrived before March 1856, Carvalho and Rocha should "ship hides and coffee on board any vessel to the consignment of Messrs. Figaniere Brothers of this city." These letters were not only published in the Parliamentary Papers in 1857 but also used by the Massachusetts district attorney to indict Cunha Reis. The district attorney had issued warrants against the *Mary E. Smith* before its departure from Boston, but the vessel had escaped because of "the imbecility of one of the revenue cutter officers." Also in 1856, another Portuguese official was accused of connivance with slave-trading interests. Augusto Lopes Baptista, the Portuguese vice-consul in Baltimore, was tried for his participation in the outfitting of the *C. F. A. Cole* (4214), a US vessel that had disembarked three hundred slaves in Cuba earlier that year for the house of Pedro Martinez.[39]

It was not long before US authorities asked for clarification from the Portuguese government on the relations between César Figanière and Manuel Basilio da Cunha Reis and on the role of Augusto Lopes Baptista in the case of the *C. F. A. Cole*. After Secretary of State William L. Marcy and the US minister in Lisbon contacted the Portuguese government, the Portuguese prime minister wrote to Joaquim César de Figanière e Morão for explanation. Joaquim's reaction was to meet with Marcy, and their conversation was later described in a long letter to the prime minister. Perhaps unaware of the recent findings aboard the *Mary E. Smith* and the new indictment prepared by the district attorney of Boston against Manoel Basílio da Cunha Reis, the Portuguese minister argued that his son's partnership with the slave trader started only a year and a half after the first accusation against Cunha Reis (for outfitting the *Altiva*) had appeared. The case had just been tried, with the acquittal of Cunha Reis. During the conversation, the minister acknowledged that "there were some Portuguese who were in the traffic," but stressed that he was "persuaded that many Americans were implicated in it; and in fact it is generally reported that the principal persons engaged in New York in this traffic are Americans; and such is the tenor of numerous articles which appear in the New York Papers." Those were, as discussed in Chapter 7, the same articles by Republicans and Democrats that had been using the New York traffic in their mutual accusations during the second half of the 1850s. He also argued that he had gone over all the books of his son's firm, and that it was impossible, considering the huge profits made in the slave trade, that his son could have been engaging in the illegal business (an argument that obviously ignored the many ways one could participate in the slave trade).[40]

After these events, the Portuguese government discharged César de la Figanière of his consular duties, but he and his brother continued to engage in suspicious transactions. When District Attorney McKeon ordered the capture of the *W. G. Lewis* as outfitted for the slave trade, the *New York Tribune* immediately published a note saying that the vessel was owned, at least in part, by "the same Mr. Figaniere who was not long since deprived of his position of Consul at this port for Portugal." The article mentioned that Lima Vianna had some interest in the suspicious cargo being shipped to Luanda, Angola, and that District Attorney "McKeon deserves the public thanks for his zeal in breaking up this business." It added, "If the laws were adequate to the work, the traffic would soon cease to have its center at New York."[41] César Figanière quickly wrote to the newspaper, complaining that he had no interest in the vessel and asking for a correction. The *New York Tribune* complied but added another note: true, the former consul was not the owner of the vessel; the actual owner was his brother, who sold it earlier in 1857 to an individual named Benjamin S. Wenberg. The article also stressed that their business partner, Cunha Reis, had been reported to be a slave trader in documents published by the US Senate in the preceding years. "If one partner sells a vessel to a man suspected of being concerned in the trade, which vessel is shortly afterward arrested as a slaver, and if another partner is himself engaged in it," the writer asked, "is it to be supposed that the third partner is entirely ignorant and uncompromised?" The issue continued to be the same one that we have seen in the controversies about US vessels sold in Cuba and Brazil in the previous decades: How does one prove intent? In this case, not only would the district attorney have to prove that the vessel had been sold intentionally to be employed in the slave trade, but the vessel itself would have to be examined as being truly outfitted for the slave trade, something the court ultimately failed to do. The vessel continued its course to Africa, with Joaquim César de Figanière e Morão taking the opportunity to accuse McKeon of persecuting his sons, who had never been found guilty of involvement in the slave trade. He did not foresee that the US Africa Squadron would capture the vessel once it reached the African coast. The Portuguese minister also complained of another article published by the *New York Tribune*—according to him, instigated by McKeon—about suspicions that a vessel with supplies to Cape Verde was supposedly redirected to the slave trade afterward. The initial information in the case, however, came from British officers, who accused the *North Hand* of having disembarked slaves in Cuba after leaving Cape Verde. The *New York Tribune*, based on information printed in the Parliamentary Papers, published a note stressing the presence of Figanière, Reis & Co. in the accusations. "Our suspended friend of the Portuguese Consulate is not quite so spotless as he would have us believe," the note read. "The idea of making the 'N. Hand' do double duty and fill the coffers of Messrs Figaniere, Reis & Co. at the same time that she relieved the famine from which the Cape de Verdes people were suffering, is certainly a novel one, and does great credit to its originator."[42]

Although the only evidence against Figanière, Reis & Co. is that it had a slave trader among its partners, the Figanière brothers were certainly operating in the gray area between legitimate commerce and the slave trade, as had Maxwell, Wright & Co. and other merchant houses previously around the Atlantic. The case also generated a reply from Guilherme Figanière to Lord Napier, whose accusations had been published in the Senate documents. He argued that no evidence could be found against his vessels and that, in the case of the *North Hand,* the firm had nothing to do with the vessel after it had completed the voyage to Cape Verde. "If she, after having delivered her cargo, went to the Coast for negroes," he continued, "the firm was no more accountable for the unlawful act than it would be for the commission of a murder in an office it had once occupied and from which it had moved before the crime was committed."[43]

To Joaquim César de Figanière e Morão, District Attorney Mc-Keon's actions were politically motivated. This view was also shared by slave traders, who argued that "approaching elections and the desire for popularity" were behind the *Grey Eagle* case—which resulted in John Albert Machado's temporary arrest and George Marsden's flight to Canada. Political capital may have indeed motivated McKeon and other US officers who fought US involvement in the transatlantic slave trade. That their actions had political significance, however, was a sign of how deeply entrenched opposition to the transatlantic slave trade had become within the North Atlantic. The British consul in New York observed that the number of articles against the slave trade printed in local newspapers indicated "an improvement in the tone of public sentiment in this country in regard to the defects of the laws, and the insufficiency of the means provided for the suppression of the traffic, no less than to the want of vigilance and energy in the conduct of the officials entrusted with the execution of the laws and treaties." When George William Gordon—one of the most active anti-slave-trade consuls in Brazil during the 1840s—ran for governor of Massachusetts in 1856, his party immediately published a short description of his past activities. Pedro Tovookan Parris, one of two Africans rescued by Gordon in the case of the *Porpoise,* supposedly made a series of campaign speeches for his election.[44]

The Portuguese consul general in New York after 1858, Thomas Ribeiro dos Santos, had a completely different attitude toward the involvement of Portuguese New Yorkers in the slave trade. In one of his

first messages to his government, he stated that "the Portuguese resident here are the ones who engage the most in this illicit commerce."
He mentioned cases of US vessels being taken to Africa by these men
without going through the required legal proceedings at his consulate.
In other letters Ribeiro dos Santos denounced the Portuguese slave traders, referring to Antonio Augusto de Oliveira Botelho as an "insolent"
slave trader responsible for having disembarked nine hundred Africans
in Cuba in 1858. The consul also accused Abranches, Almeida & Co. and
other Portuguese New Yorkers of engaging in the illegal slave trade. In
a conversation with the master of a Portuguese brig and a French merchant, Ribeiro dos Santos allegedly said that every Portuguese in New
York was a slave trader. Afterward he described his efforts to curb the
traffic and added that "if we had a Minister of a different quality than
the one we have, then I could do more than I have done. Since I am not
supported by the Minister, Mr. Figanière, I have been forced to look
for Lord Napier, through my internal friend, the consul of your British
Majesty. Nothing escapes me: as soon as I receive information about the
organization of an expedition I immediately communicate it to the English Minister." The consul had in fact provided information about the
Panchita, the *Ellen*, and the *Isla de Cuba*. The story was told by Figanière
himself, who angrily told the Portuguese minister of foreign affairs that
he would have to do something about the consul general's disrespectful
behavior.[45]

The increased pressure on the Portuguese New Yorkers led to a reorganization of the business in the late 1850s. The consul general in New
York and the vice-consul in Baltimore were first suspended and then
removed from their positions by the Portuguese government. Manoel
Basílio da Cunha Reis was arrested in 1858, which led him to move to
Havana later that year. According to a later report, the transformations
led to the reorganization of the business around two key figures: "For a
while there was one grand junta or monopoly in whose hands the business was concentrated, but divisions arising, the Slave-trading Company
split, one faction being led by Albert Horn and the other by Machado
and his mistress, Mary J. Watson." John Albert Machado continued to
provide intermediary services for Cuban slave traders while organizing
a few voyages himself. Albert Horn probably also worked as an inter-

mediary for foreign slave traders most of the time, but in the case of the *City of Norfolk,* there is no evidence that connects him to third parties. It is possible that Horn, like Machado, had owned a few vessels himself. As discussed in Chapter 7, both became the main slave traders operating in New York around 1860.[46]

Conclusion

Back in Cuba in 1858, Cunha Reis and a planter named Luciano Fernandez Perdones formed a company and sent a proposal to the captain general for a scheme to introduce contract laborers. The authors began by describing how Cuba entered the nineteenth century with great material progress through sugar and coffee production. However, deadly blows to the Cuban industry had been dealt, first, by the treaty of 1817 with Britain and, second, by the cholera outbreak of 1833. The main problem then became how to repopulate the Cuban fields, the basis of all wealth on the island. According to the authors, native Spanish immigrants would certainly be of interest for both Cuba and Spain, but they posed immense difficulties, starting with their high cost. Asian immigration had been tried with no success, since the individuals who came to the island were "perverse men, eminently criminals, used to stealing and killing." Indians in turn were weak and indolent. The solution was to be found—as had been the case throughout the century—in Africa, the source of laborers capable of enduring hard work during every season of the year. The company asked for authorization to introduce sixty thousand African contract laborers over the following decade.

The contract Cunha Reis and Fernandez Perdones presented can be read as an attempt to establish in Cuba a renewed version of the services offered by New York Portuguese slave-trading networks. The fourth article observed that if Spanish possessions in Africa could not provide enough contract laborers, these should be sought in Portuguese dominions such as Cabo Verde, Beaso, Cachio, Loanda, Benguela, Ambriz, and other ports. The fifth article was also key: if not enough workers could be found in Portuguese dominions either, the company should then be permitted to buy enslaved individuals (precisely where Cunha Reis and other Portuguese slave traders had factories). These enslaved

Africans would immediately "arrive in full liberty" and enter into a ten-year labor contract, after which they could renew their contract or return to their country. Other articles established that the workers would receive four pesos per month, two of which should be discounted to pay for clothes, shoes, and a sombrero. After these were paid, the remaining two pesos would be collected by the company to fund the voyage back to Africa for those who decided to return.[47]

The Spanish government did not accept the proposal, and it is unclear whether Cunha Reis was able to continue his slave-trading activities after moving to Cuba. In New York, however, the remaining Portuguese slave traders developed new strategies and continued to organize slave voyages to Cuba until the advent of the Civil War in 1861. The use of the US flag, citizens, vessels, and ports in the transatlantic slave trade persisted widely during the political crisis of the 1850s. The direct connection made by Republicans—and incorporated by part of the subsequent historiography—between a federal government dominated by slave power and the negligence of US authorities toward US participation in the transatlantic slave trade was less clear-cut. This interpretation was, of course, reinforced by the emergence of a pro-slave-trade movement in the South, which in fact managed to protect the few Southerners who organized slave-trading expeditions as well as, in a few cases, some individuals involved in the networks operating among New York, Africa, and Cuba. Although a consensus against the slave trade suffered setbacks in the South, it became more entrenched in the North with the growth of abolitionism after the later 1840s. The public's rejection of the nefarious traffic led many authorities to act with vigor against the slave-trading networks that had turned US ports into the bases of their operations, forcing them to adapt constantly to new situations.

On a deeper level, the survival of slavery in Cuba—which kept the transatlantic slave trade alive—depended on its North American counterpart. The central role played by the United States in the growth, persistence, and defense of slavery in the nineteenth century served as a guiding example for proslavery ideologues in both Brazil and Cuba. As Don Fehrenbacher argues, in international diplomacy, the US government "habitually assumed the role of a protector, and sometimes spoke even as a vindicator, of slavery." Not surprisingly, many Cuban Creoles saw annexation to the United States as the best way to keep slavery alive, using this prospect to curb the anti-slave-trade actions of the Spanish and British governments. Only the advent of the Civil War would shift the geopolitical configuration that kept those tensions alive.[48]

Crisis, 1859–1867

I n April 1864, the Lincoln administration undertook a controversial action. After a request from the Spanish government, Secretary of State William Seward ordered the immediate detention and extradition of a Spanish subject in New York. That man was José Agustín Arguelles, lieutenant governor of the district of Colón, Matanzas, and he had been in New York since March. On April 11, the *New York Herald* published a letter from its correspondent in Havana describing the recent case of a Cuban officer who had disappeared after selling two hundred Africans. The Africans were part of the cargo of more than a thousand captives found aboard the *Cicerón,* a slave steamer owned by the notorious Cuban slave trader Julián Zulueta. Cuban authorities, including Arguelles, captured the ship in November 1863. Though the letter did not mention his name, Arguelles immediately wrote a lengthy reply, entitled "Captain-General Dulce and the Slave-Traders of Cuba." He gave many details of the vessel's seizure and accused Cuba's captain general, Domingo Dulce y Garay, of having close connections to Zulueta. According to Arguelles, Dulce had ordered him to release all the slave traders who had been arrested in that seizure. He also detailed slave-smuggling strategies and named a number of individuals involved. By the time the story became public, however, Captain General Dulce had already contacted the US secretary of state, requesting Arguelles's extradition. US Marshal Robert Murray and other officers arrested the Spanish lieutenant-governor and put him on board a ship to Havana.[1]

The extradition generated mixed reactions in the United States. Abolitionists and some moderates praised the government's actions. "For the good of humanity this was demanded," said a letter published in the *New York Times*. "It is true that this Government, without an extradition treaty with Spain, was not legally obliged to do this; but, according to the custom and moral obligation devolving upon a nation, it was due." Many others, however, criticized the action. The British journalist George Augustus Sala, working in the United States as a reporter for the *Daily Telegraph*, wrote, "All New York is in a fever of indignation at the kidnapping, spiriting away, and ultimate deportation to Havana of Colonel Arguelles." Sala reproduced Arguelles's story without completely endorsing it. But to Sala, the slave trade was not the issue. A man had just been abducted from a country and delivered to the government of another without explanation. Sala argued that it was unlikely that Arguelles would ever again be seen alive: "Dead men tell no tales; and José Augustín Arguelles must know a great many things of a nature to compromise some of the most respectable people in Havana." Congressman Samuel S. Cox of Ohio in turn indicted the federal government for having violated the Constitution and the right of asylum. Twenty years later federal judge Henry Wade Rogers termed the executive action "an enormous usurpation of power."[2]

Considering Rogers's later comment, the response from Secretary of State Seward to the accusations was less than convincing. A committee was established to investigate, and Seward was called to testify. Although his response may have been largely unpersuasive, it provides a fascinating example of the radical changes wrought by the Civil War. Seward started by describing some of the reasons that called for actions from the executive under the auspices of the law of nations and the Constitution (without specifying how exactly the latter empowered the president for such actions). First, the country, "the refuge of the innocent and oppressed," should not offer asylum for "the guilty betrayer of human freedom." Second, the efforts of every government department to extinguish the slave traffic should not be checked. Finally, the victims of slave traffic should not be kept in captivity while the United

States sheltered a criminal (Arguelles's presence in Cuba was necessary, according to the Spanish minister, to prove that the 141 slaves had been illegally sold). Seward then cited a number of specialists on the law of nations and described a few other historical cases to assert that the action had been legitimate.

At one point Seward cited the opinions of William Wirt, US attorney general between 1817 and 1829. That period, as we have seen in Chapter 3, was marked by a number of legal cases in the United States involving foreign-owned slave ships. The cases decided by Wirt involved *slaves,* Seward warned, "a subject, under the general law of nations, falling more properly under the head of extradition of persons, than of delivery of property." "In neither of these cases, besides," he continued, "were the slaves charged as criminals, so that their cases fell within the privilege of *asylum,* which civilized nations, and this nation more than all others, so strenuously and so resolutely maintain in protection of all refugees from political prosecution or personal oppression." Seward then described the decisions in the cases of the *Jeune Eugenie* and the *La Pensée,* the two slave ships captured by the US Navy in the early 1820s that were later restored to their original French owners. The *Pensée* had, in fact, been seized with slaves on board, and all of them were returned to the French government even before a legal case could be started in the United States. Seward also quoted Wirt on the case of a slave from the Danish island of Saint Croix who had escaped to New York hidden in a US ship in 1822. The Danish minister to the United States demanded the slave's extradition, and the government promptly complied. The implications of Seward's arguments were clear: the federal government had been extraditing people since the 1820s without being charged with usurping power or violating the Constitution.[3]

The same system of international laws that had been protecting the contraband slave trade during the first fifty years of peace after 1815 was now being used to justify the deportation of a slave trader. The contrast could not have been more striking. The United States had repeatedly refused to establish any treaty with Britain that implied the establishment of the mutual right of search or mixed commission courts for four decades. These issues had united people across political and sectional divisions. When, in 1860, Seward and others proposed new measures to suppress US involvement in slave traffic, most congressmen had agreed with all of them, except for those calling for concerted actions with Britain. Yet here was Seward, four years later, defending the actions of the federal government as part of a joint effort with the British government. Both countries had "united in an urgent appeal to the government of Spain to execute the laws of that country so effectually as to suppress the introduction of African slaves into the island of Cuba." What caused such a sudden shift?[4]

The Renewal of Tensions

As discussed in Chapter 6, the United States had been at the center of geopolitical tensions that allowed the contraband human traffic to Cuba to continue, and the US flag had become the preferred disguise of slave traders in the 1850s. As the obstacles to the suppression of the slave traffic in a world of sovereign nation-states became clear, the British, who had been the greatest advocates of this new world order, eventually decided to violate those limits. The late 1840s and the late 1850s were marked by many such events. Starting in 1848, as we have seen, the British launched a series of naval strikes in Brazilian waters. The attacks had an immediate impact and combined with new political developments in Brazil to stimulate the definitive suppression of the traffic to the country in the early 1850s. In 1858, Britain launched a new strike, this time against the traffic to Cuba. After Palmerston became prime minister for a second term in 1855 and the Crimean War ended the following year, the Royal Navy resumed its more aggressive attitude toward the transatlantic slave trade. Because the US flag covered most of the slave trade to Cuba, British actions inevitably led to the boarding and seizures of US vessels. Anglo-American tensions rose again.

The slave traders explored and maximized these frictions, pressuring both governments with claims for losses in what they claimed was legitimate commerce with Africa. In the case of the *North Hand*, Guilherme de la Figanière wrote to Secretary of State Lewis Cass in 1858 complaining that "so long as improper direct British interference with our vessels continues, and unwarrantable suspicion is created against them, our legitimate trade with Africa will not only be injured—as I know to my cost—but destroyed." John Albert Machado also made his contributions to heighten tensions. When his vessel the *Thomas Watson* was seized and taken to Sierra Leone by the British navy earlier that same year, he immediately contacted the US secretary of state to complain about the destruction of his lawful business. He also took the opportunity to make a claim for the *Mary Varney*, another vessel captured by the British that had been employed, according to him, in a lawful voyage to Africa. Both vessels had actually been restored, but Machado asked for compensation of eighty thousand dollars for the interference in the voyage of the *Thomas Watson* and fifty thousand dollars for the *Mary Varney*. The British government considered these values too high, especially because Machado did not furnish any vouchers or accounts of his losses (and waited four years before making a claim for one of the vessels).[5]

Authorities did realize how slave traders had been exploring the spaces opened by international tensions. The Royal Navy's seizure of the *Lydia Gibbs* generated the usual complaints from the US government, with the minister in Britain protesting to the Foreign Office that, first, there was no evidence that the ship had been employed in an illegal voyage and that, second, and more important, the British had no right to search or seize vessels under US colors. According to the British foreign secretary the Earl of Malmesbury, however, the captain had sold the vessel in Havana and had received six thousand dollars to sail it to Africa. Moreover, Malmesbury observed, part of the evidence used in the US complaint was an anonymous report of the ship's capture. That report was published with some changes in the *Charleston Mercury* and reprinted in other Northern newspapers, including the *New York Times* and *New York Herald*. It focused on the right-of-search issue and essentially depicted the British commander as a pirate. According to the article, Captain Watson of the *Lydia Gibbs* (a Scot who had become a naturalized American) and the British commander of the *Trent* were childhood friends. After friendly interactions on the coast of Africa, the right-of-search issue became a topic of conversation, and Captain Watson allegedly declared that in the event of a war, he would fight for the flag under which he was sailing. The declaration irritated the British commander, who left "swearing that he would find means to search the damned Yankee schooner yet." The following morning the British commander boarded the *Lydia Gibbs* and ordered his men to search for money (which would prove that the vessel had been engaged in a slave-trading venture). "So exasperated was he at not finding his darling prize-money," the report continued, "that he robbed every man on board, of not only money, but clothing, even to their shirt-buttons and rings." Malmesbury repudiated the accusations and concluded his letter by observing that parties connected to the slave trade "endeavor to make use of a foreign government in order to prevent the interference of British cruisers with the slave trade." And, in fact, in a subsequent complaint from the US government (about rumors that British officers had been pressing US captains to destroy their papers so that they could be taken as British prizes instead of facing criminal charges in US courts), the US minister had based his arguments on a report by a sailor who later proved to have been engaged in the slave trade.[6]

Anglo-American tensions during 1858—stimulated in part by the deliberate actions of slave traders—generated angry responses from all sides in Congress. A few congressmen actually called for the seizure of British warships as a form of payback. Unlike in Brazil ten years earlier, the loud US reactions led the British government to back off. Malmesbury emphasized the difficulties faced by British officers in a letter to the US representative in London but assured him that new instructions had been issued to the commanders of British cruisers. They should continue their duties in a "manner as little calculated as possible to give occasion to complaints." The British minister at last declared that his government recognized the principles of international laws as spelled out in a previous letter sent by Secretary of State Cass. The US government celebrated the declaration as a capitulation by the British. Although British officers continued on occasion to board US vessels, they did it on a much smaller scale after mid-1858.[7]

As international pressure decreased, tensions within the United States rose. A deeper conflict over the transatlantic slave trade had been in the making since the early 1850s. Opposition to the illegal business in the South remained unchanged for most of the period of the Second Party System, in which Whigs faced off against Democrats. The reappearance of the issue in the US political sphere at the turn of the

1840s, however, immediately provided new arguments to Northern abolitionists. In 1845, a few Northern newspapers published the short story "Wise and the Slaver," a fictitious account of an encounter between the US minister to Brazil, on his way back to the United States, and a vessel engaging in the US domestic slave trade from Virginia to Louisiana. Initially thinking that the vessel was engaging in the transatlantic slave trade, an outraged Wise presented himself to the captain as "the great slave-trade-exterminator." Once learning from the captain that the ship was actually coming with slaves from Virginia, Wise changed his attitude and, relieved, explained the difference between the domestic and the transatlantic slave trades. On the way back to his ship, all misunderstandings now resolved, Wise heard a voice shouting from the hatchway: "Massa Wise, Massa Wise!" It was Tom, a slave owned by his neighbor, whose wife and kids were the properties of Wise himself. Sold into the domestic slave trade, the slave implored Wise to return him to his family. Wise bought the slave from the captain and took him to his ship, thinking about the case for the rest of the day. Before sleep that night, he muttered to himself, "D——n it! I verily believe, if I had been raised in New England, I should have been as red-hot an Abolitionist as Garrison himself." A newspaper from Philadelphia, on the other hand, expressed real hopes that such a change could have taken place after noting that Wise had "returned from Brazil quite a reformer" and reminding readers of Wise's relentless struggle against the complicity of US citizens in the Brazilian slave trade.[8]

The views of Henry Wise indeed went through changes, but not in the direction expected by Northern abolitionists. When Nehemiah Adams, a pastor from Boston, wrote Wise inquiring about Southern slavery, the Virginian was extremely offended by what he saw as another Northern attempt to interfere with what was an exclusively Southern affair. In a long reply, Wise described the horrors of the slave trade that he had witnessed as minister to Brazil and made his traditional denunciations of British and New England merchants for profiting from the illegal business. Surprisingly, however, despite all the horrors, Wise argued that "if called on tomorrow to say, as a man of humanity, of honor, of truth, of love for the African race, of hatred to the slave-traders, of fear and love to my own Almighty Master, whether the coast trade in human beings would cease, I would advise steps the very contrary of those taken by the civilized world at the present day." Like many other Southern slaveholders, Wise had incorporated some of the British antico-ercionist arguments and turned them into a critique of the US slave trade acts of the early nineteenth century. All laws against the traffic should be repealed because the contraband worsened the conditions of the Middle Passage. Moreover, Brazil was a "heaven" for Africans compared to Africa, "where they may acquire a right to freedom, to intermarriage, to social equality, and where they do become useful artisans" (Wise reproduced here some Brazilian proslavery arguments that emphasized the social mobility of former slaves during the Segundo Reinado, 1840–99). His point was that, as in Brazil, slaves fared much better in the United States than in Africa. "That barbaric horde of heathens who were brought to the New World, in the economy of Providence, to hew away the rocks, and to make the rough places smooth for a more chosen and superior race," Wise concluded, "who, in turn for the slavery, have given to Africa the arts of civilization, and the knowledge and the worship of the only true and living God."[9]

Although the argument that Africans were better off in the Americas than in Africa had been a recurrent motif of proslavery arguments, Wise's call for a repeal of all anti-slave-trade legislation was new and must be understood as part of the general crisis over slavery that marked the 1850s. It was related more to the defense of slavery in face of Northern criticism than to real projects to reopen the transatlantic slave trade (after all, Wise was on his way to becoming the governor of the state that had been the supplier of captives for the domestic slave trade par excellence). The decade had started with the debates that accompanied the end of the Mexican War (1846–48). With the Treaty of Guadalupe-Hidalgo, negotiated by the former US consul in Cuba, Nicholas Trist, vast amounts of land were incorporated into the Union in 1848, renewing some of the tensions that had already marked the inclusion of Missouri in the late 1810s. The following years would be marked by debates around slavery—not least because of the political significance of slave resistance, as James Oakes argues—that led to fractures within political parties and, ultimately, the country. The African slave trade issue repeatedly appeared in these discussions. The controversies involving US citizens and the traf-

fic in the early 1840s kept the issue alive for Free-Soilers and abolitionists, despite the consensus against it in the political sphere. The 1840s
policy of the Liberty Party, a forerunner of the Republican Party, for
example, called for a complete divorce of the federal government from
slavery through, among many other things, actions against slavery in the
District of Columbia and the complete enforcement of laws against the
transatlantic slave trade.[10]

The subsequent debates that accompanied the Compromise of
1850 and the Kansas-Nebraska Act of 1854 brought the slave trade topic
back to discussion. One of the main issues in the debates of the Thirty-
First Congress (1849–51), besides the extension of slavery into the recently conquered territories and the demand for a new fugitive slave law
by Southerners, was the call from Northerners for the abolition of slavery and the slave trade in the District of Columbia. When Henry Clay
suggested that Congress lacked the power to regulate the trade in slaves
between slaveholding states, Senator Salmon P. Chase, one of the leaders
of the Free-Soil Party, immediately reacted by comparing the interstate
slave trade to its transatlantic variant. "We hear much of the cruelty of the
African slave trade," the senator from Ohio argued in a long speech, but
"is it less cruel, less deserving of punishment, to tear fathers, mothers,
children, from their homes and each other, in Maryland and Virginia,
and transport them to the markets of Louisiana or Mississippi? If there
is a difference in cruelty and wrong, is it not in favor of the African
and against the American slave trade?" It was not a surprise, then, that
almost every Southerner opposed ending the slave trade in the capital.
Prohibiting the sales of slaves would be, as historian Paul Finkelman argues, "an admission that buying and selling slaves was morally wrong—
which southerners would not admit, and most did not believe."[11]

The slavery issue reemerged even stronger after the Kansas-
Nebraska Act, which repealed the Missouri Compromise ban on slavery
in most of the western territories that had come with the purchase of
Louisiana in 1803. Two main consequences of the act were the bloody
conflict between antislavery militants and slaveholders in Kansas, a Civil
War in miniature, and the formation of the Republican Party. Like the
Newport, Rhode Island, petitioners of 1820, some saw a straight connec-
tion between the incorporation of new territories and the transatlantic

slave trade. One of them was the future leader of the Republican Party, Abraham Lincoln. In what was perhaps his first great speech against slavery, Lincoln described the Kansas-Nebraska Act as a tool for the expansion of slavery and directly connected it to a possible reopening of the African slave trade. "The law which forbids the bringing of slaves *from* Africa; and that which has so long forbid the taking them *to* Nebraska," he argued, "can hardly be distinguished on any moral principle; and the repeal of the former could find quite as plausible excuses as that of the latter." Lincoln also challenged the argument that the opening of slavery in the new territories would not increase the number of slaves by suggesting that the African slave trade had not been completely closed and that the new demand would stimulate its growth. He made a few other references to the subject during his three-hour speech, but his conclusion was always the same: the principle that slaveholders had the right to carry slaves into the new territories could be used to support the transatlantic slave trade. "If it is a sacred right for the people of Nebraska to take and hold slaves there, it is equally their sacred right to buy them where they can buy them cheapest; and that undoubtedly will be on the coast of Africa; provided you will consent not to hang them for going there to buy them."[12]

The national crisis also led some Southerners to explore those same connections between the expansion of slavery and the transatlantic slave trade. Unlike Lincoln and other Northerners, however, these individuals reinterpreted those links in a positive light, calling for the reopening of the transatlantic slave trade as a strategy to strengthen slavery. South Carolina Fire-Eaters led the movement and became increasingly influential there and in other Southern states. The crusade had its most vocal defender in Leonidas W. Spratt, who in 1853 bought the *Charleston Southern Standard* to publicize his views. The movement, however, gained momentum only after slavery became the center of national debates with the Kansas-Nebraska Act. In November 1856, the governor of South Carolina defended the project in a message to the legislature. The core of his argument was that, first, the basis of slaveholding in the South needed to be widened if the institution was to survive and, second, that more slaves were needed to keep cotton prices low enough for the region to maintain its monopoly over the production of the crop. Other important proslavery writers defended the revival of the slave trade for different reasons. Whereas George Fitzhugh believed that a renewed flow of Africans could strengthen the South and maintain the region within the Union, William L. Yancey defended the cause in hopes that it could create divisions within the Democratic Party and stimulate secession. Secessionists were certainly the majority of reopeners, and in that sense, winning victories at state legislatures and Southern commercial conventions seemed more important than repealing the ban on the slave trade through Congress.[13]

Their major target may have been the South, but their writings immediately reverberated in the North. In May 1856, a presidential election year, the *Albany Evening Journal* published an article with the title "Will the North Be Forced into the African Slave Trade?" in which the author connected Southern schemes for the expansion of slavery, the compliance of Northern politicians, and the transatlantic slave trade. His accusations were based on an article published in the *Charleston Standard* calling for a repeal of the slave trade acts so that Western planters could take advantage of African labor at the same pace that Northerners had been using the "pauper labor from Europe." According to the *Albany Evening Express* the repeal of the restrictions of the Missouri Compromise had been only the first step in the complete destruction of the obstructions to the transatlantic slave trade. "The profane hands of Northern Congressmen and Politicians laid upon the Missouri Compact," the article continued, "are now ready, for a price, to tear down the barriers which our Fathers built to check the Foreign Trade in Human Slaves." The differences between violently carrying slaves from, on the one hand, Virginia to Kansas, and, on the other, Guinea and Charleston, were minimal. Southern designs for reopening the traffic were approaching reality, especially because not only had a number of Northern politicians supported the Kansas-Nebraska Act but also "New York and Boston are not largely, though stealthily, interested in the horrid traffic, and have wealthy and high-walking traders, whose regular business is to supply Cuban and Brazilian plantations with 'cheap African labor.'" Moreover, reopening the traffic was merely the first step. The ultimate goal was announced in a counterfactual explored by the *Charleston Standard*. If the slave trade had been allowed to continue since the early nineteenth century, then "slavery would now have been the common form of social development in the whole Union."[14]

The *New York Herald,* which would in fact support the election of the Republican candidate John C. Frémont that year, responded to the article in the *Albany Evening Journal* three days later with a short note: "Such are the miserable shifts of the nigger worshipping alliance to keep up the excitement. We shall next probably hear that the 'slave oligarchy' are plotting for the annexation of Africa, in order to secure an inexhaustible supply of slaves at less than prime cost." As Election Day approached, however, the newspaper became less critical of those depictions of Southern extremism, since such attacks could be directed against the election of James Buchanan. According to a correspondent, one consequence of the election of Buchanan would inevitably be the reopening of the transatlantic slave trade. "The new field operated by the re-establishment of the African slave trade for the employment of capital," the letter continued, "will actively engage all interests in its prosecution, and thus the North and the South will once more unite, as a band of brothers, in the ties of a common interest."[15]

The movement, nevertheless, generated controversy in the South, with many opposing the reopening on classic paternalistic grounds. South Carolinian J. J. Pettigrew argued that the introduction of "one hundred thousand idle, slovenly, insubordinate barbarians among our educated, civilized negroes" would destroy the great improvement toward Africans that Southern paternalists had achieved during the nineteenth century. Walter Brooke of Mississippi argued along similar lines, claiming that Southern slaveholders would become, "instead of the patriarchal friend and master of his slave—a bloody, brutal, and trembling tyrant." Three state legislatures—South Carolina, Georgia, and Louisiana—came very close to reopening the trade but ultimately rejected the proposition. The infiltration of the topic into the public sphere was sufficiently strong to generate a congressional debate on a resolution condemning attempts to revive the traffic in enslaved Africans. In December 1856, after debates on the wording of the resolution, a final version was approved, 183 to 8, a nearly unanimous vote. The main issue in the debate was the wording of the resolution, not its necessity.[16]

The Democrats' Assault on the Slave Trade

Neither the end of elections nor the passing of the resolution settled the issue outside Congress. But it was clear to many that the movement for reopening the trade faced unsurpassable obstacles. One day after Buchanan's election, the *New York Herald* printed a long article with the title "Revival of the African Slave Trade—Shall the King of Dahomey Be Brought into Competition with Governor Wise?" that exposed the clear limits of the reopening movement. According to the author, the election had brought the price of slaves issue to the forefront and, consequently, the question about whether the African slave trade should be revived. Some in the South had not only been defending the reopening but had also been advocating the incorporation of Cuba, Nicaragua, and other countries as slave states. The "proposition for the revival of this direct trade with the King of Dahomey in the cash article of niggers," however, faced some steep difficulties. The first problem, and probably the main one, was that "the traffic stands condemned by the public opinion of the civilized world, by international treaty stipulations between this country and the great Powers of Europe, and by the laws of the United States, as piracy. That is the word—piracy." To restore the traffic, therefore, it would be necessary to go back one or two hundred years "and repeal the public opinion of the world denouncing this inhuman traffic as piracy." It would also be necessary to repeal the US slave trade legislation and all the treaties with European powers while securing "their consent to the restoration of the traffic, or run the hazards of the inevitable war into which the experiment would plunge us." The author had no doubt that reviving the traffic would result in war with England and France, as would the attempt to "wrest" Cuba from Spain (paraphrasing passages from the Ostend Manifesto). The article continued to expose the difficulties and concluded: "Finally, let Governor Wise cheer up. There is no possible danger of a reduction in the price of Virginia niggers from the revival of the trade with the King of Dahomey."[17]

The issue, however, continued to be discussed, especially because some proponents of reopening decided to put their beliefs into practice. In 1859, the British consul in Charleston wrote that "a majority of the southern people is, still, decidedly opposed to a renewal of the slave trade, but, in view of the changes of the last two years, it may not be unsafe to predict that it will not long continue so." His comments were inspired by recent cases of a few Southerners who had organized voyages to Africa for slaves against US laws. In the famous case of the *Wanderer,* Charles Lamar, a wealthy slaveholder from Savannah, organized a voyage that disembarked 303 captives on the coast of Georgia in 1858. There were rumors at the time that his other vessel, the *E. A. Rawlins,* also disembarked slaves in the United States. The British consul noted that these violators received protection from local authorities and the public. The *Charleston Mercury* had, in fact, defined the slave trade act of 1808 as a dead letter after the acquittal of the captain of the *Wanderer* in 1859.

According to the consul, most people in South Carolina were delighted with the offenders' lack of punishment not only in this case but also in the case of the *Echo,* a US vessel captured by the US Navy off the coast of Cuba in 1858 with more than four hundred slaves on board. Pro-slave-trade ideologues in South Carolina took the opportunity of these court cases to promote their views and generate what Manisha Sinha has called "judicial nullification." In the case of the *Echo,* Leonidas W. Spratt and a few other secessionists actually represented the crew of the captured vessel in the Charleston Circuit Court. No one involved in the case was convicted. The *Charleston Mercury* termed the decision of the jury an act of "resistance." Other rumors abounded that the consensus against the traffic had suffered a serious setback. In late 1858, the district attorney for Northern Florida communicated to the State Department his difficulties in stopping the suspected slaver *Ardennes,* arguing that "this community is strongly opposed to the execution of the laws prohibiting the slave trade, and every obstacle is thrown in the way of the officers who are endeavoring to discharge their duty." Southern newspapers published different accounts of other slave disembarkations in the South, but these seemed to be more the product of provocations than reality, since reopeners inflated those events to make their point. Historians may yet uncover other voyages and attest to the veracity of some of those rumors, as historian Sylviane Diouf has done, but it seems unlikely that the number of slave disembarkations in the United States during the 1850s will change radically. Thus it is important to note that in terms of their numbers, these voyages were exceptions in the broader history of the transatlantic slave trade.[18]

In terms of politics, however, their impact was inversely proportional to their size. Despite the signs that the movement was far from consensual in the South, the Republican Party had been exploring the connections between the expansion of slavery and the reopening of the slave trade even before the cases of the *Wanderer* and the *Echo* became public. Already in his classic "irrepressible conflict" speech of 1858, William Seward included a reopened traffic as part of the apocalyptic future that would be brought by the expansion of the slave system. Not only would slavery be introduced in future territories and the treaty-making powers of the nation be used to incorporate foreign slaveholding states, but also "they will induce Congress to repeal the act of 1808, which prohibits the foreign slave-trade, and so they will import from Africa, at the cost of only $20 a head, slaves enough to fill up the interior of the continent." To support his argument, Seward then described a number of instances in which the Democratic Party had unashamedly supported the expansion of slavery. "This dark record shows you, fellow citizens, what I was unwilling to announce at an earlier stage of this argument," he continued, "that of the whole nefarious schedule of slaveholding designs which I have submitted to you, the Democratic Party has left only one yet to be consummated—the abrogation of the law which forbids the African slave trade."[19]

Earlier that same year, during the campaign for the position of senator for Illinois, Abraham Lincoln commented in his famous "house divided" speech that a newspaper had defended the election of his opponent, Stephen A. Douglas, as a necessary step to curb the attempts to reopen the traffic. The argument was puzzling. After all, Lincoln argued, Douglas had "labored to prove it a *sacred right* of white men to take negro slaves into the new territories." Douglas had, in fact, been the main figure behind the Kansas-Nebraska Act of 1854. Lincoln revived some of the arguments that he had made in his 1854 Peoria speech. "Can he possibly show that it is less a sacred right to buy them where they can be bought cheapest? And unquestionably they can be bought cheaper in Africa than in Virginia." According to the Republican candidate, Douglas had reduced the question of slavery to an issue of right of property. Consequently, if the right to property should be "perfectly free," the only opposition to the slave trade that he could possibly defend was on the ground of a threat to the home production (the supplying slave states of the East). "And as the home producers will probably not ask the protection," Lincoln concluded, "he will be wholly without a ground of opposition."[20]

With the reduction of British pressure in 1858, Republicans could also call for the enforcement of US laws or the passing of new legislation against the slave trade in the Senate without facing accusations of being British puppets. The slave-trading cases in the South and the wide coverage they received in the North had also been adding to the growing popularity of the Republicans, especially because the cases appeared as an early materialization of the predictions of Seward and others critics of the Slave Power. The *New York Tribune* denounced the acquittal of the captain of the *Echo* as a sign that "it will not be long before the slave-trade will be carried on with as much open contempt of the laws against it, and with as much impunity, as our New-York City liquor trade now is." Their criticisms, however, were not limited to the movement to re-open the slave trade. Republicans frequently cited the traffic carried on from New York by the Portuguese Company in their indictment of the federal government for its inability to stop the transatlantic slave trade. The innumerable slave-trading cases in New York—which as we have seen were largely disconnected from the South—were interpreted as another reflection of the collusion between slaveholders and the federal government that had marked the nation's history. This collusion was manifested locally in the recent acquittal of slave captains in the South and nationally in the transformation of New York into a new capital of the transatlantic slave trade. The *New York-Enquirer,* owned by the Republican James Watson Webb, proclaimed that although New York was the source of the best possible ships used in the traffic, government officials did very little to stop the illegal business. The main problem, according to the author, was that the Democratic Party had yielded to proslavery demands, which were "not only willing to have that institution carried into the free Territories, but it regards the slave trade with apathy." Slave traders, consequently, laughed at US laws. "No more weighty reason," the article concluded, "for wishing our Government placed under the control of a different party could be desired, than is found in the action of the Democratic party in regard to the suppression of this African slave trade."[21]

The answer from the Buchanan administration to these pressures was to launch the largest assault on the transatlantic slave trade in US history since independence. The actions could at once eliminate a source of Republican criticism and alleviate Anglo-American tensions. Howell Cobb, secretary of the Treasury, instructed collectors in Boston, New York, New Orleans, Savannah, and Charleston to examine cases of suspected slavers and to refuse to issue clearances when evidence of the illegality of the voyage was compelling. The secretary of the navy increased the number of ships in the Africa Squadron from four to eight and in the Home Squadron from five to thirteen, most of them steamships. He also moved the supply base from the Cape Verde Islands to a point closer to where slave embarkations took place. Twenty vessels were captured in 1859 and 1860, more than twice the total number of prizes taken by American warships between 1851 and 1858.[22]

Despite the unprecedented assault, slave-trading vessels continued to depart from the United States flying the Stars and Stripes. Although the new initiatives were unparalleled in US history, they were insufficient to curb the traffic. And more important, as the actions of the British government had shown, ending the illegal business depended on the willingness of the Spanish government to suppress it. The number of slaves disembarked in Cuba under US colors between 1858 and 1861 reached unmatched levels (although their numbers decreased almost by half between 1859 and 1860). Theodore Sedgwick, who replaced John McKeon as district attorney for Southern New York, described the difficulties of enforcing the anti-slave-trade legislation. The circumstances he described—which were largely based on the case of the *Haidee,* a vessel that had embarked 1,145 enslaved Africans at Kilongo, in West Central Africa, and disembarked the surviving 903 at Cardenas in 1858—also showed how slave traders continued to circumvent anti-slave-trade efforts. The difficulties started with the fact that vessels employed in the legal trade in palm oil between Africa and the United States went to many of the same places that slave ships embarked captives, making the efforts of US authorities extremely delicate. The risks of disrupting the legitimate commerce with their actions were not small, and US officers feared the charges that could ensue from mistaken detentions. Second, the articles used by slave traders were no longer as distinctive, making seizure based on equipment much more difficult. According to Sedgwick, manacles stopped being used and the deck was prepared during the voyage itself. Assessing a voyage's illegality based exclusively on its provisions and water casks was extremely difficult. Moreover, some slave voyages, as had been the case with the *Haidee*, went to other ports before sailing to Africa, and the crew was often unaware of the ship's destination and thus could not provide enough evidence for the condemnation of the vessel. To complicate things even further, some vessels took on water casks and even crews only after being cleared.[23]

US commanders complained about similar difficulties, as the letter of instructions from the secretary of the navy to the main commander of the Africa Squadron made clear. "It is not to be supposed that vessels destined for the slave trade will exhibit any of the usual arrangements for that traffic," the secretary observed. "They take especial care to put on the appearance of honest traders, and to be always prepared, as if in pursuit of lawful commerce." The consequence was that positive proof of slavers' involvement in the slave trade came only after enslaved Africans had been taken on board. Still, he observed, some signs should make commanders suspicious, such as double sets of papers and logbooks, an unusual number of water casks and provisions, shipping lists with wages higher than the usual, and forged consular certificates. The utmost care should still be taken not to disrupt the lawful business carried on by US citizens and foreigners. Even if a slave ship could be identified as such, proving nationality remained problematic. The fourth and fifth sections of the act of 1820 made the condemnation of foreigners involved in the slave trade dependent on US ownership of the vessel. This was precisely the problem in the case of the *Haidee*, where all the accused members of the crew were foreigners and the US ownership of the vessel could not be proved.[24]

In Cuba, similar problems persisted. The last consul to Havana before the Civil War, Kentuckian Charles J. Helm, later reappointed Confederate consul to Cuba, was particularly concerned with the dangers of affecting legitimate commerce. One of his first actions in November

1858 was to clear the *Enterprise* and the *Ardennes*, the two vessels that Vice-Consul Savage had detained as suspected slavers. According to Helm, one of the captains provided all the documents of the *Ardennes* and assured him that the vessel would be employed on a legal trading voyage to Africa, "insisting that he never had been, directly or indirectly, engaged in the slave trade." After investigating the background of the captain, Helm allowed the vessels to proceed to Jacksonville before going to Africa. In another letter he described how he cleared the *J. J. Cobb* after the interested parties assured him that the vessel would not be employed directly or indirectly in the slave trade. He complained, however, of the lack of instructions for US consuls from State Department regarding suspected slavers.[25]

Despite the lack of guidelines, Helm did refuse to provide documents for some vessels that he believed had been fraudulently sold to Cuban slave traders. In the case of the *White Cloud,* a vessel sold at New York to José Pernias of Havana, Helm allowed its departure only after canceling the American documents. The vessel ultimately sailed under the colors of Buenos Aires. Helm continued to complain about the lack of instructions on the slave trade, describing in one letter the case of the *Erie,* a slaver that was subsequently captured on the African coast and made famous by the conviction and hanging of its captain, Nathaniel Gordon, in 1862. Helm was "morally convinced" that the vessel would carry slaves from Africa to Cuba. He could not detain it, however, because "every person connected with her would asseverate that she was intended for legal trade." If there was in fact a legal trade between Cuba and the coast of Africa as well as between the coast of Africa and the United States, he believed that he did not have the right to detain the vessel. Captain General Serrano wrote to the consulate saying that he had permitted the *Erie* to proceed on its voyage because the Cuban customhouse was not authorized to detain foreign vessels employed on lawful voyages. Because he suspected the vessel was a slaver, however, Serrano had communicated his suspicions to the British consul general so that a British cruiser could be sent to watch the suspected vessel. The note generated a long response from Helm, who was extremely offended by the captain general's actions. He reminded Serrano that the United States had been one of the earliest nations to abolish the slave trade and emphasized that the traffic should be regulated by each individual nation for itself. The United States did not allow its merchant ships—even suspected slavers—to be searched by any other nation. The country had its own vessels of war both on the coasts of Africa and Cuba, the only ones allowed to stop and search US vessels.[26]

It was in this context that Helm proposed to the State Department that the onus of the slave trade should be placed on Spain. He suggested communicating to the captain general that all US vessels cleared at the Havana customhouse would be allowed to proceed on their voyage, with the clearance standing as enough evidence that Spanish authorities had made all the necessary inspections to ensure that the vessel would not be employed in the slave trade. His wish was granted, and by late May 1860, Helm wrote to Captain General Serrano informing him that all US consulates in Cuba would merely dispatch the vessels that had already been cleared by the customhouse, since "the Spanish government has better and greater sources of information as to their objects and destination or connexion with the slave trade than the consul general of the United States resident at Havana possibly can have."[27]

Despite their limited interventions, Blythe, Savage, and Helm did have some impact on the slave trade carried on under the US flag from Cuba. Savage was especially optimistic during his most militant phase in 1858, when he wrote to the State Department that he was convinced that "my course, if it should meet with the approbation of the government, has put a stop to the use of our flag by Spanish slavers in this port." An increasing number of captured US slavers were fraudulently sold and carried forged documents or had no documents at all during this final era of the transatlantic slave trade. But slave traders seem to have had an infinite array of strategies. As US authorities increased their efforts to take their flag out of the business, slavers flew the Mexican and other flags. As a correspondent of the *New York Herald* wrote from Cuba, "Nearly all the slavers are now leaving the island with Mexican papers, and three steamers are fitting out in Havana. So long as there is a demand for negroes so long will interested parties find the means of escaping from the men-of-war employed to check the traffic." The US consul general in Cuba wrote to the secretary of state that during 1859 "several American vessels have been sold at this port and put under the

Mexican and Chilean flags, and were, no doubt, purchased for the slave trade, and if they used the American flag, it was hoisted at sea, as it is only used for the protection of this illegal traffic by foreigners."[28]

Thus Buchanan was correct to state that the annexation of the Spanish colony was one of the few possible ways to stop the traffic. Without annexation the United States might increase its efforts to re-duce US involvement, but completely stopping the trade was beyond its reach. Ironically, Buchanan's policy turned part of the Cuban popu-lation against the annexationist cause. In July 1860, the lieutenant of a US steamer wrote to the secretary of the navy that whereas in the past he had met many Cubans who were proud of having been educated in the United States or associated with the country in some other way, this was no longer the case. "The whole population of Cuba appears to be warmly in favor of the slave trade," the officer observed, attributing the shift in US popularity to their efforts to suppress the use of their flag in the illegal business. The consequence would be that even if Spain agreed to sell Cuba to the United States, the inhabitants of the island would disapprove of it. "The feeling of the people are turning against us," he concluded, "and those who still like us tell me it is dangerous for them to show it, as it causes them to be marked men."[29]

With the Buchanan administration unable to halt the traffic, oppo-nents continued to exploit the issue. There was another way of stopping the traffic to Cuba, which certainly never crossed Buchanan's mind: end-ing US slavery, the cornerstone of the nineteenth-century slave Americas. That was precisely what some in the Republican Party had set out to do. They continued to denounce US involvement in the transatlantic slave trade, and a few of them at least believed that the traffic to Cuba could not be ended as long as geopolitical tensions hindered Anglo-American cooperation. Republican senators William Seward and Henry Wilson pressed for new measures to curb US participation in the traffic, with Wilson making three propositions to Congress in 1860. Wilson pro-posed, first, that five steamers should be built and taken to the coast of Africa; second, that the death penalty for convicted slave traders should be reduced to imprisonment for life (thus facilitating convictions); and, third, that some inquiry should be made toward establishing the mutual right of search with Britain for vessels within two hundred miles of the

African coast. "The Democrats express cheerful concurrence in the first two," a report from Washington described, "but question the propriety of the third, in view of the difference in navies of this and European Governments, and our national repugnance to the right of search."[30]

Despite the decrease in British seizures of US vessels, or perhaps because of it, the British continued to call for concerted actions against the traffic. In July 1860, the Foreign Office sent a letter to the US government describing the long history of British efforts to curb the traffic and its recent growth in Cuba. The letter, which was also sent to the French government, argued that the United States needed to improve its laws for the seizure of vessels equipped for the slave trade and increase, along with their British and Spanish counterparts, the number of cruisers surrounding Cuba. The letter concluded by quoting Buchanan's presidential message of that May: "It is truly lamentable that Great Britain and the United States should be obliged to expend such a vast amount of blood and treasure for the suppression of the African slave trade, and this when the only portions of the civilized world where it is tolerated and encouraged are the Spanish Islands of Cuba and Puerto Rico." The answer from the US secretary of state stressed that, in the president's opinion, only when Britain enforced the terms of its 1817 treaty with Spain would the traffic end. "But with this," the secretary observed, "the government of the United States has no right to interfere."[31]

Republican newspapers, especially the *Evening Post,* readily picked up the exchanges in order to criticize the Buchanan administration. In August the newspaper critically assessed the quoted passage from Buchanan's speech. It then recalled a list of one hundred slavers in New York that it had published in its pages just one week earlier. The success of the traffic in the city, in fact, derived "its main encouragement from the direct interference of the President himself, who pretended in his message that the only places where it was encouraged were the Spanish islands of Puerto Rico and Cuba." According to the newspaper, it was under his administration and influence that European newspapers described New York as "the greatest slave-trading mart in the world." That this was the case was better known in London than in New York itself. Earlier that year the newspaper had argued that the only "achievement" of the Buchanan administration was a nullification of the slave trade acts. "By putting the peaceful relations between this country and England in peril, upon a pretended violation of our rights on the high seas," the article concluded, "he has succeeded in discouraging English cruisers, while at home his officers and agents are of a class who are too sagacious to execute the laws in a spirit hostile to the obvious policy of the Administration." The *World* in turn argued that the British efforts to end the traffic and the calls for mutual collaboration should be praised, but that the answer from the secretary of state was anything but encouraging. No desire to cooperate for the end of the traffic was shown. "We confess that there is no single thing," the article argued, "which so reconciles us to a change of administration as the prospect that the change will bring with it a new line of action toward the African slave trade." Not surprisingly, therefore, the critique of the transatlantic slave trade had been included in the Republican platform of 1860, which condemned the attempts to reopen the slave trade to the nation and called for new measures against "that execrable traffic."[32]

Multiple reactions to the Republican indictments came from Southerners and Democrats, many of them also criticizing the efforts to reopen the traffic. Some, however, sought to indict Northerners and, more specifically, Republicans for New York's persisting involvement in the slave trade. Florida lawyer William G. M. Davis emphasized that the judge had made the correct decision in face of the available evidence in the case of the *Echo* and that more slavers had been condemned at Key West during 1858 than in New York, "where no doubt there are not a few fitted out." Other Southern newspapers made similar arguments, emphasizing that a large part of the transatlantic slave trade was carried from Northern ports while it continued to be widely rejected by Southerners. Democrats, in turn, noted how the Republican Party had been exploiting the reopening issue. The *New York Evening Express* claimed that the story of a cargo of slaves that had been landed in Mobile Bay, widely publicized by Republican newspapers, was a hoax. The rumors, however, were "probably worth many thousand votes, for Lincoln, out in Ohio, in some portions of this State, and in parts of New England, where by consequence, the readers thereof, cannot ever get at the truth." As historian Sylviane Diouf has shown, however, this was far from a hoax. The *Clotilda* had indeed disembarked 110 captives in Mobile in 1860.[33]

Some responses had a more conspiratorial bent. One article argued that Northerners profited from the slave trade while Southern slaveholders had not the slightest interest in its revival. According to another article, "New York and New England, which are claimed as preserves by the friends of the 'almighty nigger,' furnished the vessels, the capital wherewith to fit them out, the officers to command them, and the men to sail them. The profits went into Northern pockets." These vessels were sent to Southern ports in order to stir sensibilities against the South and generate an issue in the 1860 election. At the same time, the profits of the business would help "elect the rum seller Seward President of these United States." These theories were supported by the *New York Herald* during 1860 with the additional accusation that abolitionist newspapers had so much information about the slave trade that Republicans must have had some interest in those voyages (whereas, in fact, many of the details were actually coming from Emilio Sanchez y Dolz, a Spanish broker from New York who worked as a British informant and published articles under the pseudonym "South Street"). "The profits of the trade are so great," one report concluded, "that they can well afford to contribute a hundred thousand dollars or more towards the election of an anti-slavery President." The Democrats' efforts to use the slave trade to indict Republicans were obviously not successful. Their party had already been shattered by the actions of Southern expansionists, the same individuals who had been providing signs for a Northern audience that some Republican indictments may have been right since the beginning. On November 6, 1860, the antislavery party achieved victory.[34]

The Republican Assault on the Slave Trade

The secession of the South that followed the election of Lincoln and the subsequent start of a civil war gave Britain scope to negotiate new measures against the transatlantic slave trade, since both US sections needed British support (although many in the North were already giving signs that they were predisposed to concessions before the beginning of the war). Although the Constitution of the Confederate States of America assured the protection of slavery in the South, its ninth article prohibited the "importation of negroes of the African race from any foreign country other than the slaveholding States or Territories of the United States of America." The British consul in Charleston remained highly skeptical of the prohibition, arguing that although it was great to see the human traffic being repealed by the Confederacy, the ban did not proceed "from the dictates of principle or from a conviction of the cruelty and infamy of the traffic." According to him, not even the most moderate Southerners opposed the trade. "If the slave trade be prohibited just now," he continued, "it is simply from considerations of expediency, which they openly say might disappear at any given period. In such case, they add, it would be revived without sample, and I feel quite certain that such would be the case."[35]

A few events in South Carolina probably contributed to the consul's skepticism. Earlier in 1861, on its way to Norfolk, Virginia, bad weather forced the USS *San Jacinto* into Charleston. The ship had seized the *Bonita* off the coast of Africa with 750 slaves on board. While in South Carolina, a writ of habeas corpus was procured requiring the US lieutenant to explain the detention of the captain of the *Bonita*, Joseph Stackpole. The Charleston judge denied the habeas corpus, but on the way from the court to the vessel, Stackpole "was, as it is alleged, rescued by a gang of men in the streets of Charleston." The consul also had strong suspicions that the lieutenant facilitated the escape. The USS *San Jacinto* was ultimately taken to Savannah, where Confederate forces seized and auctioned it. In July 1861, the same consul mentioned rumors that slave traders in Southern ports were preparing to take advantage of the Africa Squadron's withdrawal to fly the US flag openly, thus protecting them from British interference. At the same time, in New York it was rumored that "the Confederate privateers will not molest the slavers should they fall in with them." That year would, in fact, see the successful completion of at least two voyages originating in Southern ports, those of the *John Bell* and the *Potomac*. Both took place, however, before the British consul's denunciations. The rumors that rebel forces would leave slavers untouched also seemed unfounded, since Confederates in North Carolina captured the *Thomas Watson*, owned by the Portuguese New Yorker John Albert Machado, after the vessel reportedly disembarked slaves in Cuba.[36]

The Union also acted quickly in its attempts to gain British support, especially after the government recalled the US vessels in the Africa Squadron. "Ironically," Don Fehrenbacher notes, "the first antislavery administration in American history found it necessary to discontinue the vigorous offensive against the slave trade that had been launched by its generally proslavery predecessor." Squadrons were recalled from different parts of the world to blockade Southern ports. Robert W. Shufeldt, consul general to Cuba, wrote to the State Department that, in the absence of US men-of-war, he should be empowered to refuse clearance to any US vessels departing from Cuba to Africa as the only way of preventing the use of the US flag by slave traders. The US consul in Trinidad de Cuba complained about how powerless he was to act against the transatlantic slave trade in the absence of a single US steamer of war.[37]

By recalling the Africa Squadron, the Union was, in fact, violating the Webster-Ashburton Treaty of 1842. Before stronger reactions came from the British government, Secretary of State William Seward gave signals in 1861 that the new administration was more flexible toward the right-of-search issue. The following year the two nations signed the Lyons-Seward Treaty, which, in article 1, established a mutual right of search within delimited distances of the coast of Africa and Cuba. The remaining eleven articles established, among other things, a slave-trading equipment clause and the institution of mixed courts in New York, Sierra Leone, and the Cape of Good Hope. By the time the treaty was ratified in mid-1862, however, the outfitting of slavers at US ports as well as the volume of slaves carried on vessels flying the US flag had significantly decreased. The Anglo-American mixed courts did not adjudicate a single case and were dissolved in 1870. The use of US ports for the organization of slave voyages nearly ended during 1861, and there is evidence of only one voyage departing New York in 1863.[38]

The Republican administration continued the assault on US participation in the slave trade initiated by Buchanan, but the election of Lincoln and the outbreak of war gave a new symbolic power to the anti-slave-trade initiatives of 1861. The new context suddenly removed US participation in the slave trade as a political issue. Accusations that Republicans were taking slave-trading money or that Southern Fire-Eaters were on the brink of reopening the slave trade disappeared. The classic

Republican interpretation became the predominant narrative. During 1861–62 articles and notes observed the negligence of previous administrations (dominated as they were by the Slave Power) and highlighted the anti-slave-trade efforts of the new Republican government. Although historians should be careful not to take the Republican discourse about its own anti-slave-trade efforts at face value, the predominance of this discourse in the public sphere seems indeed to have ensured stronger court decisions against US citizens involved in the traffic.

During 1861 newspapers constantly reported the anti-slave-trade actions of US Marshal Robert Murray and District Attorney of Southern New York Delafield Smith. The arrest of a customhouse broker named Joseph E. Sanchez for complicity in the slave trade was publicized in a short, but epic, description: "At the moment of his arrest, there was a company of persons in his office cursing the 'abolitionists,' etc. He [Marshal Murray] spoke to them in Spanish, and they were silent in an instant." Around the same time appeared many reports of US marshals of Northern states meeting for more effective ways to stop the slave trade carried from US ports. In one of them, according to the *New York Post,* Marshal Murray reported "the names of the principal slave-dealers of this city, several of whom associate in our highest society. He indicated their methods of procedure, the amount of capital they employed, their devices to secure counsel and bail for their accomplices when arrested, and the whole particulars." Another report described Murray leading a visit to the Tombs (the colloquial name of the famous municipal jail in Lower Manhattan) with other marshals to see captured slavers, with the meeting furthering "the purposes of the general government by interchange of sentiments, agreement upon a concerted plan of operations, etc. In this way they are sanguine of success in utterly breaking up the piratical commerce, so far as the free states are concerned." Murray increasingly appeared as the hero of the moment, acting against slave-trading interests and threats. By the end of the year, a note in the *New York Times* said that "his success has not only met the highest praise of the Government, but has received the commendation of the London News, which states that he had done more for the suppression of the Slave-trade than both national fleets have done for ten years."[39]

Newspapers also described the conditions and tribulations faced by US individuals who had been arrested for their complicity in the business. Like the US marshals, the *Evening Post* also paid a visit to the "slavers on the tombs" (the title of the article). They were the captains and mates of the *City of Norfolk, Nightingale, Montauk,* and *Erie.* Captain Nathaniel Gordon of the *Erie* observed that during the Buchanan administration, when he was arrested, he had been treated with much "kindness." He was allowed to use the prison yard, and friends could visit him. "The new Administration," he said, "has been very strict; none except his wife are allowed to visit him." Gordon, as we have seen in the Introduction, had been arrested in 1860 aboard the *Erie,* a vessel captured by the US Navy off the coast of Africa after the embarkation of 897 slaves.[40]

It was no coincidence that all the prisoners interviewed by the *Evening Post* were captains and mates, rather than owners. As we have seen, despite the increasing importance of US ports for the organization of slave voyages, the trade remained under the control of Portuguese and Spanish nationals. Therefore, the vast majority of individuals who were taken to US courts were the intermediaries, captains, mates, supercargoes, and crews of slave voyages. Seamen, captains, and mates comprised 75 percent of all 207 individuals prosecuted between 1839 and 1862 (table 7.1). The twelve buyers who appear were the receivers of the slaves carried to Georgia by the *Wanderer* in 1859.

Despite the difficulties in tracking down the ownership of vessels during the illegal era, it seems that most of those taken to US courts as owners of vessels and ventures were indeed intermediaries. Some were both, operating as agents for Cuban slave traders while holding a share in some vessels. Manoel Basílio da Cunha Reis and John Albert Machado, two of the main figures among the Portuguese New Yorkers, were within this category. Two US citizens who were arrested in this last phase of the slave trade, Appleton Oaksmith and Albert Horn, may also have been in this group. Oaksmith, however, had been acting in conjunction with his brother and three New York individuals: José Pietra-hita, Ramondella Zone, and a man named Aymar. It seems likely that these last three were simply agents of Cuban slave traders such as Julián Zulueta. Oaksmith wrote to the US secretary of state from prison arguing that he was "not a man of means" and that his partner in the firm of Appley &

Table 7.1. Number of individuals prosecuted for
involvement in the transatlantic slave trade by
role, 1839–62

Role	Individuals	Percentage
Seamen	92	44.4
Captains	44	21.3
Mates	20	9.7
Owners/agents	28	13.5
Buyers	12	5.8
Charterers	6	2.9
Supercargoes	5	2.4
Total	207	100

Note: Eleven captains also appeared as owners, but I left them
as captains since most of them were not the actual owners of
the seized vessels. The *Bonita* was excluded from this sample
because the number of seamen prosecuted is not specified in
the source.

Source: Howard, *American Slavers*, 224–35.

Oaksmith was the actual owner of the suspected slaver. Albert Horn, as
we have seen, probably acted in the same way as John Albert Machado,
working primarily as an agent and perhaps owning a share in a few vessels. According to one newspaper, Horn had been "Machado's alleged
great rival in the abominable traffic."[41]

Most of the indicted individuals employed the same tactics that
had acquitted others in previous years, but the new context was certainly more complicated. The recurrent strategy of forfeiting bail, for
example, became much more expensive, with judges trying to ensure
the presence of these individuals in their trials. Joseph E. Sanchez, who
was accused of helping the captain of the *Cora* to escape, and Pierre L.
Pierce, supposedly the owner of the *Brutus,* were each held to a ten-
thousand-dollar bail, while Appleton Oaksmith was bound to five
thousand dollars. Officials suspected of connivance with slave traders
were also arrested, such as Deputy Marshal John F. Cullingan, who had

to explain the escape of the captain of the *Cora*. The British consul in Boston hailed the condemnation of Captain Samuel Skinner at New Bedford as perhaps the first based solely on the intent of engaging in the slave trade. Combined with the condemnation of Nathaniel Gordon of the *Erie,* the consul believed that it would have a great impact on the illegal business.[42]

The effect of the Gordon case on the New York slave-trading community was indeed great. Captured in August 1860, the vessel was condemned and sold on October 4. The captain and two mates were taken to New York, where they were indicted under the acts of 1800 and 1820. They were ready to plead guilty to a misdemeanor in order to avoid the death penalty, but the attorney general indicated that the government would probably still prosecute them under the piracy act. When Republican Delafield Smith assumed the post of attorney general in April 1861, he complained that no preparations for the Gordon case had been made. Whether this was an exaggeration or not, Smith worked hard to convict the US captain. After a first trial failed to convict Gordon in July, Smith indicated that he would file for a new trial. He sent detectives to find the seamen of the *Erie* in the New York and Boston ports so to serve as witnesses against Gordon. Four were found and testified that Gordon was still the captain of the vessel after the Africans had been embarked. During the trial the defense used familiar arguments: Gordon was not the captain but a passenger; he was not a US citizen; the vessel had been sold to foreigners in Havana. While many accused individuals had been released on similar grounds, this time Justice Samuel Nelson—who had been the judge in similar cases during the previous decade—decided that the evidence of Gordon's innocence was not enough. The jury took just twenty minutes to render a verdict of guilty. The strongest indication of the new times, however, was perhaps in Abraham Lincoln's refusal to issue a presidential pardon to Gordon. During the previous twenty years, at least eight individuals had been granted presidential pardons for their involvement in the slave trade. On February 21, 1862, Gordon was hanged. Lincoln would grant a pardon to Albert Horn in May 1863, but by then it was clear that US involvement in the slave trade was coming to an end.[43]

At the time of Gordon's conviction, the British consul was skeptical that the sentence would be carried out but believed that, whether Gordon was executed or not, his condemnation "cannot fail to have a very salutary effect; and will, in my judgment, greatly diminish the activity with which the slave trade has been carried on hitherto from this country." In fact, shortly after this letter, the consul received comments about the impact of the arrests and convictions on the slave-trading community operating out of New York. "The slave traders are so alarmed," his informant reported in December 1861, "that it is surmised that those who are under bonds will prefer forfeiting their bail rather than stand their trials. The following slave traders were forewarned of their being under indictment and left for foreign ports before the order for their arrest was issued: Abranches; Almeida; Rosl; J. Lima Viana; & Mrs Watson."[44]

"Then there came a thunder-clap," said the *New York Tribune* in reference to the Republican assault on the slave trade. The coverage of the arrests and convictions of slave traders during 1861 and 1862 was massive, but special attention was given to the cases of Albert Horn and John Albert Machado, the two main agents and organizers of slave voyages after Manoel Basílio da Cunha Reis left New York in the 1850s. Horn was indicted for being the owner and having fitted out, equipped, and loaded the steamship *City of Norfolk* to be used in the slave trade. The vessel embarked 987 slaves at Whydah, in West Africa, and sold the surviving 562 at Cardenas. Horn was sentenced to five years in prison in October 1862, and his motion for a new trial was almost immediately refused. John Albert Machado was arrested in 1861 and again in 1862. At the time of his first arrest, the *New York Times* described him as "the king of the slave-traders in this City," remarking that rumors were that Machado outfitted more than half of all slavers that departed New York in the previous five years. By the time of his second arrest in 1862, the paper wrote that his arrest "may be considered the 'last of the Mohicans,' and with it the nest of Slavers in this city is completely broken up, and the trade has received a quietus which it will not recover from for the present." The authorities managed to prevent slave voyages from being outfitted in their ports and to significantly diminish the use of the Stars and Stripes in the illegal business. After 1862, there is evidence of only three voyages under the US flag, the *Mariquita,* the *Venus,* and an unnamed vessel, and only the *Mariquita* departed from a US port. The

New York Tribune observed that "in the short space of eighteen months, a brave, conscientious Marshal, backed by an honest prosecuting attorney, and an upright judge, has broken up, root and branch, an illegal traffic, which commanded unbounded capital, and had so suborned our public officers that it laughed the cruisers of two nations to scorn."[45]

When comparing the volume of the traffic between 1859–62 and 1863–66 the impact of the Republican assault (and the Anglo-American treaty that came with it) becomes clear. There is, of course, the general decline of the trade as a whole caused by the war. But the second period still saw the embarkation of more than fifteen thousand captives, a relatively high number. The numbers for both periods, distributed by flag of ship, are shown in table 7.2. Between 1859 and 1862, the number of voyages flying the US flag increased compared to the previous four years (see table 6.4), reaching a total of 73.3 percent, or 105 voyages. The previous period saw a comparable ratio (67.4 percent), but a much smaller total number of voyages (61) because the traffic as a whole had increased since then. The high volume of slaves embarked under US colors was a product of the tensions that led the British government temporarily to stop boarding US vessels. What becomes evident is how incapable of enforcing the law the Buchanan administration had been. Still, pressures brought by US officers in Cuba did lead slave traders to employ alternative flags, despite the growth in the number of voyages under the US flag during 1859–62. The "Other" category of table 7.2 is based on the evidence of one voyage under the flag of Argentina and seven under Mexican colors. More striking is the near disappearance of the US flag, which becomes clear in a comparison of the two periods. The participation of the Stars and Stripes dropped from 73.3 percent to 20 percent. This was obviously a result of Republican efforts, but probably less connected to the actions of authorities in New York than to the 1862 treaty permitting the mutual right of search between Britain and the United States. As had been the case with treaties involving Britain and other nations, slave traders were forced to resort to other flags or abandon them altogether, a common strategy in the final years of the traffic.

The actions of US officers had a clearer impact on the number of voyages actually outfitted in the nation (table 7.3). One could perhaps argue that the attacks on the trade during the Buchanan period had

Table 7.2. Estimated number of vessels and the slaves they embarked by flag flown at the point of departure from the Americas to Africa, 1859–66

	1859–62			1863–66		
	Voyages	Slaves	Percentage	Voyages	Slaves	Percentage
Spain	25	17,265	17.2	12	8,303	53.3
Portugal	1	863	0.9	3	2,076	13.3
United States	105	73,377	73.3	5	3,114	20.0
France	2	1,727	1.7	3	2,076	13.3
Other	10	6,906	8.0	—	—	—
Total	143	100,138	100	23	15,569	100

Note: Caribbean here means mainly Cuba, but there is evidence of at least one slave voyage organized in the Danish West Indies during this period.

Source: www.slavevoyages.org

some effect on the number of voyages departing from the United States. By comparing tables 6.4 and 7.3, we see that the Buchanan administration at least contained the increase of slave voyages outfitted from the United States. Although 51 voyages were organized from US ports between 1855 and 1858, the number decreased slightly in the following four years to 46. The trade as a whole in turn increased from the first to the second period from 90 to 143 voyages. Such a conclusion, however, would be based on the assumption that slave voyages organized in the United States would rise along with the rest of the traffic. It appears that the Portuguese slave traders of New York managed to maintain their business without major disruption, despite the changes that resulted in the move of Cunha Reis to Cuba and the more active role of John Albert Machado and Albert Horn. More than thirty thousand captives disembarked in Cuba were carried on voyages that had started in the United States. In terms of voyages dispatched, the United States was second only to Cuba (which accounts for the vast majority of voyages under the label Caribbean) (table 7.3). A comparison between tables 6.4 and 7.3 also shows the reappearance of Europe as an important region for the departure of slave voyages. Here is where the effects of the actions of US

Table 7.3. Estimated number of vessels and the slaves they embarked by broad
region of departure from the Americas to Africa, 1859–66

	1859–62			1863–66		
	Voyages	Slaves	Percentage	Voyages	Slaves	Percentage
Europe	21	14,427	14.4	19	12,822	28.3
United States	46	32,248	32.2	1	916	4.3
Caribbean	73	50,918	50.8	3	1,832	67.4
Other	4	2,546	2.5	—	—	
Total	143	51,682	100	23	15,669	100

Source: www.slavevoyages.org

authorities during the Republican administration are more evident. The number of voyages dropped from 46 to 1 between 1859–62 and 1863–66. After 1861 only three slave voyages are known to have departed from the United States. The Royal Navy, which could search US vessels from 1862, captured all three. And it was not just the United States that had taken action against the fitting out of slaving vessels. In Cuba, too, the authorities were cracking down on the slave trade and pushing dealers to outfit their voyages in alternative cities, since voyages starting in Cuba also dropped significantly in the second period.[46]

In the final years of the traffic, most slave traders transferred their operations to Europe, especially Spain and France. The British consul in New York described with satisfaction to the Foreign Office the vigor of the US federal officers in dismantling the slave-trading networks established in the city. "It would be perilous to attempt such an adventure in the face of the recent convictions, the vigilance of the police, and the change in the public sentiment in reference to the execution of the laws for the suppression of the slave trading." He noted, however, that although New York would probably cease being an important port for slave-trading operations, other actions were necessary to prevent the transference of the business to other ports, including British ones. According to his informant, despite all the exultation in the press over the condemnation of Captain Gordon, slave traders were already establishing new strategies to continue in the business. "Their vessels will be purchased here," the informant described, "and the voyages will be made up at Liverpool, London, Antwerp, Cadiz, Lisbon, Gibraltar, Barcelona & Marseilles." He pointed out that a number of slavers had cleared from New York precisely to those ports.[47]

John Albert Machado reportedly dispatched eight vessels with legitimate cargos to various ports in Spain and Portugal between his first and second arrests. The vessels were supposed to be refitted for the slave trade after arriving in Europe, but US consuls in both countries detained seven of the eight vessels. After absconding from the New York authorities, Mary J. Watson, Machado's wife, traveled to Cadiz to take care of these transactions. The US minister at Madrid, however, cancelled her passport and forced her to move permanently to Spain. "After the detention of the vessels by our Consuls," a report sent to the British consulate stated, "it is said she commenced drinking very hard, and subsequently died of Delirium Tremens." Although US authorities were able to detain Machado's vessels, other slaving ventures continued to be organized from European ports(see table 7.3). The informant from New York continued to be paid by the British Foreign Office because "the system lately inaugurated by the slave dealers of purchasing vessels in the US and sending them to Europe to be equipped will most likely be followed up."[48]

The changes brought by the war had led to a radical assault on most of the US-based components of the slave trade to Cuba. Local authorities in New York effectively suppressed the outfitting of slave voyages in the city, and the Lyons-Seward Treaty of 1862 ensured that slave traders would abandon the US flag, since their ships would now be liable for seizures by the British navy. That did not mean an immediate end to the traffic. A report from 1863 stated "the slave trade is now carried on by Spaniards, under the French flag, evasion being comparatively easy on account of the absence of the French Squadron, engaged on other duties." The absence of the US flag also did not mean that US-built vessels would not be employed in the business, since the US had as much control over the destiny of their vessels as the British had over the steamships built within their dominions.[49]

Yet something had changed. Ending the slave trade to Cuba depended ultimately on the will of Spanish and Cuban elites, and it was precisely the Civil War in the United States that had prepared the ground for a shift there as well. The beginning of the war almost immediately strengthened a reformist movement in the Spanish Empire that sought to, among other things, stamp out the transatlantic slave trade to Cuba. A proslavery reformism was part of the actions of Captains General Francisco Serrano y Domínguez (1859–62) and Domingo Dulce y Garay (1862–66), who believed that the slave trade had to be eliminated in order to preserve slavery. Serrano pressured Madrid for an increase in the number of vessels patrolling the coasts of Cuba and called for the transformation of the slave trade into a crime of piracy. Captain General Dulce continued the pressure and employed harsher measures against some slave traders, although the events involving José Augustín Arguelles stimulated some skepticism among British authorities regarding his intentions. He allegedly entered into direct conflict with slave traders including Julián Zulueta, Antonio Durañona, and other individuals who controlled the traffic in its final years. In 1863, he deported Durañona and Francisco Tuero from Cuba for their involvement in the illegal business. That same year the Portuguese consulate in Cuba received Portuguese individuals who were about to meet the same fate. One was a member of Abranches, Almeida & Co. in New York who had moved to Cuba after the company dissolved. That spring at least eight Portuguese slave traders were deported from Cuba. Cunha Reis, who had been living there since the late 1850s, also left. By 1865, he was living in Mexico, still pursuing colonization schemes.[50]

The exact nature of the engagement of Cuban authorities with local slave-trading elites is unclear, but their actions did lead to the extinction of slave-trading operations in Cuba. Dulce continued to complain of a loophole in the law of 1845, however, and called for new measures against the traffic. The trade could not be stopped, he argued, until Spanish officials were allowed to search for illegally disembarked slaves inside the plantations themselves. The Spanish government remained hesitant. Actions against the slave trade needed to be calibrated so as not to threaten the existence of slavery in Cuba, and a new anti-slave-trade project appeared in the Spanish senate only in 1866. The following year the bill was approved and became law, providing ample means, as British authorities attested, for the Spanish to suppress the illegal traffic.

By then, however, the traffic had nearly disappeared. In 1866, one vessel successfully disembarked 700 enslaved Africans in Cuba, and two others were seized before embarking the captives. During 1867, there were a few rumors of slave voyages being organized to the island, and at least one vessel successfully disembarked slaves, according to Captain General Manzano and the Royal Navy. In late 1866, the British commissioner in Luanda, Angola, believed that a Portuguese named Leivas was the last person to persist in the transatlantic slave trade, "notwithstanding his heavy losses, in dispatching slave-vessels to this part of the coast of Africa." By that October, Leivas had prepared a new slave expedition with the *Pepito*. When slaves were being embarked, however, a crew member warned the captain of the presence of what supposedly was a man-of-war steamer. and the captain scuttled the vessel. The aborted shipment, intended for Cuba, was apparently Leivas's final attempt. According to the British commissioner in Loanda, "Leivas has suffered such severe losses, not only by the capture of his ships, and the great expense of maintaining so many slaves for so long a period, but also by the refusal of the planters in Cuba to pay him a very large sum of money due for previous shipments." As a British commodore pointed out in June 1867 at Loanda, "Everyone thinks the Slave Trade is over in consequence of the failure of the demand from Cuba." A later report confirmed Leivas's withdrawal from the business: "The whole of the Slaving establishment belonging to this man have recently sold or broken up by his agent who has quitted the Coast for Portugal." The report concluded that "Native Dealers as well as the Europeans remaining in the country who were formerly engaged in the slave traffic, have I believe without exception embarked in legitimate trade in which they find ample employment for their slaves and realize large profits." The history of slavery in Latin America was far from concluded, but the transatlantic slave trade that kept it alive had finally come to an end.[51]

Conclusion

The history of the Republic's relationship with slavery starts and ends with wars. The first, the Revolution, created a nation-state based on liberal principles that protected slavery. Historians from Donald Robinson to George van Cleeve have described how independence spurred the growth of slavery. Such emphasis, correct in my view, is hardly surprising, considering that the nation's number of enslaved people reached four million by the time a second war tore the institution apart. In some ways, the potential for similar growth was present in the history of the US slave trade. Merchants aggressively entered into the slave-trading business and, with their efficient sailing ships and large supplies of rum, broke through trade restrictions in transoceanic empires and helped create the world of freer trade and commercial growth that became a hallmark of the nineteenth century. The forceful entrance of US merchants into the transatlantic slave trade, however, was cut short in the incipient stages of that new world. Changing attitudes to the traffic, which redefined it as the apotheosis of evil, generated tensions that pervaded the North Atlantic. By 1808, not only the United States but also Britain and Denmark had passed legislation prohibiting their citizens from engaging in the foreign commerce in human beings. By 1820, the US branch of the transatlantic slave trade, as the world knew it, had been dismantled.

Unlike Britain, however, where the condemnation of the traffic ultimately led to the end of slavery (although with an interval of thirty years), US planters were remarkably successful in separating the institution itself from the transatlantic traffic that supplied it. The process that led to this distinction between slavery and the slave trade—an alternative counter to the broader shift in attitudes—reached its peak in the United States by 1820. Abolitionists, of course, continued to explore the tensions inherent in that artificial separation, but the subsequent Second Party System ensured that these critiques would remain outside the political sphere. The efforts to link slavery with the slave trade were also weakened after a large number of US citizens withdrew from the business. The Rhode Island slave-trading community vanished. In the years between 1820 and 1835, US participation in the traffic was not markedly different from that of other nations, as crews of slave ships became increasingly internationalized. If the issue emerged, Southerners could (and did) claim that the shipping of enslaved human beings had been essentially a Northern business since independence.

The transatlantic slave trade came back into the US political sphere with the help of pressure from the outside. Whereas US planters were able to create a "peculiar institution" insulated from Africa, their counterparts in Cuba and Brazil were unable to establish such a distinction. Based on a consensus on the necessity of slavery for the development of both economies, and the acknowledgment that, unlike the United States, such a system could not survive without a supply of slaves directly from Africa, a massive contraband slave trade emerged. The United States was then brought back into the story, with US colors reappearing in the traffic. The demand for US-built vessels had already been on the rise since the 1810s, but the real shift came with increasing British pressure to suppress the contraband slave trade after 1835. From that point on, the role of US captains, mates, brokers, and other middlemen steadily increased. The reappearance of the US flag inevitably led to the growth of British pressure on the United States, bringing the issue back to discussion by the late 1830s. At first the US response was solid and strengthened by the growing power of the slaveholding South. If in the aftermath of the War of 1812 the rejection of cooperation had been connected to nationalist motivations, by the late 1830s these motives combined with the rising suspicions of the abolitionist designs of Britain. The United States would persistently refuse to establish the mutual right of search or mixed-commission courts with Britain.

The nation, however, continued to position itself against the transatlantic traffic. John C. Calhoun would openly criticize the slave trade to Brazil and Cuba. As secretary of state, he investigated cases of US involvement in the slave trade to Brazil and ordered several arrests. In the aftermath of the Webster-Ashburton Treaty, Calhoun argued that Brazil and Cuba had enough slaves and that it was actually in the US interest to end the international slave trade. The fraudulent use of the US flag would then no longer be an issue, and US cruisers on the African coast would have the sole purpose of protecting US commerce in the region. For Southern slaveholders the demise of the transatlantic slave trade to Brazil meant just the weakening of another competitor.[1]

An Anglo-American treaty establishing the mutual right of search and mixed commissions would have had little direct impact on the traffic to Brazil. The US flag was less important to the Brazilian traffic than some historians have supposed. None of the British treaties with countries other than the United States had brought the Brazilian slave trade to an end, and there is no reason to believe that an Anglo-American pact would have been different. Events in Brazil were perhaps more important for prefiguring some of the strategies that would connect the United States and Cuba in the 1850s. In the aftermath of slave-trade suppression in Brazil, the strong opposition the United States offered to British pressure in the 1840s induced slave traders to reconfigure their networks to include the United States. These traders, many of them involved in the traffic to Brazil, realized the advantages of slave trading in the slaveholding republic. The United States provided an easier access to their vessels and a much stronger basis for conducting their operations in face of growing British pressure. In the short run, the option was effective. Resources from the United States became part of the traffic to Cuba to a much larger extent than in Brazil, and traders took advantage of the geopolitical chessboard that involved the United States, Britain, and Spain.

From a broader political perspective, however, the move was extremely dangerous. The separation between slavery and the transatlantic slave trade could not be sustained indefinitely. The activities of these slave traders, combined with rising perceptions of Southern expansionism in the North, brought the transatlantic slave trade issue back to the public sphere. Here we see the importance of the earlier shifting attitudes that led to the abolition of slavery in many Northern states and the slave trade in the country in 1808. Those sensibilities remained entrenched in the North, even though for three decades the issue had not inflamed political tensions. Thus it is not surprising that when the slave trade issue reemerged in the 1850s, every political force other than the Southern Fire-Eaters sought political and moral capital in trying to suppress the traffic. Antebellum efforts to suppress the trade, most clearly pursued in the Buchanan administration, bumped against some of the same limits that the British government had faced since its abolition of the traffic. These limits were a consequence of tensions that accompanied the reconfiguration of historical capitalism in the long nineteenth century, with, on the one hand, the growth of slavery in Cuba, Brazil, and the United States (and the highly internationalized contraband slave trade that supplied the first two) and, on the other hand, the reestablishment of an interstate system regulated by the law of nations following the Napoleonic Wars. British courts established the parameters of governmental action against the slave trade by acquitting British merchants indirectly involved in the traffic and restoring seized ships of other nations. It was unlikely that other Atlantic states such as France and the United States would have acted differently in the wake of these British responses. As long as Atlantic states respected the rule of law and competed in the capitalist world economy, they would find obstacles to the ultimate suppression of the traffic insurmountable. President Buchanan was correct to stress that one of the few US actions that could suppress the traffic to Cuba was annexing the island, but that option faced growing opposition in both Cuba and the United States. Britain in turn refrained from repeating the methods it had successfully employed in Brazil because of the possibility of US annexation. The problems in curbing the traffic, therefore, had less to do with governmental apathy, as commonly depicted in the historiography, than with the consolidation of the post-1815 order, characterized by the reestablishment and expansion of a system of sovereign nation-states and the creation of a

liberal ideology that ensured the accumulation of capital on an unprecedented scale.

Members of the Republican Party during the 1850s, of course,
would not recognize these wider obstacles faced by their opponents in
office. They presented Southern attempts to reopen the traffic in the
South and the frustrated attempts of the federal government to curb
it in the North as signs of an expanding Slave Power. Such a coherent
narrative touched on many of the predominant sensibilities toward the
traffic and brought to the fore what many considered the evilest dimensions of slavery.

The most effective way of ending the transatlantic slave trade, as
many abolitionists pointed out at the time, was to abolish slavery altogether. And in this the Civil War played a role that can hardly be overestimated. The first impact was economic, the second ideological. By
disrupting cotton and sugar production in the United States, the war
created opportunities for planters in Cuba and Brazil. At the same time,
by destroying the stronghold of nineteenth-century slavery, the conflict
threw a shadow over the institution that had been at the center of their
connections to the world economy. By 1867, the slave trade to Cuba was
dead, even though Captain General Domingo Dulce y Garay continued
to argue that the slave trade legislation contained loopholes, advocating
plantation searches for and deportations of illegally imported captives.
Yet the issue was no longer the slave trade but rather the continued existence of slavery itself. Dulce himself came to see total suppression of
the traffic as the first step toward gradual emancipation. The concern
of slaveholding elites, thus, became how to prolong slavery, especially
with the new economic opportunities created by slavery's destruction
in the United States. Planters debated a number of bills, but their disagreements were over how rather than whether to end the institution.
Slavery in the Spanish Empire entered its final phase with the passing
of the Moret Law of July 4, 1870, which established that every newborn
after September 1868 or slave with more than sixty years of age would
be emancipated. The passing of the law, of course, did not eliminate
conflicts regarding slavery, and Cuba's sugar planters attempted to circumvent the law and postpone abolition for as long as they could. But
the system could not endure for much longer.[2]

Similar dynamics, although at a slower pace, marked the end of slavery in Brazil. During the Civil War, Brazilian planters contributed to the defeat of the Confederacy by participating in the reconstituted global networks of cotton that emerged with the disruption of cotton production in the South. After the end of war, the growth of coffee consumption in the United States reached unprecedented levels, which in turn stimulated radical transformations in Southeast Brazil. Two symbols of this new moment were the expansion of railroads and the emergence of a massive domestic slave trade, with slave prices rising steadily for three decades after the suppression of the transatlantic slave trade in 1850.[3]

This new expansion, however, took place in a context of crisis that had also been unleashed by the end of slavery in the United States. Although abolitionist newspapers and ideas were disseminated in Brazil in the early 1850s, the issue was not much discussed after 1854. This silence was reflected in the behavior of the Emperor Dom Pedro II in 1861. The US minister to Brazil since 1857 had been Richard K. Meade, a Virginian who tried to gain Brazil's support for the Confederacy in 1861 by pointing to common slaveholding interests before being relieved of his duties by Washington. His replacement, Republican James Watson Webb—whom we saw denouncing the apathy of the Democratic administration toward the transatlantic slave trade in the pages of his newspaper—prepared a long speech to the emperor. Webb claimed that his predecessor had "indulged in language derogatory to our country, and at war with the facts of the case" before leaving his post. The Brazilian secretary of foreign affairs requested a copy of the speech and, after analyzing it, requested that no allusion to slavery should be made. But because Meade had touched on the issue, Webb saw it as his duty to clarify it. The minister's reply, according to Webb, was that the emperor recognized his right to discuss the point, but that "he would be embarrassed in making a reply, and equally embarrassed in not replying to what I said in condemnation of slavery."[4]

That silence was directly connected to the efforts of proslavery Brazilians to curb governmental intervention against the institution. Despite their tendency to see the suppression of the transatlantic slave trade as the death of Brazilian slavery, notorious politicians such as Carneiro Leão and J. M. Pereira da Silva seriously considered projects that stimulated the natural growth of the Brazilian slave population. The shining example of such a possibility was, of course, the United States. Brazilian slaveholding elites therefore followed the events of the Civil War carefully, fearing that emancipation in the United States would alter Brazil's destiny. Only after the Battle of Gettysburg did slavery become once more a central topic of discussion in the parliament, with a number of deputies calling for its gradual abolition. The impact of the war's outcome is clear in the contrast between Dom Pedro II's reluctance even to mention the issue of slavery around 1861 and his actions after 1865. Now he would use his moderating power to pressure cabinets and ministers toward the reform and gradual abolition of slavery. The new climate ultimately led to the debates that culminated in the passing of a free-womb law in 1871. That legislation set in motion a process that ultimately led to the extinction of slavery in Brazil, and, therefore, in all of the Americas.[5]

Abbreviations

ANRJ	Arquivo Nacional do Rio de Janeiro
AST	The African Slave Trade: A Selection of Cases from the Records of the US District Courts in the states of Alabama, Georgia, North Carolina, and South Carolina, National Archives and Records Administration, Atlanta, GA
BPP, Slave Trade	*British Parliamentary Papers,* Slave Trade, 95 vols. (Edgware, Middlesex, UK: Irish University Press)
BHPS	Bristol Historical and Preservation Society, Bristol, RI
CHC	Cuban Heritage Collection, University of Miami Libraries, Miami, FL
FO 84	Foreign Office: Slave Trade Department and successors: General Correspondence before 1906
HCA	Records of the High Court of Admiralty and Colonial Vice-Admiralty Courts
JCBL	John Carter Brown Library, Brown University, Providence, RI
NA	National Archives, Kew, Richmond, Surrey, UK
NARA	National Archives and Records Administration, Washington, DC
TSTD2	Voyages: The Transatlantic Slave Trade Database, www.slavevoyages.org

Notes

ONE Introduction

1. James Dickinson, *Trial of James Parks, Otherwise Dickinson for the Murder of William Beatson, at Cuyahoga Falls, Ohio, on the Night of the Thirteenth of April, 1853: Embracing the Opening Statements of Counsel, Confessional Plea, Motions, Decisions, Evidence, Judge's Charge, Verdict, Sentence, Together with a History of His Life!* 2nd ed. (Akron, OH: Laurie and Barnard, 1854), 32–33; James D'Wolf last will and testament, Bristol, RI, 1836. Bristol Town Hall. The name D'Wolf appears in the documentation with different spellings, including D'Wolf, de Wolf, DeWolf, and DWolf. I chose to use D'Wolf, the form most common in the nineteenth-century documents. There has been a growing interest in the history of the D'Wolfs and other Rhode Island families with involvement in the slave trade as part of a broader scholarly and public awareness of the history of slavery and the slave trade in the northern United States. In Rhode Island, the 2003 appointment of the Brown University Steering Committee on Slavery and Justice to study the university's historical connection to slavery and the slave trade stimulated great public interest. In the committee's final report, the D'Wolfs were described as "the largest slave trading family in all of North America, mounting more than eighty transatlantic voyages." Since then, several works have specifically discussed the history of the D'Wolf family, some of them produced by descendants of the family themselves. See Thomas Norman DeWolf, *Inheriting the Trade: A Northern Family Confronts Its Legacy as the Largest Slave-Trading Dynasty in U.S. History* (Boston: Beacon, 2009); the documentary film *Traces of the Trade: A Story from the Deep North*, written by Alla Kovgan and directed by Alla Kovgan and Jude Ray (San Francisco: California Newsreel, 2008); and Cynthia Mestad Johnson, *James DeWolf and the Rhode Island Slave Trade* (Charleston, SC: History Press, 2014).

2. James A. Rawley, "Captain Nathaniel Gordon, the Only American Executed for Violating the Slave Trade Laws," *Civil War History* 39, no. 3 (1993): 216–24.

3. Dale W. Tomich, *Through the Prism of Slavery: Labor, Capital, and World Economy* (Lanham: Rowman and Littlefield, 2003); Márcia Regina Berbel, Rafael de Bivar Marquese, and Tâmis Parron, *Escravidão e política: Brasil e Cuba, c. 1790–1850* (São Paulo: Editora Hucitec and FAPESP, 2010). For the US edition, see Márcia Regina Berbel, Rafael de Bivar Marquese, and Tâmis Parron, *Slavery and Politics: Brazil and Cuba, 1790–1850* (Albuquerque: University of New Mexico Press, 2016). For an interpretation of the long nineteenth century as a third stage of historical capitalism, see Giovanni Arrighi, *The Long Twentieth Century: Money, Power, and the Origins of Our Times* (London: Verso, 1994). On the concept of historical capitalism, see Immanuel Maurice Wallerstein, *Historical Capitalism: With Capitalist Civilization* (London: Verso, 1995).

4. David Eltis, *Economic Growth and the Ending of the Transatlantic Slave Trade* (New York: Oxford University Press, 1987), 50; Jeannine Marie DeLombard, *In the Shadow of the Gallows: Race, Crime, and American Civic Identity* (Philadelphia: University of Pennsylvania Press, 2012), 272.

5. Ralph Waldo Emerson, *An Address Delivered in the Court-House in Concord, Massachusetts, on 1st August, 1844, on the Anniversary of the Emancipation of the Negroes in the British West Indies* (Boston: James Munroes, 1844), 19. The critique of the consumption of slave-grown products had a more practical version in the "free produce movement," based on the establishment of stores selling goods produced by free laborers. A number of these shops were opened at the turn of the 1830s but never had the support that the movement for the boycott of slave-grown sugar had in early nineteenth-century Britain. By the 1850s most free produce stores had closed, and the movement was criticized or simply ignored by most abolitionists. See Lawrence B. Glickman, "'Buy for the Sake of the Slave': Abolitionism and the Origins of American Consumer Activism," *American Quarterly* 56, no. 4 (2004): 889–912. On the boycotts of slave-grown sugar in Britain, see Clare Midgley, *Women against Slavery: The British Campaigns, 1780–1870* (London: Routledge, 1992), 35–40; and Mimi Sheller, *Consuming the Caribbean: From Arawaks to Zombies* (London: Routledge, 2003), 88–95. On the narrative of a white New England, see Joanne Pope Melish, *Disowning Slavery: Gradual Emancipation and "Race" in New England, 1780–1860* (Ithaca, NY: Cornell University Press, 1998).

6. Eltis, *Economic Growth*, 84.

7. Thomas C. Holt, "Explaining Abolition," *Journal of Social History* 24, no. 2 (1990): 371–78; Christopher Leslie Brown, *Moral Capital: Foundations of British Abolitionism* (Chapel Hill: University of North Carolina Press, 2006).

8. James A. McMillin, *The Final Victims: Foreign Slave Trade to North America, 1783–1810* (Columbia: University of South Carolina Press, 2004); Gerald Horne, *The Deepest South: The United States, Brazil, and the African Slave Trade* (New York: New York University Press, 2007); Ernest Obadele-Starks, *Freebooters and Smugglers: The Foreign Slave Trade in the United States after 1808* (Fayetteville: University of Arkansas Press, 2007); Sarah Batterson, "'An Ill-Judged Piece of Business': The United States and the Failure of Slave Trade Suppression" (PhD diss., University of New Hampshire, 2013);

Dale Torston Graden, *Disease, Resistance, and Lies: The Demise of the Transatlantic Slave Trade to Brazil and Cuba* (Baton Rouge: Louisiana State University Press, 2014); Stephen M. Chambers, *No God but Gain: The Untold Story of Cuban Slavery, the Monroe Doctrine, and the Making of the United States* (London: Verso, 2015).

9. W. E. B. Du Bois, *The Suppression of the African Slave-Trade to the United States of America, 1638–1870* (New York: Longmans, Green, 1896); Obadele-Starks, *Freebooters and Smugglers.*

10. This is most evident in Horne, *Deepest South.* Although few historians would agree with his depiction of the US role in the traffic to Brazil, some important works have, nonetheless, reproduced this view (see Chapter 5).

11. Jay A. Coughtry, "The Notorious Triangle: Rhode Island and the African Slave Trade, 1700–1807" (PhD diss., University of Wisconsin, Madison, 1978), 569–70. Coughtry's dissertation was later published as *The Notorious Triangle: Rhode Island and the African Slave Trade, 1700–1807* (Philadelphia: Temple University Press, 1981). All references here come from his dissertation. Warren S. Howard, *American Slavers and the Federal Law, 1837–1862* (Berkeley: University of California Press, 1963), 206–10; Don Edward Fehrenbacher, *The Slaveholding Republic: An Account of the United States Government's Relations to Slavery* (Oxford: Oxford University Press, 2001); David F. Ericson, *Slavery in the American Republic: Developing the Federal Government, 1791–1861* (Lawrence: University Press of Kansas, 2011); Robert Edgar Conrad, *World of Sorrow: The African Slave Trade to Brazil* (Baton Rouge: Louisiana State University Press, 1986), 144.

12. Philip D. Curtin, *The Atlantic Slave Trade: A Census* (Madison: University of Wisconsin Press, 1969); Herbert S. Klein, *The Atlantic Slave Trade* (Cambridge: Cambridge University Press, 1999); David Eltis and David Richardson, eds., *Extending the Frontiers: Essays on the New Transatlantic Slave Database* (New Haven: Yale University Press, 2008); Manolo Florentino, *Em costas negras: Uma história do tráfico Atlântico de escravos entre a Africa e o Rio de Janeiro, séculos XVIII e XIX* (São Paulo: Companhia das Letras, 1997); Eltis, *Economic Growth.*

13. Donald L. Robinson, *Slavery in the Structure of American Politics, 1765–1820* (New York: Harcourt Brace Jovanovich, 1970); Paul Finkelman, *Slavery and the Founders: Race and Liberty in the Age of Jefferson,* 2nd ed. (Armonk, NY: M. E. Sharpe, 2001); Fehrenbacher, *Slaveholding Republic;* Matthew Mason, *Slavery and Politics in the Early American Republic* (Chapel Hill: University of North Carolina Press, 2006); David Waldstreicher, *Slavery's Constitution: From Revolution to Ratification* (New York: Hill and Wang, 2009); George Van Cleve, *A Slaveholders' Union: Slavery, Politics, and the Constitution in the Early American Republic* (Chicago: University of Chicago Press, 2010).

14. Tomich, *Through the Prism of Slavery;* Dale Tomich, "The Wealth of Empire: Francisco Arango y Parreño, Political Economy, and the Second Slavery in Cuba," *Comparative Studies in Society and History* 45, no. 1 (2003): 4–28; Tâmis Parron, *A política da escravidão no Império do Brasil, 1826–1865* (Rio de Janeiro: Civilização Brasileira, 2011); Berbel, Marquese, and Parron, *Escravidão e política;* Rafael B. Marquese and Tâmis P. Parron, "Internacional escravista: A política da segunda escravidão," *Topoi: Revista de História* 12 (2011): 97–117; Christopher Schmidt-Nowara, *Empire and Antislavery: Spain,*

Cuba, and Puerto Rico, 1833–1874 (Pittsburgh: University of Pittsburgh Press, 1999); Anthony E. Kaye, "The Second Slavery: Modernity in the Nineteenth-Century South and the Atlantic World," *Journal of Southern History* 75, no. 3 (2009): 627; Edward E. Baptist, *The Half Has Never Been Told: Slavery and the Making of American Capitalism* (New York: Basic Books, 2014).

TWO North American Slave Traders in the Age of Revolution, 1776–1807

1. *Oracle of Dauphin,* May 3, 1802; George Howe, *Mount Hope: A New England Chronicle* (New York: Viking , 1959), 108–9. It must be noted that Moses Brown, who had been an abolitionist since the last decades of the eighteenth century, believed that Thomas Jefferson had been duped in the appointment of Collins, an argument with which historian Jay Coughtry seems to agree. See Jay A. Coughtry, "The Notorious Triangle: Rhode Island and the African Slave Trade, 1700–1807" (PhD diss., University of Wisconsin, Madison, 1978), 582n72. On the *Thomas Jefferson,* see TSTD2, voyageid 36757.

2. James A. Rawley and Stephen D. Behrendt, *The Transatlantic Slave Trade: A History* (Lincoln: University of Nebraska Press, 2005), 305; Rachel Chernos Lin, "The Rhode Island Slave-Traders: Butchers, Bakers and Candlestick-Makers," *Slavery and Abolition* 23, no. 3 (2002): 21–38.

3. Eric J. Hobsbawm, *The Age of Revolution: Europe, 1789–1848* (New York: Praeger, 1969). There is another debate related to the classic work of R. R. Palmer. For some reviews of these debates, see the introductory chapters of Gabriel B. Paquette, *Imperial Portugal in the Age of Atlantic Revolutions: The Luso-Brazilian World, c. 1770–1850* (Cambridge: Cambridge University Press, 2013); David Armitage and Sanjay Subrahmanyam, eds., *The Age of Revolutions in Global Context, c. 1760–1840* (Houndmills, UK: Palgrave Macmillan, 2010); and Rafael Marquese and João Paulo Pimenta, "Latin America and the Caribbean: Traditions of Global History," in *Global History, Globally,* ed. Sven Beckert and Dominic Sachsenmaier (Cambridge: Cambridge University Press, forthcoming). On the distinction between societies with slaves and slave societies, see Moses I. Finley, *Ancient Slavery and Modern Ideology* (New York: Viking, 1980).

4. Alex Borucki, David Eltis, and David Wheat, "Atlantic History and the Slave Trade to Spanish America," *American Historical Review* 120, no. 2 (2015): 433–61; Alex Borucki, "The Slave Trade to the Río de La Plata, 1777–1812: Trans-Imperial Networks and Atlantic Warfare," *Colonial Latin American Review* 20, no. 1 (2011): 81–107; Elena Schneider, "African Slavery and Spanish Empire," *Journal of Early American History* 5, no. 1 (2015): 3–29; I. K. Sundiata, *From Slaving to Neoslavery: The Bight of Biafra and Fernando Po in the Era of Abolition, 1827–1930* (Madison: University of Wisconsin Press, 1996), 18–19; and Gabriel Aladrén, "Sem respeitar fé nem tratados: Escravidão e guerra na formação da fronteira sul do Brasil (Rio Grande de São Pedro, c. 1777–c.1835)" (PhD diss., Universidade Federal Fluminense, Rio de Janeiro, 2012), 148–50.

5. Borucki, Eltis, and Wheat, "Atlantic History and the Slave Trade." See also Josep M. Delgado Ribas, "The Slave Trade in the Spanish Empire (1501–1808)," Luiz Fe-

lipe de Alencastro, "Portuguese Missionaries and Early Modern Antislavery and Pro-slavery Thought," and the excellent introduction by Josep Maria Fradera and Christopher Schmidt-Nowara, all in *Slavery and Antislavery in Spain's Atlantic Empire,* ed. Josep Maria Fradera and Christopher Schmidt-Nowara (New York: Berghahn Books, 2013). For a comparison between the Spanish and British Empires, see John Huxtable Elliott, *Empires of the Atlantic World: Britain and Spain in America, 1492–1830* (New Haven: Yale University Press, 2006). On the traffic to South Carolina, see Jed Handelsman Shugerman, "The Louisiana Purchase and South Carolina's Reopening of the Slave Trade in 1803," *Journal of the Early Republic* 22, no. 2 (2002): 263–90; and James A. McMillin, *The Final Victims: Foreign Slave Trade to North America, 1783–1810* (Columbia: University of South Carolina Press, 2004).

6. See the estimates page of the TSTD2; and Franklin W. Knight, "The American Revolution and the Caribbean," in *Slavery and Freedom in the Age of the American Revolution,* ed. Ira Berlin and Ronald Hoffman (Charlottesville: University Press of Virginia, 1983).

7. Joyce Oldham Appleby, *Inheriting the Revolution: The First Generation of Americans* (Cambridge, MA: Belknap Press of Harvard University Press, 2000), 58; Coughtry, "Notorious Triangle"; Borucki, "Slave Trade to Río de la Plata."

8. TSTD2: *Cristiana* (voyageid 19061), *Louisiana* (voyageid 36797), *Columbia* (voyageid 36864), *Ascension* (voyageids 36570, 36590, and 37294). On the *Ascension,* see also Samuel Chase to William Vernon, Apr. 9, 1797, New-York Historical Society, Slavery Collection, Series I: Samuel and William Vernon, available online at: http://cdm128401 .cdmhost.com/cdm/ref/collection/p15052coll5/id/21658/show/21656. On the British and US shipping industries in the eighteenth century, see Ralph Davis, *The Rise of the English Shipping Industry in the Seventeenth and Eighteenth Centuries* (London: Macmillan, 1962); Samuel Eliot Morison, *The Maritime History of Massachusetts, 1783–1860* (Boston: Houghton Mifflin, 1961); and Curtis P. Nettels, *The Emergence of a National Economy, 1775–1815* (New York: Holt, Rinehart and Winston, 1962).

9. On the early history of Cuba, see Alejandro de la Fuente, *Havana and the Atlantic in the Sixteenth Century* (Chapel Hill: University of North Carolina Press, 2008).

10. Elliott, *Empires of the Atlantic World,* 303.

11. Adam Rothman, *Slave Country: American Expansion and the Origins of the Deep South* (Cambridge, MA: Harvard University Press, 2005), 17; Shugerman, "Louisiana Purchase and South Carolina's Reopening"; Edward E. Baptist, *The Half Has Never Been Told: Slavery and the Making of American Capitalism* (New York: Basic Books, 2014), ch. 2.

12. See TSTD2 (General Variables>Ship, nation, owners>Place registered); and McMillin, *Final Victims,* 81.

13. *Geribita* was a type of Brazilian rum used by Luso-Brazilian merchants in the slave trade in Central Africa. On the role of geribita in the Rio de Janeiro–Angola trade, see Roquinaldo Ferreira, "Dinâmica do comércio intra-colonial: Geribita, panos asiáticos e guerra no tráfico angolano de escravos," in *Antigo regime nos trópicos: A dinâmica imperial portuguesa (séculos XVI–XVIII),* ed. J. Fragoso, M. F. Bicalho, and M. F. Couvêa

(Rio de Janeiro: Civilização Brasileira, 2001), 339–78. On the Bahia–Bight of Benin connection, see Pierre Verger, *Trade Relations between the Bight of Benin and Bahia from the 17th to 19th Century* (Ibadan, Nigeria: Ibadan University Press, 1976); Coughtry, "Notorious Triangle," 301 (quotation). For a detailed discussion of one specific voyage organized by Rhode Island slave traders and their interactions with the Eurafrican community on the Upper Guinea coast, see George E. Brooks and Bruce L. Mouser, "An 1804 Slaving Contract Signed in Arabic Script from the Upper Guinea Coast," *History in Africa* 14 (1987): 341–48. On US merchants in Upper Guinea, see Bruce L. Mouser, *American Colony on the Rio Pongo: The War of 1812, the Slave Trade, and the Proposed Settlement of African Americans, 1810–1830* (Trenton, NJ: Africa World Press, 2013).

14. Philip D. Morgan, "Ending the Slave Trade: A Caribbean and Atlantic Context," in *Abolitionism and Imperialism in Britain, Africa, and the Atlantic,* ed. Derek R. Peterson (Athens: Ohio University Press, 2010), 103 (quotation), 107–8; Justin Roberts, *Slavery and the Enlightenment in the British Atlantic, 1750–1807* (Cambridge: Cambridge University Press, 2013).

15. Peter S. Onuf, *Jefferson's Empire: The Language of American Nationhood* (Charlottesville: University Press of Virginia, 2000), 140.

16. Paul Finkelman, "Regulating the African Slave Trade," *Civil War History* 54, no. 4 (2008): 379–405.

17. Donald L. Robinson, *Slavery in the Structure of American Politics, 1765–1820* (New York: Harcourt Brace Jovanovich, 1970), 299–301.

18. Richard S. Newman, *The Transformation of American Abolitionism: Fighting Slavery in the Early Republic* (Chapel Hill: University of North Carolina Press, 2002), 39, 48–49, 57–58.

19. Richard S. Newman, "Prelude to the Gag Rule: Southern Reaction to Antislavery Petitions in the First Federal Congress," *Journal of the Early Republic* 16, no. 4 (1996): 593–94; Robinson, *Slavery in the Structure of American Politics,* 307–9; George Van Cleve, *A Slaveholders' Union: Slavery, Politics, and the Constitution in the Early American Republic* (Chicago: University of Chicago Press, 2010), 195.

20. "An Act to Prohibit the Carrying on the Slave Trade from the United States to Any Foreign Place or Country," 3d Cong., 1st Sess., Act of Mar. 22, 1794, Chap. 11, 1 Stat. 347, 349, available online at: http://avalon.law.yale.edu/18th_century/sl001.asp; "An Act in Addition to the Act Intituled 'An Act to Prohibit the Carrying on the Slave Trade from the United States to any Foreign Place or Country,'" Act of May 10, 1800, available online at: http://avalon.law.yale.edu/19th_century/sl002.asp; Finkelman, "Regulating the Slave Trade," 398–99.

21. Newman, *Transformation of American Abolitionism,* 74; *Impartial Register,* Aug. 14, 1800; Gary B. Nash and Jean R. Soderlund, eds., *Freedom by Degrees: Emancipation in Pennsylvania and Its Aftermath* (New York: Oxford University Press, 1991), 183–85; Donald L. Canney, *Africa Squadron: The U.S. Navy and the Slave Trade, 1842–1861* (Washington, DC: Potomac Books, 2006); on the *Prudent,* see TSTD2, voyageid 36707; on the *Phoebe,* see ibid., voyageid 36992.

22. Lin, "Rhode Island Slave-Traders."

23. Howe, *Mount Hope,* 186–87.

24. Ibid., 101–2; on the *Punch,* see TSTD2, voyageid 36742; on the *Ann,* see ibid., voyageid 36856.

25. See, e.g., the sloop *Baltimore* with 60 slaves, *Charleston Courier,* July 13, 1807; the brig *Three Sisters* with 122 slaves, *City Gazette and Daily Advertiser,* July 25, 1807; and the brig *Betsy and Polly* with 106 slaves, *Charleston Courier,* Aug. 25, 1807.

26. As a whole, the transatlantic slave trade was responsible for a small share of the total external commerce of the United States. David Eltis, "The U.S. Transatlantic Slave Trade, 1644–1867: An Assessment," *Civil War History* 54, no. 4 (2008): 366.

27. "John Cranston's testimony to the Grand Jury, June 15, 1791," box 43, folder 24, Newport Historical Society, Newport, RI; Jay Coughtry, ed., *Papers of the American Slave Trade* (Bethesda, MD: University Publications of America, 1996); Marcus Rediker, *The Slave Ship: A Human History* (New York: Viking, 2008), 343–47; Isidor Paiewonsky, *Eyewitness Accounts of Slavery in the Danish West Indies: Also Graphic Tales of Other Slave Happenings on Ships and Plantations* (New York: Fordham University Press, 1989); Leonardo Marques, "Slave Trading in a New World: The Strategies of North American Slave Traders in the Age of Abolition," *Journal of the Early Republic* 32, no. 2 (2012): 233.

28. Charles Rappleye, *Sons of Providence: The Brown Brothers, the Slave Trade, and the American Revolution* (New York: Simon and Schuster, 2006).

29. The main source for the voyage of the *Rebecca* is Jay Coughtry's "Notorious Triangle," but he does not specify the specific origin of his data. It is important to note that Welcome Arnold had been part of a committee that prepared a bill to prevent the sale of Rhode Island slaves to other states without their consent in 1779 (which would be a violation of the manumission act of 1774). I thank Kimberly Nusco of the JCBL for most of the information on the Arnolds used here. See the *Rebecca,* TSTD2, voyageid 36611.

30. Elizabeth Donnan, *Documents Illustrative of the History of the Slave Trade to America,* vol. 4: *The Border Colonies and the Southern Colonies* (Washington, DC: Carnegie Institution, 1935), 344; Coughtry, "Notorious Triangle," 523. Vermont's 1777 constitution freed slaves (and thus by implication made the slave trade illegal). See Stanley L. Engerman, *Slavery, Emancipation, and Freedom: Comparative Perspectives* (Baton Rouge: Louisiana State University Press, 2007), 5n9. On the *Hope,* see the TSTD2, voyageids 36536, 36549, and 36554.

31. BB & Ives to Martin Benson, Nov. 29, 1794, Brown Family Papers, box 513, JCBL; for the involvement of Brown & Ives in the legitimate commerce with Africa, see George E. Brooks, *Yankee Traders, Old Coasters, and African Middlemen: A History of American Legitimate Trade with West Africa in the Nineteenth Century* (Brookline, MA: Boston University Press, 1970), 65–66; and Coughtry, "Notorious Triangle," 536–46.

32. John Brown to Moses Brown, Nov. 17, 1797, Moses Brown Papers, Rhode Island Historical Society, Providence; Coughtry, "Notorious Triangle," 543; on the *Ann,* see TSTD2, voyageid 36628; on the *Hope,* see ibid., voyageid 36630.

33. Coughtry, "Notorious Triangle," 545.

34. *Columbian Courier,* June 10, 1803; Coughtry, "Notorious Triangle," 560. On the *Fanny,* see TSTD2, voyageid 36733.

35. Peter J. Coleman, *The Transformation of Rhode Island, 1790–1860* (Providence, RI: Brown University Press, 1963), 56; Coughtry, "Notorious Triangle," 568.

36. Edward Field, *State of Rhode Island and Providence Plantations at the End of the Century: A History* (Boston: Mason, 1902), 275.

37. Michel-Rolph Trouillot, "Motion in the System: Coffee, Color and Slavery in Eighteenth-Century Saint Domingue," *Review, A Journal of the Fernand Braudel Center* 3 (1982): 331–88.

38. Michelle Craig McDonald, "From Cultivation to Cup: Caribbean Coffee and the North American Economy, 1765–1805" (PhD diss., University of Michigan, 2005), 236–45; David Geggus, "The French Slave Trade: An Overview," *William and Mary Quarterly*, 3rd ser., 58, no. 1 (2001): 119–38; on the *Elizabeth,* see TSTD2, voyageid 26071; on the *Betsey,* see ibid., voyageid 25297.

39. The governor of Santiago de Cuba, Sebastián Kindelan y O'Regan, estimated 19,635 migrants arriving in the island between 1800 and 1804. See Matt D. Childs, *The Aponte Rebellion in Cuba and the Struggle against Atlantic Slavery* (Chapel Hill: University of North Carolina Press, 2006), 40; Gabriel Debien, "The Saint Domingue Refugees in Cuba, 1793–1815," in Carl A. Brasseaux and Glenn R. Conrad, eds., *The Road to Louisiana: The Saint-Domingue Refugees, 1792–1809* (Lafayette: University of Eastern Louisiana Press, 1992), 33 (quotation); María Elena Orozco Melgar, "La implantación francesa en Santiago de Cuba," in *Les Français dans L'Orient cubain,* ed. Jean Lamore (Bordeaux: Maison des Pays Iberiques, 1993), 48. By comparing documentation from Haiti and Cuba and tracking names in a list of Cuban coffee farms of 1807, historian Gabriel Debién has found that, of the 62 names (from a total of 138) that he was able to identify, at least 35 had been coffee planters in Saint Domingue.

40. Rafael de Bivar Marquese, "A ilustração luso-brasileira e a circulação dos saberes escravistas caribenhos: A montagem da cafeicultura brasileira em perspectiva comparada," *História, Ciências, Saúde-Manguinhos* 16, no. 4 (2009): 866–67; William C. Van Norman, *Shade-Grown Slavery: The Lives of Slaves on Coffee Plantations in Cuba* (Nashville, TN: Vanderbilt University Press, 2013), 20–21, 161n52.

41. Laird W. Bergad, Fe Iglesias García, and María del Carmen Barcia, *The Cuban Slave Market, 1790–1880* (Cambridge: Cambridge University Press, 1995), 28, 82, 95–96; Ada Ferrer, "Cuban Slavery and Atlantic Antislavery," in Fradera and Schmidt-Nowara, *Slavery and Antislavery in Spain's Atlantic Empire,* 140–41 (quotation); Manuel Moreno Fraginals, *O engenho: Complexo sócio-econômico açucareiro cubano,* 3 vols. (São Paulo: Hucitec, 1988); Gabriel Debién, "The Saint-Domingue Refugees in Cuba, 1793–1815," in Brasseaux and Conrad, *Road to Louisiana,* 33, 74.

42. Debién, "Saint-Domingue Refugees in Cuba," 74; David R. Murray, *Odious Commerce: Britain, Spain, and the Abolition of the Cuban Trade* (Cambridge: Cambridge University Press, 1980), 11–12; David Wheat, *Atlantic Africa and the Spanish Caribbean, 1570–1640* (Chapel Hill: University of North Carolina Press, 2016).

43. Ada Ferrer, "A sociedade escravista cubana e a Revolução haitiana," *Almanack* (Brazil), no. 3 (2012): 40; Ferrer, "Cuban Slavery and Atlantic Antislavery," 138; Rafael

Bivar Marquese, "Comparando imperios: O lugar do Brasil no projeto escravista de Francisco de Arango y Parreño," in *Francisco Arango y la invención de la Cuba azucarera*, ed. Maria Dolores González-Ripoli and Izáskún Álvarez Cuartero (Salamanca, Spain: Ediciones Universidad de Salamanca, 2009), 69; Manuel Barcia Paz, *The Great African Slave Revolt of 1825: Cuba and the Fight for Freedom in Matanzas* (Baton Rouge: Louisiana State University Press, 2012), 51 (quotation).

44. The revolt started when two captives, Romualdo and Joseph, the latter a French-speaking man, attacked their master and ran away, recruiting slaves from a number of plantations on their way. At the beginning of the affair, when the master ordered Joseph to tie Romualdo up, the French-speaking slave answered: "Tie him up? Why would I tie him up? Nobody here has a master any longer: we are all free." Barcia Paz, *Great African Slave Revolt of 1825*, 53–54; Childs, *Aponte Rebellion*, 39.

45. José Guadalupe Ortega, "Cuban Merchants, Slave Trade Knowledge, and the Atlantic World, 1790s–1820s," *CLAHR: Colonial Latin American Historical Review* 15, no. 3 (2006): 235–37; Pablo Tornero Tinajero, *Crecimiento ecónomico y transformaciones sociales: Esclavos, hacendados y comerciantes en la Cuba colonial (1760–1840)* (Madrid: Ministerio de Trabajo y Seguridad Social, 1996), 71–72.

46. Dale Tomich, "The Wealth of Empire: Francisco Arango y Parreño, Political Economy, and the Second Slavery in Cuba," *Comparative Studies in Society and History* 45, no. 1 (2003): 10; Howe, *Mount Hope*, 123.

47. John Catalogne to John Sabins, Havana, Dec. 18, 1806, Wilsons' Papers, BHPS; reproductions of the plants can be found in Coughtry, *Papers of the American Slave Trade*, and in Stephen Chambers, "At Home among the Dead: North Americans and the 1825 Guamacaro Slave Insurrection," *Journal of the Early Republic* 33, no. 1 (2013): 61–86. For a document showing Sabins as a slave captain, see Brooks and Mouser, "1804 Slaving Contract."

48. David Brion Davis, *Inhuman Bondage: The Rise and Fall of Slavery in the New World* (New York: Oxford University Press, 2006), 158. On the historiographical debates over the impact of Saint Domingue on the Americas, see David Barry Gaspar and David Patrick Geggus, eds., *A Turbulent Time: The French Revolution and the Greater Caribbean* (Bloomington: Indiana University Press, 1997); and Robin Blackburn, *The American Crucible: Slavery, Emancipation, and Human Rights* (London: Verso, 2011), pt. 3.

49. Darold D. Wax, "'The Great Risque We Run': The Aftermath of Slave Rebellion at Stono, South Carolina, 1739–1745," *Journal of Negro History* 67, no. 2 (1982): 140.

50. Patrick S. Brady, "The Slave Trade and Sectionalism in South Carolina, 1787–1808," *Journal of Southern History* 38, no. 4 (1972): 609–10; Rawley and Behrendt, *Transatlantic Slave Trade*, 352.

51. Douglas R. Egerton, *Gabriel's Rebellion: The Virginia Slave Conspiracies of 1800 and 1802* (Chapel Hill: University of North Carolina Press, 1993); Alfred N. Hunt, *Haiti's Influence on Antebellum America: Slumbering Volcano in the Caribbean* (Baton Rouge: Louisiana State University Press, 1988), 112; Thomas B. Wait and Sons, *State Papers and Publick Documents of the United States: Thomas B. Wait and Sons, Propose to Pub-*

lish, *the State Papers and Publick Documents of the United States, Commencing with the Accession of Mr. Jefferson to the Presidency* . . . (Boston: Thomas B. Wait and Sons, 1814), 487–88.

52. Laurent Dubois, *Avengers of the New World: The Story of the Haitian Revolution* (Cambridge, MA: Belknap Press of Harvard University Press, 2004), 284–86; Wait, *State Papers and Publick Documents of the United States,* 487–88.

53. Robinson, *Slavery in the Structure of American Politics,* 316–18; *U.S. vs Planters Adventure,* 1801, AST, box 3; *U.S. vs Brig Ida,* 1802, ibid., box 4; *Ida,* TSTD2, voyageid 36745.

54. *U.S. vs Schooner Amelia,* 1803, AST, box 4; *U.S. vs Brig Lady Nelson,* 1803, ibid.; Lacy K. Ford, *Deliver Us from Evil: The Slavery Question in the Old South* (Oxford: Oxford University Press, 2009), 90–91.

55. David P. Geggus, "The Caribbean in the Age of Revolution," in Armitage and Subrahmanyam, *Age of Revolutions in Global Context,* 89; Thomas Cooper, *The Statutes at Large of South Carolina: Acts Relating to Charleston, Courts, Slaves, and Rivers* (Columbia, SC: A. S. Johnston, 1840), 450; Brady, "Slave Trade and Sectionalism in South Carolina"; Shugerman, "Louisiana Purchase and South Carolina's Reopening."

56. Ford, *Deliver Us from Evil,* 105–11.

57. Ibid., 112–21; Peter J. Kastor, *The Nation's Crucible: The Louisiana Purchase and the Creation of America* (New Haven: Yale University Press, 2004), 55–62.

58. "Act to Prohibit the Importation of Slaves into any Port or Place within the Jurisdiction of the United States, from and after the First Day of January, in the Year of Our Lord One Thousand Eight Hundred and Eight," 2 Stat. 426, enacted Mar. 2, 1807, available online at http://avalon.law.yale.edu/19th_century/sl004.asp; Robinson, *Slavery in the Structure of American Politics,* 331; Matthew E. Mason, "Slavery Overshadowed: Congress Debates Prohibiting the Atlantic Slave Trade to the United States, 1806–1807," *Journal of the Early Republic* 20, no. 1 (2000): 71.

59. The New York Manumission Society in fact warned African Americans in the city in 1809 that their celebrations of the abolition of the slave trade had been "improper" and that "both their procession, and Politicks in their orations should be discontinued for the future." See David Nathaniel Gellman, *Emancipating New York: The Politics of Slavery and Freedom, 1777–1827* (Baton Rouge: Louisiana State University Press, 2006), 198–99; Seymour Drescher, *Abolition: A History of Slavery and Antislavery* (Cambridge: Cambridge University Press, 2009), 137; Julie Winch, "Self-Help and Self-Determination: Black Philadelphians and the Dimensions of Freedom," in *Antislavery and Abolition in Philadelphia: Emancipation and the Long Struggle for Racial Justice in the City of Brotherly Love,* ed. Richard S. Newman and James Mueller (Baton Rouge: Louisiana State University Press, 2011), 75; Robin Blackburn, *The Overthrow of Colonial Slavery, 1776–1848* (London: Verso, 1988), 268; and William B. Gravely, "The Dialectic of Double-Consciousness in Black American Freedom Celebrations, 1808–1863," *Journal of Negro History* 67, no. 4 (1982): 303.

60. *Providence Gazette,* Aug. 29, 1807; Howard Albert Ohline, "Politics and Slavery:

The Issue of Slavery in National Politics, 1787–1815" (PhD diss., University of Missouri–Columbia, 1969), 252–53.

THREE Transitions, 1808–1820

1. Joseph Story, "A charge, delivered to the grand juries of the circuit court, at October term, 1819, in Boston, and at November term, 1819, in Providence, and published at their unanimous request," in *The African Slave Trade and American Courts: The Pamphlet Literature*, ed. Paul Finkelman, vol. 1 (New York: Garland, 1988), 5. Story does not refer to violations of the 1818 law, and there is no evidence that he had worked in any slave trade–related case during 1819. Paul Finkelman suggests that this charge might be connected to the indictments of the cases of Captains La Coste and Smith, which could have started already in 1819, but in fact, both vessels were seized only in 1820. See Paul Finkelman, *Slavery in the Courtroom: An Annotated Bibliography of American Cases* (Washington, DC: Library of Congress, 1985; reprint ed., Lawbook Exchange, 1998), 214. The *Cyane* seized the *Endymion* (see TSTD2, voyageid 3874), the *Esperanza*, the *Plattsburg* (ibid., voyageid 7651), and the *Science* (ibid., voyageid 4967); the *Hornet* seized the *Alexander* (ibid., voyageid 34173); and, finally, the *Alligator* seized the *Jeune Eugene* (ibid., voyageid 4966), the *Mathilde* (ibid., voyageid 34253), the *Daphne* (ibid., voyageid 120), and the *Eliza* (ibid., voyageid 34223). For US citizens onboard the *Endymion*, see *Franklin Gazette*, July 11, 1820. The US Navy also captured a few other suspected slavers off the coast of Africa at the time, but they were either destroyed or released. The US African Squadron would be established only in 1843, but the US government did make some relatively small investments for the enforcement of anti–slave trade legislation starting in 1819. See David F. Ericson, *Slavery in the American Republic: Developing the Federal Government, 1791–1861* (Lawrence: University Press of Kansas, 2011), ch. 2.

2. That same year, the *Hornet* captured the *Alexander*, but the vessel had been denounced by its own crew before the embarkation of slaves at Cape Verde. *Boston Recorder*, July 15, 1820; National Messenger, published as *National Messenger*, July 14, 1820; *Columbian Centinel*, July 8, 1820; *Rhode-Island American*, Jan. 30, 1821.

3. *Repertory*, July 8, 1820; *Franklin Gazette*, Nov. 13, 1820. On the *Esperanza*, see Society of Friends, Philadelphia Yearly meeting, *A View of the Present State of the African Slave Trade* (Philadelphia: William Brown, 1824), 33–34; Pedro Malibran later became the owner of one of the largest and better-equipped sugar plantations on the island. Antonio Bachiller y Morales, *Prontuario de agricultura general: Para el uso de los labradores i hacendados de la isla de Cuba* (Havana: Barcina, 1856), 7; *Planter and Sugar Manufacturer* 29 (1902): 411.

4. Henry Wheaton, *Reports of Cases Argued and Adjudged in the Supreme Court of the United States*, vol. 10 (New York: R. Donaldson, 1825), 135–45.

5. *Repertory*, Oct. 7, 1820.

6. African Institution, *Report of the Committee of the African Institution*, vol. 16 (London: Ellerton and Henderson, 1822), 281; Society of Friends, *Present State of the*

African Slave Trade, 34, 36, 40; see Chapter 4 for a discussion of the important decision of Justice Joseph Story in the *Jeune Eugenie* case.

7. David R. Murray, *Odious Commerce: Britain, Spain, and the Abolition of the Cuban Trade* (Cambridge: Cambridge University Press, 1980), 40–42. Vice-Admiralty courts were scattered around the English-speaking world, including Sierra Leone. These records are grouped in the British National Archives under the HCA 49/97 code. For more details of specific voyages, see TSTD2: *Esperanza* (voyageid 7619), *Nueva Constitución* (voyageid 7579), *Pepe* (voyageid 7571), *Dolores* (voyageid 7589), and *Nueva Paz* (voyageid 7594).

8. The owner of the *Amelia* also noted that slaves in Bahia were abundant and cheap and that if the captain could buy them for prices ranging somewhere between $80 and $100, he could abandon the voyage to Africa. The ship, however, never completed that voyage. Captives rose in revolt while at sea and took over the ship. A Liverpool brig would later find it and take the surviving slaves to Sierra Leone. *Sixth Report of the Directors of the African Institution, Read at the Annual General Meeting on the 25th of March, 1812* (London: J. Hatchard, 1812), 36–42; TSD2: *Amelia* (voyageid 7659), *Hermosa Rita* (voyageid 7658).

9. *Carlota Teresa* (TSTD2, voyageids 14505, 14512, 14557, and 14571).

10. Josep M. Fradera, "La participació catalana en el tràfic d'esclaus (1789–1845)," *Recerques: Història, Economia, Cultura* no. 16 (1984): 119–39, esp. 132–33 (tables); Martín Rodrigo y Alharilla, "Spanish Merchants and the Slave Trade: From Legality to Illegality, 1814–1870," in *Slavery and Antislavery in Spain's Atlantic Empire,* ed. Josep Maria Fradera and Christopher Schmidt-Nowara (New York: Berghahn Books, 2013), 182.

11. See the data in TSTD2.

12. See the estimates in ibid.

13. Bruce L. Mouser, *American Colony on the Rio Pongo: The War of 1812, the Slave Trade, and the Proposed Settlement of African Americans, 1810–1830* (Trenton, NJ: Africa World Press, 2013), 11; Boubacar Barry, *Senegambia and the Atlantic Slave Trade* (Cambridge: Cambridge University Press, 1998), 136; *Eugenia* (TSTD2, voyageid 7565), *Juana* (ibid., voyageid 7566).

14. Manuel Moreno Fraginals, *O engenho: Complexo sócio-econômico açucareiro cubano,* 3 vols. (São Paulo: Hucitec, 1988), 343.

15. *U.S. vs Schooner P.D. or Fauna,* 1811, AST, box 7; Hugh Thomas, *The Slave Trade: The History of the Atlantic Slave Trade, 1440–1870* (London: Picador, 1997), 578; José Guadalupe Ortega, "The Cuban Sugar Complex in the Age of Revolution, 1789–1844" (PhD diss., University of California, Los Angeles, 2007), 70n25.

16. *U.S. vs Schooner P.D. or Fauna.*

17. *Amedie* (TSTD2, voyageid 7661), *Fortuna* (ibid., voyageid 7683).

18. Murray, *Odious Commerce,* 40–41, 81; David Eltis, *Economic Growth and the Ending of the Transatlantic Slave Trade* (New York: Oxford University Press, 1987), 108–10; *Donna Mariana* (TSTD2, voyageid 7552).

19. Lance Edwin Davis, Robert E. Gallman, and Karin Gleiter, *In Pursuit of Levi-*

athan: Technology, Institutions, Productivity, and Profits in American Whaling, 1816–1906 (Chicago: University of Chicago Press, 1997), 265. On Carredano, see *Mulata* (TSTD2, voyageid 14700), *Segundo Campeador* (ibid., voyageid 14705), *Minerva* (ibid., voyageid 14704), and *Palafox* (ibid., voyageid 7515). The *Palafox,* however, was seized by the British in 1815 before the embarkation of slaves. Later documents point to Carredano as a respected Santander merchant, being compensated by the Spanish crown in 1828 for the seizure of the *Palafox.* This is probably the same Juan Carredano who became the *alcalde* of Santander in the early 1820s. See *Colección legislativa de la deuda pública de España* (Madrid: Imprenta Nacional, 1860), 469; and "Acto de propiedad y matrícula del bergantín 'La Unión,' propiedad de Nicolás Antonia Allona, ante Juan Carredano, alcalde primero y president del ayuntamiento constitucional de Santander," Archivo Histórico Provincial de Cantabria.

20. Peter J. Coleman, "The Entrepreneurial Spirit in Rhode Island History," *Business History Review* 37, no. 4 (1963): 335; George E. Brooks, *Yankee Traders, Coasters, and African Middlemen: A History of American Legitimate Trade with West Africa in the Nineteenth Century* (Brookline, MA: Boston University Press, 1970), 71–72.

21. "Answers from Sierra Leone to the Queries of Viscount Castlereagh," April 1817, in *Papers Presented to Parliament in 1819,* vol. 1 (London: R. G. Clarke, 1819), 184 (quotation), 203; TSTD2: *Rosa* (voyageid 7562), *Dolores* (voyageid 7589), *Nueva Paz* (voyageid 7594), *Triumphante* (voyageid 7604), *Dorset* (voyageid 7609), *Paz* (voyageid 14633).

22. Moreno Fraginals, *O engenho,* 344–54; Robin Law, *Ouidah: The Social History of a West African Slaving "Port," 1727–1892* (Athens: Ohio University Press, 2004), 173; Alberto da Costa e Silva, *Francisco Félix de Souza, mercador de escravos* (Rio de Janeiro: EdUERJ–Nova Fronteira, 2004). Some alternative spellings of their name were Zangronie, Sangron, Sangronio, and Zangromis. For the seized ships taken for trial in Sierra Leone, see TSTD2, voyageids 2548, 2549, and 2831.

23. Feliciano Gámez Duarte, "El desafío insurgente: Análisis del corso hispano-americano desde una perspectiva peninsular: 1812–1828" (PhD diss., Universidad de Cádiz, 2004), 320–21. On Blanco, see the *Montserrat* (TSTD2, voyageid 41894); and Marcus Rediker, *The Amistad Rebellion: An Atlantic Odyssey of Slavery and Freedom* (New York: Viking, 2012). He also worked as a captain in a number of other voyages until 1825. Madrazo in turn had one of his vessels seized by the British in 1814 and condemned at Sierra Leone. In 1818 the British navy captured another of his slavers, but this time the British judge decided in his favor. The *Antelope* was seized off the coast of Africa, with a number of captives already on board, by a privateer operating under a commission issued by the South American revolutionary José Artigas. The original crew of the *Antelope* was then discharged and a new one put on board under the command of the US captain John Smith (the privateer had been outfitted at Baltimore and had a large number English-speaking sailors, many of them probably US citizens, as part of its large crew). After passing through Northeast Brazil, where the privateer wrecked and the survivors, including captives, were taken aboard the *Antelope,* the ship then left for

Surinam, where the captain tried to sell the cargo of captives without success. After another unsuccessful attempt to sell the slaves in Saint Bartholomew, the vessel proceeded to Florida, where US authorities seized the vessel for trying to smuggle slaves into the country (although the captain later argued that he was at Florida only to get supplies for the Portuguese- and Spanish-owned captives). On the *Antelope,* see John Thomas Noonan, *The Antelope: The Ordeal of the Recaptured Africans in the Administrations of James Monroe and John Quincy Adams* (Berkeley: University of California Press, 1977).

24. Coleman, "Entrepreneurial Spirit in Rhode Island History," 335; *U.S. vs Brig Columbia,* AST, box 6; *Columbia* (TSTD2, voyageid 36914); David M. Williams, "Abolition and the Re-Deployment of the Slave Fleet, 1807–1811," *Journal of Transport History* 11 (1973): 103–15; Leonardo Marques, "Slave Trading in a New World: The Strategies of North American Slave Traders in the Age of Abolition," *Journal of the Early Republic* 32, no. 2 (2012); Edward E. Baptist, *The Half Has Never Been Told: Slavery and the Making of American Capitalism* (New York: Basic Books, 2014), 432n41; Gardner & Dean to Mess. Phillips & Gardner, Apr. 10, 1807, New-York Historical Society, Slavery Collection, Series II: Gardner and Dean, 1771–1807.

25. "Record of Policy Mt Hope Insurance Co—1810–1812 for ships," John DeWolf Papers, BHPS; *Arrogancia* (TSTD2, voyageid 14586).

26. J. Buch to Charles D'Wolf, Dec. 6, 1818, Edward Spalding Papers, box 1, folder 2, CHC, available online at: http://merrick.library.miami.edu/cdm/compoundobject/collection/chc0184/id/2293/rec/40.

27. Letter from William Ellery, December 1815, Sedgwick Papers, Stockbridge Library, Stockbridge, MA. I thank Nancy Kougeas for providing me a copy of this document. In his recent book, Stephen Chambers disagrees with my argument that James D'Wolf had already withdrawn from the slave trade by the turn of the 1820s, arguing that "there is ample evidence that New Englanders such as D'Wolf and his agent Edward Spalding remained active in the slave trade into the 1820s." It is possible that James D'Wolf continued to engage in the traffic into the 1820s, but I still fail to see ample evidence for this. Chambers cites Noonan's book, The Antelope, which argues that James and Charles D'Wolf owned the Rambler. George Howe, however, says that James D'Wolf had already sold the ship in 1809, as we will see. The problem here is that neither Noonan nor Howe provides references to primary sources that indicate ownership of the vessel. On Edward Spalding, I completely agree with Chambers. We will see that he not only continued to be involved in the traffic into the 1820s but also appears connected to Nicholas Trist when Trist was accused of aiding the slave trade to Cuba in the late 1830s. See Chambers, No God but Gain, 85–86.

28. George Howe, *Mount Hope: A New England Chronicle* (New York: Viking, 1959), 209–10.

29. On George D'Wolf and his plantation, see ibid., 209–10; *Enrique* (TSTD2, voyageids 14690 and 14671); for references on the MacDonough, see John Wendeurer to Edward Spalding, Dec. 25, 1819, Edward Spalding Papers, box 1, folder 2, CHC, available online at: http://merrick.library.miami.edu/cdm/compoundobject/collection/chc0184/id/1323/rec/42.

30. *Fortuna* (TSTD2, voyageid 14267); Howe, *Mount Hope,* 234; in 1810, Morice bought a house on Hope Street 1795 from Jacob Babbitt and Bernard Smith. Richard V. Simpson, *Bristol: Montaup to Poppasquash* (Charleston, SC: Arcadia, 2002), 47; *Empresa* (TSTD2, voyageids 14653 and 14730); Disdier S. Morphy to John A. Smith, Dec. 28, 1815, Edward Spalding Papers, box 1, folder 1, CHC, available online at: http://merrick.library.miami.edu/cdm/compoundobject/collection/chc0184/id/508/rec/21.

31. See "El Ministro Eguía, a Morillo, sobre lo ofrecido por don Enrique Disdier, vecino y del comercio de La Habana, que posee un importante cargamento de armas," Madrid, May 27, 1819, Real Academia de la Historia—Signatura: Sig. 9/7655, leg. 12 (a), fols. 67–67v, available online at: http://bibliotecadigital.rah.es/dgbrah/i18n/consulta/registro.cmd?id=1406; on the plantations owned by Disdier and Gowen, see Manuel Barcia Paz, *The Great African Slave Revolt of 1825: Cuba and the Fight for Freedom in Matanzas* (Baton Rouge: Louisiana State University Press, 2012), 84.

32. "Slave Trade in 1816," *Publications of the Rhode Island Historical Society,* n.s., 6 (1898): 226–27; Howe, *Mount Hope,* 208.

33. Samuel Aborn to Brown & Ives, Jan. 4, 1817, Brown Family Papers, BFBR Miscellaneous Letters, box 392, JCBL.

34. *Weekly Recorder,* May 28, 1819.

35. Brown & Ives to W. H. Leigh, June 26, 1818, Brown Family Papers, box 636, folder 4, JCBL. Ironically, the Providence branch had George D'Wolf among its directors.

36. On Babbitt, see Jay Coughtry, ed., *Papers of the American Slave Trade* (Bethesda, MD: University Publications of America, 1996); on Dooley, see C. Malcom, "A Slave Ship Letter from the Gallinas River, 1819," *Navigator: Newsletter of the Mel Fisher Maritime Heritage Society* 23, no. 5 (2007): 3–14.

37. David Turnbull, *Travels in the West: With Notices of Porto Rico, and the Slave Trade* (London: Longman, Orne, Brown, Green, and Longmans, 1840), 146; *Cintra* (TSTD2, voyageid 2317). On US slave plantations in Cuba, see Stephen Chambers, "At Home among the Dead: North Americans and the 1825 Guamacaro Slave Insurrection," *Journal of the Early Republic* 33, no. 1 (2013): 61–86.

38. Howe, *Mount Hope,* 202, 210–11; *Farmer's Repository,* July 26, 1820; Noonan, *Antelope,* 27–28; *Niles' Register,* June 17, 1820.

39. Howe, *Mount Hope,* 212 (quotation).

40. Copy, P. C. Greene to Mr. Fletcher, Second inclosure in Gregory & Fitzgerald to Castlereagh, May 11, 1820, *BPP,* Slave Trade, 1821 (003), vol. 22, class A, 85.

41. The case of the schooner St. Salvador, Second inclosure in Gregory & Fitzgerald to Castlereagh, May 11, 1820, *BPP,* Slave Trade, 1821 (003), vol. 22, class A, 82–84. See also Graden, *Disease, Resistance, and Lies,* 22–23. The commissioner of arbitration was J. Cezar de La Figaniere e Morão, Portuguese minister to the United States in the 1850s, as discussed in Chapter 6.

42. The case of the Schooner the Cintra, First inclosure in Gregory to Castlereagh, Nov. 30, 1819, Feb. 12, 1820, *BPP,* Slave Trade, 1821 (003), vol. 22, class A, 69–70. Voyages that had Allen Munro among their owners, TSTD2: *Mary* (voyageid 36697), *Commerce* (voyageid 36719), *Aurora* (voyageid 36747), and *Ann and Harriot* (voyageid 36907).

43. P. C. Greene to T. W. Payton, Aug. 21, 1820, Edward Spalding Papers, box 1, folder 3, CHC, available online at: http://merrick.library.miami.edu/cdm/compound object/collection/chc0184/id/171/rec/1.

44. Financial records of Edward Spalding, 1816–1820, ibid., box 2, folder 10, available online at: http://merrick.library.miami.edu/cdm/compoundobject/collection/chc 0184/id/980/rec/349. Pages 61 to 70 show the transactions of the *Francisco* (TSTD2, voyageid 2320). Inclose in Gregory to Castlereagh, May 8, 1820, *BPP,* Slave Trade, 1821 (003), vol. 22, class A, 78.

45. Charles DeWolf to Edward Spalding, Sept. 26, 1821, Edward Spalding Papers, box 1, folder 3, CHC, available online at: http://merrick.library.miami.edu/cdm/com poundobject/collection/chc0184/id/159/rec/64.

46. Howe, *Mount Hope,* 205.

47. James A. McMillin, *The Final Victims: Foreign Slave Trade to North America, 1783–1810* (Columbia: University of South Carolina Press, 2004), 109–10; *Africa* (TSTD2, voyageid 7632).

48. David Head, "Sailing for Spanish America: The Atlantic Geopolitics of Foreign Privateering from the United States in the Early Republic" (PhD diss., State University of New York–Buffalo, 2010), 33; William C. Davis, *The Pirates Laffite: The Treacherous World of the Corsairs of the Gulf* (Orlando, FL: Harcourt, 2005), ch. 10; Sarah Batterson, "'An Ill-Judged Piece of Business': The United States and the Failure of Slave Trade Suppression" (PhD diss., University of New Hampshire, 2013), ch. 2.

49. David Head, "Slave Smuggling by Foreign Privateers: The Illegal Slave Trade and the Geopolitics of the Early Republic," *Journal of the Early Republic* 33, no. 3 (2013): 439–42; Don Edward Fehrenbacher, *The Slaveholding Republic: An Account of the United States Government's Relations to Slavery* (Oxford: Oxford University Press, 2001), 150; Rafe Blaufarb, "The Western Question: The Geopolitics of Latin American Independence," *American Historical Review* 112, no. 3 (2007): 743; for an overview of the vast literature on independence, see Gabriel Paquette, "The Dissolution of the Spanish Atlantic Monarchy," *Historical Journal* 52, no. 1 (2009): 175–212.

50. *U.S. vs Schooner Hal & Cargo,* 1815, AST, box 21.

51. There is actually evidence of only one disembarkation organized by Aury after seizing a Portuguese slaver in 1810. See Adam Rothman, *Slave Country: American Expansion and the Origins of the Deep South* (Cambridge, MA: Harvard University Press, 2005), 89.

52. H.R. Doc., 15th Cong., 1st Sess., No. 12 (Serial 6), 8–9.

53. H.R. Doc., 16th Cong., 1st Sess., No. 36 (Serial 33), 6; Rafe Blaufarb, "The Western Question: The Geopolitics of Latin American Independence," *American Historical Review* 112, no. 3 (2007): 753.

54. S.Doc.; 16th Cong., 1st Sess., No. 93 (Serial 60), 13, 53; Batterson, "Ill-Judged Piece of Business," ch. 2; TSTD2: *Isabelita* (voyageid 5050), *Jesus Nazareno* (voyageid 41885).

55. *De Bow's Review* 13 (1852): 380–81; H.R. Doc., 16th Cong., 1st Sess., No. 36 (Serial 33), 5.

56. Robert E. May, "Manifest Destiny's Filibusters," in *Manifest Destiny and Empire: American Antebellum Expansionism,* ed. Sam W. Haynes and Christopher Morris (College Station: Texas A&M University Press, 1997), 150–51.

57. David Eltis, "The U.S. Transatlantic Slave Trade, 1644–1867: An Assessment," *Civil War History* 54, no. 4 (2008): 352–53.

58. Seymour Drescher, *Abolition: A History of Slavery and Antislavery* (Cambridge: Cambridge University Press, 2009), 229.

59. J. R. Oldfield, *Transatlantic Abolitionism in the Age of Revolution: An International History of Anti-Slavery, c. 1787–1820* (Cambridge: Cambridge University Press, 2013), 213; Matthew Mason, "Keeping Up Appearances: The International Politics of Slave Trade Abolition in the Nineteenth-Century Atlantic World," *William and Mary Quarterly,* 3rd ser., 66, no. 4 (2009): 810n2 (quotation); Matthew Mason, "The Battle of the Slaveholding Liberators: Great Britain, the United States, and Slavery in the Early Nineteenth Century," *William and Mary Quarterly,* 3rd ser., 59, no. 3 (2002): 665–96.

60. Eugene Kontorovich, "The Constitutionality of International Courts: The Forgotten Precedent of Slave-Trade Tribunals," *University of Pennsylvania Law Review* 158, no. 1 (2009): 39–115.

61. Leon Fink, *Sweatshops at Sea: Merchant Seamen in the World's First Globalized Industry, from 1812 to the Present* (Chapel Hill: University of North Carolina, 2011), 10–23; Paul A. Gilje, *Free Trade and Sailors' Rights in the War of 1812* (New York: Cambridge University Press, 2013).

62. Paul Michael Kielstra, *The Politics of Slave Trade Suppression in Britain and France, 1814–48* (Basingstoke: Macmillan, 2000), 76, 157–60.

63. Alfred P. Rubin, *Ethics and Authority in International Law* (Cambridge: Cambridge University Press, 1997), 110–15.

64. J. C. A. Stagg, "George Mathews and John McKee: Revolutionizing East Florida, Mobile, and Pensacola in 1812," *Florida Historical Quarterly* 85, no. 3 (2007): 277.

65. Jane Landers, *Black Society in Spanish Florida* (Urbana: University of Illinois Press, 1999); Daniel Walker Howe, *What Hath God Wrought: The Transformation of America, 1815–1848* (New York: Oxford University Press, 2007), 97–99; Angela Pulley Hudson, *Creek Paths and Federal Roads: Indians, Settlers, and Slaves and the Making of the American South* (Chapel Hill: University of North Carolina Press, 2010), 121–44.

66. H.R. Doc., 16th Cong., 1st Sess., No. 42 (Serial 33), 5.

67. John Craig Hammond, "Slavery, Settlement, and Empire: The Expansion and Growth of Slavery in the Interior of the North American Continent, 1770–1820," *Journal of the Early Republic* 32, no. 2 (2012): 175–206; John Craig Hammond, "'Uncontrollable Necessity': The Local Politics, Geopolitics, and Sectional Politics of Slavery Expansion," in *Contesting Slavery: The Politics of Bondage and Freedom in the New American Nation,* ed. John Craig Hammond and Matthew Mason (Charlottesville: University of Virginia, 2011), 138–60.

68. Howe, *What Hath God Wrought,* 98–111; Jennifer Heckard, "The Crossroads of Empire: The 1817 Liberation and Occupation of Amelia Island, East Florida" (PhD diss., University of Connecticut, 2006); Royce Gordon Shingleton, "David Byrdie Mitchell

and the African Importation Case of 1820," *Journal of Negro History* 58, no. 3 (1973): 327–40.

69. *Annals of Congress,* H.R., 15th Cong., 1st Sess., Jan. 12, 1818, 97–98. On King and the right of search, see Mason, "Battle of Slaveholding Liberators," 670–71.

70. "Slaves Brought into the United States from Amelia Island," *American State Papers,* H.R. Doc., 15th Cong., 1st Sess., 458–59.

71. Oldfield, *Transatlantic Abolitionism,* 215; Ericson, *Slavery in the American Republic,* 36–37.

72. David L. Lightner, *Slavery and the Commerce Power: How the Struggle against the Interstate Slave Trade Led to the Civil War* (New Haven: Yale University Press, 2006), 50 (quotation); on the Missouri Compromise, see Robert Pierce Forbes, *The Missouri Compromise and Its Aftermath: Slavery and the Meaning of America* (Chapel Hill: University of North Carolina Press, 2007).

73. *American State Papers,* S., 16th Cong., 1st Sess., Miscellaneous: vol. 2, 568–69; *Vermont Intelligencer,* Apr. 3, 1820.

74. *An Act to continue in force "An act to protect the commerce of the United States and punish the crime of piracy," and also to make further provisions for punishing the crime of piracy;* Finkelman, *Regulating the Slave Trade,* 404.

75. Head, "Sailing for Spanish America," 169–70; William C. Davis, *The Pirates Lafitte: The Treacherous World of the Corsairs of the Gulf* (New York: Houghton Mifflin Harcourt, 2006), ch. 21; Peter Earle, *The Pirate Wars* (London: Methuen, 2003), ch. 12.

76. The second round of debates was generated by a clause in the Missouri constitution that prohibited the entrance of free blacks into the state, which was the true object of Smith's speech. After long considerations on the compatibility of democracy and slavery and on the natural exclusion of slaves and their descendants from the body politic, the senator bashed those northerners who criticized the Missouri constitution. "Had Christophe, the famous chief of Hayti, come to some sections of our country, before he blew his own brains out," Smith argued, "if he could have obtained the naturalization which our free negroes and mulattoes have done, by a residence merely, he might, under the spirit of these times, soon have found his way here [the US Congress]." Henri Christophe, a US congressman: what a unique form of stimulating white anxieties. It is not surprising that the aftermath of the debates would see many in the North reexamining their positions on race only to find some common ground with racist southerners such as Smith. See Matthew Mason, *Slavery and Politics in the Early American Republic* (Chapel Hill: University of North Carolina Press, 2006), 210–11.

77. James D'Wolf to John D'Wolf, Dec. 21, 1821, John DeWolf Papers, BHPS.

78. David Brion Davis, "The Impact of British Abolitionism on American Sectionalism," in *In the Shadow of Freedom: The Politics of Slavery in the National Capital,* ed. Paul Finkelman and Donald R. Kennon (Athens: Ohio University Press, 2011), 23.

79. Moreno Fraginals, *O engenho,* 345–47; José Guadalupe Ortega, "Cuban Merchants, Slave Trade Knowledge, and the Atlantic World, 1790s–1820s," *CLAHR: Colonial Latin American Historical Review* 15, no. 3 (2006): 238–39.

FOUR The Consolidation of the Contraband Slave Trade, 1820–1850

1. Theophilus Conneau, *Captain Canot; or, Twenty Years of an African Slaver* (New York: Appleton, 1854), 127, 361.

2. Alexander Hamilton, "Defence of the Funding System," in *The Works of Alexander Hamilton,* ed. Henry Cabot Lodge, vol. 8 (New York: G. P. Putnam's Sons, 1904), 462; P. J. Cain and A. G. Hopkins, *British Imperialism: Innovation and Expansion, 1688–1914* (London: Longman, 1993), 84; Shearer Davis Bowman, *Masters and Lords: Mid-19th-Century U.S. Planters and Prussian Junkers* (New York: Oxford University Press, 1993); Brian Schoen, *The Fragile Fabric of Union: Cotton, Federal Politics, and the Global Origins of the Civil War* (Baltimore: Johns Hopkins University Press, 2009); Paul Bairoch, "European Trade Policy, 1815–1914," in *The Cambridge Economic History of Europe: The Industrial Economies: The Development of Economic and Social Policies,* vol. 8, ed. Peter Mathias and Sidney Pollard (Cambridge: Cambridge University Press, 1989), 8–9; Alfredo Bosi, "A escravidão entre dois liberalismos," *Estudos Avançados* 2, no. 3 (1988): 4–39. According to Cain and Hopkins, this financial expansion, in the case of the cotton industry at least, impaired the industry's profits. Martin Daulton in turn sees a more synergetic connection between finances and manufacturing. See M. J. Daunton, "'Gentlemanly Capitalism' and British Industry, 1820–1914," *Past and Present* no. 122 (1989): 119–58.

3. A. G. Hopkins, "The United States, 1783–1861: Britain's Honorary Dominion?" *Britain and the World* 4, no. 2 (2011): 238.

4. The Aberdeen Act of 1845 prohibited British subjects from purchasing slaves, but the company lobbied the British government to include a provision that allowed British citizens to keep slaves purchased before the passing of the law. Marshall G. Eakin, "Business Imperialism and British Enterprise in Brazil: The St. John D'el Rey Mining Company, Limited, 1830–1960," *Hispanic American Historical Review* 66, no. 4 (1986): 711; David Eltis, *Economic Growth and the Ending of the Transatlantic Slave Trade* (New York: Oxford University Press, 1987), 59. On the symbiosis of legitimate commerce and the slave trade, see George E. Brooks, *Yankee Traders, Old Coasters and African Middlemen: A History of American Legitimate Trade with West Africa in the Nineteenth Century* (Brookline, MA: Boston University Press, 1970).

5. The pervasive presence of the US merchant fleet in the whaling industry led some slave traders to use the business as a cover for illicit operations. In the annual report of the slave trade during 1843, British authorities in Rio de Janeiro complained that slave traders such as José Bernardino de Sá were using US vessels supposedly engaged in the whale and seal fisheries to actually carry slaves from Africa. In 1847, the US consul to Rio, Gorham Parks, described the case of the *Fame* (TSTD2, voyageid 4949), a whaler from New London captained by the Portuguese captain Anthony Marks. According to the consul, Marks consigned the vessel to Rio de Janeiro slave traders without the consent of its owners and captained the voyage that disembarked 527 enslaved Africans in Southeast Brazil in 1847. Gorham Parks to James Buchanan, Aug. 20, 1847, H.R. Doc., 30th Cong., 2d Sess., No. 61, 5–6. During the 1850s, this strategy became even more common as US ports became important centers for the organization of slaving expeditions. The *Montauk* (TSTD2, voyageid 4375), *Wildfire* (ibid., voyageid 4362), *Laurens* (ibid.,

voyageid 4320), and *Augusta* (ibid., voyageid 4960) were outfitted as whalers before proceeding to slave-trading ventures. At the turn of the decade, the *World* constantly denounced the widespread use of the whaling industry to cover slave-trading operations. *World*, New York, Aug. 27, 1860. In 1863, a whaling agent was actually convicted for fitting the whaler *Tahmaroo* in 1860 for the transatlantic slave trade. Lance Edwin Davis, Robert E. Gallman, and Karin Gleiter, *In Pursuit of Leviathan: Technology, Institutions, Productivity, and Profits in American Whaling, 1816–1906* (Chicago: University of Chicago Press, 1997),402.

6. Robert Paquette, *Sugar Is Made with Blood: The Conspiracy of La Escalera and the Conflict between Empires over Slavery in Cuba* (Middletown, CT: Wesleyan University Press, 1988), 17–24, 187; Louis A. Perez Jr., *Cuba and the United States: Ties of Singular Intimacy* (Athens: University of Georgia Press, 1988), 24, 25 (quotation); Mary Gardner Lowell and Karen Robert, *New Year in Cuba: Mary Gardner Lowell's Travel Diary, 1831–1832* (Boston: Northeastern University Press, 2003), 102–7.

7. Schoen, *Fragile Fabric of Union,* 122–23; Robert W. Fogel and Stanley L. Engerman, *Time on the Cross: The Economics of American Negro Slavery* (Boston: Little, Brown, 1974), 25; Philip D. Curtin, *The Atlantic Slave Trade: A Census* (Madison: University of Wisconsin Press, 1969), 74–75. This is much lower than the numbers offered by W. E. B. Du Bois, who did not distinguish the disembarkations in Cuba and Brazil under the US flag. For a discussion of the numbers of the US slave trade, see David Eltis, "The U.S. Transatlantic Slave Trade, 1644–1867: An Assessment," *Civil War History* 54, no. 4 (2008): 347–78; Robert W. Fogel, "Problems in Measuring the Extent of Slave Smuggling" in *Without Consent or Contract: Evidence and Methods,* ed. Robert W. Fogel, Ralph A. Galantine, and Richard L. Manning (New York: W. W. Norton, 1992), 50–52.

8. Adam Rothman, "The Domestication of the Slave Trade in the United States," in *The Chattel Principle: Internal Slave Trades in the Americas,* ed. Walter Johnson (New Haven: Yale University Press, 2004), 32–54; Michael Tadman, *Speculators and Slaves: Masters, Traders, and Slaves in the Old South* (Madison: University of Wisconsin Press, 1989), ch. 2; Elizabeth Fox-Genovese and Eugene D. Genovese, *The Mind of the Master Class: History and Faith in the Southern Slaveholders' Worldview* (Cambridge: Cambridge University Press, 2005), 283 (quotation).

9. W. E. B. Du Bois, *The Suppression of the African Slave-Trade to the United States of America, 1638–1870* (New York: Longmans, Green, 1896), 254; Steven Deyle, *Carry Me Back: The Domestic Slave Trade in American Life* (Oxford: Oxford University Press, 2005), 181–82, 213; Thomas C. Thornton, *An Inquiry into the History of Slavery; Its Introduction into the United States; Causes of Its Continuance; and Remarks upon the Abolition Tracts of William E. Channing, D. D.* (Washington, DC: W. M. Morrison, 1841), 22.

10. Thomas R. Dew, *Review of the Debate in the Virginia Legislature of 1831 and 1832* (Richmond, VA: T. W. White, 1832), 46; *African Repository and Colonial Journal* 19:336. For Hodgson's slaves, see William Kauffman Scarborough, *Masters of the Big House: Elite Slaveholders of the Mid-Nineteenth-Century South* (Baton Rouge: Louisiana State University Press, 2003), 440. For other examples of proslavery apologists condemning the transatlantic slave trade before 1850, see Edward B. Rugemer, "The Southern Response

to British Abolitionism: The Maturation of Proslavery Apologetics," *Journal of Southern History* 70, no. 2 (2004): 237–38; and David Brion Davis, "The Impact of British Abolitionism on American Sectionalism," in *In the Shadow of Freedom: The Politics of Slavery in the National Capital,* ed. Paul Finkelman and Donald R. Kennon (Athens: Ohio University Press, 2011), 23.

11. Don Edward Fehrenbacher, *The Slaveholding Republic: An Account of the United States Government's Relations to Slavery* (Oxford: Oxford University Press, 2001), 159; John Thomas Noonan, *The Antelope: The Ordeal of the Recaptured Africans in the Administrations of James Monroe and John Quincy Adams* (Berkeley: University of California Press, 1977), 70.

12. Henry Wheaton, ed., *United States Reports: Cases Adjudged in the Supreme Court* (Washington, DC: US Government Printing Office, 1883), 53.

13. Fehrenbacher, *Slaveholding Republic,* 160; David Brion Davis, *Inhuman Bondage: The Rise and Fall of Slavery in the New World* (New York: Oxford University Press, 2006), 211, 225–26. On the connection between French abolitionists and the Haitian Revolution, see David P. Geggus, "The French and Haitian Revolutions and Resistance to Slavery in the Americas: An Overview," *Revue Française d'Histoire d'Outre-Mer* 282–83 (1989): 107–23.

14. Oakes, "Conflict vs. Racial Consensus in the History of Antislavery Politics," 293–94; Davis, *Inhuman Bondage,* 220; Fehrenbacher, *Slaveholding Republic,* 161.

15. TSTD2: *Esencia* (voyageid 129), *Ceylon* (voyageid 645), *William Gardner* (voyageids 39044 and 39048), *Atrevido* (voyageid 3047); John Parkinson to Lord Palmerston, Dec. 18, 1833, *BPP,* Slave Trade, 1835 (007), vol. 51, class B, 41; J. Brackenbury to H. U. Addington, Apr. 29, 1830, ibid., 1831 (004), vol. 29, class A, 8.

16. Leslie Bethell, *The Abolition of the Brazilian Slave Trade: Britain, Brazil and the Slave Trade Question, 1807–1869* (Cambridge: Cambridge University Press, 1970), 27–61.

17. Ibid., 72; Tâmis Peixoto Parron, "A política da escravidão no império do Brasil, 1826–1865" (MA thesis, Universidade de São Paulo, 2009), 80–84. Historians have been reconsidering the classic interpretation of the law as a dead letter. See the dossier organized by Beatriz Mamigonian and Keila Grinberg, "Para inglês ver? Revisitando a lei de 1831," *Estudos Afro-Asiáticos* nos. 1–2–3 (2007).

18. Parron, "A política da escravidão," 128–29; Eltis, *Economic Growth,* 195–96. On the connection between sugar-producing areas in the province of São Paulo and the illegal slave trade, see Carlos A. M. Lima, "São Paulo, o açúcar, o café e o rearranjo da década de 1840," in *IX Congresso Brasileiro de História Econômica e 10a Conferência Internacional de História de Empresas—Anais* (Curitiba, Brazil: Universidade Federal do Paraná, 2011), 1–25.

19. See estimates in TSTD2. The rise in sugar production in the Brazilian Northeast was also a consequence of the equalization of duties on sugar imports by the British government in 1846, which automatically led to an increase in the demand for slave-grown sugar; Nathaniel H. Leff, "Economic Development and Regional Inequality: Origins of the Brazilian Case," *Quarterly Journal of Economics* 86, no. 2 (1972): 243–62; H. Augustus Cowper to Earl of Aberdeen, Jan. 1, 1844, *BPP,* Slave Trade, 1845 (633), vol. 50, class B, 407

(quotation); Parron, "A política da escravidão," 133 (quotation), 145. Opponents of the Regresso occasionally referred to them as the *partido negreiro* (slave-trading party) as well as *português e africanista* (Portuguese and Africanist).

20. Rafael Bivar Marquese and Dale W. Tomich, "O vale do paraíba escravista e a formação do mercado mundial do café no século XIX," in *O Brasil imperial,* ed. Keila Grinberg and Ricardo Salles (Rio de Janeiro: Civilização Brasileira, 2009); Michelle Craig McDonald and Steven Topik, "Americanizing Coffee: The Refashioning of a Consumer Culture," in *Food and Globalization: Consumption, Markets and Politics in the Modern World,* ed. Alexander Nützenadel and Frank Trentmann (Oxford: Berg, 2008), 110.

21. Manuel Moreno Fraginals, *O engenho: Complexo sócio-econômico açucareiro cubano,* 3 vols. (São Paulo: Hucitec, 1988), 191–201.

22. Berbel, Marquese, and Parron, *Escravidão e política,* 144–49; Tâmis Peixoto Parron, *A Política da Escravidão na Era da Liberdade, 1787–1846* (PhD diss., Universidade de São Paulo, 2015), 135–36.

23. Christopher Schmidt-Nowara, *Empire and Antislavery: Spain, Cuba, and Puerto Rico, 1833–1874: Spain, Cuba, and Puerto Rico, 1833–1874* (Pittsburgh: University of Pittsburgh Press, 1999), 20–21; José Antonio Piqueras Arenas, *Sociedad civil y poder en Cuba: Colonia y postcolonia* (Madrid: Siglo XXI de España Editores, 2005), 132–34.

24. David R. Murray, *Odious Commerce: Britain, Spain, and the Abolition of the Cuban Trade* (Cambridge: Cambridge University Press, 1980), 199–202; Eltis, *Economic Growth,* 201.

25. Laird W. Bergad, Fe Iglesias García, and María del Carmen Barcia, *The Cuban Slave Market, 1790–1880* (Cambridge: Cambridge University Press, 1995), 28; Oscar Zanetti Lecuona, *Sugar and Railroads: A Cuban History, 1837–1959* (Chapel Hill: University of North Carolina Press, 1998); Louis A. Pérez, *Cuba: Between Reform and Revolution* (New York: Oxford University Press, 2011), 58–59, 62. For a broader discussion of the ecological impact of sugar production, see Jason W. Moore, "Sugar and the Expansion of the Early Modern World-Economy: Commodity Frontiers, Ecological Transformation, and Industrialization," *Review, A Journal of the Fernand Braudel Center* 23, no. 3 (2000): 409–33.

26. *American State Papers,* 19th Cong., 2d Sess., Foreign Relations: vol. 6, 277; *Jornal do Commercio* (Rio de Janeiro), Apr. 14, 1828.

27. Alberto da Costa e Silva, *Francisco Félix de Souza: Mercador de escravos* (Rio de Janeiro: EdUERJ–Nova Fronteira, 2004), 128; Macaulay & Lewis to Palmerston, Nov. 30, 1837, *BPP,* Slave Trade, 1837–38 (132), vol. 50, class A, 19; *Florida* (TSTD2, voyageid 2556). The work of Daget is based on sources that detail the places of construction on a level unparalleled by the existing documentation for other nations involved in the illegal business. See Serge Daget, *Répertoire des expéditions négrières françaises à la traite illégale (1814–1850)* (Nantes: Université de Nantes, 1988).

28. W. G. Ouseley to Palmerston, Apr. 13, 1840, *BPP,* Slave Trade, 1841 (331), vol. 30, class B, 154. The new interpretation was put to test when, on May 30, a British commander seized and brought to Rio de Janeiro the *Maria Carlota* (TSTD2, voyageid 3085) and the *Recuperador* (ibid., voyageid 3086), both captured on their outbound voyages to

Africa fully equipped for the slave trade. The Royal Navy continued to capture Brazilian vessels based on their equipment—slave irons, excessive water casks, large boilers for food preparation—while the Brazilian government continued to contest the practice. Bethell, *Abolition of the Brazilian Slave Trade*, 167–68, 242–66; Fehrenbacher, *Slaveholding Republic*, 161.

29. Ouseley to Palmerston, Apr. 13, 1840, *BPP,* Slave Trade, 1841 (331), vol. 30, class B, 154.

30. William Hunter to John Forsyth, Apr. 16, 1838, S. Doc., 28th Cong., 1st Sess., No. 217, 9–10.

31. Cole & Macaulay to Palmerston, Jan. 5, 1835 (Second Enclosure in No. 2), *BPP,* Slave Trade, 1836 (005), vol. 50, class A, 6; H. S. Fox to John Forsyth, Oct. 29, 1839, ibid., 1840 (268), vol. 47, class D, 168.

32. Schenley & Madden to Palmerston, Oct. 25, 1836, *BPP,* Slave Trade, 1837 (001), vol. 54, class A, 191–92.

33. Rumors that the sugar harvest of D'Wolf failed in 1825 had already reached Rhode Island by July, and the bankruptcy of Samuel Williams around three months later certainly contributed to increasing the suspicions. Williams, a US expatriate established in London, had been a fundamental figure in the commercial networks connecting New England merchants to Britain. When a number of US merchants failed to repay their loans, with George D'Wolf probably among them, Williams's bank broke. In December, George abandoned Bristol with his family and moved to Cuba. His bankruptcy had a deep impact on a number of other Bristolians who had speculated in his ventures in previous years. If the slave trade act of 1820 had already disrupted his slave-trading operations, the crackdown on privateering in the following years probably added to his problems. Howe, *Mount Hope,* 233–34.

34. Palmerston to Fox, Jan. 21, 1837, *BPP,* Slave Trade, 1837 (002), vol. 54, class B, 143; Richard Kerwin MacMaster, "The United States, Great Britain and the Suppression of the Cuban Slave Trade 1835–1860" (PhD diss., Georgetown University, 1968), 72 (quotation), 74–75; Lewis Tappan, "Correspondence of Lewis Tappan and Others with the British and Foreign Anti-Slavery Society [Part 1]," *Journal of Negro History* 12, no. 2 (1927): 192.

35. Her Majesty's Judge to Palmerston, Aug. 22, 1838, *BPP,* Slave Trade, 1839 (180), vol. 48, class A, 126; A Calm observer, *A Letter to Wm. E. Channing, D.D.: In Reply to One Addressed to Him by R.R. Madden, on the Abuse of the Flag of the United States in the Island of Cuba, for Promoting the Slave Trade* (Boston: William D. Ticknor, 1840), 8–9.

36. Du Bois, *Suppression of the African Slave Trade,* 267; Murray, *Odious Commerce,* 105–6; Strohm v. U.S., 23 F. Cas. 240.

37. Edward Bartlett Rugemer, *The Problem of Emancipation: The Caribbean Roots of the American Civil War* (Baton Rouge: Louisiana State University Press, 2009); Steven Heath Mitton, "The Free World Confronted: The Problem of Slavery and Progress in American Foreign Relations, 1833–1844" (PhD diss., Louisiana State University, 2005); David Turnbull, *Travels in the West: With Notices of Porto Rico, and the Slave Trade* (London: Longman, Orne, Brown, Green, and Longmans, 1840), 139–40.

38. Eltis, *Economic Growth,* 57, 84.

39. Cited in Lawrence C. Jennings, "French Policy towards Trading with African and Brazilian Slave Merchants, 1840–1853," *Journal of African History* 17, no. 4 (1976): 519; Chevalier d'Azeglio to R. Abercromby, Jan. 15, 1850 (Inclosure 1 in No. 230), *BPP,* Slave Trade, 1850 (1291), vol. 55, class B, 318.

40. "Answers from Sierra Leone to the Queries of Viscount Castlereagh, dated April 1817," in *Papers Related to the Slave Trade Presented to Parliament in 1819,* vol. 1 (London: R. G. Clarke, 1819), 211.

41. Eltis, *Economic Growth,* 83.

42. David F. Ericson, "Slave Smugglers, Slave Catchers, and Slave Rebels: Slavery and American State Development, 1787–1842," in *Contesting Slavery: The Politics of Bondage and Freedom in the New American Nation,* ed. John Craig Hammond and Matthew Mason (Charlottesville: University of Virginia, 2011), 187.

43. Eliga H. Gould, *Among the Powers of the Earth: The American Revolution and the Making of a New World Empire* (Cambridge, MA: Harvard University Press, 2012), 175–76.

FIVE The United States and the Contraband
Slave Trade to Brazil, 1831–1856

1. Henry A. Wise to Hamilton Hamilton, Dec. 1, 1844, H.R. Doc., 28th Cong., 2d Sess., No. 148, 61. The growing internationalization of the business also stimulated the connection of Portuguese and Brazilian slave traders with other countries. Between 1832 and 1835, a large number of ships disembarking enslaved Africans in Rio de Janeiro had a connection with Uruguay. See Alex Borucki, "The 'African Colonists' of Montevideo: New Light on the Illegal Slave Trade to Rio de Janeiro and the Río de La Plata (1830–42)," *Slavery and Abolition* 30, no. 3 (2009): 427–44.

2. Wise to Maxwell, Wright, & Co., Dec. 9, 1844, H.R. Doc., 28th Cong., 2d Sess., No. 148, 88.

3. John Quincy Adams, *Memoirs of John Quincy Adams: Comprising Portions of His Diary from 1795 to 1848,* ed. Charles Francis Adams, vol. 12 (Philadelphia: J. B. Lippincott, 1877), 195–96.

4. Ilmar Rohloff de Mattos, *O tempo saquarema: A formação do estado imperial* (São Paulo: Hucitec, 2004). On the history of the Conservative Party, see Jeffrey Needell, *The Party of Order: The Conservatives, the State, and Slavery in the Brazilian Monarchy, 1831–1871* (Stanford, CA: Stanford University Press, 2006); and Tâmis Peixoto Parron, "A política da escravidão no império do Brasil, 1826–1865" (MA thesis, Universidade de São Paulo, 2009).

5. Carlos A. M. Lima, "Como se Cuba não existisse: Observações sobre Jaime Balmes, a escravidão e o tráfico de escravos (Espanha, década de 1840)," *História: Questões & Debates* 50 (2009): 240.

6. Warren S. Howard, *American Slavers and the Federal Law, 1837–1862* (Berkeley: University of California Press, 1963); Don Edward Fehrenbacher, *The Slaveholding Re-*

public: An Account of the United States Government's Relations to Slavery (Oxford: Oxford University Press, 2001).

7. Gerald Horne, *The Deepest South: The United States, Brazil, and the African Slave Trade* (New York: New York University Press, 2007); Dale Torston Graden, "O envolvimento dos Estados Unidos no comércio transatlântico de escravos para o Brasil, 1840–1858," *Afro-Ásia* 39 (2007): 9–35.

8. David Tod to John M. Clayton, Jan. 8, 1850, S. Doc., 31st Cong., 2d Sess., No. 6, 25; Seymour Drescher, *Abolition: A History of Slavery and Antislavery* (Cambridge: Cambridge University Press, 2009), 316.

9. Michelle Craig McDonald and Steven Topik, "Americanizing Coffee: The Refashioning of a Consumer Culture," in *Food and Globalization: Consumption, Markets and Politics in the Modern World,* ed. Alexander Nützenadel and Frank Trentmann (Oxford: Berg, 2008), 120. Daniel Rood argues that "enslaved workers from Central and East Africa—illegally purchased and transported by New England merchants—were other significant, though unreported items in North America's foreign trade with Brazil—a line of business that actually reached a peak of approximately of over sixty thousand souls per year at the end of the 1840s." See Daniel B. Rood, "Plantation Technocrats: A Social History of Knowledge in the Slaveholding Atlantic World, 1830–1865" (PhD diss., University of California, 2010), 131.

10. Horne, *Deepest South,* 33.

11. Besides the two regions, Pernambuco and Amazonia received, respectively, 22,858 and 3,432 enslaved Africans. A further 5,236 slaves were disembarked in unspecified parts of Brazil. See estimates in TSTD2.

12. It is important to note that a growing number of ships abandoned registration documents and flags altogether on inbound voyages to circumvent the authorities, a practice that does not appear in the TSTD2 data. Information on the number of vessels that abandoned documents and flag would result in lower ratios for all flags presented in table 5.1.

13. Rafael Bivar Marquese and Dale W. Tomich, "O vale do paraíba escravista e a formação do mercado mundial do café no século XIX," in *O Brasil imperial,* ed. Keila Grinberg and Ricardo Salles (Rio de Janeiro: Civilização Brasileira, 2009); David Eltis, *Economic Growth and the Ending of the Transatlantic Slave Trade* (New York: Oxford University Press, 1987), 150–51.

14. In fact, by the early 1840s, a few Cuban slave traders had redirected their operations to Rio de Janeiro. Rovirosa, who also appears in the documents as Ruviroza y Urzellas, had been the most successful one, becoming the fourth largest slave trader in Rio by the mid-1840s; Eltis, *Economic Growth,* 151, 157; Edward Porter to Lord Palmerston, Apr. 25, 1848, *BPP,* Slave Trade, 1849 (1128), vol. 55, class B, 82. By the 1860s, Rovirosa was working as an informant to the British about the slave trade to Cuba, as shown in a number of letters in the papers of the Wylde Family, held at the Durham University Library, Archives and Special Collections. For an extended discussion of Fonseca, Rovirosa, and other slave traders operating in Rio de Janeiro, see Roquinaldo Ferreira, "Dos sertões ao Atlântico: Tráfico ilegal de escravos e comércio lícito em Angola, 1830–1860"

(MA thesis, Universidade Federal do Rio de Janeiro, 1996), ch. 6; on Joaquim Pereira Marinho, see Cristiana Ferreira Lyrio Ximenes, "Joaquim Pereira Marinho: Perfil de um contrabandista de escravos na Bahia, 1828–1887" (MA thesis, Universidade Federal da Bahia, 1999), 79–82.

15. Joaquim de Paula Guedes Alcoforado, "História sobre o infame negócio de africanos da África Oriental e Ocidental, com todas as ocorrências desde 1831 a 1853," transcribed by Roquinaldo Ferreira, *Estudos Afro-Asiáticos,* no. 28 (1995): 219–29. In their effort to suppress the transatlantic slave trade in the 1850s, Brazilian authorities employed some of the clandestine methods used by the British. It was in this context that they hired Joaquim de Paula Guedes Alcoforado, a former slave trader who had been supplying the British with intelligence on the contraband slave trade to Brazil. Leslie Bethell, *The Abolition of the Brazilian Slave Trade: Britain, Brazil and the Slave Trade Question, 1807–1869* (Cambridge: Cambridge University Press, 1970), 290, 351–52; on Fonseca's network in Angola, see Phyllis M. Martin, "Family Strategies in Nineteenth-Century Cabinda," *Journal of African History* 28, no. 1 (1987): 65–86; and Maria Cristina Cortez Wissenbach, "As feitorias de Urzela e o tráfico de escravos: Georg Tams, José Ribeiro dos Santos e os negócios da África Centro-Ocidental na década de 1840," *Afro-Ásia,* no. 43 (2011): 43–90; on Mozambique, see Aurélio Rocha, "Contribuição para o estudo das relações entre Moçambique e o Brasil—século XIX," *Studia* 51 (1992): 109–10. See the specific voyages owned by Fonseca, Cunha Reis, and other slave traders by searching for "Vessel owners" in TSTD2.

16. Bethell, *Abolition of the Brazilian Slave Trade,* 290; W. G. Ouseley to Palmerston, Jan. 21, 1839 (enclosures), *BPP,* Slave Trade, 1839 (189), vol. 49, class B (further series), 124–25; Jackson & Grigg to Palmerston, Jan. 2, 1841 (enclosures), *BPP,* Slave Trade, 1842 (402), vol. 42, class A, 271–72. The *embargoes* were especially problematic in the case of the *Brilhante* (TSTD2, voyageid 1724), a US vessel converted into a Portuguese slaver in 1836. British commissioners would accept the embargo presented at the time only under the condition that it would not constitute a precedent for the future, something the Brazilian government refused for some time to accept. The sentence took five months to be executed, with the slaves staying onboard the captured vessel and resulting in the death of twenty-two Africans during this period.

17. Hesketh & Grigg to Lord Aberdeen, Aug. 1, 1842 (thirteenth enclosure), *BPP,* Slave Trade, 1843 (482), vol. 58, class A, 280–81; Jackson & Grigg to Palmerston, Mar. 24, 1840, *BPP,* Slave Trade, 1841 (330), vol. 30, class A, 293–94; *Jornal do Commercio,* June 26, 1842. The newspaper version mentions only Brazil as the target of British efforts to destroy agriculture.

18. [João Manoel Pereira da Silva], *Inglaterra e Brasil: Tráfego de escravos, por um deputado* (Rio de Janeiro: Typographia do Brasil, de J. J. da Rocha, 1845), 34, 76, 94, 175, 233–34, 267–68. For a discussion of the authorship of *Inglaterra e Brasil,* with the convincing conclusion that it was written by Pereira da Silva, see Parron, "A política da escravidão," 172. A few years earlier he had translated and published the *Histoire criminelle du gouvernement anglais,* adding two hundred pages of observations about relations between Brazil and Britain. Pereira da Silva also criticized Brazilians who opposed

the slave trade, such as Manuel Alves Branco, the man responsible for the additional articles allowing the capture of Brazilian vessels equipped for the slave trade. Pereira da Silva suggests that Branco, a member of the Liberal cabinet in power between 1844 and 1848, had been "indoctrinated according to the bible of Wilberforce and his saints, and following the principles of these philanthropic sects that call for the liberty of Africans; he sacrificed the real interests of his country, the primary basis of the calculations of a statesman, in order to satisfy *this great and beautiful idea of the extinction of the slave trade!*" See [Pereira da Silva], *Inglaterra e Brasil,* 114.

19. [Pereira da Silva], *Inglaterra e Brasil,* 65; Bethell, *Abolition of the Brazilian Slave Trade,* 182–86.

20. Aberdeen to Louis M'Lane, Jan. 14, 1846 (enclosure 1, Matson to Percy, Feb. 2, 1843), *BPP,* Slave Trade, 1847 (857), vol. 66, class D, 116.

21. A month later, the British officer boarded the vessel once more after receiving a message from three British subjects onboard the *John A. Robb* with complaints of ill treatment. Matson allowed one of them, whose documents seemed to be irregular, to go with him on the *Waterwitch,* generating some diplomatic discussions between Britain and the United States. Ibid., 113.

22. George W. Slacum to Daniel Webster, July 1, 1843, H.R. Doc., 29th Cong., 1st Sess., No. 43, 18–20; Slacum to Abel P. Upshur, Oct. 6, 1843, ibid., 22.

23. *Jornal do Commercio,* Jan. 15, 1840; see also Carlos Gabriel Guimarães, "La independencia e las finanzas de Brasil: Comentarios sobre la dependencia de Brasil a partir del comportamiento de las empresas británicas, 1820–1850: O caso da Samuel Phillips & Co," paper presented at the Tenth International Congress of the AEHE, Universidad Pablo de Olavide, Seville, September 2011; Slacum to Webster, July 1, 1843, H.R. Doc., 29th Cong., 1st Sess., No. 43, 18–20; Laura Jarnagin, *A Confluence of Transatlantic Networks: Elites, Capitalism, and Confederate Migration to Brazil* (Tuscaloosa: University of Alabama Press, 2008), 128. In 1846, the *Jornal do Commercio* published a report on Brazilian exports. Seven merchant houses were responsible for half of all coffee exported to the United States, with Maxwell, Wright & Co. at the top of the list. The other six houses were Charles Coleman & Co., Miller, Le Cocq & Co., F. Le Breton & Co., Phipps Brothers & Co., Schroeder & Co., and Astley, Algorri & Co. See *Jornal do Commercio,* Jan. 26, 1846.

24. Slacum to Webster, Sept. 4, 1841, May 1, 1842, H.R. Doc., 29th Cong., 1st Sess., No. 43, 3, 25 (quotation); on the *Sofia,* see TSTD2, voyageid 3139; on the Bella União, see TSTD2, voyageid 900192.

25. Slacum to Webster, Sept. 14, 1841, H.R. Doc., 29th Cong., 1st Sess., No. 43, 10.

26. Fehrenbacher, *Slaveholding Republic,* 108–9; Hunter Miller, ed., *Treaties and Other International Acts of the United States of America,* vol. 4: *Documents 80–121, 1836–1846* (Washington, DC: US Government Printing Office, 1934).

27. Fehrenbacher, *Slaveholding Republic,* 166–67. The Quintuple Treaty never went into effect because the French refused to ratify it.

28. John C. Calhoun, *Speeches of John C. Calhoun: Delivered in the Congress of the United States from 1811 to the Present Time* (New York: Harper and Brothers, 1843), 539–40.

29. Edward Bartlett Rugemer, *The Problem of Emancipation: The Caribbean Roots of the American Civil War* (Baton Rouge: Louisiana State University Press, 2009); Steven Heath Mitton, "The Free World Confronted: The Problem of Slavery and Progress in American Foreign Relations, 1833–1844" (PhD diss., Louisiana State University, 2005); Matthew Jason Karp, "'This Vast Southern Empire': The South and the Foreign Policy of Slavery, 1833–1861" (PhD diss., University of Pennsylvania, 2011).

30. Upshur to George Proffit, Aug. 1, 1843, in *Diplomatic Correspondence of the USA—Inter-American Affairs, 1831–1860,* vol. 2: *Bolivia and Brazil,* ed. William R. Manning (New York: Simon and Schuster, 2007), 125–26 (quotation); Slacum to Upshur, Oct. 6, 1843, S. Doc., 28th Cong., 1st Sess., No. 217, 28 (quotation). "Of the vast amount of capital invested, and the great number of English houses supported and enriched by the African trade," Slacum wrote, "this city furnishes abundant proof; samples of 'coast goods,' as they are called, are sent home to Manchester, where orders are constantly filled, goods manufactured to suit the taste or fancy of the negroes, sent, here, and sold by English agents to notorious slave traders." Since no English vessel was allowed to carry the cargo to Africa, US merchants were occupying that space. A consequence of the captures of Portuguese and Brazilian vessels by the British navy, argued the consul, was that "the slave dealer has now to look to the commercial marine of the United States to supply his factories on the coast with British manufactures and other products, (articles of exchange for slaves,) or vessels in which to transport the victims of his cupidity and avarice." And where goes the profit?, he asked. "It accrues to the British manufacturer, the British merchant, and the slave dealer," ignoring the profits of US merchants indirectly involved in the slave trade to Brazil. See Slacum to Webster, May 1, 1842, S. Doc., 28th Cong., 1st Sess., No. 217, 24.

31. In an often quoted passage from this letter, John C. Calhoun argued that "Brazil has the deepest interest in establishing the same policy, especially in reference to the important relation between the European and African races as it exists with her and in the Southern portion of our Union. Under no other can the two races live together in peace and prosperity in either country. The avowed policy of Great Britain is to destroy that relation in both countries and throughout the world. If it should be consummated, it would destroy the peace and prosperity of both and transfer the production of tobacco, rice, cotton, sugar and coffee from the United States and Brazil to her possessions beyond the Cape of Good Hope. To destroy it in either, would facilitate its destruction in the other." Calhoun to Wise, May 25, 1844, in Manning, *Diplomatic Correspondence,* 127. In 1843, the Brazilian representative sent to London to renegotiate the commercial treaty between Brazil and England heard some very similar comments from a non-official US agent at the city. According to the Brazilian representative, the US agent—probably Duff Green, given the mentioned connections to Calhoun and Hammond—told him that the British efforts to convince Brazil and Cuba to emancipate their slaves bothered the US government, who considered these practices to be illegal interventions in the internal business of other peoples. See Rafael B. Marquese and Tâmis P. Parron, "Internacional escravista: A política da segunda escravidão," *Topoi: Revista de História* 12 (2011): 106–7.

32. The message produced some reaction in Parliament, where Prime Minister

Robert Peel argued that Tyler confused the status of recently emancipated Africans with the apprenticeship period, which had already come to an end. He did not deny the possible British involvement in the slave trade, observing that "if the law could reach the owners of British capital embarked in the Slave Trade, every exertion should be made to enforce it to the utmost." The following year President James Polk reproduced some of Tyler's arguments in his message to the Congress, carrying forward the interpretation of British anti-slave-trade policies as economically motivated. James Polk, "Slaves and Slavery," *United States Magazine and Democratic Review* 19 (1846): 243–54; Edward Bartlett Rugemer, *The Problem of Emancipation: The Caribbean Roots of the American Civil War* (Baton Rouge: Louisiana State University Press, 2009), 258.

33. George William Gordon to Alexander Tyler, Sept. 27, 1844, Tyler to Gordon, Oct. 13, 1844, and Wise to Gordon, Oct. 25, 1844, H.R. Doc., 28th Cong., 2d Sess., No. 148, 50, 50–51, 52–54. See also Howard, *American Slavers*, 296n6; *Sooy* (TSTD2, voyageid 3869).

34. Jason S. Pendleton, captain of the *Montevideo* (TSTD2, voyageid 3429), Cornelius E. Driscoll, captain of the *Hope*, Hiram Gray, captain of the *Agnes* (ibid., voyageid 3426), Thomas Duling, captain of the *Washington's Barge*, Joshua M. Clapp, captain of the *Panther* (ibid., voyageid 4926), Peter Flowery, captain of the *Spitfire* (ibid., voyageid 4943), and Cyrus Libby, captain of the *Porpoise*, as well as the crews of the *Cacique* (ibid., voyageid 3493) and the *Pons* (ibid., voyageid 4925). Slacum to Upshur, Feb. 12, 1844, H.R. Doc., 28th Cong., 1st Sess., No. 43, 25; Howard, *American Slavers*, 224–26; on the *Albert*, see all the letters and documents in H.R. Doc., 29th Cong., 1st Sess., No. 690.

35. Wise to Buchanan, May 1, 1849, H.R. Doc., 30th Cong., 2d Sess., No. 61, 150; Wise to Hamilton, July 31, 1846, *BPP*, Slave Trade, 1847 (855), vol. 56, class B, 220.

36. Deposition of Gilbert Smith, May 9, 1845, H.R. Doc., 29th Cong., 1st Sess., No. 690, 64; copy from the private journal or memorandum book of Captain Gilbert Smith, master of the brig *Sea Eagle*, of Boston, ibid., 71 (quotation).

37. The agent was probably Julio Augusto da Cunha. See Martin, "Family Strategies in Cabinda," 75; Wise to Calhoun, Jan. 12, 1845, in *The Papers of John C. Calhoun*, ed. Clyde N. Wilson, vol. 21: *January–June 1845* (Columbia: University of South Carolina Press, 1993), 94–95 (quotation); Howard, *American Slavers*, 176–77 (quotation). Driscoll was referring here to Judge Samuel Betts from New York.

38. The *Kentucky*, an American vessel turned into a slaver, became famous after the outbreak of a slave rebellion on the voyage from Mozambique to Rio de Janeiro. Some of the passengers described in detail the brutality of the repression that took place on board. See Robert Edgar Conrad, *In the Hands of Strangers: Readings on Foreign and Domestic Slave Trading and the Crisis of the Union* (State College: Penn State University Press, 2004), 101–4.

39. Wise to Calhoun, Feb. 18, 1845, H.R. Doc., 30th Cong., 2d Sess., No. 61, 82.

40. Karp, "This Vast Southern Empire," 158–59 (quotation); Adams, *Memoirs*, 196–97 (quotation); Buchanan to Wise, Sept. 27, 1845, in *The Works of James Buchanan, Comprising His Speeches, State Papers, and Private Correspondence*, ed. James Buchanan, John Bassett Moore, and James Buchanan Henry (Philadelphia: J. B. Lippincott, 1908),

267–71 (quotation). Wise was recalled in 1847 because of an issue unrelated to the slave trade.

41. The article was reproduced in the *Daily Atlas,* Aug. 27, 1846, 1 (quotation); *Oberlin Evangelist,* Aug. 19, 1846, 135 (quotation).

42. Wise to Calhoun, Dec. 14, 1844, H.R. Doc., 28th Cong., 2d Sess., No. 148, 55 (quotation); Wise to Maxwell, Wright & Co., Dec. 9, 1844, ibid., 74–75, 84, 88 (quotation).

43. Wise to Hamilton, July 36, 1846, S. Doc., 30th Cong., 1st Sess., No. 28, 21–22.

44. Deposition of Joshua M. Clapp to Gorham Parks, Nov. 26, 1847, H.R. Doc., 30th Cong., 2d Sess., No. 61, 25; on the *Panther,* see TSTD2, voyageid 4926.

45. Wise to Hamilton, Dec. 1, 1844, H.R. Doc., 28th Cong., 2d Sess., No. 148, 55–63.

46. Palmerston to Lord Howden, July 30, 1847, *BPP,* Slave Trade, 1847–48 (976), vol. 64, class B, 202–3.

47. Howden to Palmerston, Apr. 8, 1848, *BPP,* Slave Trade, 1849 (1128), vol. 55, class B, 14.

48. Gorham Parks to James Buchanan, Aug. 20, 1847, H.R. Doc., 30th Cong., 2d Sess., No. 61, 7.

49. TSTD2: *C. H. Rogers* (voyage id 4010), *Safira* (voyageid 3729), *Tolerante* (voyageid 4108). Other documents point to the proximity between Ventura Fortuna and Fonseca. Fortuna exported a thousand muskets on board the *Flora,* a vessel owned by Fonseca and bound to Montevideo (but supposedly prepared to engage in the African slave trade, as discussed below). James Hudson to Palmerston, Jan. 13, 1849 (enclosures), *BPP,* Slave Trade, 1849 (1128), vol. 55, class B, 75–77. Another vessel owned by Ventura Fortuna, the *Assombro* (TSTD2, voyageid 3802), was captured and destroyed by British authorities in 1849. See Return of vessels captured on the ground . . . (inclosure in no. 278), *BPP,* Slave Trade, 1851 (1424-II), vol. 56, pt. 2, class B, 533.

50. On the voyages of the *Brazil,* see TSTD2, voyageids 900221 and 900228. Parks to Buchanan, Aug. 20, 1847, H.R. Doc., 30th Cong., 2d Sess., No. 61, 7. According to the US consul, Jenkins had already been one of the main figures behind the case of the *Fame* (TSTD2, voyageid 4949), a whaler turned into a slaver without the knowledge of the American owners. Jenkins convinced the master to turn it into a slaver and was responsible for receiving the enslaved Africans in Brazil as well as paying for the crew, duties that apparently became common among the US brokers of the second half of the 1840s in Brazil. Krafft continued to engage in the slave trade to Cuba during the 1850s (see Chapter 6).

51. List of Slave-Merchants residing at Rio de Janeiro (Inclosure 3 in no. 262), *BPP,* Slave Trade, 1851(1424-II), vol. 56, pt. 2, class B, 509–10; Pessoas comprometidas nos crimes de moeda falsa e tráfico de escravos, 1836–1864, IJ6, pasta 468, ANRJ.

52. On the *Camargo,* see TSTD2, voyageid 4154. *Jornal do Commercio,* May 10, 1847, July 7, 1850; Henry Southern to Earl of Malmesbury, Jan. 7, 1853, and Southern to Francisco Felix de Souza, Jan. 22, 1853 (Inclosure 1 in No. 100), *BPP,* Slave Trade, 1852–53 (0.5), vol. 53, pt. 2, class B, 209–10 (quotation), 250 (quotation).

53. On the *Ann D. Richardson,* see TSTD2, voyageid 4952. Tod to Webster, June 11, 1851, S. Doc., 32d Cong., 1st Sess., No. 73, 4 (quotation); Hudson to Palmerston, Jan. 13,

1849, *BPP*, Slave Trade, 1849 (1128), vol. 55, class B, 75; *New York Herald (1840–1865),* Jan. 30, 1849 (quotation); Clapp was also part owner of the *Martha,* captured under similar circumstances. See Donald L. Canney, *Africa Squadron: The U.S. Navy and the Slave Trade, 1842–1861* (Washington, DC: Potomac Books, 2006), ch. 9.

54. On the *Gannicliffe,* see TSTD2, voyageid 3427. Tod to Webster, June 11, 1851, S. Doc., 32d Cong., 1st Sess., No. 73, 4 (quotation); *Jornal do Commercio,* July 10, 1847; J. J. C. Westwood to Palmerston, Feb. 17, 1848, *BPP,* Slave Trade, 1849 (1128), vol. 55, class B, 144.

55. "List of vessels sold at this port . . . ," S. Doc., 31st Cong., 2d Sess., No. 6, 41. Some of the advertisements of Clapp were: the *Camila* for sale, *Jornal do Commercio,* Feb. 24, 1848, the *France* on freight, ibid., Aug. 23, 1848, and the *Fiora* for sale, ibid., Jan. 9, 1849.

56. "The deposition of Captain W. E. Anderson, taken at the instance of Mr. Tod, envoy of the United States," S. Doc., 32d Cong., 1st Sess., No. 73, 7. For a longer description of this voyage, see Graden, "O envolvimento dos Estados Unidos," 15–19.

57. The British commander probably misspelled "Maneta" for "Minetta." The additional "Don Juan" remains a mystery; Roderick Dew to George F. Hastings, Jan. 30, 1850 (Inclosure 4 in no. 185), *BPP,* Slave Trade, 1851 (1424-II), vol. 56, pt. 2, class A, 250; Robert T. Hesketh to Palmerston, May 4, 1847, *BPP,* Slave Trade, 1847–48 (976), vol. 64, class B, 262; Melville and Hook to Aberdeen, June 28, 1845 (Enclosure in No. 50), and Melville and Hook to Aberdeen, Nov. 12, 1844 (Enclosure 2), *BPP,* Slave Trade, 1846, vol. 50, class A, 266, 313.

58. Hudson to Her Majesty's Chargé d'Affaires at Montevideo, Dec. 25, 1848 (Inclosure 1 in No. 54), *BPP,* Slave Trade, 1849 (1128), vol. 55, class B, 75; Parks to Buchanan, Nov. 30, 1847 (deposition of Joshua Clapp), H.R. Doc., 30th Cong., 2d Sess., No. 61, 22; Tod to Webster, June 11, 1851, S. Doc., 32d Cong., 1st Sess., No. 73, 4 (quotation).

59. Extract of letter enclosed in Parks to Buchanan, Aug. 31, 1847, H.R. Doc., 30th Cong., 2d Sess., No. 61, 17–18 (quotation); Enoch Lewis, *Friends' Review: A Religious, Literary and Miscellaneous Journal* (Philadelphia, 1850), 206 (quotation). The vessel was also carrying almost twenty thousand dollars in gold and silver coin, which led to legal discussion regarding the destiny of the prize; see Report C.C., H.R., 34th Cong., 3d Sess., No. 47.

60. Tod to Buchanan, Jan. 27, 1848, S.Doc., 31st Cong., 2d Sess., No. 6, 8 (quotation); Hesketh to Palmerston, Mar. 14, 1850, *BPP,* Slave Trade, 1851 (1424-II), vol. 56 pt. 2, class B, 507 (quotation); Hudson to Palmerston, Feb. 21, 1850, BNA, FO84/801.

61. Bethell, *Abolition of the Brazilian Slave Trade,* 333; Parron, *A política da escravidão,* 186 (quotation—the translation is mine). For reviews of the debates on abolition, see Jeffrey D. Needell, "The Abolition of the Brazilian Slave Trade in 1850: Historiography, Slave Agency and Statesmanship," *Journal of Latin American Studies* 33, no. 4 (2001): 681–711; and Márcia Regina Berbel, Rafael de Bivar Marquese, and Tâmis Parron, *Escravidão e política: Brasil e Cuba, c. 1790–1850* (São Paulo: Editora Hucitec and FAPESP, 2010).

62. Webster to Schenck, May 8, 1851, S. Doc., 33d Cong., 1st Sess., No. 47, 2. Martha Abreu, "O Caso Bracuhy," in *Resgate: Uma Janela Para o Oitocentos,* ed. Hebe Maria Mat-

tos de Castro and Eduardo Schnoor (Rio de Janeiro: Topbooks, 1995); Thiago Campos Pessoa Lourenço, "O império dos Souza Breves nos oitocentos: Política e escravidão nas trajetórias dos comendadores José e Joaquim de Souza Breves" (PhD diss., Universidade Federal Fluminense, 2010).

63. Southern to Malmesbury, May 1, Nov. 30, 1852, *BPP,* Slave Trade, 1852–53 (0.5), vol. 103 pt. 3, class B, 98, 203 (quotation); Robert C. Schenck to Alexander Everett, Feb. 5, 1853, *BPP,* Slave Trade, 1854–55 (0.4), vol. 56, class B, 638. Roquinaldo Ferreira discusses Marsden and the Bracuhi case in more detail based on his vast research at the Brazilian National Archives. See Ferreira, "Dos sertões ao Atlântico," 137–47.

64. Bethell, *Abolition of the Brazilian Slave Trade,* 370–71; Abreu, "O Caso Bracuhi"; Lourenço, "O império dos Breves nos oitocentos"; Schenck to Everett, Feb. 5, 1853, *BPP,* Slave Trade, 1854–55 (0.4), vol. 56, class B, 638 (quotation).

65. Ferdinand Coxe to William L. Marcy, July 21, 1853 (A 65, H 65), S. Doc., 33d Cong., 1st Sess., No. 88, 8–9 (quotation), 15; Coxe to Paulino de Souza, Aug. 13, 1853, ibid., 29 (quotation).

66. Cong. Globe, 31st Cong., 2d Sess. 246–47, 304–9 (1851).

67. João Pedro Marques, *The Sounds of Silence: Nineteenth-Century Portugal and the Abolition of the Slave Trade* (Oxford: Berghahn Books, 2006), 217; Southern to Malmesbury, Nov. 30, 1852, *BPP,* Slave Trade, 1852–53 (0.5), vol. 103, pt. 3, class B, 203 (quotation).

68. On the *Grey Eagle,* see TSTD2, voyageid 4190; Howard, *American Slavers,* 178; *Relatório da repartição dos negócios estrangeiros apresentado à assembléa geral legislative na primeira sessão da decima legislatura* (Rio de Janeiro: Typographia Universal de Laemmert, 1857), 20; José Honório Rodrigues, *Brazil and Africa* (Berkeley: University of California Press, 1965), 177.

69. Brasil, Ministério da Fazenda, Comissão de Inquérito, *Relatório da Comissão de Inquérito: Nomeada por aviso do Ministério da Fazenda de 10 de Outubro de 1859,* app. A (Rio de Janeiro: Ministério da Fazenda, 1859), 24. Sergio Buarque de Holanda quotes this passage in his classic work exploring the tensions between liberalism and slavery. This particular aspect would later be developed under the concept of "misplaced ideas" by Roberto Schwarz, who, not surprisingly, quotes the same nostalgic words of Maxwell, Wright & Co. See Sergio Buarque de Holanda, *Raízes do Brasil* (São Paulo: Companhia das Letras, 1995); and Roberto Schwarz, *Ao vencedor as batatas* (São Paulo: Duas Cidades, 2000). The translated version used here comes from Roberto Schwarz and John Gledson, *Misplaced Ideas: Essays on Brazilian Culture* (London: Verso, 1992), 33–34. For a more recent discussion of this source, see Rafael de Bivar Marquese, "Estados Unidos, segunda escravidão e a economia cafeeira do império do Brasil," *Almanack* 1, no. 5 (2013): 58.

70. For a list of steamships employed in the slave trade, select "steamer" in the rig variable in TSTD2.

71. On the *Piratinim* case, see Beatriz G. Mamigonian, "In the Name of Freedom: Slave Trade Abolition, the Law and the Brazilian Branch of the African Emigration Scheme (Brazil—British West Indies, 1830s–1850s)," *Slavery and Abolition* 30, no. 1

(2009), 53–54. On the proposal made by the Brazilian minister of foreign affairs, Paulino Soares, to hand the coastal trade to the US flag, see Parron, "A política da escravidão," 245; and John J. Crittenden to Schenck, Oct. 25, 1851, in Manning, *Diplomatic Correspondence of the USA*, 480–81 (quotation).

s i x Slave Trading in the Slaveholding Republic, 1851–1858

1. *Charleston Mercury,* Aug. 26, 1856.

2. The *Junta Cubana* of New York nominated John A. Quitman (who had been involved to some degree in the failed filibustering adventure of Narciso Lopez a few years earlier) to be the leader of a new liberating invasion of the island. Ramiro Guerra, *Manual de historia de Cuba: Económica, social y política; [desde su descubrimiento hasta 1868]* (Havana: Editorial Nacional de Cuba, Editora del Consejo Nacional de Universidades, 1964), 496–500; Arthur F. Corwin, *Spain and the Abolition of Slavery in Cuba, 1817–1886* (Austin: University of Texas Press, 1967), 115–25; Robert E. May, *Manifest Destiny's Underworld: Filibustering in Antebellum America* (Chapel Hill: University of North Carolina Press, 2002), 33–35; Gould, *Among the Powers of the Earth*, 211–12.

3. David Eltis, *Economic Growth and the Ending of the Transatlantic Slave Trade* (New York: Oxford University Press, 1987), 187; David R. Murray, *Odious Commerce: Britain, Spain, and the Abolition of the Cuban Trade* (Cambridge: Cambridge University Press, 1980), 246; Manuel Moreno Fraginals, *O engenho: Complexo sócio-econômico açucareiro cubano,* 3 vols. (São Paulo: Hucitec, 1988).

4. J. T. Crawford and W. D. Ryder to Lord John Russell, Jan. 2, 1860, *BPP*, Slave Trade, 1860 (2749), vol. 70, class A, 12.

5. E. M. Archibald to Richard Lyons, Oct. 4, 1859, BNA, FO 84/1086.

6. Commodore Thomas Crabbe, Feb. 14, 1857, NA89, Letters to the Secretary of the Navy from the African Squadron, 1843–1861, microfilm edition, reel 108, NARA.

7. The railroad would connect Barreiros to Setúbal and Vendas Novas, regions south of Lisbon. João Pedro Marques, *The Sounds of Silence: Nineteenth-Century Portugal and the Abolition of the Slave Trade* (Oxford: Berghahn Books, 2006), 217; Leslie Bethell, *The Abolition of the Brazilian Slave Trade: Britain, Brazil and the Slave Trade Question, 1807–1869* (Cambridge: Cambridge University Press, 1970), 353; *Hansard*, ser. 3, 118:686; Extrato das cartas, G. J. Motta a Antonio Silvestre (Avellar), IJ6, pasta 480, Série Justiça, ANRJ. Many of the sources from the Arquivo Nacional do Rio de Janeiro explored here have been analyzed by Roquinaldo Ferreira, who also offers great detail on the African side of slave-trading operations. See Roquinaldo Ferreira, "Dos sertões ao Atlântico: Tráfico ilegal de escravos e comércio lícito em Angola, 1830–1860" (MA thesis, Universidade Federal do Rio de Janeiro, 1996).

8. Henry Bulwer to Lord Palmerston, Mar. 10, 1851, NA, FO 84/856.

9. Corwin, *Spain and the Abolition of Slavery,* 118–19; Eltis, *Economic Growth,* 202–3; for a discussion of the profits of Captain General Concha during 1851–52, see José Gregorio Cayuela Fernández, "Los capitanes generales ante la cuestion de la abolicion (1854–1862)," in *Esclavitud y derechos humanos: La lucha por la libertad del negro en el*

siglo XIX, ed. Francisco de Solano and Agustín Guimerá Ravina (Madrid: Consejo Superior de Investigaciones Científicas, 1990), 415–53.

10. Interrogatório feito ao indiciado em crime Antonio Severino de Avellar, IJ6, pasta 480, Série Justiça, ANRJ; Archibald to Foreign Office, Dec. 12, 1859, BNA, FO 84/1086; Eltis, *Economic Growth,* 149–50; Ferreira, "Dos sertões ao Atlântico," ch. 6; Alfonso W. Quiroz, "Implicit Costs of Empire: Bureaucratic Corruption in Nineteenth-Century Cuba," *Journal of Latin American Studies* 35, no. 3 (2003): 489–90.

11. J. G. Cayuela Fernández, *Bahía de Ultramar: España y Cuba en el siglo XIX; El control de las relaciones coloniales* (Madrid: Siglo XXI Editorial, 1993), 238; Eltis, *Economic Growth,* 140–50.

12. Auto de Perguntas e Interrogatório feito a Francisco Riverosa y Urgelles, May 11, 1853, IJ6, pasta 468, Série Justiça, ANRJ; Ferreira, "Dos sertões ao Atlântico," ch. 6.

13. Henry Kilbee to William Hamilton, Feb. 8, 1820, NA, FO 84/6; Extract given by Her Majesty's Commissary Judge, transmitted to Earl of Aberdeen on December 15th, 1845, *BPP,* Slave Trade, 1847–48 (975), vol. 64, class A, 7 (quotation); Lieutenant Pike to Commodore Wise, Aug. 16, 1858 (Inclosure in No. 141), *BPP,* Slave Trade, 1859 (2569), class A, 194 (quotation).

14. José S. Maia Ferreira a Avelar, Feb. 8, 1855, Extrato das cartas apprehendidas a Antonio Severino de Avellar, IJ6, pasta 468, Série Justiça, ANRJ. Ferreira was the author of the first poetry book from Portuguese Africa, published in 1849. See José da Silva Maia Ferreira, *Espontaneidades da minha alma* (Loanda: Imprensa do Governo, 1849). For a short biography of Ferreira, see William P. Rougle, "José da Silva Maia Ferreira: Poeta angolano, correspondente brasileiro, homem de negócios Americano," *Revista Colóquio/ Letras,* Notas e Comentários, 120 (1991): 184–88.

15. Guilherme José da Silva Correa to João José Vianna, Apr. 21, 23, 1855, Intercepted letters annexed to William Stafford Jerningham to Lord Clarendon, June 13, 1856, *BPP,* Slave Trade, 1857 (2282), vol. 64, class B, 131 (quotation).

16. Archibald to Russell, Feb. 5, 1861, BNA, FO 84/1138; James C. Van Dyke to Mr. Guthrie (Inclusure 3 in No. 25), *BPP,* Slave Trade, 1856 (0.1), vol. 62, class A, 56; Ferreira, "Dos sertões ao Atlântico," 138; *Grey Eagle* (TSTD2, voyageid 4190).

17. Archibald to Russell, Sept. 17, 1861, BNA, FO 84/1138 (quotation). "He has at one time acted as contractor with the United States Government, having purchased and imported the camels for domestication in Texas (and incidentally for the profit of the gallant repudiators and Secessionists who have come into power in that section of late). He tells us himself that he has had as many as fifteen vessels at a time engaged in the African trade, which would seem to indicate that he must have brought oceans of oil and mountains of ivory from the torrid and inhospitable region."

18. Archibald to Russell, May 14, 1866, BNA, FO 84/1261 (quotation). He used the name of his wife to cover his operations only by the end of the 1850s, as discussed in the next chapter.

19. Marques, *Sounds of Silence,* 179; *New York Herald,* May 7, 1856. For the list of contributions, see Relação especial dos Portugueses que contribuíram a favor dos destrituídos habitantes de Cabo Verde, Documentos do Consulado Português em Nova

Iorque, Arquivo Histórico-Diplomático de Lisboa (henceforth AHDL); Fonseca's last will and testament is full of donations to many churches and other institutions both in Brazil and Portugal. Arquivo Nacional da Torre do Tombo (Lisboa), Arquivo Histórico do Ministério das Finanças, Testamentos, Livro 20, Tabelião, António Simão de Miranda, Testamento de Manuel pinto da Fonseca, May 22, 1854.

20. According to Palmerston, the fact that "the present Portuguese Minister at Rio de Janeiro has not imitated the misconduct of his predecessors with respect to Slave Trade, must dispose this Government to give every consideration possible to the representations of M. Figaniere." Palmerston to W. G. Ouseley, Feb. 29, 1840, *BPP,* Slave Trade, 1840 (271), vol. 47, class B, 96.

21. C. Figanière to Visconde de Atouguia, Apr. 20, Mar. 29, 1853, Legação de Portugal em Washington, N. 4, 1851–1861, AHDL (quotation); Ferreira, "Dos sertões ao Atlântico," 144–45. Barboza was a merchant from Benguela who had engaged in the slave trade in the late 1830s and early 1840s. See the ventures where he appears as owner in TSTD2.

22. Archibald to Earl of Malmesbury, Oct. 9, 1858, NA, FO 84/1059; Robert Bunch to Malmesbury, Apr. 21, 1859, ibid., FO 84/1086 (quotation).

23. Extrato das cartas apprehendidas a Anto. Severino de Avellar, IJ6, pasta 480, Série Justiça, Arquivo Nacional do Rio de Janeiro (quotation); see also the documents and letters related to the voyage of the Pierre Soulé in National Archives (Washington), NA89, Letters to the Secretary of the Navy from the African Squadron, 1843–1861, microfilm edition, reel 108, 190–97; Eltis, *Economic Growth,* 351n74 (quotation); Ferreira, "Dos sertões ao Atlântico," ch. 6.

24. The British officer describes them as Messrs. Goldenbon and Sesparre, 75 Camp street, New Orleans. Memorandum of Information relative to Slavers (Inclosure 1 in No. 156) in F. Grey to Secretary of Admiralty, Aug. 14, 1857, *BPP,* Slave Trade, 1857–58 (2443), vol. 61, class A, 122; William Mure to Clarendon, Dec. 18, 1857, ibid., (2443-1), vol. 61, class B, 463 (quotation); Moreno Fraginals, *O engenho,* 370.

25. W. E. B. Du Bois, *The Suppression of the African Slave-Trade to the United States of America, 1638–1870* (New York: Longmans, Green, 1896), 162.

26. Eltis, *Economic Growth,* 182; *Quevedo* (TSTD2, voyageid 4350), *Cicerón* (ibid., voyageid 4988).

27. The interviewer replied: "'But I thought Concha was the great enemy of the slave trade.' 'So he is—in words. He talks a great deal, but Pezuela acted. From time immemorial, the planter's estate has been sacred. But Pezuela respected nothing. He seized the negroes wherever he could find them, even on the plantations. By this he incurred the enmity of the planters; and he would probably have been assassinated if he had not been recalled.'" *De Bow's Review* 18, p. 226 (reprinted from the *Evangelist*).

28. The numbers in this paragraph where I refer to the data instead of estimates can be seen by selecting the tab "Tables" on the link above and organizing the rows by individual years and the columns by flag.

29. Eltis, *Economic Growth,* 158; Thomas Savage to T. H. Hatch, Aug. 6, 1857, H.R. Doc., 36th Cong., 2d Sess., No. 7, 72. The highly competitive nature of the contraband business also occasionally led slave traders to use the law to damage their competitors.

The informant of the British consul in New York describes such an event: "I have also been informed that the 'Antelope' was purchased for a man by the name of Valencia, and it appears that she was detained at the instigation of the Captain Drinkwater who was looking out for his own interest. That since her arrival out Captain D. had written to some parties here, requesting them to inform the authorities where the 'Antelope' could be captured, stating the latitude and longitude. The vessel was chartered by A. M. Ros to San Juan de Los Remedios and when detained he made and extended his protest against the captain for the detention." According to the vice-consul, the arrival was never reported in the newspapers. Archibald to Malmesbury, Apr. 30, 1859, BNA, FO 84/1086.

30. Memorandum of Information relative to Slavers (Inclosure 1 in No. 156) in Grey to Secretary of Admiralty, Aug. 14, 1857, *BPP*, Slave Trade, 1857–58 (2443), vol. 61, class A, 122 (quotation).

31. Leon Fink, *Sweatshops at Sea: Merchant Seamen in the World's First Globalized Industry, from 1812 to the Present* (Chapel Hill: University of North Carolina, 2011), 22–23. In early 1853, a Portuguese official in Cabo Verde denounced the presence of a US slavers under the command of Krafft. See Guilherme Peixoto to Joaquim César Figanière e Morão, Feb. 28, 1853, Legação de Portugal em Washington, N. 4, 1851–1861, AHDL. Two years later the Foreign Office received information "respecting the employment of Don Jaime Robirosa and of a person named Krafft as agents for fitting out slave vessels in the United States." See Draft, Clarendon to John F. Crampton, Oct. 26, 1855, NA, FO 84/973. For Rauch's activities in the Cuban slave trade, see "List of Vessels which, under American colors, are known or believed to have engaged in or been fitted out for the slave trade," H.R. Doc., 36th Cong., 2d Sess., No. 7, 200.

32. Cushing to Marcy, Feb. 12, 1857, H.R. Doc., 36th Cong., 2d Sess., No. 7, 51–55.

33. Savage to Appleton, Oct. 14, 1858, H.R. Doc., 36th Cong., 2d Sess., No. 7, 267. For an overview of Savage's actions, see Warren S. Howard, *American Slavers and the Federal Law, 1837–1862* (Berkeley: University of California Press, 1963), 111–23. On the *Lyra*, see TSTD2, voyageid 4910; on the *Charles Perkins*, see ibid., voyageid 4277.

34. Savage to Lewis Cass, Aug. 9, 1858, H.R. Doc., 36th Cong., 2d Sess., No. 7, 172, 194 (quotation).

35. J. A. Thomas to John McKeon, June 20, 1856, H.R. Doc., 36th Cong., 2d Sess., No. 7, 40.

36. Crampton to Clarendon, Sept. 25, 1854 (Inclosure in No. 618), *BPP*, Slave Trade, 1854–55 (0.4), class B, 676 (quotation). The note was originally published in the *Democrat* from Rochester, being reprinted on Frederick Douglass' Paper and a few other newspapers. *Frederick Douglass' Paper*, Dec. 1, 1854 (quotation).

37. Visconde d'Atouguia to Joaquim César de Figanière e Morão, Nov. 17, 1854, and Joaquim de la Figanière e Morão a C. H. S. de la Figanière, Nov. 13, 1854, Legação de Portugal em Washington, N. 4, 1851–1861, AHDL.

38. See the slips taken from newspapers that were annexed to Figanière e Morão to Visconde de Atouguia, Feb. 27, 1855, Legação de Portugal em Washington, 1851–1861, AHDL.

39. *New York Herald-Tribune*, Sept. 24, 1856 (quotation); Intercepted letters an-

nexed to Jerningham to Clarendon, June 13, 1856, *BPP,* Slave Trade, 1857 (2282), vol. 64, class B, 132 (quotation); B. F. Hallett to William L. Marcy, Jan. 5, 1857, H.R. Doc., 36th Cong., 2d Sess., No. 7, 48 (citation); Joseph T. Crawford to Clarendon, Mar. 25, 1857, *BPP,* Slave Trade, 1857–58 (2443-I), vol. 61, class B, 315.

40. Figanière e Morão to Ministro dos Negócios Estrangeiros, 1856, Legação de Portugal em Washington, 1851–1861, AHDL.

41. *New York Herald-Tribune,* July 14, 16, 1857 (quotations); on the *W. G. Lewis,* see TSTD2, voyageid 4910.

42. Figanière e Morão to Marquez de Loulé, Aug. 22, 1857, Legação de Portugal em Washington, 1851–1861, AHDL; *New York Herald-Tribune,* Aug. 7, 1857.

43. G. J. de la Figanière to Lord Napier, May 25, 1858, Legação de Portugal em Washington, 1851–1861, AHDL.

44. 9a. carta de G. J. da Motta a Antonio Silvestre Esq. (Avellar) de New York 8 de Outubro de 1854 para Trinidade in Extrato das cartas apprehendidas a Antonio Severino de Avellar (quotation), IJ6, pasta 480, Série Justiça, ANRJ; Archibald to Lord John Russell, Mar. 5, 1860, BNA, FO 84/1111 (quotation); American Party (Mass.), and African American Pamphlet Collection (Library of Congress), *The Record of George Wm. Gordon: The Slave Trade at Rio de Janeiro, Seizure of Slave Vessels, Conviction of Slave Dealers, Personal Liberation of Slaves, &c. Practice against Theory. Lovers of Freedom, Read! Read!! Read!!! and Vote for the Best Man* (Boston: American Head-Quarters, 1856); Percival J. Parris, "Pedro Tovookan Parris," *Old-Time New England* 63, no. 231 (1973): 60–68.

45. See Thomas Ribeiro dos Santos to Duque da Terceira, Apr. 25, 1859 (quotation), Dos Santos to Duque da Terceira, Aug. 6, 1859 (quotation), and Figanière e Morão to Duque da Terceira, May 23, 1859 (quotation), Legação de Portugal em Washington, 1851–1861, AHDL.

46. *New York Tribune,* Oct. 31, 1862.

47. Suarez Ardugin, Cunha Reis y Perdones, *Proyecto de Immigracin Africana presentado al superior gobierno de esta isla* (Havana: Imprenta de la Habanera, 1860).

48. Don Edward Fehrenbacher, *The Slaveholding Republic: An Account of the United States Government's Relations to Slavery* (Oxford: Oxford University Press, 2001), 132.

SEVEN Crisis, 1859–1867

1. For a description of Arguelles's arrest, see *New York Tribune,* May 13, 1864; Joseph T. Crawford to Lord John Russell, May 10, 1864 (Inclosure 1 in No. 256), *BPP,* Slave Trade, 1865 (3503-I), vol. 56, class B, 241; David R. Murray, *Odious Commerce: Britain, Spain, and the Abolition of the Cuban Trade* (Cambridge: Cambridge University Press, 1980), 313–14; *Cicerón* (TSTD2, voyageid 4988).

2. "The Extradition of Arguelles," *New York Times,* July 14, 1864; George Augustus Sala, *My Diary in America in the Midst of War* (London: Tinsley Brothers, 1865), 24, 28, 30; Samuel S. Cox, *Eight Years in Congress, from 1857–1865* (New York: D. Appleton, 1865), 104–7; William G. Weaver and Robert M. Pallitto, "The Law: 'Extraordinary Rendition' and Presidential Fiat," *Presidential Studies Quarterly* 36, no. 1 (2006): 106, 108 (quota-

tion). Weaver and Pallitto stress the very exceptional character of the Arguelles affair in US history. Until the late twentieth century the executive branch generally followed the idea that it did lacked the power to extradite foreign individuals unless authorized by treaties or statutes with other foreign powers. Shifts in this conduct became clearer during the George W. Bush administration and the employment of the so-called extraordinary renditions as a tool against terrorism. On George Augustus Sala, see Peter Blake, "George Augustus Sala and the English Middle-Class View of America," *19: Interdisciplinary Studies in the Long Nineteenth Century,* no. 9 (2009).

3. "Message of the President of the United States and Accompanying Documents," H.R. Doc., 38th Cong., 2d Sess., No. 1, 1864, 37, 50–52.

4. Ibid., 36.

5. G. J. de la Figanière to Lewis Cass, New York, May 27, 1858, Legação Portuguesa nos Estados Unidos, AHDL. When Machado resuscitated these cases in the 1860s, the British consul in New York, based on information collected with the US attorney, argued that, considering his vast involvement in the slave trade, "the consciousness of his claim on our government furnished an additional motive for trying to appear virtuous." See E. M. Archibald to Lord Clarendon, May 12, 1866 (Inclosure n. 1), BNA, FO 84/1261.

6. *Lydia Gibbs* (TSTD2, voyageid 4264); Earl of Malmesbury to G. M. Dallas, Apr. 30, 1859, H.R. Doc., 36th Cong., 2d Sess., No. 7, 335–36; *Charleston Mercury,* Oct. 29, 1858; *New York Herald,* Nov. 2, 1858; *New York Times,* Nov. 4, 1858.

7. Malmesbury to Dallas, June 1, 1858, H.R. Doc., 36th Cong., 2d Sess., No. 7, 93. Don Edward Fehrenbacher, *The Slaveholding Republic: An Account of the United States Government's Relations to Slavery* (Oxford: Oxford University Press, 2001), 186–87.

8. *Cambridge Chronicle,* Aug. 27, 1846 (originally published in the *Boston Whig*). The explanation of the author, through the voice of a fictitious Wise, pointed to the competition between slave societies in the Americas: "Every negro carried from Africa into Brazil, Porto-Rico, or Cuba, helps to swell the amount of sugar produced in those countries, and consequently to lower its price in the markets of the world. The result of this is to lessen the profits of the Louisiana sugar-planters, and consequently to diminish the demand for slaves. In such a state of things, the slave-breeding States must either keep their negroes at home, or sell them for a mere song. The latter they would not do, and the keeping them at home would soon lead to the abolition of Slavery in all the Northern slave States. You see, Sir, we *must* put down the African Slave-Trade." *Pennsylvania Freeman,* Feb. 6, 1851. The author of the Pennsylvania newspaper in turn had been informed that the "frequent official and social intercourse which he [Wise] had occasion to hold with distinguished persons of African descent, have had the effect to remove in a great degree, some of his old American prejudices, and that his views and feelings on the subject of color have undergone quite a commendable change."

9. *Liberator,* Sept. 9, 1854; Tâmis Peixoto Parron, "A política da escravidão no império do Brasil, 1826–1865" (MA thesis, Universidade de São Paulo, 2009), 252.

10. James Oakes, "The Political Significance of Slave Resistance," *History Workshop,* no. 22 (1986): 89–107; Eric Foner, *Free Soil, Free Labor, Free Men: The Ideology of the Republican before the Civil War* (Oxford: Oxford University Press, 1995), 117; Paul Fin-

kelman and Donald R. Kennon, eds., *Congress and the Crisis of the 1850s* (Athens: Ohio University Press, 2012).

11. David L. Lightner, *Slavery and the Commerce Power: How the Struggle against the Interstate Slave Trade Led to the Civil War* (New Haven: Yale University Press, 2006), 122 (quotation); Paul Finkelman, "The Appeasement of 1850," in Finkelman and Kennon, *Congress and the Crisis of the 1850s*, 46.

12. Lincoln argued that the "African slave trade is not yet effectually suppressed." In his view, a comparison of the white and black populations would show that the black populace was growing more rapidly in part because some of them might have been coming from Africa. "If this be so, the opening of new countries to the institution, increases the demand for, and augments the prices of slaves, and so does, in fact, make slaves of freemen by causing them to be brought from Africa, and sold into bondage." Roy P. Basler, ed., *The Collected Works of Abraham Lincoln*, vol. 2 (New Brunswick: Rutgers University Press, 1953), 256, 263, 268–69; for a discussion of this speech, see William E. Gienapp, *Abraham Lincoln and Civil War America: A Biography* (Oxford: Oxford University Press, 2002), 50–52.

13. The classic study on the topic is Ronald T. Takaki, *A Pro-Slavery Crusade: The Agitation to Reopen the African Slave Trade* (New York: Free Press, 1971). It has also been more recently explored in Walter Johnson, *River of Dark Dreams: Slavery and Empire in the Cotton Kingdom* (Cambridge, MA: Belknap Press of Harvard University Press, 2013).

14. *Albany Evening Journal,* May 2, 1856.

15. *New York Herald,* May 5, Oct. 13, 1856.

16. William W. Freehling, *Road to Disunion,* vol. 2: *Secessionists Triumphant, 1854–1861* (New York: Oxford University Press, 2007), 177; Fehrenbacher, *Slaveholding Republic,* 180–83.

17. *New York Herald,* Nov. 5, 1856.

18. Robert Bunch to Malmesbury, Jan. 20, 1859, NA, FO 84/1086; Bunch to Malmesbury, Dec. 16, 1858, NA, FO 84/1059; L. J. Flemming to Cass, Dec. 9, 1858, H.R. Doc., 36th Cong., 2d Sess., No. 7, 284; Sylviane A. Diouf, *Dreams of Africa in Alabama: The Slave Ship Clotilda and the Story of the Last Africans Brought to America* (Oxford: Oxford University Press, 2007); TSTD2: *Wanderer* (voyageid 4974), *Clotilda* (voyageid 36990), *Echo* (voyage id 4284). On the Africans liberated by the US Navy from slave ships between 1858 and 1860, including the *Echo,* see Sharla M. Fett, "Middle Passages and Forced Migrations: Liberated Africans in Nineteenth-Century US Camps and Ships," *Slavery and Abolition* 31, no. 1 (2010): 75–98.

19. The irrepressible conflict, a speech by William H. Seward, delivered at Rochester, Monday, Oct. 25, 1858, in *The Campaign of 1860 Comprising the Speeches of Abraham Lincoln, William H. Seward, Henry Wilson, Benjamin F. Wade, Carl Schurz, Charles Sumner, William M. Evarts, &c.* (Albany, NY: Weed, Parsons, 1860).

20. Republican Principles, a speech of Hon. Abraham Lincoln of Illinois, at the Republican State Convention, held at Springfield, Illinois, June 16, 1858, in ibid.

21. *New York-Enquirer,* July 31, 1860.

22. See the various instructions from Howell Cobb in H.R. Doc., 36th Cong., 2d

Sess., No. 7, 632–45; Fehrenbacher, *Slaveholding Republic,* 187; Ericson, *Slavery in the American Republic,* 44–46.

23. See the slip "The Slave Trade: Its Prevention, Detection and Punishment by the Late Theodore Sedgwick" annexed to Archibald to Malmesbury, June 26, 1860, NA, FO 84/1111. Organized by the Portuguese New Yorker Antonio Augusto de Oliveira Botelho, the *Haidee* (TSTD2, voyageid 4285) had departed New York with him aboard. After the slaves were disembarked, the mate and part of the crew sailed back to Montauk Point, where they sank the ship. The mate and part of the crew were arrested, and Sedgwick played a central role in the case.

24. H.R. Doc., 36th Cong., 2d Sess., No. 7, 577–78; *Boston Daily Advertiser,* July 26, 1860. The Sedgwick document also became the object of political disputes, with Republicans using it to accuse Democrats and vice-versa. See other slips in Archibald to Malmesbury, June 26, 1860, BNA, FO 84/1111.

25. Charles J. Helm to Cass, Nov. 15, Dec. 27, 1858, H.R. Doc., 36th Cong., 2d Sess., No. 7, 280 (quotation), 292–94.

26. Helm to Francisco Serrano, May 5, 1860, H.R. Doc., 36th Cong., 2d Sess., No. 7, 428–29.

27. Helm to Cass, Apr. 11, 1860, H.R. Doc., 36th Cong., 2d Sess., No. 7, 419–20; Helm to Serrano, May 29, 1860, ibid., 436.

28. W. H. Robertson to Marcy, Jan. 31, 1856 (annex 1), H.R. Doc., 36th Cong., 2d Sess., No. 7, 29 (quotation); Helm to Cass, Mar. 12, 1860, ibid., 396; *New York Herald,* Feb. 18, 1860; see, e.g., TSTD2: *Cortez* (voyageid 4878), *Mary Elizabeth* (voyageid 4794), *Venus* (voyageid 4290), *St. Andrew* (voyageid 4793).

29. Fabius Stanly to Isaac Toucey, July 10, 1860, H.R. Doc., 36th Cong., 2d Sess., No. 7, 622 (quotation).

30. *New York Times,* Mar. 21, 1860.

31. Russell to Cowley, July 11, 1860, *BPP,* Slave Trade, 1861 (2823-I), vol. 64, class B, 65–67; Trescot to Irvine (Inclosure in No. 192), Aug. 10, 1860, ibid., 169–71.

32. *Evening Post,* Aug. 15, July 24, 1860; *World,* Aug. 21, 1860. The ninth declaration of the Republican platform states: "That we brand the recent reopening of the African slave trade, under the cover of our national flag, aided by perversions of judicial power, as a crime against humanity and a burning shame to our country and age; and we call upon Congress to take prompt and efficient measures for the total and final suppression of that execrable traffic." Republican Party Platforms: "Republican Party Platform of 1860," May 17, 1860. Available online at Gerhard Peters and John T. Woolley, The American Presidency Project: http://www.presidency.ucsb.edu/ws/?pid=29620.

33. See the slips in Archibald to Russell, Aug. 28, 1860, NA, FO 84/1111; *New York Evening Express,* July 14, 1860; Diouf, *Dreams of Africa in Alabama.*

34. *New York Herald,* Aug. 10, 1860 (quotation). See the slips in Archibald to Russell, June 5, 1860, NA, FO 84/1111, for many other examples.

35. James D. Richardson, *A Compilation of the Messages and Papers of the Confederacy including the Diplomatic Correspondence, 1861–1865* (Nashville, TN: United States Publishing, 1905); Bunch to Russell, Mar. 8, 21, 1861, NA, FO 84/1138.

36. Bunch to Russell, Jan. 1, 1861, Archibald to Russell, May 28, 1861, Bunch to Russell, July 6, 1861, and Archibald to Russell, Sept. 17, 1861, BNA, FO 84/1138; TSTD2: *Bonita* (voyageid 4656), *John Bell* (voyageid 4656), *Potomac* (voyageid 4390).

37. Fehrenbacher, *Slaveholding Republic,* 189; Robert W. Shufeldt to William Seward, July 5, 1861, and Russell to Seward, Oct. 15, 1862, S. Doc., 38th Cong., 1st Sess., No. 56, 3, 9.

38. Matthew Mason, "Keeping Up Appearances: The International Politics of Slave Trade Abolition in the Nineteenth-Century Atlantic World," *William and Mary Quarterly,* 3rd ser., 66, no. 4 (2009): 830.

39. *Philadelphia Inquirer,* Aug. 17, 1861; *New York Herald,* July 19, 1861; *New York Times,* Dec. 3, 1861. See the slips in Archibald to Russell, Sept. 5, 1861, NA, FO 84/1138.

40. TSTD2: *City of Norfolk* (voyageid 4366), *Nightingale* (voyageid 4955), *Montauk* (voyageid 4375), *Eerie* (voyageid 4653). See *Evening Post* slip in Archibald to Russell, July 10, 1861, NA, FO 84/1138.

41. See the slips in F. Lousada to Russell, June 24, 1862, NA, FO 84/1172, and in Archbald to Russell, Sept. 5, 1861, BNA, FO 84/1138; *New York Daily Tribune,* Feb. 5, 1862.

42. See the slips annexed to Archibald to Russell, Sept. 5, 1861, the letter from the British informant annexed to Archibald to Russell, Dec. 31, 1861, slips annexed to Archibald to Russell, May 28, 1861, and Lousada to Russell, Dec. 2, 1861, NA, FO 84/1138.

43. Howard, *American Slavers,* 224–35.

44. Archibald to Russell, Nov. 11, 1861, letter from the informant annexed to Archibald to Russell, Nov. 12, 1861, letter from the informant annexed to Archibald to Russell, Dec. 3, 1861, NA, FO 84/1138.

45. *New York Times,* Aug. 28, 1861, Nov. 17, 1862; TSTD2: *Mariquita* (voyageid 4829), *Venus* (voyage id 4888), unnamed vessel (voyage id 4851).

46. For the voyages departing from the United States after 1861, see TSTD2: voyageids 4884, 4820, and 4829.

47. Archibald to Russell, Nov. 17, 1862, NA, FO 85/1172; Archibald to Russell, Nov. 11, 1861, letter from the informant annexed to Archibald to Russell, Nov. 11, 1861, NA, FO 84/1138.

48. Memorandum annexed to Archibald to Russell, May 12, 1866, BNA, FO 84/1261; letter annexed to Archibald, Feb. 1, 1862, BNA, FO 84/1172.

49. Charles V. Dyer and Timothy R. Hubbard to Seward, Feb. 21, 1864, BNA, FO 84/1222.

50. Fernando de Caver para Ministro de Estado e Negócios Estrangeiros, Feb. 20, Mar. 2, 1863, Consulado Português em Havana, AHDL; Murray, *Odious Commerce,* 312. On December 8, 1865, Cunha Reis signed a contract allowing him to form the Asiatic Colonization Company, which was entitled to an exclusive right to introduce Asian immigrants into Mexico for the following ten years. Apparently no immigrant ever entered Mexico through this contract. Clinton Harvey Gardiner, "Early Diplomatic Relations between Mexico and the Far East," *Americas* 6, no. 4 (1950): 401–14. Two years later, the Mexican government authorized him to construct a railroad connecting Mexico City to Tuxpan River, in the province of Veracruz. See *Report of the Secretary of Finance of the United States of Mexico,* Jan. 15, 1879, 56.

51. W. Vredenburg to Stanley, Dec. 14, 1866, *BPP,* Slave Trade, 1867–68 (4000), vol. 64, class A, 16; Hornby to the Secretary of Admiralty, June 7, 1867, ibid., 53; Vredenburg to Stanley, Sept. 18, 1868, *BPP,* Slave Trade, 1868–69 (4131), vol. 56, class A, 26; W. G. Romaine, Admiralty to Foreign Office, BNA, FO 84/1310, ff. 132–33; W. Dowell to the Secretary of Admiralty, Feb. 7, 1869, *BPP,* Slave Trade, 1870 (C.140), vol. 61, class A, 46; for the cases of 1866, see TSTD2, voyageids 4998, 4898, and 4899.

EIGHT Conclusion

1. Calhoun also argued that Cuba and Brazil were rivals on the production of many articles, especially cotton. "Brazil possesses the greatest advantages for its production, and is already a large grower of the article," continues the report of his speech, "towards the production of which the continuance of the market for imported slaves from Africa would contribute much." *Speeches of John C. Calhoun: Delivered in the Congress of the United States from 1811 to the Present Time* (New York: Harper and Brothers, 1843), 539–40.

2. Christopher Schmidt-Nowara, *Empire and Antislavery: Spain, Cuba, and Puerto Rico, 1833–1874* (Pittsburgh: University of Pittsburgh Press, 1999), 137–38; Seymour Drescher, *Abolition: A History of Slavery and Antislavery* (Cambridge: Cambridge University Press, 2009), 334. On the relation between the wars of independence and the abolition of slavery, see Rebecca J. Scott, *Slave Emancipation in Cuba: The Transition to Free Labor, 1860–1899* (Pittsburgh: University of Pittsburgh Press, 2000); and Ada Ferrer, *Insurgent Cuba: Race, Nation, and Revolution, 1868–1898* (Chapel Hill: University of North Carolina Press, 1999).

3. Rafael B. Marquese and Tâmis P. Parron, "Internacional escravista: A política da segunda escravidão," *Topoi: Revista de História* 12 (2011): 112.

4. Cited in Gerald Horne, *The Deepest South: The United States, Brazil, and the African Slave Trade* (New York: New York University Press, 2007), 160. See also Tâmis Peixoto Parron, "A política da escravidão no império do Brasil, 1826–1865" (MA thesis, Universidade de São Paulo, 2009), 234.

5. Parron, "A política da escravidão," 254–55; certain regions in the Vale do Paraíba actually presented some small positive rates of demographic growth among the slave population. See Ricardo Salles, *E o vale era o escravo: Vassouras, século XIX: Senhores e escravos no coração do império* (Rio de Janeiro: Civilização Brasileira, 2008). Bibliography on the abolition of slavery in Brazil is vast. See, among others, Emília Viotti da Costa, *Da senzala à colônia* (São Paulo: Livraria Editora Ciências Humanas, 1982); Emília Viotti da Costa, *The Brazilian Empire: Myths and Histories* (Chicago: University of Chicago, 1985); Rebecca J. Scott, *Abolition of Slavery and the Aftermath of Emancipation in Brazil* (Durham, NC: Duke University Press, 1988); Hebe Maria Mattos de Castro, *Das cores do silencio: Os significados da liberdade no sudeste escravista, Brasil seculo XIX* (Rio de Janeiro: Arquivo Nacional, 1995); and Celso Castilho and Camillia Cowling, "Funding Freedom, Popularizing Politics: Abolitionism and Local Emancipation Funds in 1880s Brazil," *Luso-Brazilian Review* 47, no. 1 (2010): 89–120.

Index